Territorial Politics
in Industrial Nations

edited by
**Sidney Tarrow
Peter J. Katzenstein
Luigi Graziano**

The Praeger Special Studies program, through a selective worldwide distribution network, makes available to the academic, government, and business communities significant and timely research in U.S. and international economic, social, and political issues.

Territorial Politics
in Industrial Nations

Praeger Publishers   New York   London

Library of Congress Cataloging in Publication Data

Main entry under title:

Territorial politics in industrial nations.

  Includes bibliographical references and index.
  1. Decentralization in government—Addresses, essays,
lectures. 2. Comparative government—Addresses, essays,
lectures. I. Tarrow, Sidney. II. Katzenstein, Peter J.
III. Graziano, Luigi, 1939-
JS113.T47   351'.093   77-83439
ISBN 0-03-040961-6

PRAEGER SPECIAL STUDIES
200 Park Avenue, New York, N.Y., 10017, U.S.A.

Published in the United States of America in 1978
by Praeger Publishers,
A Division of Holt, Rinehart and Winston, CBS, Inc.

789   038   987654321

ACKNOWLEDGMENTS

This volume is a product of the Program of Training and Research on Center-Periphery Tensions of the Center for International Studies of Cornell University. Financed by a three-year grant from the Ford Foundation, the program brought together scholars in political science, anthropology, history, economics, and regional planning with a common interest in the changing territorial conflict structure of industrial societies. In addition to sponsoring a number of occasional papers and individual works, the program was responsible for another collective volume, Ethnic Conflict in the Western World, edited by Milton J. Esman (Ithaca, N.Y.: Cornell University Press, 1977). The present volume was the result of a continuing workshop on center-periphery tensions in industrial societies that was run under the aegis of the program. We would like to thank our colleagues at Cornell, and especially M. Gardner Clark, Pierre Clavel, Milton J. Esman, Davydd Greenwood, Jerome Milch, and Lawrence Scheinman for their continuing participation in this workshop. We would also like to thank the staff of the Center for International Studies for assisting us with its organization, and the Ford Foundation for financing it. The volume would not have been possible without the editorial assistance of Nicole Ball and the typing and editorial skills of Renee Pierce. To our fellow authors we would like to record our thanks for their patience over the years and months since their papers were first delivered.

CONTENTS

LIST OF TABLES AND FIGURES

LIST OF ABBREVIATIONS

AG	Agudat Israel
AMC	Association of Municipal Corporations
BHA	Boston Housing Authority
BRA	Boston Redevelopment Authority
BSEIU	Building Service Employees International Union
CAR	Conférence administrative regionale
CCA	County Councils Association
CELIB	Comité d'études et de liaison d'intérêts bretonnes
CODER	Regional Economic Development Committees
CV	Cartell-Verband
DATAR	Délégation à l'aménagement du territoire et à l'action régionale
DC	Christian Democratic Party
DDE	Direction départementale de l'équipement
DN	New Democracy Party
EEC	European Economic Community, Common Market
ENI	National Hydrocarbons Agency
EPA	Etablissement public d'aménagement
EPAREB	Etablissement public d'aménagement des Fives de l'étang de Berre
FIAT	Fonds pour l'intervention à l'aménagement du territoire
FPÖ	Austrian Freedom Party
HSA	Home and School Association
IGAMES	Inspecteurs généraux de l'administration en mission extraordinaire
IPE	index of party experience
IRI	Institute of Industrial Reconstruction
LDP	Liberal Democratic Party
MIAFEB	Interministerial Mission for the Planning of Fos and the Etang de Berre
MRP	Movement républican populaire
MSI	Italian Fascist Party
MSIDN	Movimento sociale italiano–destra nationale
NRP	National Religious Party
PAG	Orthodox Labor Movement
OREAM	Metropolitan Area Planning Agency
ÖVP	Austrian Peoples' Party
PCI	Italian Communist Party
PCF	French Communist Party
PDUP	Democratic Party of Proletarian Unity
PLI	Italian Liberal Party
PMI	Italian Monarchist Party
PRI	Italian Republican Party

PSDI	Italian Social Democratic Party
PSI	Italian Socialist Party
PSIUP	Italian Socialist Party of Proletarian Unity
PUWP	Polish United Workers Party
SCA	community planning syndicates
SFIO	French Socialist Party
SPÖ	Austrian Socialist Party
SVM	syndicat à vocation multiple
SVU	syndicat à vocation unique
UDR	Union des démocraires pour la république
UFT	United Federation of Teachers
UPA	United Parents Association
WWO	Naamat (Women's Workers Organization)
WIZO	World Zionist Organization

Territorial Politics
in Industrial Nations

1

INTRODUCTION
Sidney Tarrow

This book is about the territorial politics of industrial nations. By this term, we do not intend to analyze politics about territory but rather politics about other issues that are fought out across territory. By one of those peculiar but natural divisions of labor in the social sciences, the study of class and economic conflict has become separated from the study of the relations among territorial units—the former under the rubric of political sociology and the latter under the heading of intergovernmental relations. While the first deals with vast issues, roiling conflicts, and deep-seated social and economic cleavages, the second, all too often, has been limited to seeing the pirouettes of pettifogging bureaucrats fighting apparently abstract battles over local autonomy, federalism, and revenue sharing.

But it is through the territorial units they live in that men organize their relations with the state, reconcile or fight out conflicts of interest, and attempt to adapt politically to wider social pressures. Through these same units, central governments distribute grants and services, organize consent, and, when forced to do so, offer correctives to the pressures of economy and society. Thus, how central governments and their territorial subunits are linked politically is

For their very useful comments on an earlier version of this chapter, I am grateful to my coauthors and coeditors as well as Samuel Beer, Terry Clark, Davydd Greenwood, Richard Hofferbert, and L. J. Sharpe. None of these colleagues is in any way responsible for assertions or interpretations put forward here. I am particularly in debt to Professor Beer, whose essay on "The Modernization of American Federalism" (Publius 3 [Fall 1973]) was the starting point for many of the ideas developed here.

not only a problem of intergovernmental relations but also one of managing the class and interest conflicts of modern societies. No more
can intergovernmental relations be separated from political sociology
than can the current fiscal crisis be separated from the inner logic
of the economic system. Both take territorial forms, but both are ultimately related to conflicts of interest and ideology that emerge from
the functional cleavages of a modern society.

It would be foolish to deny that there are deep functional cleavages in industrial societies that are fought out mainly at the summit
of the political system or in the conflicts between capital and labor;
in any case, independent of the vertical relations between central governments and their territorial subunits. But it is becoming increasingly clear that—in contrast to what was thought to be true in the 1960s
—territorial conflicts are not declining. They are reinforced by cultural and regional identities, fiscal imbalances, and by the massive
urbanization that has everywhere led to new service functions for
local governments. While in some global sense the demand for these
services—and for the national subsidies to provide them—has led to a
decline in local autonomy, it has also increased the importance of the
linkages between center and periphery of the political system and of
the skills and resources of the politicians and administrators who
serve as gatekeepers between each level.

It is thus not surprising that, in face of the cultural standardization, the mass markets, and the administrative centralization of modern states, there has been surprisingly little change in the attachment
of ordinary citizens to their territorial subunits. For the linkages
between the latter and higher levels of government cut across the economic dependency, the administrative stratification, and the cultural
differences between nation and locality. How these linkages are organized and utilized by actors at either end of the center-periphery continuum may thus tell us more about the cohesion of industrial societies
than the intensity of the cleavages or the financial dependency of subnational or national governments. That, at least, was the idea that
guided the selection of the chapters in this book. It led us to organize
them according to the following questions:

- First, what tasks does the periphery perform for the center of the
  political system: merely the provision of the services to furnish a
  private economy with public infrastructure? Or the mobilization
  of consent and demands that can be communicated to the center?
  Or, also, the preservation of enclaves of diversity in which social
  experimentation can be carried out?
- Second, what are the uses of the center for the periphery, and what
  strategies of access typify peripheral elites trying to capture policy
  goods from higher levels of government? Is the center merely a

source of financial support or also of the initiatives needed to overcome the impersonal forces of the market? And which strategies
appear to work best for local elites seeking policy support from the
center?

• Third, how do existing networks of center-periphery exchange respond to crisis and change? By stubborn resistance to changes in
the way decisions are made and resources allocated? By a blind
rush to embrace new solutions at the cost of local autonomy and diversity? Or by attempts to combine new technical and administrative solutions with the preservation of inherited political values and
institutions?

In this chapter, drawing wherever possible on the chapters that
follow, I will turn to some of these questions. My basic argument
will be that, as the migration of functional conflicts to the summit of
the political system erodes the effectiveness of national parliaments,
citizens turn more and more not to "functional" representation but to
the territorial institutions around them, reinforcing the territorial
dimension in representation just as it is being displaced in policy making and administration. The result is to create a greater and more
sophisticated range of demands upon local political leaders and a
need for leaders who can link center and periphery of the political
system.

FUNCTION VERSUS TERRITORY: POLICY MIXES
AND REPRESENTATIONAL POLARITIES

The problem of relating political authority to territorial administration is as old as political science itself. As James Fesler points
out in his magisterial Area and Administration, "It has been traditional since Aristotle to think of this problem [of the distribution of
authority] primarily in terms of the distribution of functions among
the officials at the capital city of a defined geographical area." But
"there is another phase of the problem on which the experience of the
Greek city-states cast little light. This is the distribution of governmental authority by area."[1] The main problems canvased in Fesler's
book revolve around the dichotomy between administration by function
and administration by territory, and this is typical of the intergovernmental relations literature as a whole. Such questions possess an essential uniformity of purpose: how to find, within the limits of political realism, the optimal territory and size of territory for administration by policy function.

Far more complex, however, is relating policy and policy implementation to different principles of political representation. Doug-

las Ashford touches on this aspect of the question when he writes of
"the historic and continuing conflict of how to reconcile territorial influence based on political representation and party organization with
the growing functional powers of central governments and the changing
functional relationship between the center and the subunits."[2] For in
mobilized political systems—whether liberal-democratic, social-
democratic, or Leninist—there are two basic principles of representation: territorial representation based on the choice of officials
through geographic areas, and functional representation based on professional, class, and interest organization.[3] These two principles,
which go back, respectively, to the national and industrial revolutions
of the eighteenth and nineteenth centuries, do not admit of even the
kind of practical reconciliation found in the study of functional versus
territorial administration. It is not merely political realities that
prohibit finding the "optimal" territory and size of territory as arenas
for functional representation, but a difference in the character of the
constituencies of each. Function versus territory can find a proper
mix in terms of administration; but they are the bases of representational polarities that will always conflict in any fully mobilized political system. Thus, the liberal critique of the U.S. House of Representatives—that it reflects a multitude of cracker-barrel territorial interests—is not qualitatively different in this sense from the recent
Italian Communist controversy over the devolution of industrial planning functions to the regions—many of them controlled by the left.
Both are responding to a logic of functional (versus territorial) representation.[4]

Historically, territorial representation arose in two waves:
first, in the development of western European city-states during the
Renaissance, especially in the trading communities on Europe's
northern and southern coasts; and second, in the practice that developed in Europe and North America of localities sending delegates to
legislative assemblies at higher levels of government. Though this
practice in most cases went back to the middle ages, it was only when
infused by the ideologies of the national revolutions that it took on a
representative quality. Though the relationship varied from country
to country, where they survived, autonomous jurisdictions of the
past generally sustained and forwarded movements toward parliamentary representation. This was reflected in one form in the United
States where, as Heinz Eulau points out, the Federalist papers reveal
an early commitment to combining federalism with representation.[5]
In other systems, such as Britain, localism got progressively weaker
in Parliament as representation took national forms, but local groups
and communities had vigorously pursued the movement toward parliamentary representation. In Italy, in contrast, though the provincial-
ism of its city-state tradition impeded national unity, local clientele

groupings would profit from their links to parliamentary representatives once a unified nation was achieved. (See the historic section of Chapter 9, pp. 297-304.)

Functional representation, in contrast, if we ignore the much earlier organization of the European estate system, was a quintessential product of the Industrial Revolution, particularly of the concentration of industrial ownership that led to consistent organized pressures on policy makers at the national level. Of course, functional representation developed in local forms as well—typically through the informal control by propertied interests over local governments. But its formal expression was to be national from the start: through the creation of social and economic councils or advisory bodies around national ministries, and especially around the institutions of national economic planning that would flourish during and after the two world wars.[6]

The most collective forms of organized functional representation would ultimately be found in authoritarian regimes.[7] But far more influential on policy—because cast in the framework of liberal states—has been organized interest representation in the recent postwar period, symbolized for many by the French commissions de modernisation.[8] However, even in the less étatiste tradition of Great Britain, Samuel Beer found a politics of collectivism every bit as organized as across the channel.[9] State capitalism has privileged the distinct representation of organized functional interests, in contrast to classical liberal democracies, in which functional interests were largely channeled through parliamentary representatives.

If there is a secular relationship between functional and territorial representation, it has been for the latter to become less relevant at the same time as the more recent corporate forms of functional representation have appeared. This has led many to the inference that the two processes were causally related: that as interests became more concentrated, governments more centralized, and societies and cultures less localized, functional representation would increasingly edge classical forms of territorial representation to one side.[10]

This argument should, however, be divided into two parts: first, that the decline of Parliament meant that national representation would increasingly shift from territorial to functional axes; and, second, that the territorial subunits of government—in uneven competition with increasingly technocratic central governments—would become less able to take initiatives in regard to the policy problems of their inhabitants. Underlying both strands of the argument is the assumption that changes in the focuses of representation follow the curve of the modernization process—with its increasing scale and differentiation—in substituting functional for territorial cleavages as the major

axes of politics and forcing demands upward to the summit of the political system where they are dealt with by technocratic elites in contact with the national representatives of functional groups and parties.

The national strand of this argument can best be seen in Shonfield's Modern Capitalism.[11] There is not sufficient space here to
analyze in detail his prediction of a gradual shift from parliamentary
to "corporatist" representation as economic planning made the work
of the individual member of Parliament irrelevant. Suffice it to say
that Shonfield's predictions were perhaps swayed by his fascination
with France, a country that, in the mid-1960s, was in the forefront
of both "functional" planning and parliamentary decline. What needs
emphasis in the French case, however, is that the two phenomena had
different roots: the first in the innovative planning machinery developed in the 1950s, which, in France, as elsewhere, led to a visible
consultative role for functional interest groups; and the second in the
antiparliamentary bias of the Fifth Republic, which, for political reasons, favored doctrines of corporatist representation over parliamen-
tarism. That the favored role of business in French planning never
extended to labor was evident even when Shonfield wrote; that the commissions de modernisation were so much window dressing would emerge
soon after;[12] and that Parliament was in decline seems, in retrospect,
to have been more closely linked to the identity between De Gaulle's
presidential and legislative majority than to secular trends in French
capitalism.

We are more concerned here with the "vertical" corollary of
the argument from functional representation. The argument runs as
follows: As social and economic problems began to gravitate to the
level of greatest centralization—the national state—territorial units,
such as the cities, towns, provinces, and regions, which had participated in the earlier wave of democratization, found their representative function in decline. The role of economic modernization in this
process is frequently underscored. Beer writes, in a stimulating
analysis of American federalism:

> In the United States, as in other modernizing societies,
> the general historical record has spelled centralization.
> While in recent years a new phase of this centralizing pro-
> cess has set in—which I call technocratic federalism—
> the main reasons for this change are not to be found in the
> personal, partisan or ideological preferences of office-
> holders, but in the new forces produced by an advanced
> modernity.[13]

Centralization, for Beer, is not produced automatically by growing economic scale and interdependence. Interdependence leads to

centralization through politics, especially through "the formation of coalitions to influence the action of government."[14] These coalitions have evolved in scale and in character: from "pork barrel" coalitions of particularistic interests of the early modernization period, to "spillover" coalitions demanding national action for policy problems that escape the boundaries of subunit political interest, to the class coalitions that produced the welfare state, "which in turn involved that vast extension of the public sector that has been a main ground for the present tendencies toward technocracy."[15]

In the age of technocratic politics, the core of political pressure and policy proposals moves to "within government and its associated circles of professionals and technically trained cadres."[16] Although functional groups in society persist from earlier phases of modernization, those that correspond to programs of the technocratic coalition "typically arise after the program is established and are shaped in membership and basic aims by the corresponding features of the program."[17] These new clientele groups are both public and private, but the important point is that they are functionally organized and cut across the levels of government of the traditional governmental system. Deil Wright writes of the highway lobby in the United States, "Policy control in this area usually rests less with governors than with alliances of highway engineers at all levels plus construction contractors and cement and equipment manufacturers."[18]

What happens to territorial units of representation at the base of societies that have reached such stages of modernization? First, they suffer from their obvious financial weakness vis-a-vis central governments during a period in which massive social investments are demanded by constitutents.[19] Second, technocracy is based upon scientific rationalism. Since this, by definition, is abstract and general, the professional and scientist tend to "turn to that government which can deal with all such problems on the widest possible scale"—the central government.[20] Third, though national officials take pains to enlist the cooperation of local elites in the implementation of their programs, the central governments they work for are responding primarily to functional interests, business in particular, but also organized labor where it is powerful. As Ashford writes:

> In our effort to build a welfare state, concern has been
> with the aggregation of similarities regardless of their
> territorial location or contiguity. . . . The emergence
> of functionally specific groups, usually detached from
> territorial units, means that the existing system of demo-
> cratic checks and control is diminishing.[21]

For these reasons, territorial representation may indeed have been dealt a mortal blow by the growth in the influence of functional interest groups and a shift in industrial societies from territorial to functional modes of organization. But before concluding that all industrial states have become some version of a national "co-optative polity" based on privileged negotiation among organized functional interests at the national level,[22] let us look more deeply into the fiscal, technocratic, and functional arguments listed above. I shall argue that a new equilibrium between policy centralization and territorial representation can be detected in the relations between center and periphery in industrial nations. It is to exploring this essentially political balance that this book is devoted.

CENTRAL FINANCE AND THE EROSION OF LOCAL AUTONOMY

It is impossible even to summarize adequately the vast literature that has grown up in both Europe and America on central governmental subsidization of local government activities.[23] In all industrial countries, the growth in urban functions and services of the postwar period has led to a large increase in external financing of local governments—usually on the part of higher levels of government. The general tendency among students has been to conclude from these transfers of funds that central governments have gained increased leverage —for some a stranglehold—over the autonomy of policy choice of local units of government. As G. Ross Stephens writes of the United States, "There has been considerable verbalization about the increasingly influential role of the national government in state and local affairs. Much of this has presumably resulted from a massive increase in federal monetary support."[24]

But the circumstances under which such transfers occur can vary greatly, influencing political and policy outcomes in equally varying ways. In the first place, central government grants and loans differ in their impact in terms of how closely their use must be linked to specific policy areas and programs. A general grant impairs local policy autonomy less than a categorical one, and the latter will vary in its effects on local autonomy according to whether or not it allows local discretion in the use to which such funds are put.

Hansen and Kjellberg put these distinctions nicely for Norway, a country in which many local politicians and administrators have complained of local government being "regulated into a mere subordinate administrative branch of central government." They write:

In some cases grants must be used for specific tasks, but in other cases they take the form of general grants to be appropriated by the municipal authorities according to

their own discretion and specific priorities. And even
the fact that some financial transfers are earmarked does
not automatically imply a restriction with respect to local discretion. In some instances they take the form of
offers from the central government, which the local authorities may avail themselves of.[25]

In the United States, categorical grants have increased in number and variety since the 1950s but decreased as a proportion of federal aid to local governments from 98 percent in 1966 to 75 percent
in 1975, according to Beer's insightful analysis.[26] And despite an
overwhelming impression of local authority dependency on central
government grants, one finds in Britain a heavy reliance on an automatic transfer of general funds and relatively little use of categorical
grants.[27] Only in France and Japan has there been consistent recourse to high levels of categorical grants-in-aid and, in the latter
case, at least, the goal has been less central control over local governmental activity than the center's macroeconomic aim of regulating
the rate of growth of the economy.[28]

Also, many subnational units of government, such as the American states, have increased their shares of both taxing and spending
vis-a-vis both the federal and local levels of government. "If they
have not been notable innovators," writes Beer," the states have
nonetheless continued and increased their massive efforts to finance
the traditional welfare state."[29] And far from losing out financially
to the center, American state revenue structures, according to
Stephens' analysis, are becoming more viable. "It might be hypothe-
sized," he observes, "that the states have been prodded, propped-up
and provisioned by the federal government."[30]

Is this a deviant outcome of the American federal system or,
as Beer suggests, does "the way a political system divides power between levels of government . . . have little to do with how it will divide resources and responsibilities between the public and the private
sector?"[31] When Ashford analyzed the proportion of national income
disbursed by all levels of government from the UN Yearbook of National Accounts over a ten-year period, he found that in France,
West Germany, Canada, and the United States total local spending had
either kept up with the growth in public spending as a whole (Canada
and Germany) or was growing more rapidly than the public sector as
a whole (France and the United States).[32] The only country in the
UN figures he studied in which public spending was growing less rapidly
in the localities than in general was Britain, and even here opinions
are divided. Newton, for example, cites figures that lead him to conclude that "local expenditure has outpaced the gross domestic product" and "has increased more rapidly than public expenditure" as a
whole.[33]

Capital formation has been a special area of growth in public spending in the postwar period, and here Ashford found the ratio of central to local capital formation to be more favorable to the center in four out of five of the countries he analyzed.[34] However, even in Britain, for many the nation with the most unqualified trend toward centralization, some observers calculate that local expenditure on capital projects has increased more rapidly than spending in the public sector as a whole.[35] If nothing else, local authorities in Britain can rely on the private capital market as well as on publicly controlled investment funds, a factor that, in Alberta Sbragia's words, "makes it more difficult for the center to constrain local policy choices."[36]

The financial dependence of localities on central governments has not, as was expected, led to a high degree of standardization of local expenditure. Even in uniform administrative systems like Norway[37] and France,[38] there are substantial variations between local units in their per capita expenditure. And in Britain, "nearly twenty years of central government funding has barely changed the amount of variation among the subunits of the British political system."[39] In federal systems like the United States, West Germany, Canada, and Switzerland, the variability in local spending—for example, in the important field of educational policy[40]—is very striking. Only in Japan, of the countries I have surveyed, does a complicated equalization grant formula appear to "go a long way towards equalizing access to general purpose resources among local authorities."[41] Even in Japan, however, the equalization grants are partially offset by the categorical grants used by the center for purposes of macroeconomic policy.

The disparities in per capita spending among local units brings us to the important, but still obscure, question of the impact of politics and political alignments on local policy making. For the "erosion of local autonomy" model suggests either one of two things: that the central, or centrally controlled, financing of local governments must be politically neutral (in systems with an apolitical civil service); or (in systems where the bureaucracy is politicized) that it redounds mainly to the benefit of friends of the government.

Unfortunately, neither generalization can be made with any confidence. While numerous political variables have, for one or another country or set of expenditures, been related to urban policy outputs, few consistent or strong relationships have emerged across systems. As Robert Fried writes, expenditure levels can be related to

the preferences and orientations of community leaders;
the distribution of power among them; the forms and extent of citizen participation; the leftism of the civic elite;

the power and routines of the municipal bureaucracies;
the form of municipal government; the form of municipal
elections; the strength and diversity of urban interest
groups; the number of urban governments per city; the
competitiveness of the party system; the dominant type
of local mass political culture. [42]

But after citing so impressive a list of indicators from a number of countries, Fried can only cautiously conclude that "political
variables have relatively less direct and independent impact than
socio-economic variables."[43] Few would go so far as he when he
writes that "the weakness of party differences even in apparently more
polarized urban party systems seems to suggest that all urban political systems are, in effect, non-partisan systems."[44] But many
would concur that the inconsistency of the cross-national results "may
be the result of the pluralism of urban political systems—a reflection
of the possibility that they are exposed to pressures from a variety
of local and central groups"[45] (in any case, not only from the center).
    With respect to countries with a neutral civil service tradition,
the findings are mixed. In Norway, "political variables seem to exert
an independent influence in these areas of policy where local authorities enjoy some degree of autonomy from central control." Thus, the
Socialist vote in Norway is significantly correlated to the level of expenditures, especially in the social services.[46] In Britain, although
many public services—for example, parks, sewers, police, fire protection, and housing investment—show little impact of voting patterns
on local spending, "on the other hand," concludes Newton, "there is
a fair weight of evidence to show that the more costly and highly politicized services such as education, housing, and personal services are
influenced by political control, the Labour cities generally spending
more and producing a different pattern of services in contrast to the
Conservative cities."[47] Though Newton, like other observers of the
British scene, is impressed with the powerful effect of "the huge redistribution grants which central government makes to local government," he concludes that "local politics in Britain has not been without its influence in bringing about this state of affairs.[48]
    As for countries with a more politicized civil service, the scat-
tered results we possess do not support the "central financial control"
model any more consistently. Conservative governments may wish
to help bourgeois communities, but these normally spend less, bor-
row carefully, and—in any case—possess substantial fiscal resources
of their own. And while they may wish to penalize industrial communities for supporting the opposition, there is evidence from France
that left-wing municipalities spend more freely and from Italy that
they enjoy central financial aid above the national average, in order
to provide a high level of social services.[49]

In summary, the empirical case that financial centralization has robbed subnational governments of their vitality has yet to be made. Though national public spending has increased, subnational spending has increased still more and, while numerous categorical grants tie down the activities of many local governments, the general revenue sharing that is more common leaves them far more freedom; finally, the continued high level of variation across subunits within industrial nations argues against the financial centralization hypothesis as well, especially where local political factors are closely linked to variations in spending.

The problem with using measures of financial subsidization of local government as an indicator of centralization is to know what political meaning to give to them. While the centralization of governmental expenditure may be an index of local policy dependency, its allocation to particular municipalities or urban functions may be a measure of the political clout of local officials, of the potential for mobilization of the urban public or interorganizational decision making, or of the coalitional strategies of national elites; in other words, of political exchange. But in the absence of independent measures of the centralization of government decision making and of the political influence of local elites and the mass public, the centralization of expenditures is a totally neutral indicator with respect to who has power over whom. This leads to the argument from technocracy.

TECHNOCRACY AND LOCAL POLITICAL ELITES

Beer writes:

> There is, I think, an inherent tendency for professional knowledge to promote governmental centralization. . . . Not only do professionals outside government tend to seek out the wider jurisdiction as the appropriate vehicle for problem-solving. Within government when similarly trained professionals work with one another across different systems, this common discipline constitutes a ground for harmony and cooperation tending to offset the Madisonian checks and balances that might otherwise arise from intergovernmental differentiation. Vertical hierarchies cutting across different levels of government are a main feature of the new phase of American federalism. [50]

With suitable changes, Beer's comments could be repeated with equal validity for a number of other industrial nations. Jean-Claude

Thoenig shows that the Ponts et chaussées corps gained increasing leverage over French urban policy in the late 1960s as part of the Ministry of Equipment's reorganization.[51] In Japan, Michio Muramatsu writes, economic growth policies increased the number and importance of specialists and experts in economics and planning within the bureaucracy.[52] And in Britain, Ashford argues in this volume, local government is conceived in extremely functional terms, which gives central governmental experts a technological and psychological advantage over the local councils that receive their aid.

These points are too well known to require elaboration here. But they should not obscure for us some complementary and countertrends that, to some extent, modify this picture of technocratic centralization. First, as Beer himself is quick to point out, if the new professionalism is spatially centralizing, it may be functionally decentralizing,[53] creating a proliferation of new agencies and programs. These can give territorial units a number of competing contact points from which to seek central governmental largesse, helping the local political entrepreneur who can pyramid resources from these various sources.[54] I have made this argument with respect to the Italian bureaucracy, which, despite the relative paucity of resources that it transfers to local governments, provides through its dispersion a variety of channels of access for local elites to use in seeking central financial support.[55]

Second, though many have seen technocracy as the antithesis of politics, I would adopt a different view: even the most technocratic of administrators respond to the demands of the political leadership at the level of government closest to them. The proliferation of experts and specialists to local and intermediate levels of government in recent years thus not only creates professional hierarchies between center and periphery; it also gives local elected officials technological advocates to use in their relations with the center. Thus, the highly skilled housing administrators of Milan, Sbragia found, were able to use their expertise and professionalism to extract financial resources from Rome that less qualified personnel in other cities failed to get so easily.[56] In Britain, what L. J. Sharpe has called the "nonexecutant tradition of central government" means that "whatever the legal and financial controls exercised over local government by central government, there remains an irreducible element of autonomy exercised by local government because it controls its own professional staff."[57] In Japan, as Muramatsu shows, in the 1960s "local governments were modernized in the sense that they acquired trained statisticians, planners, computer programmers, and others who were providing their skills in making master plans for development."[58]

In the United States, "the technocratic potential of state administration has been strengthened and refined in many instances," though frequently at the cost of the municipalities. As Beer concludes,

> With their new technocratic equipment they [the states]
> perform functions of planning, coordination and control
> in regard to essentially national programs. On the
> other hand, looking toward the local governments, the
> state can perform the critical function of adjusting local
> jurisdictions and boundaries to correspond with program
> needs. [59]

Stephens shows that there has been a high degree of centralization in
the American states. [60] But if the cause of this is technocracy, and if
technocracy is already gravitating from the federal center to the
states, can it not ultimately settle in the federal periphery—the cities
—as well?

Technological conformity may threaten local political elites
where they permit it to embarrass them vis-a-vis local citizens'
groups. Thus, nuclear energy, air pollution, and airport controversies in many countries have made local officials wary of adopting the
technological positions of central administrators and anxious to consult experts of their own before agreeing to their communities' becoming sites for environmentally troublesome projects. For instance,
after the first successful residents' movements against air and water
pollution in Japan, "local governments were quick to change their attitudes toward the problem of pollution; the central government re-
acted much more slowly." [61] The political reaction of the Port Authority of New York in the Concorde controversy is an example of the
political lessons learned from earlier technological confrontations.

Local techniques of dealing with the central "technocratic-pro-
fessional complex" have been quick to develop. One such reaction is
of dubious value to local communities: adopting the language of management and essentially accepting the vision of modernization of the
center, which comes bearing subsidies for potentially costly improvements. This was widespread in France—especially in provincial
France—in the 1960s. But is such a managerial stance ever truly
apolitical? In an analysis of a sample of small-town French mayors
in the 1960s, I found a strong relationship between such apolitisme
and ideological conservatism. [62] The lesson could have been learned
from American history, when a municipal reform movement developed
that essentially aided local business circles in the name of taking politics out of local government. [63] As in the earlier American experience,
the local advocates of French apolitisme regarded themselves as modernizers, a stance that dovetailed neatly with the then-dominant ideology of the ruling Gaullist regime.

Another widespread technique has been to coopt technocrats into
local political office. This is described by Peter Katzenstein in Chapter 5 of this volume: the Austrian valley community he studied chose

the former communal secretary, with his links to higher administrators and his technical expertise, as mayor. This can also be seen in Italy in the 1960s, where a large number of urbanists and municipal civil servants became city council members and mayors.[64] It should be added, however, that even an urban planner with the national reputation of a Kenneth Logue has difficulty translating technologically based influence into political power, as was shown by his loss of the Boston mayorality election to Kevin White.

As technocracy is diffused from the summit of the political system to the base, it takes on different ideological colorations. Thus, the French Communists, content to stew locally in their own ideological juices in the 1950s, by the end of the 1960s had developed a managerial style and a cadre of urban planners and engineers to oppose to the technocracy of the right a new technocracy of the left.[65] The technologically backed movements against environmental pollution in the United States, western Europe, and Japan show that technocracy is as easily politicized as were earlier ideologies.

Another aspect of technocratic government that ultimately works in favor of localities is its tendency to lead to what Beer calls an "intergovernmental lobby": the "governors, mayors, country supervisors, city managers and other office-holders, usually elective, who exercise general responsibilities in state and local governments."[66] These lobbies, though formally antagonistic to the professionals who allocate resources from the center, are actually interdependent with, and to some extent owe their existence to, the stimulus of central programs of local assistance.

One impact of local and regional interest lobbies was to help bring about the shift from categorical grants to general revenue sharing and block grants discussed earlier.[67] Another, less easy to trace, was an increase in the proportion of national spending directed to the cities. A third was to help increase interest in some countries in a regional level of government, as Peter Gourevitch points out about France in Chapter 2 of this volume. And in Italy, newly chosen regional officials tended to coordinate their pressures on the central government, leading to fears of "panregionalism" on the part of the center.

In summary, the new centralism may have created a new localism, a localism based not on parochialism and privilege but on the effects of technocracy, while sharing its language if not its goals. While the new localism seems particularly well organized in the United States through various forms of intergovernmental lobbies, it is also apparent in other industrial nations in which the technical expertise to administer complex national programs has been developed by municipalities. This is true even in Italy, where since 1975 the partisan stratification of the territorial system is so pronounced that

the left—and especially the Communist Party—is developing its own
"technocracy of the base" to oppose the technocracy of the center.
When a technocracy of the base and a technocracy of the left are opposed to a technocracy of the summit and a technocracy of the right,
then politics takes over once again and, in Katzenstein's words, the
shape of our political future may be determined by the shape of our
political past.

FUNCTIONAL CENTRALIZATION AND
TERRITORIAL REPRESENTATION

This takes us back to the problem raised at the outset: the relationship between the growth of functional programs and administration at the center and the forms of representation through which industrial nations are governed. Through an unfortunate but perhaps symbolic linguistic accident, the term "function" has come to relate to
two distinct meanings (even excepting the somewhat arcane one given
to it by Parsonian sociology): the specialized policy activities of modern governments and a mode of representation that is based upon social and professional interests. These two meanings are explicitly
linked in Ashford's succinct summary. "The growth of governmental
functions," he writes, "especially under central control and specifica-
tion, has meant the dilution of the political authority of the territorial
subunit." And, "those interested in influencing policies increasingly
find that they do not need a territorial base, but operate through their
functional organization."[68]
Leaving aside the vexed question of the causal relationship between these two trends, what should be stressed is that functional
centralization is about policy making, which must take account of deep
territorial forces that have representative linkages to the center and
perform key services for the state. In systems in which the formal
bases of representation are territorial, this sets objective limits on
the degree of functional centralization of decision making that will be
possible or desirable. Indeed, one could argue, of greater danger to
democracy than functional representation is the fact that policy making is both centralized and technocratic, while policy implementation
is decentralized and—in many cases—politicized. Functional interests thus range themselves around both poles of the political system
—center and periphery—and use their territorial leverage to fight
out their conflicts of interest.
These are very broad questions and go well beyond the scope
of this chapter or the ones that follow. Rather than stray so far beyond our empirical base, I would like to deal with one specific aspect
of the representation problem: the impact of types of territorial rep-

resentation on the implementation of central policy. I will start with
the observation made by numerous authors, among them several in
this volume. If there is a central tendency in territorial politics in
industrial nations, it is for preexisting subunits of government to become the agencies for implementation of central governmental policies
for the city. To return to Beer's American example, the states are
beginning to "perform functions of planning, coordination and control
in regard to essentially national programs."[69] But the same is true
in Britain, France, Germany, and Japan, where subnational governments—either state or local—have taken charge of administering a
large proportion of national territorial policies.

Critics of centralization may argue that this delegation of functions enhances the leverage of the center over local subunits. Where
carefully controlled, as in France, this is probably true, but in most
systems, observers concur that local implementation of national policies allows natural interorganizational factors to intervene, creating
"ever-greater pressure," in Ronald Aqua's words about Japan, "to
tolerate wider degrees of local adjustment to accommodate particular or unique local circumstances."[70] The results are not always
beneficial. As Pressman and Wildavsky showed in their study of Oak-
land, interorganizational linkages between the federal center and the
urban periphery can vitiate a program of much of its purpose.[71]

What may have led central governments to utilize existing local
governments to implement their programs locally? One answer is
utilitarian; most programs need field agencies to administer them,
so why not utilize the local governments in place and avoid a proliferation of central governmental agencies? I do not think this explanation
holds much water: first, because proliferation of national administrative agencies has occurred anyway—if only to keep a check on implementation; and second, because the logical territory or size of territory for administering a given program may vary independently of
the size of the existing city.[72]

I think the real reason lies in the vitality of territorial representation, both in its corporate (local) and individual (legislative)
forms and in the capacity of local political elites to use their representative roles to prevent their erosion of functional responsibility.
Eulau has argued that the genius of the American federal system is
that the framers combined the concepts of federalism and representation and that their work may still be observed, for example, in the
continued salience of state and local interests in the House of Representatives.[73] Certainly, the Appalachian Regional Commission,
created as an experiment in regional economic planning in the John-
son years, operates, as a result of congressional drafting to help
states "to take maximum advantage of the system" and not as an instrument of regional planning. As Martha Derthick observes, "What

was briefly an effort to transcend the states turned very quickly into an organizational device that rationalized a larger role for them."[74] What one author has called "social pork barrel" illustrates this meshing between functional programs and territorial representation quite well: the ordering principle of social policy making in America is technocratic, but the mode and logic of implementation are determined by territorial representation, which is just as potent in determining the allocation of the new social programs as of the old pork barrel legislation.[75]

Is there a sort of "polarity principle" in American federalism, one that determines that "nation and states," in Eulau's words, "are opposites that, like the poles of the magnetic field, are yet linked?"[76] Thus, Eulau speculates, "as the federal center is strengthened there is yet also a noticeable strengthening of the federal periphery." And "the glue that holds the system together is the representation of multiple constituencies"—functional and territorial—each with linkages between levels of the American system.[77] If Eulau is right, then studies of changing federalism should regard nation and localities as dualities that are linked not only by the overarching power of functional administration but also by a capillary system of territorial representation.

If Eulau has turned to the Federalist papers for hints about the nature of American federalism, where would we turn to in France, in many ways the antithesis of the United States in terms of centralization? To Tocqueville, with his notion of the all-embracing Napoleonic state? Or to Montesquieu, who defended the corporate privileges of the provincial parlements? Although some, like Tocqueville, have viewed France mainly in terms of its iron cage of bureaucracy, the evidence of empirical research is more mixed. It is true that the central government in France has many tools to use against local governments. But the most important of these tools—the integrated prefecture—is a double-edged one; because the prefect operates through a politics of complicity[78] with the local officials who administer the municipalities in his département, he is frequently loath to assist Paris in implementing policies that directly threaten their interests.

This was clearly the case of the prefect of the Bouches-du-Rhône when the government wished him to implement a ville nouvelle around the new industrial pole of Fos, studied in Chapter 4 of this volume. Evidence from the local level suggests that French mayors—at least provincial mayors—do regard the prefect as an ally,[79] a tendency that was, paradoxically, enhanced by the same Fifth Republic that attacked local autonomy in the 1969 regional reform discussed by Gourevitch (Chapter 2). This paradox was evident in the implementation of the regional planning reform of 1964, in which the prefectoral corps succeeded in dominating recruitment into the new missions ré-

gionales and local elected officials ended up heavily represented on
the new regional CODER, the regional economic development committees.[80]

Heretical as it may sound to advocates of the Tocquevillian vision of French administration, there is a "polarity principle" in French
politics too, which, with different forms and effects from the United
States, balances the power of the Napoleonic central state against the
periphery. In the past (as perhaps once again in the future) part of
the territorial principle of representation was reflected in Parliament,
particularly in a national assembly that was notoriously addicted to
rural pork barrel.[81] While the Fifth Republic did preserve an element
of territorial representation through the senate, so circumscribed
were the powers of both senate and assembly that territorial elites
were forced increasingly back on their ties with the prefecture. This
in turn privileged the representation of the commune as a corporate
entity and dovetailed with local elites' inclination to put themselves
forward as the representatives of "the municipality as a whole."[82]
However fictitious such a claim may have been, it nonetheless
strengthened the mayor, who could succeed in legitimizing himself
with broad support from within the community vis-a-vis the administration and deepened the ties of complicity between local politicians,
prefects, and other officials.

Indeed, so widespread was this system of informal ties in the
1960s that Thoenig has used the image of a "honeycomb structure" to
describe it.[83] At the same time, a parallel system of "political para-
chutage" developed between Paris and the provinces through the efforts
of the Gaullist national elite to develop grassroots presence. This
too increased the ability of local elites to elicit program support from
Paris, particularly where—as in the case of the Corrèze, for example—the "parachuted" leader was a minister or Gaullist notable.[84]
But the administrative linkages between French communities and the
state give the latter far more policy leverage than in the United
States and give priority to the corporate representation of the commune through its mayor and council rather than through individual legislators' activities at higher levels of government.

In Italy, party plays the key role in linking center and periphery,
as illustrated in the case of the south by Luigi Graziano in Chapter 9
of this volume. Clientelism takes up part of the slack of an inefficient
bureaucracy and offsets the national ideological stalemate by distribut-
ing resources incrementally—and ineffectively—to the periphery of
the political system. Parliament has become so suffused by clientelistic interests—often in the form of organized factional groupings—that
it has lost much of its capacity for coherent policy making, especially
with respect to the south. Yet while economic elites have been able
to exploit this system, it should be remembered that poor communi-

ties and those with a paucity of industrial employment—not to mention those administered by the left, as pointed out above—have been able to use it too. The major defect of the Italian system of center-periphery allocation has been the absence of collective choice in policy making at all levels and its domination forms of policy allocation that can be easily translated into individual goods. But the efforts of local political elites to extract resources through political leverage has at least prevented a mastodontic national bureaucracy from coming totally under the control of functional clientele groupings at the summit.

Can we see a "polarity principle" even in centrally planned socialist systems as well? In Chapter 7 of this volume, Jacek Tarkowski finds that the vertical <u>dirigisme</u> of the Polish economic planning mechanism is modified by the "horizontal" ties between party officers, public officials, and producers at the base and by complementary vertical ties between the localities and higher levels of government. Especially instructive for our knowledge of the workings of the Polish system is the interaction between the vertical and horizontal linkages within the local party organizations that Tarkowski describes. Tarkowski argues persuasively that these linkages build flexibility into a system in which collective social goals are set at the center. Is it possible to go one step further? In Poland is there not a collective representation of territorial interests at the base to match the setting of collective "functional" goals through economic planning at the summit?

This variety of linkages between territorial representation and functional policy making lends support to Cameron and Hofferbert's finding, using educational policy, that differences in the structure of intergovernmental relations "are systematically related to differences in [policy] distribution across [and] . . . within nations."[85] That the same is true within nations is illustrated by Martin Shefter's contribution to this volume (Chapter 6). He shows that, while state legislators in Boston work at the local level to satisfy mainly individual interests, New York City legislators must work in Albany to satisfy the organized functional interests that are so powerful in their city. The "polarity principle" for New York City legislators assimilates functional interests into constituency service, while their Boston counterparts perform neighborhood services through their ties within the city administration. Can such differences in institutional linkages and in the scale of the interests represented fail to have contributed to the policy outcomes that have so exacerbated New York City's recent fiscal crisis in comparison to Boston's?

There are many political outcomes that will become clearer once we focus on the formal and informal patterns of territorial representation that are found in industrial nations. What should be stressed here is that "local autonomy" cannot be measured as the simple residual of the administrative functions that are left over after the center takes its share, nor as the level of financing that the center bestows on the periphery (for this can be as much a sign of peripheral influence as of central governmental power), but by the political resources and mechanisms of territorial representation that allow subnational units to utilize the center to their advantage. Beer talks of the "mobilization of consent," by which he means the embedding of national territorial policy "in a context of politics which will educate the clientele, win their cooperation and endow them with some real power of influencing outputs."[86] I would refer instead to the resources for territorial representation in policy making, not merely in the pork barrel sense of influencing the allocation of policy goods in a distributional manner, but in insuring that policy emerges from political exchange between territorial and functional representatives at all levels of the system.

There is little space, and less comparative research to draw on, to discuss empirically the political resources necessary for such a role to be insured for territorial representation. At a minimum, the formal intergovernmental structure must be considered. But beyond this, there is the "informal structure" of intergovernmental relations,[87] the public's perceptions of rightness or wrongness of a particular level of government occupying a given sector of policy space,[88] and, above all, the skills and strategies of local officials as gatekeepers between center and periphery.

A whole tradition of anthropological research has shown how local leaders in traditional rural communities operate as brokers to mediate between their supporters and the state. A comparison of modern community power studies shows that there are few notable differences in the techniques used and that, indeed, the political broker as a type of local leader becomes more, rather than less, important as a community grows and its population divides into a plethora of competing groups and interests.[89] The difference, of course, is that the new brokerage deals in the language of technocracy and the new brokers specialize in the transfer and implementation of the collective goals of the welfare state within their communities, as shown in the chapters by Katzenstein, Shefter, and Tarkowski. This calls for a host of new skills and personnel but reinforces the traditional politics of territorial representation while changing its stock-in-trade.

The political issues of the 1960s and 1970s have reinforced the importance of territorial representation. Industrial and technological location problems; air and water pollution; metropolitan reorganization; above all, the structural fiscal crisis of the cities: these tend to unite groups within localities against the center and challenge the hegemony of the functional interest groups that tended to overawe localities in the 1950s and early 1960s. Even in Norway, a country in which "the overall tendency . . . has been towards a reduction of territorial strains and an increase in the importance of purely economic conflicts," territorial issues emerged once again in the mid-1970s over the sensitive problem of Norwegian entry into the Common Market. [90] And, of course, recent years have seen a more violent flare-up of territorial-ethnic identities in countries where the traditional territorial linkages have failed to encompass them. [91] Has the creation of functional interest-cooptative states had the unfortunate side effect of leaving territorial interests to fester and eventually explode?

These observations suggest that the periphery best uses the center where the political skills of its leaders and the institutional and informal linkages of territorial representation permit it to do so effectively. But the center of course uses the periphery as well: to create a coalitional majority, as Luigi Graziano's discussion (see Chapter 9) of the integration of southern Italy into the Italian state in the nineteenth century teaches; as a reservoir of issues to fight out national partisan conflicts, as Peter Gourevitch's chapter (Chapter 2) demonstrates; and even to organize national defense and keep national cartel politics balanced, as Gabriel Sheffer shows in the case of the Israeli settlement towns (Chapter 3). Even in the United States, it was not merely pressure from the "intergovernmental lobby" that led to the adoption of general revenue sharing in the 1970s, but the Nixon administration's desire to pull the rug out from under some of the "technocratic" urban elites who had been enjoying easy access to the social pork barrel of the Great Society.

The use of the center by the periphery and the use of the periphery by the center clash when national elites—for technocratic or other reasons—conceive of the need to reorganize local or metropolitan area government. Consider French regional reform proposals in the 1960s. There were sound technocratic reasons put forward by a part of the Gaullist elite for reforming subnational administration; but, as Gourevitch shows, another part of the majority had already accepted the political necessity of working with the conservative notables of the provinces, who opposed on principle any threat to their privileged conduits of influence to the center. The periphery won that battle in the regional referendum of 1969; the traditionalists' goal of coopting the local political class coincided with peripheral desire for unchanged territorial representation, against De Gaulle's plans for modernization of local government. This example comes from the "Napoleonic" state of the Fifth Republic; how much more compelling the influence of territorial forces on policy outcomes in more dispersed systems like Italy or Canada!

If a generalization can be hazarded, in closing, it is that if functional centralization has had one single effect, it has been to lead citizens at the periphery to turn more and more to the local, regional, and primordial identities around them. These, in many cases, predate the national state. Even where they do not, they are relatively close at hand and have the virtue of being responsive to local political activism. In the long run, therefore, the functional cleavages that earlier scholars saw displacing the territorial dimension in politics may actually reinforce it, channeling electorally bolstered demands to the national state, which may then come into conflict with the "functional" demands of national and international interest groups. But that, of course, is another problem, and one that is only beginning to emerge on the political scene of industrial nations.

NOTES

1. James Fesler, Area and Administration (Birmingham: University of Alabama Press, 1949), p. 2.

2. Douglas Ashford, "Territory vs. Function: Toward a Policy-Based Theory of Subnational Government," prepared for delivery at the 1976 Annual Meeting of the American Political Science Association, Chicago, September 2-5, 1976, p. 2.

3. S. M. Lipset and Stein Rokkan, Party Systems and Voter Alignments (New York: Free Press,1967), pp. 1-64.

4. Lucio Libertini, "Decentramento regionale della politica industriale," Rinascita, February 25, 1977, p. 12.

5. Heinz Eulau, "Polarity in Representational Federalism: A Neglected Theme of Political Theory," Publius 3 (Fall 1973): 153-71.

6. Charles Maier, Recasting Bourgeois Europe: Stabilization in France, Germany and Italy in the Decade after World War One, pt. 3 (Princeton, N.J.: Princeton University Press, 1975).

7. See Juan Linz, "Spain: An Authoritarian Regime," Cleavages, Ideologies, and Party Systems, ed. Eric Allardt and Y. Littunen (Helsinki: Westermarck Society, 1964), pp. 290-341.

8. These are discussed in detail in John H. McArthur and Bruce R. Scott, Industrial Planning in France (Cambridge, Mass.: Harvard University Press, 1969), chap. 3.

9. Samuel Beer, British Politics in the Collectivist Age (New York: Knopf, 1966).

10. Martin Heisler writes, "The increased saliency of . . . corporate politics" is, of course, linked with the decline in the importance of the more traditional channels for political activity. See his Politics in Europe: Structure and Processes in Some Postindustrial Democracies (New York: McKay, 1974), p. 42, and the many sources cited there.

11. Andrew Shonfield, Modern Capitalism: The Changing Balance of Public and Private Power (New York: Oxford University Press, 1965).

12. McArthur and Scott, Industrial Planning in France, especially their discussion of decision making in the steel reorganization of the mid-1960s on pp. 369-76.

13. Samuel Beer, "The Modernization of American Federalism," Publius 3 (Fall 1973): 52.

14. Ibid., p. 57.

15. Ibid., p. 58.

16. Ibid., p. 75.

17. Ibid., p. 78.

18. Deil S. Wright, "Governors, Grants and the Intergovernmental System," The American Governor and Behavioral Perspective, ed. Thad Beyle and J. Oliver Williams (New York: Harper & Row, 1972), p. 188, quoted in Beer, "Modernization," p. 79.

19. Ashford, "Territory vs. Function," is a systematic attempt to document this financial dependence cross-nationally.

20. Beer, "Modernization," p. 79.

21. Ashford, "Territory vs. Function," pp. 3, 5.

22. The term is Heisler's, Politics in Europe, pp. 63 ff.

23. The closest we have to a comparative summary on the financial aspects of local government is in Robert Fried's essay, "Comparative Urban Policy and Performance," The Handbook of Political Science, ed. Fred I. Greenstein and Nelson Polsby, vol. 6 (Reading, Mass.: Addison-Wesley, 1975).

24. G. Ross Stephens, "State Centralization and the Erosion of Local Autonomy," Journal of Politics 36 (1974): 44–45.

25. Tore Hansen and Francesco Kjellberg, "Municipal Expenditures in Norway: Autonomy and Constraints in Local Government Activity," Policy and Politics 4 (1976): 29.

26. Samuel Beer, "Political Overload and Federalism," unpublished paper to appear in Polity, Fall 1977, p. 8. The evidence in this paper is summarized from Beer's "The Adoption of General Revenue Sharing: A Case Study in Public Sector Politics," Public Policy 24 (Spring 1976). I am grateful to Professor Beer for calling his unpublished article to my attention. It ought to be read as a complement to his "The Modernization of American Federalism."

27. Ashford, "Territory vs. Function," pp. 16–17.

28. Ibid., p. 20; and Ronald Aqua, "National Aid and Local Choice in Japan," prepared for the Conference on Urban Choice and State Power, Cornell University, May 1977, p. 9.

29. Beer, "Modernization," pp. 89–91.

30. Stephens, "State Centralization," p. 46.

31. Beer, "Modernization," p. 90.

32. Ashford, "Territory vs. Function," p. 9.

33. Newton's figures, and his sources, are found in his "Financial Trends in the Local Government of England and Wales," prepared for the Workshop on the Financial Problems of West European Cities, European Consortium for Political Research Joint Workshops, Berlin, March 27–April 2, 1977, p. 5.

34. Ashford, "Territory vs. Function," p. 10.

35. Newton, "Financial Trends," pp. 5-6.

36. Alberta Sbragia, "Public Policy Decision-Making Constraints: Local Government Borrowing in the U.S., U.K., and France," presented to the 1976 Annual Meeting of the American Political Science Association, Chicago, September 2-5, 1976, pp. 35-36.

37. Hansen and Kjellberg, "Municipal Expenditures in Norway," p. 27.

38. For example, see Yves Fréville, "L'Evolution des finances des grandes villes depuis 1967," Revue de sciences financières 4 (1973): 725-58.

39. Douglas Ashford, "Democracy, Decentralization and Decisions in Subnational Politics," Sage Professional Papers in Comparative Politics, vol. 5 (Beverly Hills, Calif.: Sage Publications, 1976).

40. David R. Cameron and Richard I. Hofferbert, "The Impact of Federalism on Education Finance: A Comparative Analysis," European Journal of Political Research 2 (September 1974): 239-40.

41. Aqua, "National Aid," p. 8.

42. Fried, "Comparative Urban Policy," p. 337.

43. Ibid., p. 346.

44. Ibid., p. 345.

45. Ibid., p. 346.

46. Hansen and Kjellberg, "Municipal Expenditures in Norway," p. 46.

47. Ken Newton, "Community Performance in Britain," Current Sociology 22 (1976): 81.

48. Ibid., p. 82.

49. For evidence on spending levels for France, see Josué Kobielski, "L'Influence de la structure des communes urbaines sur leurs dépenses de fonctionnement," thesis, Faculté des sciences economiques de l'université de Rennes, 1974; for Italy, see Giogio Brosio, "Composizione politica e comportamento di spesa degli enti locali italiani," Economia pubblica, October 1975, pp. 17-25. For evidence on the relationship between central grants and loans and the left-wing vote from both countries, see my Between Center and Periphery: Grassroots Politicians in Italy and France (New Haven, Conn.: Yale University Press, 1977), chap. 3. For evidence from Japan that the Conservative government provides higher financial support to LDP-oriented poorer regions, see Aqua, "National Aid," p. 16.

50. Beer, "Political Overload," pp. 7-8.

51. Jean-Claude Thoenig, L'Ere des technocrats: Le cas des ponts et chaussées (Paris: Editions d'organisation, 1973).

52. Michio Muramatsu, "The Impact of Economic Growth Policies on Local Politics in Japan," Asian Survey 15 (September 1975): 807.

53. Beer, "Political Overload," p. 8.

54. Jeffrey Pressman, "Preconditions of Mayoral Leadership," American Political Science Review 66 (June 1973): 511–25.

55. Tarrow, Between Center and Periphery, chap. 3.

56. Alberta Sbragia, "Urban Autonomy within the Unitary State: A Case Study of Public Housing Politics in Milan, Italy," unpublished doctoral dissertation, University of Wisconsin, Madison, 1974.

57. L. J. Sharpe, "Modernizing the Localities: Local Government Reorganization in Britain," unpublished paper, January 1977, p. 4.

58. Muramatsu, "Impact of Economic Growth Policies," p. 809.

59. Beer, "Modernization," p. 85.

60. Stephens, "State Centralization."

61. Muramatsu, "Impact of Economic Growth Policies," p. 809.

62. Tarrow, Between Center and Periphery, chap. 4.

63. Samuel Hays, "The Politics of Reform in Municipal Government in the Progressive Era," Pacific Northwest Quarterly 55 (1964): 157–69.

64. Tarrow, Between Center and Periphery, pp. 114–15.

65. See the special number of the PCF's journal, La nouvelle critique, no. 78 bis, "Pour un urbanisme . . . ," the text of a conference run by the Communist Party in Grenoble, in April 1974, for the flavor of this new technocracy.

66. Beer, "Political Overload," p. 9.

67. Ibid., p. 11.

68. Ashford, "Territory vs. Function," pp. 4–5.

69. Beer, "Modernization," p. 85.

70. Aqua, "National Aid," p. 4.

71. Jeffrey Pressman and Aaron Wildavsky, Implementation (Berkeley and Los Angeles: University of California Press, 1974).

72. Mancur Olson, Jr., "The Principle of 'Fiscal Equivalence': The Division of Responsibilities between Different Levels of Government," American Economic Review 59 (May 1969).

73. Eulau, "Polarity in Representational Federalism," p. 169.

74. Martha Derthick, Between State and Nation: Regional Organizations of the United States (Washington, D.C.: The Brookings Institution, 1974), p. 87.

75. David A. Stockman, "The Social Pork Barrel," The Public Interest, no. 39 (Spring 1975), pp. 3–30.

76. Eulau, "Polarity in Representational Federalism," p. 165.

77. Ibid., p. 169.

78. Jean-Pierre Worms, "Le préfet et ses notables," Sociologie du Travail 3 (July–September 1966): 249–75.

79. Tarrow, Between Center and Periphery, chap. 5.

80. Pierre Grémion and Jean-Pierre Worms, "The French Regional Planning Experiments," Planning, Politics and Public Policy: The British, French and Italian Experience, ed. Jack Hayward and Michael Watson (London and New York: Cambridge University Press, 1975), pp. 222-23.

81. David Thomson, Democracy in France since 1870 (New York and London: Oxford University Press, 1964), 4th ed., pp. 44-45.

82. For an excellent description of the "rhetoric of apolitisme," see Mark Kesselman's The Ambiguous Consensus: A Study of Local Government in France (New York: Knopf, 1967), chap. 9.

83. Jean-Claude Thoenig, "Les Rélations entre le centre et la péripherie en France," Bulletin de l'institut international d'administration publique, December 1975, pp. 77-123.

84. J. H. G. Lord, A. J. Petrie, and L. A. Whitehead, "Political Change in Rural France," Political Studies 16 (June 1968): 162-68.

85. Cameron and Hofferbert, "Impact of Federalism," p. 225.

86. Beer, "Modernization," p. 85.

87. Hansen and Kjellberg, "Municipal Expenditures in Norway," p. 27.

88. Mark Kesselman and Donald Rosenthal, "Local Power and Comparative Politics: Notes toward the Study of Comparative Politics," Sage Professional Papers in Comparative Politics (Beverly Hills, Calif.: Sage Publications, 1974), p. 8.

89. Terry N. Clark has done more than anyone to try and systematize propositions about the effects of the structure of community influence on public policy outputs. See his "The Structure of Community Influence," People and Politics in Urban Society, ed. Harlan Hahn, Urban Affairs Annual Reviews, vol. 6 (Beverly Hills, Calif.: Sage Publications, 1972), pp. 283-314, and the studies reviewed therein.

90. Stein Rokkan, "Regional Contrasts in Norwegian Politics," in Allardt and Littunen, Cleavages, pp. 218-19.

91. See Milton J. Esman, ed., Ethnic Conflict in the Western World (Ithaca, N.Y.: Cornell University Press, 1977).

2

REFORMING THE NAPOLEONIC STATE:
THE CREATION OF REGIONAL
GOVERNMENTS IN FRANCE AND ITALY
Peter Gourevitch

REFORMING THE NAPOLEONIC STATE

The abolition of provinces in 1789 by the constitutent assembly did not, as everyone since Tocqueville has pointed out, create centralization in France. Credit (or blame) for that goes to the monarchy and the forces allied with it working over many centuries. Major alterations in the structure of subnational units (such as the creation of departments) represent modernizations of an old pattern of center-periphery relations designed to improve the effectiveness of rule from the capital by gutting or eliminating intermediate bodies. Even the principal exception to this pattern—the democratization of town and municipal councils during the nineteenth century—took place under the very firm grip of the grands corps.[1]

In the three decades since World War II, we have witnessed another of these periodic modernizations of centralized control in France: the creation of regional institutions. What is new here is the reintroduction of a governmental level lying between departments and nation; the transfer of activities out of Paris toward local bodies; and the attempt to institutionalize new forms of representation, especially corporate representation at the regional level. Though other conceptions of administrative reform (such as participatory decentralization or regional autonomy bordering on federalism) or other goals (participation, economic development, party or personal advantage) were

Most of the funds supporting the research behind this chapter came from the Center for European Studies at Harvard. I wish to thank for their comments Suzanne Berger, Stanley Hoffmann, Peter Katzenstein, Peter Lange, J. E. S. Hayward, Sidney Tarrow, Nicholas Wahl, and the members of the Comparative Politics of Atlantic Societies seminar led by James Kurth. I am particularly grateful to Judy Chubb for helping me with Italian materials.

present and at some times appeared to have some chance of success, the changes embodied in the loi Frey of 1972 represent the most limited among the reforms proposed in this period.

In Italy provinces were suppressed in 1860. Having adapted the Napoleonic model of administration to Piedmont, the House of Savoy, like all French regimes in the nineteenth and twentieth centuries, found it eminently useful for governing a divided country.[2] So did Mussolini.

As in France, regional government was revived after World War II. The constitution of 1947 provided for 17 "ordinary" regions and five "special" ones. While the latter were set up on schedule, political tensions blocked the creation of the former until the late 1960s. The second round of elections to the regional assemblies in 1975 became a major event in Italian postwar political history when sharp gains by the Communists accentuated the present phase of the Italian political crisis.

To some degree, the reforms in each country express the same thing: the confrontation between old structures (centralization based on small units designed for static, rural societies) and new social conditions (rapid urbanization, industrialization, and population growth). The response to these contradictions differs somewhat. Compared to their French counterparts, Italian regional governments have more power, superior legal status, more money, more civil servants, and, most important, directly elected assemblies.

This chapter seeks to explain this divergence in the character of the regional governments created in Italy and France. To some degree, the difference reflects the uniqueness of the problem in each country. In Italy, regional disparities are much more severe; given the lateness of national unification, regional identities and communal traditions are more intense. Ethnic problems are deeper and a number of cities balance the national capital so that no single city dominates all aspects of life in the manner of Paris. Finally, the state machinery in Italy is much weaker than its French counterpart. All these factors plausibly encourage greater decentralization in Italy than in France.[3]

What these variables do not explain in any direct way are the politics of decentralization and regional reform. Structural factors have to operate on parties and politicians to produce legislation and constitutional change. The argument here is that the difference in the content of the regional reforms in France and Italy is a consequence of the way the issue affected, and was affected by, political parties and politicians in each country. Regionalism in France, after a very long germination period, spurted forth in the hothouse thrown up by the fresh growth of the Gaullist movement and the Fifth Republic, then slowed down into a hibernation under the much cooler conditions prevailing in the Pompidou years. In Italy, regionalism took root with the opening to the left. Once implanted, it has acquired a life of its own. Today, it not only has autonomy from the vagaries of national political storms, but the capacity to make them.

In neither country has regionalism, or politico-administrative reform of any kind, been the major stake, nor even one of the major stakes of politics, nor has it been one of the central cleavage issues around which political life revolves. Regionalism has been a by-product of other forces. Its fate has depended on what impact people judge it might have on goals of much more importance to them. The last opinion poll taken in France before the referendum of 1969 showed 52 percent of the electorate in favor of regional reform, 22 percent against, and 26 percent without any opinion; several days later, 53 percent of the electorate voted against a text offering regional reform largely because it preferred to get rid of De Gaulle.[4]

Those most directly affected by the proposed change of political structures were those who operated them—professional politicians, party militants and bureaucrats, and the civil service. Other groups would certainly be affected by institutional reform, and pressure groups do play some role in the story told below. Indeed, a full understanding of the politics of administrative reform would require some account of the political strategies of social forces in different parts of each country: why, for example, did diverse social groups cooperate on a regional program in Brittany, but not in the Nord, which also faced severe economic problems of a regional character? I have some suspicions about the answer, but mostly I am impressed by the difficulty of generalizing about what social type wanted regional reform and what social type opposed it. About France, for example, it is sometimes suggested that regionalism is a movement of the economically and socially backward in protest against Paris and the dynamic elements of society that control the national government. Yet while backward Brittany has had a strong regionalist association, backward Limousin has not. Moreover, Rhône-Alpes is one of the most dynamic regions in the country and is also a center of support for regional reform; there, it appears, energetic businessmen resent the heavy hand of Paris. One can find peasant, worker, professional, big and small business groups on all sides of the regional issue, or more frequently, rather uninvolved, seeing it as beyond the limits of their most important preoccupations. Most of the time, the consequences of regional reform for the specific, concrete interests of most pressure groups were too unpredictable and the scope of most proposals too limited to require the close attention of social forces in each country.

By and large, it was the political class of Italy and France that had the most intense interest in the details of this issue, since any alteration of politico-administrative boundaries, functions, or modes of representation threatened existing power relationships. The explanatory strategy of this chapter is to focus on politicians and political parties as the critical actors determining the nature of regional reform in France and Italy. We must find those factors that shape politicians' evaluations of the costs and benefits different proposals would bring. To explain why the French reform was more limited than the Italian, we must look for factors that encouraged Italian politicians to see more opportunity in change than did French politicians.

The history of both countries suggests that the opposition tends to be more sympathetic to decentralization than those in power.[5] For governments, the Napoleonic model provides instruments of control that appear simply too attractive to do without. Given the great depth of political cleavages in each country, governments have mistrusted oppositions too much to tolerate the risk that even a few important local institutions might fall into their hands. Even when most decentralized units appear likely to take on the political coloration of the parties in power, governments have been reluctant to diminish the direct influence that the central ministries have over local life. The parties out of power have become critics of this kind of control, and the elements within them favorable to decentralization become more vocal. Once in office, though, these groups switch positions with the hitherto governing parties.*

In the postwar period, the behavior of governing parties fits this pattern. Third Force, center-right, and right-based coalitions in Italy and France opposed decentralization or the creation of new, larger political units, fearing that these would fall under Communist control. Nonetheless, some kind of regional reform did occur in each country. We must therefore find some political considerations that led governments to overcome their structurally induced reluctance to permit deconcentration or decentralization, and we must establish what it was that caused Italian governments to go farther than the French.

In what follows, I shall argue that the major factors that induced different evaluations in the two countries of the power implications of regional reform are (1) the dynamics of alliance combinations among the parties, (2) the strength of different parties at national compared with local levels, (3) the geographic distribution of voting strength,

---

*After 1815, the returned émigrés kept the whole revolutionary-Napoleonic administrative machinery, and over the next 50 years the criticism of centralization came increasingly from the left. After 1870, the positions reversed. The left used the power of Paris to root out local conservatives, while the right rediscovered the virtues of local autonomy.

(4) the efficacy of existing institutions, and (5) ideological presumptions concerning the proper areal distribution of power.

There are more or less durable features of the political landscape that change slowly. The winds of circumstance blow over this landscape, pushing the inhabitants now one way or another. These winds have causes too, but ones that are external to the particular landscape in question. That is, another factor was conjoncture—the content and context of the specific reform proposals. To understand the course of regional reform in France and Italy, we must examine the interaction of the landscape, the winds, and the inhabitants—the structures, the course of events, and the politicians themselves.

THE STORY

One of the most outstanding characteristics of the consideration of regional reform in Italy and France is its great dependence on other issues. Even when regionalism found itself in the center ring, it never had the spotlight. It is therefore appropriate to periodize the regional debate with critical turning points drawn from the most influential of these other issues, the cold war. We may identify four phases in this story:

Constitution making and opportunity (to 1947): a period of flux at the Liberation brought to an abrupt end by the cold war. The new constitutions of both countries stress democratic participation at the local level, though regions are written into these documents only in Italy.

The cold war and immobilisme (1947–60): polarization, expulsion of the left, leading to immobilisme; decentralization clauses in both constitutions not implemented.

The thaw and fluidity (1960–69): gradual erosion of antagonisms, especially in relation to the Communists; greater fluidity in politics; in Italy, legislation implementing the constitutional clauses on regions adopted; in France, creation of regional institutions by decree, and attempt at regional reform through referendum.

Detente and ambiguity (1969–present): sharpening of domestic antagonisms after the événements (events) in both countries; recrudescence of hostility toward institutional reform by governing parties, and increasing support for it on the left; in France, limited legislation on regions passed after lengthy delay; in Italy, legislation applied in a conservative way. Selection of regional assemblies in both countries attracts attention, though far more so in Italy, where they are directly elected.

Phase One: Constitution Making to 1947

The aftermath of war is always a propitious moment for important change. In both countries, a very large spectrum of opinion in
the constituent assemblies supported significant decentralization. In
neither case did this occur, but the failures were not identical in their
degree or ultimate effects.

France

The debate over regionalization after the war did not occur on
a tabula rasa. Regional boundaries for various administrative purposes had existed for some time.[6] Vichy created regional prefects,
partly as instruments of control, partly out of nostalgia for a supposedly decentralized past.[7] Like other aspects of the Vichy experience,
this innovation was retained after the Liberation, in "purified" form:
commissaires de la république, charged by the provisional government
with broad mandates to assure effective leadership in the midst of
considerable disorder and political strife.[8] The fate of these commissaires, and of the eventual character of the areal distribution of
power in postwar France, naturally became caught up in the struggle
for political control of the country between De Gaulle and the Constituent Assembly.

During the profound questioning of French institutions that went
on under German occupation, political activists on all sides attributed
part of the "strange defeat" to overcentralization and the obsolescence
of traditional politico-administrative boundaries.[9] Some Gaullists
wanted regionalization as a solution; others, like Michel Debré, proposed redrawing departmental lines to create fewer, larger "grands
départements."[10] De Gaulle himself stressed other requirements in
a new constitution, particularly the need for a strong executive and
new types of linkage between state and society, such as socioprofessional representation. The discours de Bayeux (1946), which fore-
shadows much of the constitution of 1958 and the corporatist aspect
of the referendum of 1969, does not deal with regions or departments.[11]
Before this speech, while he was still head of the provisional government, De Gaulle did want to keep the commissaires as a way of maintaining executive authority.

The parties in the assembly, competing with De Gaulle for legitimacy, defended traditional republican standards of the proper spatial
arrangement of public institutions, for example, universal suffrage,
organized in departments and communes. Having done well in the
municipal and departmental elections of 1945, the party leaders saw
no point in ceding place to an institution (the commissaires) checked
by no elective body whatever. They argued that innovation should be

in the direction of more democracy, not less. The Marxist parties advocated recall of deputies by electors, election of judges, and the transfer of executive power in departments from prefects to the presidents of the conseils généraux (general councils). The Communists wanted to suppress the prefects outright; the Socialists, to retain weakened prefects; the Mouvement républican populaire (MRP), to keep them, but to have some kind of local referendum procedure. [12]

The effect of the conflict over what kind of reform, under whose leadership, was to reduce the extent of any reform. In the final version of the constitution of 1946, only the direct election of the presidents of the departmental councils remained as evidence of the Liberation's fervor for participation. Departments and communes again formed the base of the system, safely in the hands of the central government, ruling through the grands corps. [13]

Italy

During the course of the conflict over the new Italian constitution, the major protagonists switched positions on the desirability of regionalization. For a few months, which turned out to be critical, both sides supported it, and title V was retained. At first, the Christian Democrats (DC) alone backed regions, while the Marxist parties opposed them. Christian democracy had never been a governing party. It had suffered from centralization under the monarchy and fascism, and party members tended to regard strong local government as offering a valuable bulwark of defense against Rome—what Italian discourse calls the motivazione garantista. [14] Progressive segments of the party valued popular participation in natural intermediate bodies, geographic as well as functional. Regions and provincie (Italian departments) both derived legitimacy from the past. Some regions and provinces matched the larger historic provinces (Lombardy, Veneto, and so on), the others being "artificially" drawn at the time of unification. Conservatives in the DC feared from the beginning that regionalism would hinder the fight against communism and stressed the need for strong, hierarchical control.

The Marxist parties were emerging from 20 years of underground activity, centralized leadership, and Stalinist influence. Their program—nationalization, planning, social reconstruction—required strong central authority. Hoping to share power at the national level, they opposed any weakening of the state. Regions appeared nonessential for the realization of major programmatic goals and threatened to put important arenas of power out of reach just at the moment when the left appeared closest to it. As in France, the Marxist parties sought democratization of traditional units of local government—the provincie and communes. Nonetheless, the Marxist tradition in Italy did contain elements favorable to decentralization. As with the DC, alienation from the central government spawned an appreciation of the value of local institutions in supporting the party organization: Socialists talked of the isole rosse—Socialist strongholds in the midst of a hostile bourgeois state and society. In France, the battles over the schools, the defense of the Republic, the nationalism of World War I, and the partial successes of the Popular Front helped revive a Jacobin identification with a strong centralized state. The Italian left had no comparable experiences.

Both the Marxists and the DC parties, then, had conflicting attitudes toward decentralization in general and regionalism in particular. In both cases, power considerations helped tip the balance first one way, then another. With the cold war, the left's ability to share power in Rome diminished, and the Communists and Nenni Socialists rediscovered the potential of local government as shelters in a storm. After the coup of Prague, the DC would also switch positions (out of fear of the Communists), completing the renversements des alliances; but in the short run, being publicly committed to regionalism, they stuck to it. The constitution was adopted in the interval between these two volte-faces, so that title V had the backing of both sides.

Title V of the constitution of 1947 gives regions more legal status, competences, legitimacy, and money than any of the proposals put forward by French governments over the past two decades, though it falls far short of federalism. Regions have a juridical status equal to communes and provinces.[15] Their organization follows a parliamentary model: powers are vested in a unicameral regional council, which selects from among its members a regional executive council (the giunta regionale) and a president of that executive council.[16] Regions may propose laws to the national Parliament and may initiate national referenda. Title V prevents the very common French practice of cumul des mandats (multiple elective offices) in that regional councillors may not sit in Parliament.[17] The list of competences formally mentioned seems broad—the regional aspects of urbanism, tourism, transportation, agriculture—and Parliament can delegate more.[18] Regional councillors will be territorial, not functional, though the precise number and mode of designation was left to future legislation.

The government in Rome retains vast powers of control over the regions. It can oversee regional administration through a commissario del governo (government commissioner), resident in the regional capital and an administrative council charged with supervising the legality of regional activities.[19] The government may dissolve or dismiss regional councils for any one of a variety of reasons: violation of the national constitution, national security considerations, and paralysis of the regional government. Rome may veto legislation of the regional council, which may then repass the bill, which then is sent by the national government for adjudication either to Parliament or the constitutional court.[20] Title V specifies what regions shall be created: five special ones (Sicily, Sardinia, Trentino–Alto-Adige, Friuli–Venezia Giulia, and the Valle d'Aosta) and 15 ordinary ones.

> Despite the limits and deficiencies . . . of the Constitu-
> tional design [it] was sufficiently precise to make plain
> that the Regions were conceived not just as centers of ad-
> ministrative decentralization for purposes of efficiency,
> but, on the contrary, as entities endowed with political
> autonomy, that is to say, . . . centers of democratic self-
> government, capable of elaborating, adopting and realizing
> its own political line, eventually divergent from that of
> the central government.[21]

Any constitutional text can be subverted, as we shall see below. Nonetheless, these clauses did strengthen the supporters of regional-ism in Italy by putting beyond discussion some of the issues that in France proved to be objects of controversy. These included the legal status of regions, some aspects of the organization of regional govern-ment, and the territorial and nonfunctional character of representa-tion. Not the least important were the ample powers granted to the government to protect its definition of the national interest by inter-vening in the activities of regional governments. Though it was pre-cisely this last provision that Italian governments used to weaken the regional reform, it also facilitated implementation of title V by reas-suring the conservatives. Because the Italian Constituent Assembly had gone so much farther than the French, the hurdle to be overcome in the mid-1960s was in Italy that much lower.

Phase Two: Cold War and Immobilisme, 1947–60

The sharp polarization of politics brought on by the cold war blocked regional reform in Italy and France for almost two decades.

Italy

Title V of the constitution had called for elections to the regional council within a year of ratification and implementation of the whole regional system within three years. Decentralization implied allowing the Italian Communist Party (PCI) control of some units of local gov-ernment. Unwilling to tolerate this, the DC blocked implementation of these constitutional clauses. First, it simply failed to bring for-ward the required enabling legislation that set up regional finances

and elections. Second, in 1953 the government enacted a de facto
modification of title V (the legge Scelba on regions), so that regions
would be weak if some day political pressures forced their creation.
Where, for example, the constitution gave regions enough control
over their own internal organization to permit some diversity and
autonomy, the new law imposed considerable uniformity and central
supervision over such matters as the number of vice-presidents and
secretaries of the regional council, the precise dates of its meetings,
and how to fill vacancies on the giunta regionale. It also narrowed
the definition of regional competences and provided for a prefectoral
tutela by Rome.[22] In short, it laid down detailed regulations governing the life of institutions that did not exist and whose creation it did
nothing to promote.

Without the support of the governing party, regionalism could
not progress. Support from other forces was either lacking or wholly
isolated. The Italian bureaucracy fell into the first category, for,
unlike its French counterpart, it generated no reform movement
from within. The Communists, on the other hand, were frozen out
at the national level. By becoming the most outspoken proponents of
title V, they helped to prevent its implementation.

France

Title X of the Constitution of 27 October 1946, dealing with
democratization of departments, also fell victim to the cold war.
During the social conflicts of 1947, fragile Third Force governments
revived regional prefects (IGAMES, inspecteurs généraux de l'administration en mission extraordinaire), but these declined in importance
with the end of the short-term crisis. Bills seeking to attain the
promised greater role of the presidents of departmental councils died
in committee.[23]

Blocked by politics, administrative reform in France went underground: it moved out of the public arena dominated by parties to
the less visible meeting rooms of interest group notables and high
civil servants. Dissatisfied with the maintenance of the departmental
status quo, these actors created a patrimony of structures and ideas
ready for such time as the political situation became more favorable
to reform of the French areal distribution of power.

One impetus for change came from the grassroots. In the early
1950s, small groups of local leaders in different parts of France came
to understand the problems they confronted not in a departmental or
communal framework, but in a regional one. This led them to form
voluntary associations cutting across departmental boundaries, and
often across party lines. These groups became known as comités
d'expansion régionale and were the forerunners of the CODER, created

in 1964. (The CODER, in turn, preceded the regional assemblies of
the 1972 loi Frey.) The most famous of these voluntary associations
was the Comité de'études et de liaison d'intérêts bretonnes (CELIB).
Formed in 1950, it sought to multiply the leverage of Brittany in national politics by linking together the separate pieces of influence
spread among its hundreds of member organizations.[24] Brittany's
problems, the CELIB argued, could not be solved by aggregative national policies that treated France as a single homogeneous unit. It
pressed for a regional economic plan to be used like the national plan
as a framework for public and private investment.

Another impeuts for regionalization came from parts of the bureaucracy. In 1950, the Ministry of Reconstruction and Urbanism
published the first effort at subnational spatial planning, and in 1952,
the Planning Commission accepted a CELIB invitation to help prepare
a Breton regional blueprint in time for the Second Plan.[25] In striking
contrast with Italy, the bureaucracy in France, or at least parts of it,
was a very important center of initiative for reform of its own administrative structures and political ones as well. During the next ten
years, a small but growing number of civil servants became convinced
of the need to rationalize the criteria, methods, and administrative
boundaries with which the state spent money and made decisions.*
They wanted to unburden Parisian ministries increasingly swamped
with details and to restore order to the relations among ministerial
field services. They also sought to improve the coordination of expenditures by different ministries having significant impact on geographic areas, to slow down the excessive growth of Paris, and to
supervise more intelligently the growing volume of expenditure whose
effects spilled over the boundaries of a single department. Finally,
they hoped to provide infrastructure for economic growth and to cope
with the structural depression of certain regions.

Interacting with locally based elites like the comités d'expansion
régionale, the bureaucracy produced a series of measures that gradually set up an actual regional machinery. The decree of January 5,
1955 restricted industrial location in Paris. That of June 30, 1955
created semipublic regional development societies (sociétés de développement régional). The Fonds de développement économique et
social was established in June 1955 to promote regional expansion.
A further decree of June 1955 required the dispersal of governmental
agencies away from Paris. A major step was the promulgation in
1956 of the régions de programme (planning regions): departments

---

*My understanding of this process has been greatly aided by the
study in progress by Catherine Grémion of the decrees of March 1964,
sponsored by the Groupe de sociologie des organisations.

were grouped into 22 regions, which would become the framework for regional planning and coordination. The boundaries delimiting these districts remain those of the regions today.[26] Another decree, that of January 7, 1959, foreshadowed the very important reforms of March 1964: it harmonized the administrative districts of Parisian ministries and created a regional prefect who would preside over interdepartmental conferences. Another series of measures reformed the structure of central authority in the departments. In 1963, yet another decree created the Délégation à l'aménagement du territoire et à l'action régionale (DATAR). DATAR was to be to the regions what the Commissariat au plan was for the nation: essentially a planning body, whose powers derived primarily from exhortation, superior knowledge, position in the system, bolstered by a small pot of money (the Fonds pour l'intervention à l'aménagement du territoire—FIAT).

These changes naturally provoked strong opposition inside the bureaucracy. Members of the grands corps and officials in the various ministries feared disruption of the traditional hierarchy and curtailment of their autonomy. In the country as a whole, these changes were not closely followed. Politicians complained of inefficiency and overcentralization but continued to regard reform with suspicion. The left feared erosion of its local power positions; the center and right feared sharing power with the left. The decrees of the 15 years following adoption of the constitution created a patchwork structure of institutions and communes. To go on to another stage required politics: some significant political force would have to commit itself to overcoming the resistance to further change.

Phase Three: The Thaw and Fluidity, 1960-69

By the end of the 1950s, important shifts in international and domestic politics restored an element of movement to political life in France and Italy. The attack on Stalin eventually lessened the isolation of the Communists; in the short run, Hungary widened the breach between them and the left Socialists. In Italy, this helped bring about the opening to the left. In France, these shifts were overshadowed by Algeria.

France

The constitution of 1958, designed to support strong executive leadership, took no notice of the halting development of regional institutions that had occurred since the discours de Bayeux. A regime brought in to forestall a military coup was hardly likely to disperse power. So long as the nation feared chaos and the army, the Gaullist hold on power was secure. Without that issue, however, the general, the Gaullist movement, and the Republic would have to devise a more durable way of surviving. At two different moments over the next decade, regions appeared to offer some assistance to the Gaullists in solving that problem—thus, the decrees of March 1964 and the referendum of 1969. My argument as to how Gaullist political difficulties related to these measures requires a discussion of the character of the Gaullist movement.

In 1962, the Gaullist party was a group of deputies in Paris having no local roots.[27] Municipal and departmental councils remained firmly in the hands of the other parties; even in the largest of France's 38,000 communes, it would have been hard to find evidence of a local UDR (Union des démocraires pour la république) organization. This state of affairs derived not just from the newness of the party, but also from De Gaulle's desire to maintain it as a "movement," not a party like others. He refused to use the power of the state in order to build a party machine, relying instead on the direct support of the population expressed through referenda.

Over the long run this was impossible—routinization must replace charisma, or at least the creation of charisma must be routinized. The direct election of the president of the Republic by universal suffrage helped, but not even this would suffice. Eventually, the party and the regime had to be woven into the fabric of French life at every level: local headquarters, card-carrying adherents, patronage, and the rest. To do this required the construction of an institution, the party, and the forging of links with key social groups.

I believe that after the Algerian War there were two different strategies open to the Gaullists for securing their position. First, they could attempt to sustain the aura of Gaullism as a movement appealing to all groups in French society, avoiding excessive commitment to any particular segment of it and fighting both left and right. Alternatively, they could turn the organization into the dominant right-center party by marrying the new Gaullist équipe to the traditional conservative notables, thus effecting the contemporary equivalent of the fusion between robe and sword.[28]

Each strategy represented a different combination of groups and policies. We may distinguish three wings in the Gaullist movement: loyalists, modernizers, and traditionalists. The loyalists sought in Gaullism a strong nationalist force capable of leading a divided nation. Following the general's line of analysis, they disliked the existing center and conservative parties for being excessively tied to particularistic interests, incapable of rising above petty concerns to mobilize the authority needed to run the country.[29] On social issues, however, the loyalists tended to share with the old parties an essentially conservative vision: deference to property and management, natural inequality, protection of traditional classes and structures from the harsh whip of market forces.

The modernizers, by contrast, responded to those elements in Gaullist thought that called for a transformation of French society. They advocated modernization of the economy; reform of education; an activist policy toward urbanism, transportation, housing, and so on; integration of the labor movement through some sort of "association capital-travail"; and administrative reform. Like the loyalists, the modernizers judged the old parties incapable of these tasks.

Finally, to the traditionalists, Gaullism offered the best defense against the winds of revolution and change. They wanted the regime to protect old groups from the chaos of world market forces, changing technology, shifting demography, an unruly labor force, and the like.[30] To the traditionalists, the old parties, despite their past deficiencies, constituted vitally needed allies in a common struggle.

The loyalists were the swing-group in this three-way situation. Strategy one meant a coalition between loyalists and modernists built around their vision of a strong France and their common antagonism toward the old parties. To secure the regime, the UDR would attack the existing party formations head-on, seeking to replace or bypass them. It would run Gaullist candidates in local elections against those of the MRP, the Independents, and the peasant groups, and it would undermine existing local institutions, in which the old parties were strong, by creating new ones. Regional governments with a corporatist chamber would provide new forms and forums of presentation, giving voice to the notables of the pays réel, presumed to be pro-Gaullist, at present suppressed by the anti-Gaullist party notables of the pays légal.

Strategy two combined loyalists and traditionalists around their common conservatism. Politically, this coalition required conciliation rather than confrontation. It called for the avoidance of direct electoral clashes between Gaullists and other conservative candidates, and the avoidance of institutional (or other) innovations that upset existing groups.

From 1962 until about 1966, the loyalists and the modernists pursued strategy one, providing the political basis for changes advocated by reformers. Despite the opposition of most civil servants, Michel Debré, certainly the embodiment of right-wing Jacobin thinking about the state, became convinced that reform was necessary exactly to preserve the capacity of the Jacobin state to function. Paris and the upper reaches of the bureaucracy had to be unburdened of the press of petty details and the lines of command from Paris into the field had to be unsnarled. Following the creation of the DATAR in 1963, the government promulgated in 1964 a series of very important decrees seeking to realize these goals. In the departments, these

decrees reasserted the authority of the prefects over the field representatives from other ministries. For the regions, the reform
strengthened the powers of the regional prefect and created a regional
bureaucracy, the <u>mission régionale</u>. It established an organism within
each region to apportion credits among the departments. This was
the <u>Conférence administrative regionale</u>, which was composed of departmental prefects and treasurers. The reform also set up a consultative regional assembly, the CODER (regional economic development committees). The CODER was composed of local notables, both
territorial and functional. Half were chosen by the functional groups,
one-quarter from among elected notables, and the rest were appointed
at large by the prime minister. Finally, there were a set of measures
that developed the regionalization of the national budget, the national
plan, and regional planning itself.[31] These changes constitute a kind
of streamlined Jacobinism—modernization of the rule from the center
through administrative deconcentration. It is not decentralization in
that local institutions remain subordinate to Paris, and directly elected
local officials have no real power in the new institutions.

The decrees of 1964 drew sharp criticism from the traditionalists inside the majority and from the established parties of both left
and right. The former thought the change would weaken the state too
much; the latter saw it as an attack upon traditional vehicles of republican representation in which their organizations were strong. In the
municipal elections of 1965, strategy one suffered a setback, and the
alliance behind it started to unravel. The hope of a pro-Gaullist nonparty elite yearning to be free of existing political organisms turned
out to be a myth. Gaullists did well in those elections only in alliance
with the traditional parties, and the CODER, which were to have allowed the new elites to take over French political life, instead fell
into the hands of the old ones.[32]

Pompidou and Gaullist party secretary Robert Poujade began to
prepare the ground for a reversal of alliances, for the joining of loyalists and traditionalists against the modernizers. Where De Gaulle
resisted using the power of the state to build up a party machine,
Pompidou and Poujade encouraged it. Poujade moved for better relations with the old formations, trading favors for political support.
This alliance would constitute a new majority built on the following
lines: no excessive reformism of any kind, protection of established
social groups, a moderate foreign policy including British entry into
the European Economic Community—all policy concessions by the
Gaullists—in exchange for continued preponderance of the Gaullist
team in political offices; in short, the old parties' politics carried out
by the new men. For decentralization, this strategy meant very limited change.

The events of May-June 1968 forced a choice between these alliance strategies—though I believe, in the long run, the switch to

strategy two was almost inevitable if the Gaullists were to retain their
dominance of the right and center in France. Pompidou's leadership
of the legislative recoup in June from the political blow of May thrust
him forward as the first plausible successor to the general.[33] For
the first time since 1958, therefore, there emerged a gap between
De Gaulle and the regime, now become distinct entities with differing
requirements for survival. His authority undermined, De Gaulle
needed bold action to reestablish it—hence, his reform proposals all
evoking the theme of participation: cogestion in the university, better
status for the union in factories, and less control from Paris through
regionalization. A large body of the electorate, however, pretty
clearly preferred a more authoritarian response to les événements.
In the past, De Gaulle had always been able to overcome opposition
to his proposals by threatening, "C'est moi ou le chaos." Pompidou
reduced the leverage of this argument by offering stability without
foolish experimentation.

It was this conflict between two contrasting ways of responding
to May-June that propelled the regional reform into the center of the
political arena, and it did so in a way that ultimately contributed to
the reform's demise. Never the central issue of French politics, decentralization became for ten months the medium through which other
forces worked. Since the legislative elections had been seen as Pompidou's victory, De Gaulle turned, as before whenever he sought to
bolster his personal authority, to a referendum. Of the three aspects
of the participation theme, cogestion and unions were both too controversial. Decentralization and the regions had been in the air for a
number of years and were known to be popular. Even before les événements, De Gaulle had stressed the need to go beyond the decrees of
1964. His discours de Lyon (March 1968) announced:

> The centuries-long effort at centralization, which had long
> been necessary in order to realize and maintain France's
> unity despite the divergences of the provinces that had suc-
> cessively been attached to her, is no longer of so much
> significance.[34]

When the events made a referendum politically useful, De Gaulle
turned to this theme. There were already several different projects
under consideration in various ministries, including fusing communes,
lightening prefectoral tutelle in departments, and increasing the role
of regional missions in planning and budgeting. The choice of regionalism from this array of schemes was De Gaulle's. Events forced
postponement of the referendum offered in the May 24 speech in favor
of the stronger medicine of dissolution of the national assembly. By
the time De Gaulle brought the referendum forward again, its political

meaning had totally changed. In March 1968, reform of the politico-
administrative system appeared to be a move from strength. The
president of the Republic, having revamped the political system at the
center, restored greatness to France's role in world affairs and, assured socioeconomic progress, would now, as a crowning legacy to
the nation, preside over the reconstruction of something to which he
clearly attached great importance—the state. This reformed state,
freed of the trivia of local concerns, would be better able to handle
the essentials of national life; without the heavy hand of Paris, the
periphery would weaken the corrupt parties and allow a more fruitful
participation of the population in collective life.

By autumn, the regionalism project suggested political weakness
on the part of its sponsor. Participation and reform now appeared not
as largesse from on high but concessions forced out grudgingly. After
May, to the left, the proposals were tame and shallow; to the conservatives, they were foolhardy experimentation. This negative majority
defeated the final project on April 27, 1969.

Nonetheless, some modest project might well have passed.
Regions as territorial authorities with an assembly directly elected
by universal suffrage, a divided executive on the department model,
and a modest budget—this type of regional reform had, according to
opinion polls and the evaluation of observers, widespread support.
Instead, De Gaulle so burdened the regional ship with other concerns
that it finally sank. Besides the dubious constitutionality of this particular use of the referendum process and the failure to consult Parliament, the referendum of 1969 contained two highly unpopular provisions: the representation of socioprofessional groups (harking back
to the discours de Bayeux) who were to sit in the same assembly with
territorial representatives, albeit as a separate college subordinate
to them in case of conflict, and transformation of the senate into the
equivalent of the Conseil economique et social. Together these constituted an attack upon traditional institutions of republican local government and were seen as such from the very beginning, even by the
conservative notables who had voted UDR in June 1968.[35]

Political discourse in the fall and winter of 1968-69 showed the
need for care in the framing of a referendum text. The desire to
loosen the bonds of Parisian control was real but not unlimited. Left
and right alike articulated an analysis of political institutions that indicated considerable mistrust of anything that might weaken unitary
government. Though left and right did stress somewhat different dangers (the Marxists worried about the coherence of planning, Gaullists
about the possibility of local disorder), most deputies shared some
understandings about the indivisible nature of collective goals, the
primacy of la nation over its parts, the inferior status of partial interests, and the need for a single central institution capable of identi-

fying and implementing the common good. Even the most enthusiastic
partisans of decentralization acknowledged that it implied conflict
with the central government. Yet no one developed an argument that
reconciled the tension between collective and particular interests, that
is, an argument able to demonstrate the common good could be elicited
from the pursuit of local or private ones.[36]

The popularity of decentralization could not support any and all
burdens put on it.[37] French history did confer a certain legitimacy
on local government and territorial representation. Regionalism could
be legitimated as an extension of the principles that underlie existing
structures (which is essentially the present position of the Socialist
and Communist parties). Anything that smacked of corporatism and
threatened the power base of local politicians would provoke intense
antagonism.

Why, then, did De Gaulle cause a text to be written that did precisely that? Why, moreover, did he personalize and politicize the issue till what had presumably begun as a discussion of the merits of
decentralization became a referendum on whether De Gaulle should
remain in office? Some insiders (such as the antiregionalist minister
of interior, Raymond Marcellin, who was in close touch with local
notables, and the proregionalist DATAR group around Olivier Guichard)
urged a text that focused on regionalism, kept corporatism to a minimum, and allowed Parliament to fill in the details. Others were willing to risk a wide-ranging text including socioprofessional representation and abolition of the senate. ("This was regionalism's one chance,"
a high civil servant said to me. "We have to make the public swallow
as much as possible for we will not have another chance.") But they
were willing to do this only if De Gaulle avoided personalizing the referendum campaign.[38]

It has been suggested that this was "Presidential exit by suicide,"[39] motivated by pride, or arrogance, or an obsession with the
form of departure from public life. I believe De Gaulle's behavior
can be better explained by the logic of the political situation that led
to the referendum in the first place. The point of the undertaking was
to recover the authority lost in May–June 1968, and to at least some
degree it must be granted that De Gaulle believed in his reforms.
From July onward, the situation continually worsened: the overlarge
majority became increasingly restless; the owners of capital provoked
the monetary crisis of November; in January 1969, Pompidou announced
his availability to destiny's call. To recover his freedom of action
from la classe politique, to prevent the regime from sinking to the
level of pluralistic pushing and shoving by private interests, to retain
the ability to govern independently: for these goals, De Gaulle had to
challenge Parliament and the UDR frontally, and beat them. A pro-
vocative referendum was needed, not an ameliorative one; it had to

contain elements distasteful to De Gaulle's foes, hence the clauses on the senate and socioprofessional representation. When in the winter of 1969 the referendum appeared headed for trouble, De Gaulle could not trim his sails by reefing in the text, since appearing to run before the storm blown up by the notables would undermine the meaning of any victory. The worse he fared in the polls, the more the general was driven to personalization, to the old formula, "me or chaos."

From the majority Pompidou engineered in June 1968, De Gaulle lost on April 27, 1969 big chunks of conservative and centrist voters. The bed rock of the "no" vote was, of course, the left, which, despite the popularity of regionalist issues among its members, had been driven to a test of its solidarity.[40] But the regular combined French left vote normally did not exceed 45-47 percent. What produced De Gaulle's defeat were defections by local office holders of the center and right parties (seeking to preserve the senate and their established positions) and conservative voters from all parties (who preferred Pompidou).

The principal result of this vote was, of course, De Gaulle's departure. The by-product was defeat of the most ambitious of the various proposals for reform of France's system of representation and territorial organization. Though limited (indirect election, ample controls on the decentralized units), the referendum had called for the creation of collectivités territoriales equal in status to departments and communes. What happened now depended on how politicians interpreted the meaning of the defeat; would it be blamed on the person and strategy of De Gaulle, the attempt to abolish the senate, socioprofessional representation, or the regions themselves? Different answers implied different futures for the region.

Italy

Regionalism is perhaps the principal accomplishment of the opening to the left in the 1960s, though by no means its principal goal. The shift leftward altered the position of pro- and antiregional forces. The progressive elements inside Christian Democracy who wanted regions were able to use the alliance with the proregional Socialists to free themselves, at least on this issue, from the negative influence of the antiregional right.

Hailed as the answer to immobilism, the new center-left coalition found itself unable in fact to enact much significant new legislation. Though forced to acquiesce in the new coalition strategy, conservatives inside the DC were able to block its progress. The government, increasingly embarrassed by this stalemate, pressured by the Socialists and progressive Catholics inside the majority and by the Communists from without, turned to regionalism for much the same reasons De Gaulle had in 1968. As a reform, regionalism demonstrated the will to constructive action. As decentralization, it had a demo-cratic participatory ring. Finally, since it was limited, somewhat technical, and easily rendered vague, it was less controversial than many other issues. With the approach of the elections scheduled for 1968, the coalition partners feared the Communists would score heav-ily with a campaign based on the inactivity of the great experiment in Italian politics.

The debate over the regional election law in 1967 touched off the longest filibuster in Italian history (July 10–October 31). Most of the opposition came from the Liberals (PLI), the Monarchists (PMI), the Fascists (MSI), and the conservative wing of the DC. Most of the vocal support came from the Communists. Observers of the debate found it odd that those who were formally responsible for the bill—the dominant DC bloc—sat silently while those outside the government did the talking on both sides.

On numerous points, the Italian debate foreshadowed the French one of the following year. Proponents of regionalism argued that Par-liament dealt with too many bills of purely local interest and that the geographic boundaries of provincial-based administration no longer corresponded to the realities of Italian demography and economic life. They also maintained that the provincie were too small for planning purposes, that control from the capital suffocated initiative, and so on. Opponents warned of the pettiness of local interests and of the danger of undermining the coherence of national planning and economic policy through decentralization. In addition, they worried about the Communist menace and the incompatibility of regional diversity with equality before the law.

The two debates differed in important respects. In Italy, the political value of local autonomy was more strongly appreciated. Partly this came from the experience with fascism, which led all parties to want "regional fortresses" against the day when they might be a beleaguered opposition. For the opposition, especially the Com-munists, regions made sense as part of a policy of "presence." The PCI sought to break out of isolation and extend its influence in Italy by developing links with all classes, groups, parties, and institutions. The French Communists also make a policy of taking whatever seats are offered them on government bodies. The PCI goes beyond its French homologues, though, in relating this policy to a broader pro-gram of contact with other social forces, proving commitment to democratic values, and demonstrating a capacity for good local man-agement and incorruptibility.

Another contrast between the debates in the two countries was the absence in Italy of any serious charge that regions were tainted by "fascism," corporatism, or feudalism. To some degree this came from the content of the proposals. Socioprofessional representation had no place in the constitutional scheme. Also, the Fascists had been against regionalism and decentralization. Finally, there was less quarrel in Italy about such details as boundaries, institutional machinery, and representation, since the constitution and previous legislation had settled many of them.

As in France, government spokesmen, supposedly champions of reform, spent most of their time reassuring the bill's opponents that the central government retained ample authority to control the regions. In the final vote, DC leaders were unable to stop defections from party discipline, and without Communist support the legislation would not have passed the senate.[41]

Some observers feared the government might pass this bill but then fail to bring in a regional finance law and hold the elections. The tensions associated with the "hot autumn" of 1969 (Italy's equivalent of May 1968) worked in opposite ways. In the short run, they continued the pressure on the government to carry out reforms. At the same time, they damaged the center-left coalition by polarizing politics and strengthening those in the DC who wanted to break off the alliance. The opponents of implementation managed to delay the elections to the regional councils, but its support held up sufficiently so that they were finally held on June 7, 1970. The results were as expected: Communist domination of three regions, DC domination of the rest.[42]

Detente and Ambiguity (1969 to the Present)

The immediate consequence of the May–June events of 1968 in France and the "hot autumn" of 1969 in Italy was a heightening of domestic antagonisms and a rightward shift. In both countries this development was unfavorable to regional innovation.

France

After De Gaulle's departure, Pompidou made of the governing majority quite a different force from that which had followed De Gaulle for 11 years. Inside the UDR, Pompidou brought together the loyalists and the traditionalists, isolating the modernizers. To the center and right parties, he extended the glove of cooperation and caution. Giscard and some centrists joined the cabinet and the majority. Chaban-Delmas was dropped in 1971 partly for being too reformist. While professing loyalty to De Gaulle's visions, Pompidou practiced the policy compromises his strategy required: British entry into the Common Market, protection for small shopkeepers and farmers, the law against troublemakers loi anticasseur, and no more talk of participation.[43]

Everyone knew that the referendum of 1969 had not really expressed French opinion about regionalization. Pompidou could easily
have detached regions from all the other issues De Gaulle had tied up
with it and gotten Parliament to go along with something like what Italy
had created: regions of definite though limited power comprised of
territorially based representatives. The logic of Pompidou's political
strategy led, however, to a more limiting inference from the referendum results. The construction of a broad conservative front meant
avoidance of anything that would disrupt or threaten the local notables
who had abandoned De Gaulle and whom Pompidou needed. Indeed, it
looked at first as if Pompidou would place regions in cold storage for
good. Even in 1970, Jean-Jacques Servan-Schreiber forced the government's hand by taking up the cause of regionalism as the platform
for his successful campaign in Nancy and his challenge of Chaban-
Delmas in Bordeaux.[44] Despite Servan-Schreiber's crushing defeat
in this second race, he had demonstrated the continuing existence of
sentiment on behalf of decentralization, and Pompidou moved to take
the steam out of the issue. Roger Frey, a longtime Gaullist, became
Ministre d'État chargé de la Réforme Administrative in order to write
a new bill on regional government.

Pompidou and Frey avoided everything that had provoked antagonism in 1968-69. They emphasized strengthening of existing local institutions rather than undermining them on behalf of new ones. Prefectoral tutelle of departments has been lightened. Instead of regional
development planning, the government revived city-based concepts
like the regional métropoles d'équilibre and aid to medium-sized cities
(villes-moyennes). The fusion of tiny communes follows the voluntar-
ist procedures of the loi Marcellin (1971) rather than administrative
fiat. Some measures do make use of regions, but they deal with the
administration, not participation of local society in decisions. State
expenditures are now classed into categories according to the unit of
government most affected (nation, region, department, commune);
one envelope goes to the regional administration and, through an important organism known as the Conférence administrative régionale
(CAR), is then divided up among the departments and communes. The
antiremontée decrees of 1970 prohibit the appeal back to Paris of decisions made by the regional administration.[45]

The law on regions similarly sought to appease local forces.
The change was worked through Parliament, not by referendum, and
after lengthy consultations. Regions were given juridical status inferior to that of departments and communes—établissements publiques
instead of collectivités territoriales. The senate remains the organ
of local governments. Socioprofessional representatives meet in a
separate and distinctly inferior chamber. The dominant territorial
chamber is elected indirectly by communes and departments. There

is to be a limited budget, vague powers, and no independent regional executive. Perhaps most revealing of the desire to avoid threatening anyone's power base, the deputies to the national assembly sit by right in the regional assemblies. *

The text presented in November of 1971 (over a year after Frey took the job) did draw criticisms. Some Giscardiens and centrists, feeling the Gaullists were overrepresented nationally, attacked the representation of deputies. The left attacked the number of regions, the power of the prefect, and the weakness of formal powers and financial resources. (The law limits regional taxes to 25 francs per inhabitant, and the government has transferred to the regions only the revenues from fees on drivers' licenses, a very small sum of about 50 million francs a year.) However, it was basically the indirect selection of representatives that drew the left's ire. The government's version of decentralization offered nothing worth trying to control and appeared to be deconcentration in disguise, designed less to open the government up to local populations than to streamline control from Paris.

With some minor concessions by the government, the Regional Reform Bill passed both houses in late June 1972, having been delayed once again by the April referendum on Britain's entry into the Common Market. It immediately went into cold storage till after the legislative elections of 1973. During the winter of 1973-74, the regional institutions were finally set up. Since regional councillors are chosen indirectly, the selection process lacked the political importance direct election has given them in Italy. As in 1964, the new bodies are dominated by men already prominent in French political life; presidents of the regional councils include such men as Faure, Guichard, D'Ornano, Maurois, Savary, and Pleven. The partners of the Program commun elected five presidents, all Socialists with Communist support, in the Nord, Limousin, Midi-Pyrennes, Languedoc-Roussillon, and Provence-Côte d'Azur. Most of the rest have Gaullist leadership, some with center or Giscardien presidents. [46]

Since then, regions have lived on the periphery of French politics. The change from Pompidou to Giscard appeared at first to augur well for the regions. The new presidential majority included more of the center and Republican Independents, who had both pushed for more

---

*The loi Frey was debated in the assemblée nationale April 27-29, 1972 , by the Senate May 30-June 1, 1972 , passed in amended form by both houses at the end of June and published in the Journal officiel, Lois et decrets, no. 160, July 9, 1972. Since it was considered by Parliament as a piece of legislation (unlike the referendum project, which was only debated), there are committee reports as well.

extensive reform during the debate over the loi Frey in 1972. Giscard himself had criticized as inadequate the referendum of 1969 and
the Frey plan, and he maintained ties with Jean-Jacques Servan-Schreiber, well known for his regionalist sentiments. Nonetheless, the government has been extremely cautious. Giscard has been maneuvering
very delicately in relation to the Gaullist "majority within the majority," in particular toward the traditionalist and loyalist factions. Given
the narrowness of the margin in 1974 and the approach of the municipal (1977) and legislative (1978) elections, he apparently wishes to
avoid any changes in policy toward local governments that might exacerbate tensions inside the coalition. Under Chirac's prodding, Giscard
appears to have backed off from a "Chaban" strategy (reformism) into
a "Pompidou" strategy (caution).

During 1975-76, the government moved in two different directions at the same time, hoping to satisfy contradictory pressures. In
response to representations by the Association of Presidents of Regional
Assemblies (which includes such members of the majority as Faure and
Guichard), it has deconcentrated some competences to the region.[47]
At the same time, Giscard silenced agitation for wider changes by
proclaiming (in a speech at Dijon, November 1975) his opposition to
any revision in the near future of the loi Frey. Also, he affirmed
the importance of communes and departments, and announced the
creation of a commission (conferred to Guichard, a symbol both of
Gaullist modernizers and, as creator of the DATAR, of regionalism)
to propose ways of breathing new life into these existing collectivités
territoriales.

The left continues to emphasize the importance of democratizing
the new institutions. Socialist and Communist platforms, plus the
Common Program, call for direct election of regional councillors,
more competences, more resources, and administrative autonomy.[48]
In two regions (Nord and Provence-Côte d'Azur) they have created a
veritable regional executive under the control of the elected presidents.
In the Nord, for example, though only five or six persons are formally
on the payroll as assistants to Regional President Mauroy, 40 or 50
people employed in other capacities work through that office, making
it an important center of initiative and extending the influence of Mauroy
over the whole region.

Italy

After the implementation of title V in 1970, the center-left coalition alternated between collapse and shaky existence. The regions
exist; they spend money, commission studies, select executives, hire
staff, and so on. As institutions, they are stronger than their French
counterparts. Nonetheless, governments in Rome have limited their

role by applying the regional laws in a conservative way. When the
regional governments have challenged these actions in the courts, the
constitutional court has consistently supported Rome. One ruling
says that the listing of regional competences in the constitution refers
to what the state may transfer, not what it is obligated to transfer;
another argues that these competences are not exclusively reserved to
the regions, hence the state may continue to act in them. In many
domains which were to be regionalized, the central government continues to make decisions and allocate funds. [49]

It is far from clear how important a role regions actually play in
decision making or whether they have or will ever become a significant
locus for the allocation of funds, initiatives, and so on. The regional
elections of June 15, 1975 affected Italian political life because of the
sharp gain by the left (especially the Communists), not because the officials elected have much power. Regional elections in Italy appear
to have become precisely what Pompidou and other French conservatives feared would happen in their country: highly politicized contests,
intimately linked to national rather than local political quarrels, affecting the relations among political forces in the national government.
The legislative elections of 1972 left Italian politics stalemated: all
parties got about the number of seats and votes they had before. In
the referendum on divorce, May 1974, the DC suffered a massive defeat. It remained unclear, however, to what extent this rejection of
the DC position on that issue would carry over to other political issues.
The regional eldctions occurred precisely at the point when this question dominated Italian political life. The answer profoundly jolted
Italian political life, provoking new national elections in June 1976
(see Table 2.1).

The PCI emerged from June 15, 1975 as the largest party in
every major city of Italy (including Rome, Turin, Milan, Venice, Florence, and Naples, as well as Bologna) and the largest party in 7 regions, 34 provinces, and 26 provincie capitals. To the three regions
of the traditional Red Belt (Umbria, Tuscany, and the Emilia-Romagna),
the left has now added control of Liguria, the Marches, and Piedmont.
The legislative elections of June 1976 confirmed these shifts. Though
some observers had thought PCI gains in 1975 were a function of the
type of election (local, not national), the PCI did even better in 1976. [50]

For the future of Italian politics, and consequently for the regions,
the impact of these elections is unclear. For the PCI, its gains are
not an unmixed blessing. Nationally, it must steer a journey between
pushing too hard prematurely on the one hand, and being stuck with
responsibility without power on the other. Locally the PCI is overex-
tended. Though party schools are training cadres in public administration, it is having to shift people from the party bureaucracy to public jobs. Expectations rise as the public waits for the reproduction of

TABLE 2.1

Italian Election Results, Regional and National, 1970–75
(in percent)

Parties	1970		1975			1976		
	Regional Elections	National Elections	Regional Elections	Change from 1970	Change from 1972	National Elections	Change from 1972	Change from 1975
PCI	27.1	27.5	32.4	+5.3	+4.9	34.4	+6.9	+2.0
PSI	10.6	9.7	12.1	+1.5	+2.4	9.6	-0.1	-2.5
PSIUP–PDUP[a]	3.1	2.6	1.2	-1.9	-1.4	1.5	-1.1	+0.3
PRI	3.0	2.9	3.3	+0.3	+0.4	3.1	+0.2	-0.2
DC	37.6	38.7	35.5	-2.1	-3.2	38.7	0.0	+3.2
PSDI	6.9	5.2	5.6	-1.3	+0.4	3.4	-1.8	-2.2
PLI	4.6	3.9	2.5	-2.1	-1.4	1.3	-2.6	-1.2
MSI–DN[b]	6.9	8.8	6.9	0.0	-1.9	6.1	-2.7	-0.8
Miscellaneous	0.3	0.5	0.5	+0.2	+0.1	1.9	+1.4	+1.4

[a] 1970 = PSIUP; 1972 = PSIUP + PDUP; in 1973, the PSIUP split with parts going to PCI, PSI, and PDUP; 1975 and 1976 = PDUP.
[b] 1970 = MSI + PDIUM.

Source: Rinascita, June 25, 1976.

many "Bologna miracles." So long as the DC controls Rome, however, there are severe limits on the resources available to the PCI to meet these wishes.

The DC itself is torn by dissension over how to interpret the PCI's surge, how to stop it, and how to govern in the light of it. The smaller parties in the center-left and the right have to ask the same questions. As has happened often before, gains by the left could lead to stricter rule by the right. For the regions that would mean continued tight surveillance from Rome. A government of the center-left or the compromesso storico would, conversely, be friendlier to the regions, since the left would interpret tolerance of its local fiefs as an indicator of the DC's sincerity. A Socialist-Communist government, though, might find that great historic tasks required curbs on local autonomy. The current governo del astensioni has given mixed signals to the regions.

THE DYNAMICS

The creation of regional governments in both countries is the story of reluctant governments driven into doing something about which they had grave misgivings. Each step forward expressed the pressure of some political problem on politicians. Usually this problem was weakness: for the Gaullists in 1964, weakness in local governments; for De Gaulle in 1969, weakness in relation to his own followers; for Pompidou, grumbling by his centrist allies, UDR modernizers, and potential competitors like Servan-Schreiber. In Italy, DC governments were forced to implement title V by the logic that had propelled them into the opening to the left. In both countries, the controversy over what type of regions to create reached a high-water mark of public consciousness in the late sixties. The torrents of political agitation pushed regionalism into the main channels and pools. Before the drop in water levels, previous currents had brought the two countries to different ports. It has been my argument here that this difference can best be understood as a function of six major factors.

Alliance Combinations among the Parties

Center and Right

The different fates of Christian Democracy in Italy and France have had two important consequences for the regionalist cause. In both countries, elements of the Catholic center have been among the strongest supporters of the regions. To the strain of thought exemplified by the MRP of Schumann, or the DC of De Gasperi (strongly European, anti-Marxist and anticapitalist, reformist, participatory in a corporatist way), regions permit the full play of natural social forces and help shield the citizen from both the individualistic atomism of the Jacobin model and the bureaucratic suffocation of the Soviet one. Where these ideas were strong, there regionalism had powerful supporters. Conversely, anything that weakened the Catholic center weakened regionalism. Thus, the party systems were quite important. Gaullism, by wrecking the DC position in France, skewed the political center of gravity to the right, which was more antiregional, isolating the more proregional Catholic formations. In Italy, the dominant party included those formations, while a portion of the right lay outside the organization; this facilitated center-left coalitions that pivoted around the proregional center, sloughing off part of the antiregional right.

Socialist-Communist Relations and Strategies

As relations between the Socialist and Communist parties in the two countries have varied, so has the fate of the regions. The PCI has been considerably more interested in building links to other groups than has the French Communist Party (PCF). Regions have utility, therefore, to the PCI as an arena for the development of these alliances and for the demonstration of its abilities and probity. Closer ties between PCI and the Italian Socialist Party (PSI) (again compared to the PCF and the French Socialists) have made proregionalism more rewarding by increasing the likelihood that the left could get control of some regions should they be created. In France, conversely, the PCF's greater isolation and isolationism inhibited for a long time any understanding of the political value of regional government, while poor relations with the Socialists lessened the rewards of control. The closer PS-PC relations of recent years have made regional government more attractive to both parties.

Geographical Distribution of Voting Strength

The distribution of left voting in Italy and France differs in ways that affect the incentives to support regions. Though 20 percent of the French electorate lives around Paris, the capital district has been excluded from all regional reform projects (and did not receive its own local government structure until 1975-76). That part of the left vote that lives in the Red Belt around Paris is therefore lost in a contest for control over French regions. In Italy, the Red Belt is itself regional. It has always been obvious that the left would control the

Emilia-Romagna, Tuscany, and Umbria and would be in striking distance in some others. (Indeed, it has since come to power in Liguria, Piedmont, and the Marches and plays an important role in Lombardy and elsewhere.)

The PS-PCF rapprochement in France has diminished the importance of this factor in recent years. Regional governments were set up in France during the working out of the Common Program strategy, and together the parties have elected five regional presidents (all Socialists)—in Languedoc-Roussillon, Limousin, Midi-Pyrennes, the Nord, and Provence-Côte d'Azur.

Party Strength at National and Local Levels

New political parties probably have a stronger incentive than older ones to support a shake-up of the areal distribution of power. Thus the Gaullists, who after 1958 were strong nationally and weak locally, hoped to outflank their rivals' local hold through new institutions.

Conversely, well-entrenched parties have difficulty with reform of the politico-administrative system. Change threatens not only party positions in relation to each other, but established interests within each party organization. Secure, well-integrated, disciplined, dominant parties (like the Swedish Social Democrats) can prevent threats to the party as a whole by working out these conflicts within their own organization. Looser, more poorly disciplined, and non-dominant parties like the DC find it hard to neutralize the threatening elements of change.

The Efficacy of Present Institutions

However much French local elites complain of their dependence on Paris, French centralization does give them certain benefits, particularly that of being the privileged interlocutors between the state apparatus and their constituents. Institutional reform could loosen this monopoly and disrupt established relationships. Conversely, since the Italian state apparatus functions less effectively, the benefits of established positions in relation to it are correspondingly less. Italian politicians are therefore more likely than their French counterparts to see a positive balance on the account sheets of regionalism.[51]

Ideological Assumptions Concerning the Proper
Organization of Public Authority

The entire universe of political discourse in France appears more hostile to regions and decentralization than in Italy. Left and right alike have been dominated by Jacobins who equate regions with feudalism, corporatism, fascism, anarchy, and national disintegration. The French tolerance for risks in this field appears low, though the objective danger in Italy appears much higher. An event like the 1970 riots in Reggio Calabria over the location of the regional capital would certainly have killed regional reform in France for a generation. In Italy, the two major bodies of political thought—Marxism and Christian Democracy—contain strong anticentrist currents along with centrist ones. Both traditions were excluded from power during the long stretch of rule from the center (under the monarchy and fascism) and have developed greater interests than their French equivalents in the problems of local diversity.

The Context and Content of the Reform

The circumstances that brought forth the regions, and specific features of the proposals gave them greater legitimacy in Italy. In Italy regions appeared to mean incorporation of the left and the extension of democratic participation through direct elections. In France, they appeared to be part of an attack on existing parties and institutions, a transfer of power away from direct to indirect suffrage.

It is not yet possible to evaluate the actual performance of the machinery created in each country. The French law is only just now being applied, and appears to have been emasculated even further—if this was possible—as the Giscard government has moved into deeper water. The Italian regions do function but are bogged down in juridical disputes and slowed by the more general fiscal crises of the Italian state. One can envisage two scenarios, the first narrowing the differences between the two countries, the second maintaining or accentuating them. If weak centrist governments uneasy about, or hostile toward, regionalism remain in power in Rome, they may well use the authority available to them to restrict the actions of regional institutions to the point that they begin to resemble French ones. In France, conversely, it is possible that, though participatory decentralization will remain highly limited, some significant reworking of decision making may occur inside the administrative machine, leading to administrative deconcentration to the regions. Already the Conférences administratives régionales (CAR) are being delegated broader powers, and local elites are increasingly criticizing their lack of access to it.

To the extent that spillover has real force, one can imagine administrative deconcentration provoking demands for allowing regional councils to supervise the CAR and the regional executives.

Alternatively, the differences in formal structures and the difference in national politics between Italy and France may maintain or even widen the difference in the role of regional structures. Direct election may provide Italian regions with greater strength in conflicts against the central government. Already they appear in some cases (particularly those run by the PCI) to play an important role in local decision making and may supplant the province as the main intermediary body between center and periphery.

Evaluation of the development of regional institutions requires three kinds of study. First, there should be an analysis of decision making at the regional level. Consideration should be given both to the regional units of the central bureaucracy and to the representative institutions (to what extent important resources get allocated and decisions taken at the regional level). Second, there is the need to investigate the political economy of the regions and the leading industries in them (which groups for what motive make use of regionalism). Third, there should be an evaluation of the allocation of resources at the national level to different regions (the criteria by which these decisions are made). Of particular, but not exclusive, interest should be regional economic aid. Present literature on regions either neglects these questions (especially the first two) or, when rich in detail (the third), fails to explore where decisions are really made. That is, to show how much money the central government spends on regional aid does not necessarily demonstrate whether any genuine decentralization of decision making has occurred or whether, as has been more often the case, central control is reinforced through the patronage opportunities government spending provides. Without this type of information, it will be difficult to go beyond the pure politics of the creation of the institutions toward some interpretation of their significance in the political system.

Nonetheless, the fate of regional mechanisms—whether they receive more power and money, whether we see another attempt to change the balance between the capital and various levels of local government —will remain dependent on politics, narrowly understood. Moderate shifts in the political balance among parties and a decrease in interparty tensions are likely in both countries to produce more space for the regions. Drastic political shifts, in any direction, are likely to work against the regions. In a tense political situation, rulers are likely to discover the decision rule that most governments follow: decentralization cedes advantage to your enemies.

NOTES

1. For historic treatment of the development of local institutions in France see Maurice Bourjol, Les Institutions régionales de 1789 à nos jours (Paris: Berger-Levrault, 1969); Jean Bancal, Les Circonscriptions administratives de la France (Paris: Recueil Sirey, 1945); and the books of Robert Lafont, La Révolution régionaliste (Paris: Gallimard, 1967), and Décoloniser la France (Paris: Gallimard, 1971).

2. Robert Fried, The Italian Prefects (New York: Yale University Press, 1963).

3. The literature on regionalism in Italy and France is enormous. A very useful English-language guide to the main events and literature is William G. Andrews, "The Politics of Regionalization in France," Politics in Europe, ed. Martin O. Heisler (New York: McKay, 1974). In French, see the yearbooks put out by the Institut d'Études politiques at Grenoble under the sponsorship of the DATAR, vols. 1-5 and the DATAR series Travaux et recherches de prospective. See the work produced by Groupe de sociologie des organisations, such as Michel Crozier, et al., L'Administration face aux changements; Pierre Grémion, Le Pouvoir périphérique: Essai sur la fin de l'administration républicaine (Paris: Le Seuil, 1967); Pierre Grémion and Jean-Pierre Worms, Les Institutions régionales et la société locale (Paris: Copédith, 1968); and a special number of Sociologie du travail, "L'Administration face aux problèmes du changement, July-September 1966. See also the volumes of the Centre d'études et de recherche sur la vie locale of the Institut d'études politiques de Bordeaux. French works on regionalism include: Jean-François Gravier, Paris et le désert français (Paris: Flammarion, 1st ed.: 1947, 2nd ed.: 1972); Club Jean Moulin, Les Citoyens au pouvoir: 12 régions, 2000 communes (Paris: Seuil, 1968); Yves Durrieu, Régionaliser la France (Paris: Mercure de France, 1969); René Mayer, Féodalités ou démocratie (Paris: Arthaud, 1968); Edgar Pisani, La Région: pour quoi faire (Paris: Calmann-Lévy, 1969); Morvan Levesque, Comment peut-on être breton (Paris: Seuil, 1970); Jerome Monod and Philippe Castelbajac, L'Aménagement du territoire (Paris: Presses universitaires de France, 1972); Joseph Martray, La Région: Pour un état moderne (Paris: Editions France-Empire, 1970); Michel Philipponneau, La Gauche et les régions (Paris: Calmann-Lévy, 1967); Jean de Savigny, L'Etat contre les communes (Paris: Seuil, 1971). On Italy see Note 7. Two other useful sources are Oscar Gish, A Survey of Regional Planning Research Activities in Western Europe and Yugoslavia, Information Paper no. 24 (London: Centre for Environmental Studies, 1971), and D. Kalk, ed., Regional Planning and Regional Government in Europe (The Hague: International Union of Local Authorities, 1971).

4. SOFRES poll, April 1969.

5. For some stimulating thoughts on what historic factors make for differing areal distribution of powers in the twentieth century see: Juan Linz, "Early State-building and Late Peripheral Nationalisms against the State: The Case of Spain" (mimeographed, 1972); Samuel Beer, "The Modernization of American Federalism," Publius 3 (Fall 1973): 50–95; Samuel Huntington, Political Order in Changing Societies (New Haven, Conn.: Yale University Press, 1967), chap. 2; Arthur Maass, Area and Power (New York: Free Press, 1959).

6. Bourjol, Les Institutions régionales, pp. 208–12.

7. Pierre Barral, "Idéal et pratique du régionalisme dans le régime de Vichy," Revue française de science politique 24 (October 1974): 911–39; Stanley Hoffmann, "The Vichy Circle of French Conservatives," (translation of "Aspects du regime Vichy"), Decline or Renewal? France since the 1930s (New York: Viking, 1974), pp. 3–25.

8. Bourjol, Les Institutions régionales, pp. 208–12.

9. Henri Michel and Boris Mirkine-Guetzevitch, Les Idées politiques et sociales de la résistance (Paris: Presses universitaires de France, 1954).

10. Michel Debré, La Mort de l'état républicain (Paris: Gallimard, 1947); Nicholas Wahl, "The Constitutional Ideas of Michel Debré," Theory and Practice: Festschrift for Carl Friedrich, ed. Klaus von Begme (The Hague: Martinus Nijhoff, 1972).

11. Nicholas Wahl and Stanley Hoffmann, "The French Constitution of 1958," American Political Science Review 53 (June 1959).

12. Gordon Wright, The Reshaping of the French Democracy (Boston: Beacon Press, 1948), pp. 241–42.

13. Bourjol, Les Institutions régionales, p. 221; Philip Williams, Crisis and Compromise (London: Longmans, 1964), p. 347; François Retournard, L'Assemblée des présidents des conseils généraux dans la vie publique française depuis 1945 (Paris: Fondation nationale des sciences politiques, Series recherches, no. 2, 1964).

14. On the politics surrounding the creation of regional institutions in Italy see the extremely informative series of articles, full of valuable footnote references, by France Bassanini, Relazioni sociali (1970, nos. 1–2, 3, and 4). Other useful materials include Proceedings, Acpol Congress, "Le Regioni de fronte alla crisis del sistema politico italiano" (Rome, Acpol, November 25–27, 1969); C. Palozzoli, Les Régions italiennes (Paris: Librairie générale de droit et de jurisprudence, 1966); Ettore Rotelli, L'Avvenuto della regione in Italia (Milan: Giuffré, 1967); Andrea Villani, Il Potere locale (Milan: F. Angeli, 1969). See the bibliography cited in Sidney Tarrow, "Local Constraints on Regional Reform: A Comparison of Italy and France," Comparative Politics 7 (October 1974): 1–37; also Norman Kogan, "Impact of New Italian Regional Governments on the Structure of Power within the Parties," Comparative Politics 7:3 (April 1975): 383–406.

15. Constitution of 1946, Title V, Articles 121, 122, from Norman Kogan, The Government of Italy (New York: Crowell, 1962).

16. Ibid., Article 121.

17. Ibid., Article 122.

18. Ibid., Article 117.

19. Ibid., Articles 124-25.

20. Ibid., Articles 126-27.

21. Bassanini, Relazioni sociali, p. 166.

22. Ibid., pp. 172-87.

23. See Williams, Crisis and Compromise; Retournard, L'Assemblée; Wright, Reshaping.

24. On the CELIB see J. E. S. Hayward, "Functional Representation and Group Politics," Political Studies (1969), and the works of Martray and Philipponeau.

25. On the regionalization of planning see Jacques Lanversin, L'Aménagement du territoire et la régionalisation en France (Paris: Flammarion, 1967); Kevin Allen and M. C. MacLennan, Regional Problems and Policies in Italy and France (London: Allen and Unwin, 1970); Niles M. Hansen, French Regional Planning (Bloomington: Indiana University Press, 1968); Pierre Bauchet, La Planification française, 5th ed. (Paris: Seuil, 1966); John and Anne-Marie Hackett, Economic Planning in France (London: Allen and Unwin, 1963); Stephen Cohen, Modern Capitalist Planning (Cambridge, Mass.: Harvard University Press, 1970); John McArthur and Bruce Scott, Industrial Planning in France (Cambridge, Mass.: Harvard University Press, 1969).

26. See Serge Antoine and Jean Vergeot, "Les Régions de programme," Les Cahiers français 35 (December 1958); Serge Antoine, "Réformes administratives et régions économiques," Economie et humanisme 118 (May-June 1959); René Monier, Région et économie régionale (Paris: Berger-Levrault, 1965); Léon Gormay, Les Economies regionales en France (Paris: Editions Dotec, 1958).

27. See Jean Charlot, L'UNR (Paris: Armand Colin, 1967), and Le Phenomène Gaulliste (Paris: Fayard, 1970). Also, J. E. S. Hayward and Vincent Wright, "The 37,708 Microcosms of an Indivisible Republic: The French Local Elections of March 1971," Parliamentary Affairs (1971).

28. My thoughts about the interaction of elite groups have been influenced by two studies of a similar problem in earlier epochs: Franklin Ford, The Robe and the Sword (Cambridge, Mass.: Harvard University Press, 1963); and J. H. Plumb, The Origins of Political Stability: England 1675-1725 (Boston: Houghton Mifflin, 1967).

29. On De Gaulle's views of political parties, see Charles de Gaulle, Mémoires de guerre (Paris: Plon, 1959), and the articles by Wahl and Hoffmann on the constitution of 1958.

30. On the politics of protecting traditional or declining sectors, see Suzanne Berger, "The Uses of the Traditional Sector: Why Declining Classes Survive" (mimeographed, 1972).

31. Catherine Grémion, loc. cit.

32. Elisabeth Dupoirier and Gerard Grunberg, "Vote municipal et vote législatif: Evolution de 1965 à 1971 dans les villes de plus de 30,000 habitants," Revue française de science politique 22 (April 1972). See the other articles on March 1971 elections in that issue.

33. See Pierre Viansson-Ponté, Histoire de la république gaullienne, 2 vols. (Paris: Fayard, 1970, 1971); Philippe Alexandre, Le Duel de Gaulle-Pompidou (Paris: Editions Bernard Grasset, 1970); M. -A. Burnier, ed., La Chute de général (Paris: Editions premières, 1969).

34. Le Monde, March 24, 1968. (Author's translation.)

35. See Jean-Luc Bodiguel, ed., La Réforme régionale et le référendum du 27 avril 1969 (Paris: Cujas, 1970), particularly the article by Paul Camous, "La Genèse du projet gouvernemental." Much of my interpretation of this process is based on interviews with ministers, civil servants, deputies, party leaders, mayors, the leaders of voluntary associations and interest groups, and academic researchers. During a stay in Paris from October 1971 to July 1972, I followed closely the consideration of the loi Frey. I have used a wide variety of unpublished as well as published materials from a variety of organizations, such as the Mouvement national pour la décentralisation et la réforme régionale (who publish a newsletter), Assemblée des présidents des conseils généraux et de l'association des maires de France (who publish Départements et communes), and the various party-related associations of local government politicians. Finally, I have looked at some of the primary materials that went into the great consultation of the elites of France on the regional reform in the summer of 1969, and read very closely the debates on the referendum proposal in the Journal officiel, Assemblée nationale, Débats, Quatrième législature de la constitution du 4 octobre 1968, première session ordinaire de 1968-69, sessions 104-07, December 11-14, 1968.

36. These observations on the ideas of French political elites concerning the geographic distribution of powers draw on my Ph.D. thesis: The Resilience of Ideologies in France: A Study of the Continuity of Political Ideas (Cambridge, Mass.: Harvard University, 1970), from which I intend to prepare an article on this subject. See also Suzanne Berger, Peter Gourevitch, Patrice Higonnet, and Karl Kaiser, "The Problem of Reform in France: The Political Ideas of Local Elites," Political Science Quarterly 84 (September 1969); the essays by Hoffmann, Huntington, Maass, and Ylvisaker in A. Maass, ed., Area and Power; and Henry Ehrmann, "Direct Democracy in France," American Political Science Review 57 (December 1963).

37. See the SOFRES opinion polls, and the evidence given in Burnier, ed., La Chute de général.

38. See Jean-Luc Bodiguel, ed., La Réforme régionale.

39. J. E. S. Hayward, "Presidential Exit by Suicide," Political Studies (1970).

40. For the referendum results, see Roy Macridis and Robert Ward, eds., Modern Political Systems: Europe, 3rd ed. (Englewood Cliffs, N.J.: Prentice-Hall, 1972).

41. Atti Parlementari, Cameri dei deputati, vols. 37-39 (1967).

42. Figures taken from Rinascita, June 12, 1970. See also Bassanini, Relazioni sociali, pp. 288-92.

43. Stanley Hoffmann, "The State: For What Society," Decline or Renewal?

44. See Jean-Jacques Servan-Schreiber, Le Pouvoir régional (Paris: Editions Bernard Grasset, 1971).

45. Decree no. 70-1047 of November 13, 1970. See analysis by François Lefebvre, "La Déconcentration des compétences ministerielles en maîtière d'équipement collectifs," Le Moniteur des travaux publics et du bâtiment 67 (November 21, 1970).

46. See Le Monde, January 16, 1974, for a table summarizing the results of regional council meetings, and issues of the previous six weeks for individual analyses.

47. See Decréts, nos. 76-168, 170, February 18, 1976.

48. See "Parti socialiste français," Changer la vie (Paris: Flammarion, 1972); "Parti communist français," Programme pour un gouvernement démocratique d'union populaire (Paris: Editions sociales, 1971); and Programme commun de gouvernement du parti communiste et du parti socialiste (Paris: Editions sociales, 1972).

49. Bassanini, Relazioni sociali, pp. 288-92.

50. Donald Blackmer and Sidney Tarrow, eds., Communism in Italy and France (Princeton, N.J.: Princeton University Press, 1977), paperback edition; see also Peter Lange, "The French and Italian Communist Parties: Postwar Strategy and Domestic Society" (San Francisco: American Political Science Association, September 2-6, 1975).

51. Sidney Tarrow, "Local Constraints on Regional Reform", and Between Center and Periphery: Grassroots Politicians in Provincial Italy and France (New Haven, Conn.: Yale University Press, 1977); Jean-Pierre Worms, "Le Préfet et ses notables," Sociologie du travail (July-September 1966).

3

ELITE CARTEL, VERTICAL DOMINATION, AND GRASSROOTS DISCONTENT IN ISRAEL

Gabriel Sheffer

In recent years, the malfunctioning of modern democracies has been associated with and accentuated by crises in center-periphery relations. The revolt of peripheral ethnic groups and farmers in France, the rural periphery's decisive objection to the government plans for Norwegian membership in the European Economic Community (EEC), and the increasingly tense relationship between Scotland and London serve as examples of the phenomenon of crises in center-periphery relations. But by concentrating on sudden crises and on deep permanent cleavages like those found in Northern Ireland or Lebanon, students have tended to neglect the creation of center-periphery linkages and their gradual erosion and change. As a result, the long-term impact of particular sets of center-periphery arrangements is frequently neglected. These arrangements are arrived at during relatively early periods of a state's history.[1] While they are retained under changing conditions, they can eventually deteriorate too.

The scope and pace of this deterioration may vary from state to state. It may occur through visible processes or through unnoticed undercurrents eroding established relations. It may be rapid and drastic, or gradual and incremental. The former pattern borders on revolutionary situations, a phenomenon that is outside the scope of the present study. The latter pattern, more characteristic of Western democracies, is the subject matter of this chapter, which will examine center-periphery arrangements in Israel, their establishment under conditions of nation building after 1948, and their erosion under changing political conditions.

During the long period of political stability in Israel before 1967, most attention focused on the management of the horizontal cleavages between parties and blocs of parties at the national level.[2] Political elites and Israeli commentators alike expressed satisfaction with the performance and achievements of the system,[3] thus projecting an image abroad and at home of political stability and continuity.[4] Especially in such a small system as Israel, this created an image of considerable overlap between vertical and horizontal lines of cleavage, and of the absorption of the former within the latter, as reflected in the conflicts between the major ideological-cultural blocs.

However, it is questionable whether the elite cartel that dominated Israeli national politics since independence ever succeeded in wholly incorporating the periphery into the national party system and thus in legitimizing its dominant position, even during the 1950s and early 1960s. Central political elites did institutionalize a number of devices for channeling resources to the periphery during this period, mistakenly assuming that these would permanently bridge potential cleavages without high cost, tension, or substantial local participation. But although the system worked well for some time, after 1967 elements on the periphery more vehemently demanded greater participation, a more significant role in decision making, and a redistribution of national resources.

In short, long periods of stability in elite cartel democracies such as Israel—and perhaps in other "consociational" democracies as well—may disguise erosion under the surface and fail to produce mechanisms for change in center-periphery political arrangements to adapt to new political and economic conditions.[5] Persistent erosion may eventually cause a crisis, especially where a large part of the population resident on the periphery shares a distinctive culture or sense of economic deprivation or physical insecurity. An increasing absorption of the national political elite in international problems, as is the case in Israel, can also conflict with the need to keep its ears tuned to undercurrents at the periphery.

The Israeli case provides the opportunity to examine two successive but not unrelated processes. The first is the creation of a strong central government out of highly centralized national political blocs, which controls the society and dominates the periphery. The second process is the weakening of this system under changed conditions. It includes the creation of a territorial-economic periphery mainly inhabited by culturally homogeneous groups of immigrants whose protest adds significantly to the weakening process. This case is of interest, since the processes of deterioration of Israeli center-periphery relations, I shall argue, began well before their explicit manifestations were detected in the election of 1977.

The definition of the center in this chapter is thus political: a homogeneous national elite cartel, its cabinet representatives and their senior advisers, as well as the organizational leaders of the parties in power. The definition of the periphery is a double one. It includes a political dimension—the local leaders of both the political

parties and trade unions, as well as local government elites—and a
territorial-cultural dimension—the new settlements established after
1948 under central auspices or existing towns populated mainly by
non-Western Jewish immigrants who arrived in the country after that
date. Although there is evidence of local protest throughout Israeli
society since 1967, I shall concentrate in this chapter on the communities of non-Western immigrants who are the majority population
grouping on the territorial periphery of Israeli society.

In the first section, I will analyze the relevant features of the
Israeli "stable state" from the early 1950s to the mid-1960s. In the
second section, I will deal with the symptoms and the causes of the
periphery's growing discontent. In the final section, I will briefly
discuss some possible directions of future change in Israeli center-
periphery relations. The underlying theme of the chapter is that when
cultural or economic cleavages coincide with territorial stratification
in a centralized elite cartel system, peripheral discontent, though
muffled by traditional structural arrangements and elite strategies of
domination, can receive a powerful thrust from a combination of ethnic
and economic discontent.

TWO DECADES OF A "STABLE STATE?"

Until 1977, Israel had a strong central government based on an
almost unchanging political coalition. Thus, from the very inception
of the state, an almost unchanging elite controlled Israeli politics.
The politicians were supported by highly centralized public and party
bureaucracies, and the central government dominated every major interest group in the society. As in every other aspect of current Israeli society and politics, these features of central elite domination
went back to well before 1948.

The Growth of the Center

The independent Israeli state inherited from the mandatory period (1917-48) two well-established, complementary traditions of government, both well-articulated through elaborate institutions: a strong
central government and highly developed regional administrations.
After gaining independence in 1948, Israel maintained the centralized
government buttressed by a hierarchical and obedient public bureaucracy.[6] Simultaneously, the new state inherited the traditions and
retained important segments of the autonomous central governing organizations of the Jewish community in Palestine.[7] But it did not retain the highly developed regional governments of the mandatory peri-

od. This level of government had been a most significant element in the British administration of Palestine since, for political purposes, it minimized the roles of local authorities, both Jewish and Arab.[8] The regional authorities' jurisdiction was transferred to the Israeli central government, which was increasingly interpenetrated with the institutions of the Jewish community.

This initial concentration of legitimized authority at the center partly stemmed from the acceptance of British law, which was maintained almost totally after independence. But the accumulation of greater political power by the government was also significantly enhanced by the results of the post-World War II anticolonial struggle, which coincided with a new stage of the Arab-Israeli conflict. This two-tiered struggle created a highly mobilized Jewish community. Despite a certain amount of dissent, the majority voluntarily decided to entrust the conduct of its affairs to a small, "charismatic" political elite assisted by a dedicated bureaucratic class and with close ties to the international Zionist movement. These were the same elites who had led the community since the mid-1930s. From these factors there derived a general sense of continuity and stability during the formative decade following independence.[9]

For the duration of the war of independence (1947-49), deeply rooted, traditional ideological controversies were largely brushed aside and the unifying elements in the overarching Zionist ideology were emphasized. Moreover, compliance with the government was facilitated not only by a high degree of the necessary societal mobilization but also by a general acceptance of the need to absorb the large masses of immigrants who would double the Israeli Jewish population in less than four years. This immigration changed both the territorial shape of the community and its demographic characteristics.[10]

During the initial period of nation building, the acceptance of the central government's authority was facilitated both by inherited prestate political and bureaucratic arrangements and by a high degree of consensus concerning national priorities. Furthermore, as a culmination of a process that started during the prestate period, the government emerged with almost complete control over two vital spheres for Israel—capital and manpower imports. Through a complex network of Jewish world organizations and the state's various embassies abroad, the government—and the political elites who controlled it—were the chief recipients of capital imports. These vital imports were provided by world Jewish organizations, by unilateral transfers from foreign governments, as well as by long- and short-term foreign private and governmental grants and credits.[11] Concerning manpower, the government controlled both its settlement and the means for its employment.

But there were also significant cleavages. Though culturally homogeneous, the Jewish community in Israel was still divided into

three highly structured ideological blocs, created by the main "streams"
of immigration during the colonial period. These were the "civic
bloc," the labor movement, and the religious camp. Each of these
blocs consisted of a number of political parties and factions, which
served as the main sources of political legitimization for the elites
at the national level. Through either the party system or through bloc
organizations like the Histadrut, the blocs supplied various services
to the population. These services included, among others, education,
health, welfare, banking facilities, labor exchanges, recreation and
sports, and so on.[12]

During the mandatory period, the capacity to provide these services had been deemed essential by the elites to attract additional
members to each bloc. After independence the main source of new
members came from the swelling ranks of new immigrants. An important target of the elites was to maintain stable levels of bloc and
party membership between national elections in the face of massive
immigration. These three blocs, and the parties composing them,
became the foci for the processes of political socialization, identification, and membership, as well as for the provision of social and
physical services. Thus, during the late 1940s and early 1950s, the
blocs and the parties that composed them remained the essential factors in the Israeli political game.

One important consequence of these trends was that Israeli institutions and policy-making procedures were continuously being
shaped by the interplay between demands on the part of highly ideological political parties for autonomy and by the prevailing overarching
ideological consensus and need for unity. The result was a conditional
compliance with the authority of the central government—conditional
upon the allocation of ample resources to the various political blocs
as well as the legitimization of dissent groups like the Herut party born
out of the Irgun[13] and the core of the current Likud coalition.

A second interplay was between the forces promoting a greater
governmental role in the society and those that preferred the maintenance of the prevailing patterns of vertical segmentation between
ideological blocs. The result of this standoff—in the face of the pressing policy needs of creating a state for a rapidly growing nation—was
to enhance the importance of political elites at the center. Maintaining political unity in the face of enormous policy problems could only
be accomplished—given the ideological cleavages within the society—
by the use of elite bargaining and accommodation as the main instruments of policy formation. Through these processes, the power of the
elites was enhanced, the blocs they represented were preserved, and
Israel came to reflect the politics, political arrangements, and policies of a full-fledged consociational democracy.[14]

Since neither any political bloc nor single political party com-
manded an absolute majority, there was a constant need for coalition

government. And in view of continued external threats to Israel's survival, the quest for political stability and the reduction of the potential for domestic conflict were both crucial. This accelerated the institutionalization of these complementary arrangements: a formal proportional electoral system, a strict pattern of proportional allocation of political resources,[15] and an agreement to differ in certain spheres, such as long-term ideological objectives in the realm of defense and foreign affairs. At the same time, there was informal agreement to prevent situations that could either cause struggles at the rank-and-file level of the political-ideological blocs and parties, or break the unity of the existing ruling coalition.[16]

Even so, the successful survival of this ideologically divided society and ruling elite cartel could only be explained—in a democratic system—by the remarkable voting conservatism of the Israeli public and its continued loyalty to the same parties.[17] Also important was the cartel's firm control over the state and semipublic organizations that were in charge of the distribution and redistribution of public resources. Under these conditions, it is not surprising that the cartel maintained firm control over the comparatively large and elaborate bureaucracy too. This, of course, further strengthened its hand vis-a-vis the electorate and minimized the challenges of the opposition parties.[18]

Simultaneous with the process of centralization, compartmentalization occurred inside the government and the bureaucracy. In accordance with interparty coalitional agreements, ministries and portfolios were allocated in a strictly proportional manner. Once a party was granted control over a ministry, it came to be regarded almost as its own domain. The net result was that ministerial policies were determined in accordance with party ideology and senior officials were recruited according to a mix of ascriptive (party affiliation) and merit criteria. In this system the cabinet was at best a coordinating institution. During periods of crisis and in certain spheres, such as foreign affairs and defense policies, it was also a policy-formulating and implementing body.[19] Eventually, the public sector became the most powerful single link between the grassroots and the elite cartel. But through these developments, which were steadily bureaucratized, the elite cartel became increasingly insulated and detached from the grassroots of Israeli society.

These factors caused policy making to become both highly centralized at the national level and disaggregated. Major policy guidelines were formulated secretly by senior members of the elite cartel in consultation with senior bureaucrats. Famous was the Israeli "kitchen cabinet" in its various forms. From the point of view of content, most of the grand policies were carefully designed by the elite to minimize major ideological controversies that might have resulted

in open interbloc and interparty warfare. Further, policy-making
procedures and policy content were designed to avoid cabinet crises,
which might have resulted in the breakdown of existing coalitions.[20]
Long-range planning was shunned and fuzziness with regard to controversial issues was preferred to the policy clarity that might have
created dangerous strains in the elite.

Because of its security problems and the waves of immigration
from the late 1940s on, Israel was also a highly mobilized nation.
In coping with the resulting volatility, the preferred mode of policy
implementation up until the early 1960s was the ad hoc, massive policy operation. Major problems dealt with in this manner included
housing, illiteracy, the settlement of immigrants, and large irrigation projects. Success in some of these major operations in the 1940s
and 1950s only furthered the use of this technique. Ultimately, the
adoption of this mode of policy implementation extended the scope of
central government intervention in and control of social, political,
and economic development at all levels of the society.

The Growth of the Periphery

Despite this seemingly smooth transition from colonial rule to
independence, the Israeli elite did confront some major problems during the early 1950s. These stemmed mainly from the social, economic, and political tensions that accompanied the interconnected processes
of nation building, colonization of the territorial periphery, and the
absorption of a new mass immigration. It has already been observed
that as a result of this mass immigration, the population doubled in
four years. In 1947, the Jewish population of Palestine was 867,000.
The number of immigrants for the following four years was 105,000
in 1948; 235,000 in 1949; 160,000 in 1950; and 167,000 in 1951.[21]

The sheer size of this mass immigration had an overwhelming
effect upon the new state's economy. The demographic composition
of the immigration also changed the social and educational structures
of the Jewish community. One of the most profound changes was the
introduction into the system of a large number of Oriental Jews. The
impact of this immigration upon the demographic structure can be appreciated in viewing the data presented in Table 3.1 concerning the
geographic origins of Jewish families at the beginning of the 1970s and
the size of their families.

It is interesting from a political and social point of view to contrast these figures with the ethnic composition of the members of the
Israeli Parliament during the same period. Table 3.2 dramatically
demonstrates the cohesion of the older elite and the dominant role of
politicians of European origins in Israeli society. Immigration figures

TABLE 3.1

Jewish Families by Size of Family and Continent of Birth
(average 1972)

	Israel	Asia–Africa	Europe–America	All Families
Average size of family	3.4	4.7	2.8	3.6
Number of persons in family (percent)				
Over seven	3.3	20.6	0.9	8.5
Six	3.6	10.6	2.0	5.7
Five	13.3	15.7	8.5	11.9
Four	25.1	17.4	18.4	19.2
Three	21.6	14.0	20.7	18.4
Two	16.2	13.9	33.3	23.3
One	14.9	7.8	16.2	13.0
Total	129.8	266.7	341.9	738.4

Source: Central Bureau of Statistics, Israel Statistical Abstract 1973 (Jerusalem: Government of Israel), p. 54.

also show that the vast majority of these politicians immigrated to Israel in the period 1932–47. As in business and the professions, the newer group of Asian-African immigrants has been slow to move into the national political class.

Naturally, the need to settle the new immigrants soon posed social, cultural, and political problems. Settlement was handled in a way that preserved coalitional domination. The major blocs, each of them associated with a major Jewish international "movement," were each granted proportional resources for the settlement of the immigrants who came in under their sponsorship. Once "planted" in a settlement or a "development town," the new immigrant tended to move, perceive, and, most important, to vote in line with bloc interests. Though the coalition parties had great advantages in coopting immigrants in this way, opposition parties also gained certain resources through the established national system of proportional allocation (proporz).[22]

One of the most cherished policies of successive Israeli governments was that of population dispersal.[23] This dispersal policy was based partly on defense calculations, partly on economic considerations, but also on calculations of political convenience. The main objective of the policy was the colonization of the territories along Is-

TABLE 3.2

Members of the Sixth Knesset by Party and Country of Origin
(in percent)

Country	Total	Labor Align-ment	Gahal	Ind L	State List	Free Center	NRP	AG	PAG	Haolam Haze	Maki	Rakah
Russia	20	22	19	50	50	—	—	—	—	—	—	100
Poland	32	25	35	25	—	50	58	25	100	—	100	—
Romania	3	6	—	25	—	—	—	—	—	—	—	—
Central Europe	7	3	—	—	—	—	17	50	—	50	—	—
Western Europe	1	—	4	—	—	—	—	—	—	—	—	—
English-speaking countries	1	3	—	—	—	—	—	—	—	—	—	—
Asia-Africa	12	17	8	—	—	—	—	—	—	50	—	—
Israel	24	24	30	—	50	50	17	25	—	—	—	—
Total	100	100	100	100	100	100	100	100	100	100	100	100

Source: A. Arian, ed., The Elections in Israel, 1969 (Jerusalem: Academic, 1972), p. 123.

rael's borders. The main efforts were directed at the settlement of the southern region (the Negev), the Jerusalem area, and the northern region (the Galilee), which was heavily populated by Arabs. While this policy had already been initiated during the mandatory period,[24] it was most easily implemented through the absorption of the massive waves of immigration of the early 1950s. The relatively successful results of the government's colonization efforts are shown in Table 3.3.

But the immigrants of the 1950s, largely drawn from the Middle East and North Africa, did not import capital and were less educated than previous waves of immigrants had been.[25] They were, therefore, more dependent on the state for their absorption. In accordance with the government's policy of population dispersal, the majority were settled in so-called development towns. Others found homes in clearly defined quarters within existing urban centers. Only a minority were either absorbed into existing kibbutzim or moshavim or themselves established new ones.[26] The net result was an increasing proportion of Jews of Oriental origin on the territorial periphery, as can be seen in Table 3.4. Thus, although there were Jews of Oriental origin throughout the country, a territorial-economic periphery was created in which the majority had a certain cultural unity, a low level of technical and economic skills, and the lack of historic identification with the ideology of Eastern European-derived Zionism. The need to "absorb" these immigrants economically and culturally was matched by the elite cartel's need to "absorb" and control them politically, and for this the institutions and practices of bargaining and policy making described above seemed particularly appropriate.

The Domination of Center over Periphery

There were other characteristics of the Israeli political system as it emerged after 1948 that facilitated the political absorption of the new immigrants within an increasingly centralized political system. Administrative arrangements were the most obvious factor. First, as has been observed, the regional level of government developed under the mandate was discarded. Second, local authorities were made dependent on the central government for approval of legislation, including essential budgetary legislation, which had to be approved by the ministry of the interior.[27] These procedures, of course, imposed great limitations on the freedom of action of all local authorities, but especially on those lacking a skilled middle class and an experienced local political elite.

Financial constraints also affect the freedom of action of Israeli local authorities. Direct government support accounts for a substan-

TABLE 3.3

Regional Distribution of the Israeli Population by Time Period
(in thousands)

District	November 8, 1948		December 31, 1954		December 31, 1964		December 31, 1972	
	Number	Percent	Number	Percent	Number	Percent	Number	Percent
Northern	144.0	16.8	285.7	16.6	397.0	15.7	492.2	15.2
Haifa	175.1	20.5	285.4	16.6	418.1	16.6	496.5	15.4
Central	122.3	14.3	358.5	20.9	459.9	18.2	596.0	18.4
Tel Aviv	305.7	35.7	549.2	32.0	775.8	30.7	928.2	28.7
Jerusalem	87.1	10.2	157.4	9.2	216.3	8.6	349.1	—
Southern	21.4	2.5	81.7	4.7	258.5	10.2	367.8	11.4
Total	872.7	100.0	1,717.8	100.0	2,525.6	100.0	3,232.3	100.0

Source: Central Bureau of Statistics, Israel Statistical Abstract 1964 (Jerusalem: Government of Israel), p. 17 for 1948; 1959/60, p. 12 for 1954; 1966, p. 23 for 1964; 1973, p. 27 for 1972.

TABLE 3.4

Asian and African Born in Selected Local Authorities
(percent)

	1967	1972
Municipalities		
Haifa	12.8	12.4
Jerusalem	23.9	22.3
Tel-Aviv	18.8	18.0
Ashkelon (Negev)	44.1	38.2
Beersheba (Negev)	42.3	37.2
Eilat (Negev)	31.2	27.1
Lydda (Center)	42.0	37.4
Ramla (Center)	40.1	40.5
Acre (Galilee)	42.4	41.4
Safed (Galilee)	32.4	29.7
Tiberias (Galilee)	39.2	34.6
Local councils		
Ashdod (Negev)	55.5	50.4
Dimona (Negev)	60.2	52.9
Qiryat Gat (Negev)	53.2	47.1
Afula (Galilee)	40.0	35.6
Beit Shean (Galilee)	53.1	49.8
Qiryat Shemona (Galilee)	54.0	45.0

Source: Y. Berman, ed., Profile Hevrati Shel Yishuvim
Be'Israel [A social profile of towns in Israel] (Jerusalem: Ministry
of Welfare, 1977).

tial portion of local authorities' budgets in Israel. But while this is
true even for large communities like Jerusalem (with nearly 15 percent of its ordinary revenue in 1963-64), it is far more substantial
for towns on the periphery, such as Eilat (27.5 percent), Safed (40
percent), and Beit Shean (62 percent) in the Galilee, or Dimona in the
Negev (40 percent). Illustrative data on direct support in selected local authorities, both municipalities and local councils, are presented
for selected years in Table 3.5.*

*"Municipalities" are local authorities in what is termed Hebrew
"cities"; "local councils" are local authorities in smaller communities
that have not obtained the status of "cities."

TABLE 3.5

Government Participation in the Ordinary Revenues of Selected Local Authorities, 1958-64

	1958/59		1962/63		1963/64	
	Israeli Lire per Capital	Ordinary Revenue (percent)	Israeli Lire per Capital	Ordinary Revenue (percent)	Israeli Lire per Capital	Ordinary Revenue (percent)
Municipalities						
Jerusalem	11.9	16.1	21.9	16.1	22.9	14.6
Eilat (Negev)	64.0	29.7	66.3	25.5	71.7	27.5
Ashkelon (Negev)	15.8	25.2	37.2	29.4	46.4	32.4
Beersheba (Negev)	16.8	19.5	33.2	18.4	36.4	18.4
Haifa	3.8	3.9	7.0	3.2	5.0	2.1
Tiberias (Galilee)	22.8	14.8	—	31.1	43.8	28.5
Lydda (center)	23.8	39.9	43.4	40.0	42.6	38.2
Acre (Galilee)	16.8	25.6	40.2	34.9	41.9	32.8
Safat (Galilee)	30.0	39.4	68.9	40.6	59.3	34.7
Ramla (center)	17.6	23.7	41.0	35.8	39.7	32.6
Tel Aviv-Jaffa	5.4	4.6	7.7	3.6	6.2	2.5
Local councils						
Ashdod (Negev)	—	—	30.6	37.1	23.2	20.2
Beit Shean (Galilee)	—	—	82.8	53.8	93.7	62.5
Dimona (Negev)	—	—	74.0	60.5	49.9	39.8
Afula (Galilee)	23.5	35.0	45.3	32.5	48.6	31.6
Qiryat Gat (Negev)	31.8	55.6	45.8	50.6	44.4	35.0
Qiryat Shemona (Galilee)	43.5	51.9	79.0	53.9	78.9	51.6
Other local councils	—	—	32.1	39.4	37.0	41.9
Regional councils	—	—	47.4	32.3	50.0	31.9

Source: Central Bureau of Statistics, Israel Statistical Abstract 1968 (Jerusalem: Government of Israel), p. 662-63.

Indirect support is granted to local authorities, particularly to those on the periphery, through two main channels. The first is the government's development budget;[28] the second, the investments of various ministries in local communities. These ministries include the Ministry of Education and Culture, the Ministry of Commerce and Industry, the Ministry of the Absorption of Immigrants, and the Ministry of Religious Affairs. Through such indirect grants, the central government controls the majority of services of the development towns and other peripheral communities.

The centralization of control over local government was also reinforced by developments in the party system. The parties were controlled by a small number of political leaders who had once been elected but were not periodically reelected. At the very top, there was a convergence of the elites of the coalition parties and those of the government and bureaucracy. Party elites were assisted by relatively large party bureaucracies that connected the parties' centers directly to the local chapters with no intermediate regional level. Party centralization was reinforced by the electoral machinery—a single national proportional system—which heavily reduced candidates' dependence on local bases and thus their disposition to support local demands once in office. The new immigrant communities, with their high proportion of uneducated and "unconnected" citizens, thus lacked automatic access to members of Parliament and were forced to work for local benefits through the bureaucracy or through the local party machines linked to the elite cartel.

With the benefit of hindsight, one can now see that these trends —administrative, financial, and political centralization—eroded both the government's and the political parties' ties with the grassroots and led to the center's loss of direct contact with the periphery.[29] Yet for almost two decades, the system not only functioned but managed to absorb new immigrants into the traditional voting blocs in a way that virtually perserved the original electoral balance and prevented the emergence of any significant political or social movement directly representing the political interests of postindependence immigrant groups. Table 3.6 shows a remarkable degree of continuity in Knesset election results between 1949 and 1973, except for a certain degree of change within each major political bloc. There was also a great initial similarity in patterns of voting for national and local authorities.

The remarkable thing was that the Israeli system was developing—at the center—along the classical lines of a consociational democracy, while the typical lines of cleavage that generally divide such systems vertically—ethnic or religious segmentation—were submerged within its major subcultures. What permitted this development was, in part, that new voters were added incrementally through immigra-

TABLE 3.6

Knesset Election Results

Party	Year of Election						
	1949	1951	1955	1959	1961	1965	1969
Left of center							
Communist[a]	4	5	6	3	5	4	4
Mapam	19	15	9	9	9	8	—
Ahdut Haavoda[b]	—	—	10	7	8	45	56
Mapai	46	45	40	47	42		—
Rafi	—	—	—	—	—	10	—
State List	—	—	—	—	—	—	4
Center and right							
Free Center	—	—	—	—	—	—	2
Herut	14	8	15	17	17	26	26
Liberal[c]	7	20	13	8	17	—	—
Independent Israel[d]	5	4	5	6	—	5	4
Religious							
Mafdal	16	10	11	12	12	11	12
Aguda[e] and Poalci Aguda	—	5	6	6	6	6	6
Arab and other	9	8	5	5	4	5	6
Total	120	120	120	120	120	120	120

[a]In the 1963 and 1969 elections, the New Communist List won three seats of the four.
[b]Ahdut Haavoda included in Mapam for the first two elections.
[c]"General Zionists" until 1959 election.
[d]"Progressives" until 1959 election.
[e]In the 1965 and 1969 elections, Aguda won four seats of the six.

tion, in contrast to the solid implantation of cultural voting blocs in most consociational systems. There was, however, a second reason: the territorial dispersion of many of the new immigrants into peripheral communities retarded the genesis of a sense of common grievance and of peripheral solidarity in the face of the high level of organization and well-oiled allocative procedures of the elite cartel.

During the 1950s and the first half of the 1960s, the cartel was actively engaged in what may be regarded, at first view, as contradictory efforts at integration, which had, however, tremendous implications for the future. On the one hand, the elite sought to maintain and expand the existing segmented arrangements for the management of political and social conflict. On the other hand, it was attempting to promote unifying notions of Jewish statehood through the establishment of essentially universal rather than sectoral norms for the policy guidance of central institutions.

In line with this second goal, some of the autonomous organizations established by the political-ideological blocs to supply services to their members were abolished or merged: for example, the separate "civic bloc" and Labor movement education systems, which dated from the prestate period. Also abolished were the separate paramilitary organizations created during the anticolonial struggle by the Labor movement and the rightist camp. Finally, the blocs' separate labor exchanges were merged within the state's labor exchange. But the elite cartel did not succeed in imposing a unified health system on the blocs, in merging their separate welfare organizations or their sport, cultural, and recreational services.[30] Finally, the religious school system retained operating autonomy under the religious parties in the unified Ministry of Education and Culture. The abolition of most of the blocs' redistributive mechanisms further increased the periphery's dependence on the state.

The members of the elite cartel also worked extremely hard to prevent the emergence of additional vertical interparty lines of conflict. As one means of achieving this goal, they sought to prevent cleavages within their own parties. This means that considerable effort was expended in controlling party machines as well as extending, through these machines, the size of each party's constituency. A gradual weakening of the ideological rigidity of each of the main parties took place at the same time, in part as a response to environmental change, and in part out of the political requisites of governing by elite cartel.[31]

Until the eve of the 1967 war, actual participation in governmental coalitions was broad but not universal. It was limited by ideological calculations as well as by the bitter memories of the old political rivalries and personal emnities between the leaders of the "civic bloc" and those of the Labor movement. Nevertheless, the opposition was kept relatively calm since, in allocating national resources, proporz principles were strictly adhered to. This procedure had a considerable impact on political tranquility at the periphery, complementing other mechanisms, like that of firm control over governmental investments through the development budget. It greatly curtailed the opposition's ability to capitalize on the periphery's potential dissatisfaction. The resultant greater ideological flexibility accounted for the center's successes in coopting dissident groups on the periphery. Its constant pursuit of control over the periphery and the latter's acceptance of the center's dominance created a "dynamic-conservative" atmosphere. It promoted incremental innovation and change and the appearance of stability and tranquility inside the system.

Even so, in the early 1950s, the members of the elite cartel had to make special efforts to solidify its electoral support there amid concern that the right might gain political advantage from the economically distressed peripheral towns and settlements.[32] The main tools used to prevent further advances by the right were flexible control over the economy as well as the careful and balanced allocation of national resources to politically loyal communities through various branches of the public bureaucracy.[33] In return, local party functionaries supplied party leaders with information about local needs and conditions and, more important, recruited continued political support. Only in periods immediately prior to national and local elections did the party machines assume real importance. Otherwise, they served as channels for carefully filtered communication from the periphery to the center. While the parties still served as the main channels for communication, the public administration increasingly replaced them since it became the main tool for actual investment and supply of services.

For different reasons, neither the political elite nor the bureaucracy encouraged the revival of old, or the emergence of new, local voluntary associations in response to local needs. Even voluntary action involving the needs of groups like illiterate immigrants, or environmental problems, such as the beautification of neighborhoods and the preservation of antiquities, was initiated and directed by the center in a series of highly publicized, massive, ad hoc operations. Thus, in the process of promoting the notion of statehood and national unity and in securing the periphery's compliance with the center, the spirit of voluntarism that had characterized the Jewish community in Palestine almost disappeared during the 1950s and 1960s.[34]

As a result of the new ideological flexibility during this period, there emerged a combination of distributive and redistributive sets of economic policies that affected conditions on the periphery. The preference for large development projects stemmed from nationalist tendencies. Redistributive notions derived from a combination of the

Jewish charitable and social-democratic traditions of favoring welfare arrangements. In accordance with its "distributive" orientation, the state launched large investments in housing, labor-intensive industrialization, agricultural settlement, and sizable irrigation projects.[35] An overarching ideological and strategic motivation for initiating these projects was the defense-oriented goal of population dispersal. From the point of view of redistribution of national resources, the government invested heavily in public health programs, vocational and traditional liberal education,[36] social work, and personal relief services. Little or no responsibility was left to either private initiative or to local authorities in this development of infrastructure.

The system operated smoothly until the mid-1960s. In 1952-53, and during the 1965-66 economic recession, a number of relatively minor disturbances occurred but had no visible effects on the system at large or upon the attitudes of the elite. The ease with which the elite dealt with these scattered, short-range upheavals seemed, in fact, to reinforce its political prestige and contributed to a sense of complacency concerning its ability to control the periphery. Such complacency could only be reinforced by the way the mass media were organized and run. The lack of amplification of what unrest existed on the periphery could in part be attributed to a system of mass media that is national and centrally controlled, and covers primarily international and national events. Despite its continuing economic problems, the periphery was viewed by the media as being tranquil and undemanding, and hence not worthy of extensive and regular coverage.

In summary, elite control over the periphery was increasingly implemented through the bureaucracy, with autonomous interest associations frowned upon and party machines reduced to the role of channeling demands for services upward. Only prior to national elections did the elite awaken to the periphery's special needs, since it required its electoral support to remain in office. Even in the heavily Oriental-supported religious parties, only few leaders of non-European origin rose up through the ranks during the 1950s and 1960s.[37] The center juggled distributive and redistributive policies in order to prevent local discontent. It thus created the impression that the rules of the proporz game were strictly observed at all levels. Toward the end of the period, the elite was increasingly absorbed in problems of defense and foreign affairs, leaving the affairs of the periphery in the insensitive hands of the bureaucracy. The peripheral population itself was divided among the segmented bases of the elite-controlled national political blocs.

THE EROSION OF CENTER-PERIPHERY
RELATIONS

It might be regarded as paradoxical that in the wake of a highly
successful national effort such as the 1967 war, the Israeli system
came under increasing fire. Yet only since the 1967 war have the
symptoms of the erosion of this system become apparent. Some of
these signs came to the surface as a result of the economic prosperity
that followed the war; others were a direct reaction to the war itself.[38]
However, despite such obvious symptoms as grassroots protest and
local leadership revolt, the elites at the center continued to view their
relations with its territorial-cultural periphery as basically stable
and unstrained.

The Symptoms

Whether inaccurately monitored by the elite or falsely interpreted by it, the symptoms of grassroots unrest were evident to varying degrees in all facets of Israeli life. In the midst of the economic
boom that followed the 1967 war as well as during the national gloom
and recession in the aftermath of the 1973 war, various grassroots
protests and rallies were organized. Furthermore, new kinds of demands were being advanced by both local party leaders and functionaries in the local authorities. Despite the paucity of press coverage
of these activities, it is clear that interest in the political ramifica-
tions of the periphery's situation was increasing. This interest was
reflected, for example, in the growing demands of various local organizations for lectures and visits by experts on welfare, social structure, and domestic political affairs. This tendency is clearly evident
in the reports of the Central Bureau of Information concerning its activities during that period, particularly with regard to the kinds of
lecturers requested.

The main purpose of these rallies and meetings was to promote
self-education and increase local self-awareness. Symptomatically,
most of these educational sessions and meetings were not conducted
within the framework of the local branches of the traditional parties
or of the bloc organizations. Rather, they were conducted under the
auspices of private citizens or local voluntary organizations.

Local leaders, both party and younger nonaffiliated activists,
did not content themselves with peaceful, local discussions. They
also launched symbolic actions at the local level, such as changing the
names of streets or neighborhoods. Through these symbolic actions
they both enhanced the self-awareness of their followers and demonstrated to the elite their growing dissatisfaction with the latter's pre-

dominance and politics. It is easy to imagine the impact of even these nonviolent activities on a society that is highly sensitive to the symbolic meaning of all actions in the public sphere.

The local leaders also succeeded in attracting the media's attention by some of these symbolic actions, although the effects of these actions on the parties' middle-echelon leaders and bureaucrats were wasted and were, in any case, short-lived. For these reasons, they began to seek greater public visibility through direct access to the national media. Through interviews and reports in the national press, on radio and television, which they themselves initiated, these leaders tried to build up greater popular support for their grievances as well as to influence the elite cartel directly. [39]

During the post-1967 war period, the periphery's problems were occasionally highlighted by a war of attrition on the Syrian border and by guerrilla attacks from both Jordan and Lebanon. After the 1973 war, the public's attention was once again attracted to the problems of the periphery by a series of terrorist attacks on settlements near the northern border. Local leaders were not slow in seizing upon these opportunities to promote more comprehensive and direct discussions with senior policy makers both in government and in the political parties. These talks concentrated on the economic and educational aspects of the situation of the periphery, with the question of the defense of the various towns and villages relegated to second place in the discussions.

The targets of the organized protests from the periphery were mainly in the capital, Jerusalem, and in the largest city, Tel Aviv. By Israeli standards, the 1967-75 period saw an unprecedented series of demonstrations, sit-ins, hunger strikes, and riots. Predictably, these active and sometimes violent expressions of protest were held in front of government offices and buildings and were concerned with governmental redistributive and distributive policies. The demands ranged from seeking different ratios of allocation of the development budget to greater welfare support. Very seldom were these protests directed at the patterns of policy making at the center. The degree of sophistication of the protest movement was still low and it concentrated on the symptoms, rather than on the root causes, of the situation.

Some of the new activities at the local level—and these were not limited to the periphery—were organized by new local associations and by the existing local chapters of national voluntary organizations. After a long period of inaction and relative public obscurity due to the neutralizing efforts of the center, the first to reemerge—and until recently the most persistent—were the local chapters of veteran organizations. Also included were local chambers of commerce, women's organizations such as those of the World Zionist Organization (WIZO),

the women's Histadrut-sponsored WWO, as well as local chapters of
<u>landsmenshaften</u> immigrant organizations. These organizations under-
took new operative tasks and broader social functions, and stimulated
local discussions of the situation at the local level. They also lent
new prestige to voluntary action, which had been reduced by the great
reliance upon the state and by the <u>étatiste</u> notions enhanced by the center.

    In many places, these associations were joined by newly estab-
lished neighborhood associations for specialized local action. Together all these organizations and associations began to supply some
communal services that previously had either been promised or supplied by the center. For example, some of them became increasingly
involved in supplying psychiatric social services; they financed and
professionally supported local cultural and social centers and activities; they provided grants for higher education to gifted students; they
launched programs to attract Israeli and foreign investors to local
projects; they initiated campaigns for attracting Jewish immigrants and
Israeli returnees; they were concerned with improving the environment; and they undertook to provide local civil defense functions.

    The long-range political implications of this process of grass-
roots mobilization are difficult to measure. More immediate and
measurable political effects were produced, however, by the activities
of local chapters of the various trade unions that together constitute
the Histadrut. These local chapters, which are democratically governed, became more politically active at both the local and national
levels after 1967. They experienced a process of radicalization in
which both incumbent leaders and their rivals competed in responding
to the periphery's dissatisfaction and, subsequently, in articulating
its demands. Local disputes over wages, social security, and working conditions on the shop floor were transformed on many occasions
into demonstrations regarding the general disappointment and frustration of the periphery and its protest against the center.

    One of the more important of these incidents occurred in the
Port of Ashdod in 1975, where a dispute over working conditions in
the harbor became a scene for prolonged unrest in the town itself and
attracted support from other towns on the periphery. Clashes between
workers and management and the police on the local level attracted
the mass media and, consequently, national attention. Encouraged by
this and enthusiastically supported by their followers, local union
leaders sought greater political influence, not only in the Histadrut
but also in the circles of government.

    As a result of such activities, local union leaders began to par-
ticipate in various committees that the central government set up to
examine different aspects of the social and economic deprivation, discrimination, and inequality among Oriental groups. The best known

of these was the prime minister's Committee on Children and Youth
in Distress, which extended its deliberations to more general subjects, such as poverty, education, and housing of various peripheral
social groups.

In part in response to these signs of peripheral unrest and mobilization, the number of local union leaders and other protesters in
senior positions in the national party organizations and even in the
Israeli Parliament increased dramatically from the mid-1960s on.
This occurred partly as a result of the periphery's explicit pressures
and partly as a result of the system's efforts to "absorb" emerging
dissent groups by coopting their leaders. Even after 1967, the numbers of Knesset members from towns on the periphery was still small,
as was their representation in the central bodies of the majority Labor
Party.[40] But the new leaders from these districts could at least now
apply behind-the-scenes pressure for further changes in the system.

One of the most vociferous organized protest movements that
emerged in the midst of the post-1967 war prosperity was the Black
Panthers. The group is important in this context both because of its
use of violent means of protest and for its politicization and eventual
transformation into a political party. In 1971, a group of Oriental
youngsters, supported by a few university professors, formed this
movement. Its chief goals were to protest against the discrimination
directed at Oriental Jews and, more specifically, to promote the provision of better housing, education, and employment for them.[41] Its
candidates ran both in the Histadrut elections in September 1973,
when they secured 1.7 percent of the vote, and in the December 1973
general election, when they obtained even less.[42] Although their success in the election was small, their attempt to institutionalize the
periphery's protest in a political party is indicative of the dimensions
of the erosion of the traditional system.

An emerging focus of dissent of local communities throughout
Israel since the late 1960s has been the reform of the electoral system,
which now both benefits institutionalized parties in power and blocks
the expression of local interests in the choice of candidates. Although
there has also been pressure within the elite for the adoption of a
modified British- or American-type electoral system, demands for
policy reform on the periphery have fueled the movement as it becomes
clear that the existing system of an elite cartel, plus the bureaucratic
centralization it has fostered, are the main inhibitors of reform. Demands for changes in the national electoral system were followed by
actual changes in the system of election of local authorities. Since the
1969 national elections, there has been a growing number of communities in which the contest in local elections has been based on local
issues and personalities rather than on national problems or party
lists. Thus, without changing the electoral laws—an action that is

still resisted by the established parties—local leaders are freeing themselves from the bonds of the parties. In this way, far-reaching changes are already being introduced into the Israeli political system. Further evidence of this post-1969 change in electoral behavior is found in the growing discrepancy between national and local election results, in which split-ticket voting is becoming increasingly popular. This trend may result in a growing number of floating voters in the national system, as can be seen in Table 3.7, where an analysis of split-ticket voting is presented for a number of peripheral communities.*

Finally, there have been attempts launched by the periphery itself to create, in reality, a new intermediate, regional level of government. After 1967, there emerged a growing number of joint committees for planning and executing regional projects and new metropolitan unions among formerly independent municipal units of various sizes. This trend started in the metropolitan areas but has spread to other parts of the country. There are now, for example, not only regional unions composed of similar types of municipalities but also experiments for merging the activities of agricultural and urban communities in certain spheres of mutual interest. The proclaimed objective of most of these associations is usually to enhance local efficiency in supplying services such as education, health, and transportation. At the same time, these actions are also motivated by the notion that larger and stronger local and regional units can attract both greater governmental support and private or corporate investments. The emergence of a regional level of activity is also evident in the organization of the parties, especially in the Israeli Labor Party, until recently a paradigm of central bureaucratic control.[43] Its recent electoral calamity has enhanced the centrifugal forces in the Labor Party.

The Causes

In retrospect, it seems that a gradual weakening of the party system preceded the emergence of unrest at the periphery. Concerning the center's relations with the periphery, the indifference exhibited by outstanding Israeli national leaders in the face of growing protests can only be interpreted as arising out of complacency. This, in turn, was based on the leaders' confidence in the system's ability to handle crisis situations and their belief that their control, if not complete, was at least comprehensive.

---

*Note that the phenomenon has always been widespread elsewhere in Israel.

TABLE 3.7

Selected Communities, Regions, and Split-Ticket Voting Index for
1955, 1959, 1965, and 1969 Elections

Community (Region)	1955	1959	1965	1969
Acre (Galilee)	18.5	19.9	37.9	20.4
Afula (Galilee)	1.6	3.5	3.3	12.3
Ashdod (Negev)	—	—	—	58.3
Ashkelon (Negev)	—	3.4	18.8	131.3
Beersheba (Negev)	12.3	64.0	—	9.1
Beit Shean (Galilee)	4.3	4.2	5.1	5.5
Dimona (Negev)	—	12.4	33.8	192.5
Eilat (Negev)	—	4.7	23.9	33.4
Qiryat Gat (Negev)	—	6.5	39.3	13.9
Qiryat Shemona (Galilee)	3.5	14.3	24.6	208.1
Lydda (center)	17.1	8.4	16.9	11.1
Ramla (center)	1.7	15.3	13.3	13.6
Safed (Galilee)	3.3	10.7	28.4	73.2
Tiberias (Galilee)	5.6	11.7	9.3	17.9

Source: A. Arian, ed., The Elections in Israel, 1969 (Jerusalem: Academic, 1972), p. 94.

This complacency was reinforced by the belief that the ideals of national unity would supersede any serious attempt to disrupt the system. The politically sensitive Golda Meir, then Israeli prime minister, could not possibly have missed the Black Panther demonstrations and hunger strikes in front of her office. Nevertheless, she at first dismissed these protests as insignificant, though she ultimately appointed a number of commissions to examine various aspects of the deprivation of minority social groups.

The center's failure to correctly monitor the evolving situation is partly attributable to the simple physical aging of Israel's veteran political elite. It is also related to the mechanisms used to select and recruit the next generation of leaders. The younger leaders of the mid-1960s had not been recruited from among new groups of citizens but from either the military or the civilian bureaucracies.[44] Only in rare cases was there an intentional effort to recruit young political leaders from the periphery. The military and bureaucratic elites who were recruited in this period came mainly from established non-immigrant groups, owed their allegiance to the national elite cartel, and had no direct links to the periphery. Once they assumed senior positions in the system, they did not develop a deep interest in the periphery's problems either. Lack of interest also characterized the parties' bureaucracies at the center. But in any case, the parties had by this time lost much of their importance as channels of communication from periphery to center.

The increasing gap between center and periphery of the political system was not confined to the political elite. Almost inevitably it affected the attitudes of senior bureaucrats. Like younger political leaders and party bureaucrats, senior civil servants showed an inclination to attune their actions primarily to the needs and desires of the elite cartel. The growing professionalization of the bureaucracy did not alter its apathy toward the periphery's demands either; rather, it reinforced this indifference. Greater professionalization of the bureaucracy did lead to a certain degree of sophistication in the formulation of defense and economic policies but not to a greater sensitivity and more favorable response to the periphery's demands and grievances.

An "objective" set of causes for the erosion of center-periphery relations relates to the economic situation of the latter. In particular this refers to two processes. The first is the constant gap in income, jobs, education, and housing facilities between center and periphery.[45] While it is clear that the economic situation of postindependence immigrants has improved in absolute terms, in comparison with nonimmigrant groups, their economic position is still appalling. This can be understood in comparing the average gross annual income of Israeli families from Asia-Africa and from Europe-America during the 1960s. According to many studies, occupation, level of education, age, length of residence in the country, and continent of origin are important in determining inequality. The crucial social problem of economic inequality in Israel stems from the fact that these factors aggregate in a particular way: a substantial number of the new immigrants are from Asia and Africa; they tend to congregate on the territorial periphery and have less education and a lower level of professional skills than the general population and have little direct representation at the higher levels of the bureaucracy or the political class.

Despite the fundamentally egalitarian ideology of the ruling elites, the gap between the affluent center and the relatively impoverished periphery did not narrow significantly during the boom of the late 1960s. A recent study pointed out that in the early 1970s the average standard of living of Western families was twice as high as that of Oriental families. It also showed that Westerners were represented in the higher status white-collar occupations twice as much as were Orientals and that the former were represented in institutions of higher education six to seven times as often as were Orientals, especially those from the periphery.[46]

The second process relates to what has increasingly become regarded as a distorted allocation of national resources. This has been evident not only between the cities and the territorial periphery but also between different sectors of this periphery. Thus, for example, there have been serious misgivings in the development towns about the allocation of resources to neighboring kibbutzim or moshavim as well as to towns or settlements belonging to rival blocs or parties. Residents of the heavily Oriental development towns cannot have failed to notice the remaining strong ties between the national political class and the economically dynamic kibbutz movement.

Another cause for the malaise in center-periphery relations is connected to the changing self-perception of the Oriental community after the 1967 war. This war was, in fact, the first in which Oriental groups visibly participated. They were found not only in the lower echelons of the army, but also in the middle echelons of the military command and the government. Because of this involvement in the war, a stronger sense of political deprivation emerged. The basic argument used was that an equal share in the burden of defense should be complemented by an equal share in day-to-day political participation. Such demands began to be made not only in regard to representation in central political institutions such as the Parliament and the central bodies of the various parties, but also in regard to greater autonomy in the conduct of local affairs. [47]

Finally, several factors contributed to the decline in reputation for wisdom and infallibility that the center had cultivated so carefully since Israeli independence. Most important was the debacle of the 1973 war. Also influential in this respect were the ongoing struggles within the national elite and the failure of the economy on the eve of the 1967 war. The marked decrease in the personal prestige of the central elite was soon followed by a decrease in loyalty and a reconsideration of the center's political "right" to dominate the periphery. These changes were already reflected in the results of the 1969 and 1973 elections.

FUTURE DEVELOPMENTS AND SOME
CONCLUDING NOTES

Although motivated by an unfailing urge to coopt protest movements rather than to solve problems in a fundamental manner, the Israeli political elite has introduced certain changes in its relations with the periphery. Thus, members of the political elite resumed their habit of touring the country and establishing direct contacts with local groups and leaders and dedicated more attention and energies to the periphery's problems. The political elite and the bureaucracy have reconsidered a number of programs, such as housing, industrial development, and education, and have tailored them more carefully to the needs of minority groups and the development towns. It is known, for example, that the budget bureau in the Ministry of Finance has carried out a comprehensive unpublished study of the territorial distribution of the national budget. Its main objective was to reexamine the arguments concerning neglect of the periphery. Although this may eventually be used as a weapon against the periphery's claims, the mere launching of this study showed increased sensitivity to the problem. Furthermore, some structural changes have occurred, including recruitment of local leaders into the political elite; greater autonomy for local authorities; and a willingness to experiment with larger frameworks for regional cooperation, planning, and execution of policies. [48]

Nevertheless, until new structural and procedural patterns of political communication and of division of labor emerge, a tense and uncertain atmosphere will continue to pervade center-periphery relations in Israel. It is still an open question whether the mere formulation or even implementation of more favorable policies for the periphery can fundamentally improve its situation. Only if the elite can learn to complement the introduction of new ad hoc policies with structural changes in the relations between center and periphery is there a chance that a more permanent relaxation in relations will occur.

The periphery's skepticism concerning the intentions of the center may produce new and greater pressures upon the national elite in a generally more turbulent domestic environment. Much of this skepticism is based on the periphery's assessment that, while its own interest lies in the development of great pluralism at the base, the center is still basically interested in maintaining the existing electoral system and the quasi-consociational arrangements of political accommodation and conflict management. Though it is conceivable that the proportional representation system could be maintained on the national level, there are changes evident in the way candidates are chosen within both the ruling party and some opposition parties. Furthermore, a new electoral system may be introduced at the local level through which an institutionalization of the direct personal elections of mayors and other officials might occur. Continued economic dislocation and mutual mistrust may, however, lead to more radical solutions. These include the development of greater local and regional autonomy, a greater reliance on voluntary local activities, and even the introduction of what Dahl has called "true grassroots democracy." In view of the size of the country, this might possibly be a feasible alternative. [49]

The deterioration of the established system of center-periphery relations in Israel, plus the recent electoral debacle of Labor, raise questions about the adequacy of existing explanations of the development of Israeli society and its political system. Both the notion of "dynamic conservatism" as the central characteristic of its patterns of development and adaptation and attempts to apply the consociational model to Israel should now be carefully reexamined. For example, the core of the popular notion of "dynamic conservatism" is that the Israeli political elite showed great pragmatism and flexibility in its day-to-day performance. Through this "tactical" pragmatism, which allowed a certain amount of managerial innovation at the level of national subsystems, such as the economy and education, the elite succeeded in satisfying most Israeli interest groups. This explanation suggests further that despite pressures and environmental change, the elite succeeded for 30 years in maintaining its predominant position without any need for major structural modifications. In essence, this explanation argues that while the Israeli system has shown great structural stability, it has also demonstrated procedural dynamism. When applied to center-periphery relations this explanation did not envisage any major disturbances, let alone a gradual deterioration or basic change in the system.

The main argument of the consociational model when applied to the Israeli case is that the parties have served as vertical pillars of the society. According to this assessment, the system—including its center-periphery relations—maintained its stability through the ability of those parties to fulfill three functions: to mold stable constituencies, to exert influence on senior policy makers, and to elaborate interparty patterns of accommodation through bargaining. This explanation has maintained that the parties penetrated both the center and the periphery with sufficient depth to ensure firm control over these two poles of the system.

In view of the actual developments described above, the explanatory and predictive powers of these two models are questionable. The Israeli system has lost much of its "dynamic conservatism." It is undergoing possibly far-reaching structural changes, especially in center-periphery relations. The adoption of tactical dynamism clearly was not sufficient to perpetuate structural stability. Although the system is still in the midst of change, it is clear that the absorptive and cooptive capabilities of the elite cartel are not as inexhaustible as many have thought, and the recent electoral success of the Likod bloc was based as much on the dissatisfaction of Oriental voters as it was on the scandals and inefficiency of the elite cartel.

NOTES

1. Compare with E. Shils, "Center and Periphery," Logic of Personal Knowledge (London: Routledge and Kegal Paul, 1961); S.

Lipset and S. Rokkan, Party Systems and Voter Alignments (New York: The Free Press, 1967); L. Biner, ed., Crises and Sequences of Political Development (Princeton, N.J.: Princeton University Press, 1972); S. N. Eisenstadt, Modernization, Protest and Change (Englewood Cliffs, N.J.: Prentice-Hall, 1966); S. N. Eisenstadt, State, Society and Center Formation (Jerusalem: Hebrew University, Kaplan School).

2. This academic lineage probably started with B. Akzin's "The Role of Parties in Israel's Democracy," Journal of Politics 17 (Novebmer 1955), and continued in an abundant number of articles and books that emphasized the role of parties in Israeli politics. See, for example, for an historic analysis, W. Z. Laquer, A History of Zionism (New York: Holt, Rinehart and Winston, 1972); L. J. Fein, Politics in Israel (Boston: Little, Brown, 1967); and P. Medding, Mapai in Israel (London: Cambridge University Press, 1972).

3. See the memoirs of D. Ben-Gurion, Israel: A Personal History (New York: Fink, 1971); Golda Meir, My Life (New York: Pitman and Sons, 1975); T. Prittie, Eshkol: The Man and the Nation (New York: Pitman, 1969). The only exception in this regard is the excerpted memoirs of M. Sharett, who expressed his dissatisfaction with the performance of the Israeli system in many spheres. And see G. Yaacobi, Otzmata Shel Ichut [The power of quality] (Haifa: Shikmona, 1972); B. Akzin and Y. Dror, Israel: High Pressure Planning (New York: Syracuse University Press, 1965); V. D. Segre, Israel: A Society in Transition (London: Oxford University Press, 1972).

4. See, for example, Fein, Politics in Israel; S. N. Eisenstadt, Israeli Society (New York: Basic Books, 1968); A. Etzioni, "Change in the System: Alternative Ways to Democracy, The Example of Israel," in his Studies in Social Change (New York: Holt, Rinehart and Winston, 1966).

5. K. D. McRae, ed., Consociational Democracy: Political Accommodation in Segmented Societies (Toronto: McClelland and Stewart, 1974), "Introduction"; H. Daaldẽr, "The Consociational Democracy Theme," World Politics 31, 4 (July 1974): 604-22.

6. Z. Sheref, Shlosha Yamin [Three days] (Tel Aviv: Am Oved, 1959); E. Samuel, British Traditions in the Administration of Israel (London: Valentine, Mitchell, 1957).

7. D. Horowitz and M. Lissak, "Authority without Sovereignty: The Case of the National Center of the Jewish Community in Palestine," A Reader on Israel's Government, ed. E. Gutmann and M. Lissak (Jerusalem: Akademon, 1971); D. Horowitz and M. Lissak, "From Yishuv to State," ibid.

8. J. C. Hurewitz, The Struggle for Palestine (New York: Norton, 1950); ESCO, Palestine: A Study of Jewish, Arab and British Policies, vol. 2 (New Haven, Conn.: Yale University Press, 1947).

9. Eisenstadt, Israeli Society, pp. 332-38.

10. M. Sicron, Immigration to Israel: 1948-1953 (Jerusalem: Falk Project and CBS, 1957); R. Zilberberg, Population Dispersal in Israel 1948-1972: Results of Population Dispersal Policies (Jerusalem: Economic Planning Authority, Ministry of Finance, 1973) (Hebrew).

11. D. Horowitz, Hitpathut Ha'Kalkala Be'Eretz Israel [The economy of Palestine and its development] (Tel Aviv: Mosad Bialik, 1948); R. Szereszewski, Essays on the Structure of the Jewish Economy in Palestine and Israel (Jerusalem: Falk Institute for Economic Research in Israel, 1968); N. Halevy and R. Klinov-Mallul, The Economic Development of Israel (New York: Praeger, 1968), chaps. 2 and 3.

12. H. Barkai, "The Public, Histadrut and Private Sectors in the Israeli Economy," Sixth Report 1961-1963 (Jerusalem: Falk Project, 1964).

13. See especially Horowitz and Lissak, "From Yishuv to State."

14. McRae, Consodiational Democracy; Daalder, "The Consociational Democracy Theme."

15. Fein, Politics in Israel, pp. 67-199; Eisenstadt, Israeli Society, pp. 285-368; A. Zidon, The Knesset (Jerusalem: Achiasaf, 1966); G. Sheffer, "Insulation of the Government, Disaggregation of Politics and Neutralization of the Opposition: The Israeli Case," unpublished paper, 1976; E. Gutmann, "Some Observations on Politics and Parties in Israel," India Quarterly 17 (January-March 1961).

16. Y. Elizur and E. Salpeter, Who Rules Israel? (New York: Harper & Row, 1973); M. Brecher, The Foreign Policy System of Israel (London: Oxford University Press, 1972); E. Gutmann and Y. Landau, "Political Elites and National Leadership in Israel," Political Elites in the Middle East, ed. G. Lenczowski (Washington, D.C.: American Enterprise Institute, 1975), pp. 163-99; L. G. Seligman, Leadership in a New Nation: Political Development in Israel (New York: Atherton, 1969).

17. H. Smith, "Analysis of Voting," The Elections in Israel, 1969, ed. A. Arian (Jerusalem: Academic, 1972), pp. 63-80; A. Arian, The Choosing People (Tel Aviv: Massada, 1973), pp. 103-18.

18. See especially Akzin and Dror, Israel: High Pressure Planning.

19. G. Caiden, "Israeli Administration after Twenty Years," Public Administration in Israel and Abroad 8 (1968): 9-29; Y. Dror, "Public Policy Making in Israel," Public Administration in Israel and Abroad 1 (1961): 5-16; and D. S. Felsenthal, "Hiebetim Nosafim Shel Tashlumim Koalizionim" [Additional aspects of coalition payoffs: the Israeli case] Medina U'mimshal [State and government] 4 (1975).

20. Akzin and Dror, Israel: High Pressure Planning; Dan Inbar and G. Sheffer, "Changes in Policy Making Patterns in Israel," forthcoming.

21. Central Bureau of Statistics, Israel Statistical Abstract 1973 24 (Jerusalem, 1974), p. 126. The number of immigrants in 1952, however, dropped to 11,000.

22. S. N. Eisenstadt, The Absorption of Immigrants (London: Routledge and Kegan Paul, 1954); J. T. Shuval, Immigrants on the Threshold (New York: Atherton, 1963); Eisenstadt, Israeli Society, pp. 196-208.

23. H. Pack, Structural Change and Economic Policy in Israel (New Haven, Conn.: Yale University Press, 1971), pp. 16-17, 141-68.

24. Halevy and Klinov-Mallul, The Economic Development of Israel, pp. 34-35.

25. Sicron, Immigration to Israel; G. Ofer, The Service Industries in a Developing Economy: Israel as a Case Study (New York: Praeger, 1967), chaps 5-6; Pack, Structural Change, pp. 224-25.

26. A Breler, New Towns in Israel (Jerusalem: Israel University Press, 1970); E. Cohen, "Development Towns: The Social Dynamics of 'Planted' Urban Communities in Israel," Integration and Development in Israel, ed. J. N. Eisenstadt, R. Bar-Yosef, and H. Adler (Jerusalem: Israel University Press, 1970); Eisenstadt, Israeli Society, pp. 221-25.

27. S. Weiss, "Local Government in Israel: A Study of Its Leadership" (unpublished Ph.D. dissertation, The Hebrew University, Jerusalem, 1968); S. Weiss, "Ya'hasei Gomlin Bein Ha'mimshal Ha'mercazi La'Shilton Ha'mekomi" [The interactions between central and local government], Netivei Irgun U'minhal [Management and organization], September 1970; D. Elazar, "Halukat Tafkidim Bein Ha'shilton Ha'mekomi La'Shilton Ha'mercazi" [Division of functions between local and central government], Netivei Irgun U'minhal [Management and organization], August 1974.

28. Pack, Structural Change, pp. 142-45, 154-58; Halevy and Klinov-Mallul, The Economic Development of Israel, pp. 180-89.

29. A Brichta, "Social, Political and Cultural Background of Knesset Members in Israel" (unpublished Ph.D. thesis, The Hebrew University, Jerusalem, 1973).

30. Horowitz and Lissak, "From Yishuv to State."

31. A. Arian, Ideological Change in Israel (Cleveland: Case Western University Press, 1968); D. Lazar, "Israel's Political Structure and Social Issues," Jewish Journal of Sociology 15, 1 (June 1973); E. Stack, "Foreign Policy Issues," The Elections in Israel, ed. A. Arian; M. Lissak, "Patterns of Change in Ideology and Class Structure in Israel," Jewish Journal of Sociology 7, 1 (June 1965): 46-62;

A. Arian, "Stability and Change in Public Opinion and Politics," The Elections in Israel, ed. A. Arian, pp. 202-19; R. Bilski and I. Galnoor, "Ideologiot Ve'arachim Be'Tichnun Leumi" [Ideologies and values in national planning], Likrat Ha'shiva Shitatit al Atid Medinat Israel [Toward more systematic thinking on Israel's future], ed. G. Sheffer (Jerusalem: Humanities Press, 1974), pp. 41-56.

32. M. Lissak, "Continuity and Change in the Voting Patterns of Oriental Jews," The Elections in Israel, ed. A. Arian (Jerusalem: Academic, 1972), pp. 264-77; S. Zelniker and M. Kahan, "Religion and Nascent Cleavages," Comparative Politics 9, 1 (October 1976): 21-49; A. Arian, "Electoral Choice in a Dominant Party System," in his Elections in Israel, pp. 187-201.

33. Barkai, "The Public Histadrut and Private Sectors."

34. S. N. Eisenstadt, "Change and Continuity in Israeli Society," Man, State and Society in the Contemporary Middle East, ed. Y. Landau (New York: Praeger, 1972), pp. 294-311.

35. H. Darin-Drabkin, "Housing in Israel" (mimeographed, Tel Aviv, 1957); D. Krivine, "Housing in Israel" (mimeographed, Jerusalem, 1965); E. Kleiman, The Structure of Israel's Manufacturing Industries (Jerusalem: The Falk Project, 1969); R. Weitz and A. Rokach, Agricultural Development: Planning and Implementation (New York: Praeger, 1968); Y. Mundleck, Long-Term Projections for Agricultural Research (Jerusalem: The Falk Project, 1964); Pack, Structural Change, pp. 123-26.

36. R. Klinov-Mallul, The Profitability of Investment in Education in Israel (Jerusalem: Falk Institute, 1966).

37. Zelniker and Kahan, "Religion and Nascent Cleavages."

38. E. Kanovsky, The Economic Impact of the Six Day War (New York: Praeger, 1970), pp. 86-134.

39. E. Etzioni-Halevy, "Protest Politics in the Israeli Democracy," Political Science Quarterly 90, 3 (Fall 1975): 497-520; E. Sprinzak, Nizanei Politika Shel De'Legitimiut Be'Israel, 1967-1972 [Initial de-legitimation politics in Israel, 1967-1972] (Jerusalem: Eskol Institute, 1973).

40. M. Aronoff, "Party Center and Local Branch Relations," Elections in Israel, ed. A. Arian (Jerusalem: Academic, 1972), pp. 150-83.

41. E. Cohen, "The Black Panthers and Israeli Society," Jewish Journal of Society 14, 1 (June 1972): 93-110.

42. A. Arian, "Were the 1973 Elections in Israel Critical?" Comparative Politics 8, 1 (October 1975): 152-64.

43. M. Mieseles, "The Labor Party Center Falls with the Party Regions," Maariv 15 (September 1976).

44. Elizur and Salpeter, Who Rules Israel?; Landau and Gutmann, "Political Elite and Leadership in Israel."

45. S. Smooha and Y. Peres, "The Dynamics of Ethnic Inequalities: The Case of Israel" (unpublished paper, 1974); G. Hanoch, Income Differentials in Israel (Jerusalem: Falk Project, 1961), pp. 15-130.

46. Y. Peres, Yahasei Edot Be'Israel [Ethnic relations in Israel] (Tel Aviv: Sifriat Po'alim, 1976), pp. 105-32.

47. M. Aronoff, "Party Center and Local Branch Relations," pp. 150-83; A. Brichta, "The Social and Political Characteristics of Members of the Seventh Knesset," Elections in Israel, ed. A. Arian (Jerusalem: Academic, 1972), pp. 109-31.

48. Uri Porath, "Hov Ha'rashuiut Ha'mekomiot" [The debt of the local governments], Yediot Ahronot 4 (February 1977).

49. Compare D. J. Elazar, "The Local Elections: Sharpening the Trend toward Territorial Democracy," The Elections in Israel, 1973, ed. A. Arian (Jerusalem: Academic, 1975), pp. 219-37.

4

REGIONAL POLICY, IDEOLOGY, AND PERIPHERAL DEFENSE: THE CASE OF FOS-SUR-MER

Sidney Tarrow

What is the relationship between territorial policy and the market economy? Politicians—and to a lesser extent, social scientists—often talk as if territorial policy was made, transmitted, and implemented in isolation from the interests and values of a capitalist society. Indeed, since the goal of most regional policy is to redress some of the imbalance between strong and weak regions, there is even a tendency to regard it as a kind of "spatial socialism" and therefore inimical to these interests and values. Others, most notably the Marxists, regard territorial policy as an instrument of the market economy, which either smooths out costly warps in the market's fabric or aggravates capitalism's contradictions by making peripheral regions more dependent on the center.

Much of the debate hinges on the more basic question of whether there is one actor—the capitalist state—or two—the state and capitalism—affecting the setting and implementation of territorial policy.

——————————

I wish to thank Douglas Ashford, Henry Ehrmann, Peter Katzenstein, Mark Kesselman, and John Zysman for their careful comments on an earlier version of this chapter, which was presented both to the Seminar on the State at Columbia University and to the Seminar on the State and Capitalism at Harvard University. I was also greatly helped by my conversations with Danielle Bleitrach and Alain Chenu, Didier Cultiaux, Yves Durrieux, and Paul Vieille, whose published work is cited herein. Several French government employees and former employees will recognize their anonymously given testimony. I wish to thank them without, regretfully, naming them.

For the Marxists, there is but one actor—the capitalist state—providing public funds to individual capitalists to locate plants in out-of-the-way or declining regions.[1] For liberals, there are two: the capitalist firm, with its awkward habit of concentrating in regions and cities where labor, services, and markets are within easy reach; and the state, which uses its financial weight and administrative discretion to induce industries to move to where the social benefits will be greater.[2] Even the image of the interaction between state and capitalism differs diametrically for these two schools of thought: for the liberal, the capitalist is recalcitrant, cautious, tied to the narrow interests of his firm and regional market; for the Marxist, he is devious, instrumental, making the state pay for investment in branch plants where labor is cheap and unions poorly organized.

Perhaps nowhere more than in France are the two basic views of state and capitalism in such sharp contrast. For writers like Castells and Godard, there is essentially one actor—the capitalist state—whose industrial policy serves the direct interests of capital accumulation and legitimation.[3] For liberals like Shonfield, the French capitalist—malthusian and conservative—has had to be dragged along by a technocratic state to accept the need for modernization.[4] The venerable strength and coherence of the French state likewise divides observers into those who see it as a Napoleonic tool in the hands of the capitalist elite and those who see in it an independent actor driving the economy toward new forms of integration through tools of étatisme that were developed when capitalism was in its infancy.[5]

Regional economic policy likewise divides observers into those who, like Danielle Bleitrach and Alain Chenu, see regional policy leading to an aggravation of the cleavages in capitalist society[6] and those who, like Pierre Durand, see it as a means of reorganizing economic life so as to better adapt to the needs of the regions.[7] Regional planning, to complicate matters, is often confused with decentralization, a semantic overlap as handy to governments wishing to clothe policies in democratic garb as it is to oppositions at pains to condemn central policy initiatives as attacks on local autonomy.*

Indeed, a useful distinction to be made is between regionalism as a policy or set of policies, regionalism as an ideology of governmental intervention, and regionalism as an organizing framework for peripheral defense. Taken separately, these three meanings induce different answers to the question of the relationship between territorial policy and the market economy. Taken together, they suggest

---

*The political use made of regionalism as an issue in national politics is a theme developed more thoroughly by Peter Gourevitch in his contribution to this volume.

a more synthetic answer: that regionalism can most fruitfully be studied as an element in the hegemony of the modern capitalist state, one that cushions the constraints of the market with a consensus built around regional ideology and modifies it through the give-and-take of center-periphery political negotiation. Whether it is the market or the state that is ultimately dominant, one cannot say. But regionalism mediates between governmental policy and peripheral response in many ways, one of which is to provide an ideological umbrella for policies of increased central domination.

The case of the industrial pole of Fos will illustrate these interrelationships between regionalism as policy, as ideology, and as peripheral defense. All three were, of course, major themes in the more dramatic regional policy issues of the 1960s—especially the regional referendum that cost General de Gaulle his power in 1969. But it is in regional economic policy, and in its adjunct, industrial decentralization, that the relationship between the state and capitalism in the Gaullist republic can best be seen. The case of Fos will show that when regionalism as an ideology is employed by political elites to justify policies that have little to do with regional equality, regional political defense—in part touched off by the official ideology itself—may result. Ironically, French regional policy may thus have "contributed to an increase in regional consciousness, which is at the outset awareness of frustration."[8]

REGIONALISM AS POLICY

If planning is everything, then maybe it is nothing.
                                        —Aaron Wildavsky

Fos was little more than a sleepy fishing village in the early 1960s when the French government decided to create an industrial port there, a project that reached completion in 1968. When a major industrial installation—the SOLMER plant of the De Wendel steel interests—was announced as the center of a major industrial pole to be created at Fos, political clouds began to gather. But the storm that eventually burst over the region was due not to the intrusion of big steel into a quiet backwater, but to the combination of capitalist concentration and the destruction of local autonomy that it appeared to symbolize. For, with some reason, the industrial pole of Fos-Marseilles would appear to many residents as an economic cost rather than gain, for the region, and as an extension of the power of the administrative state, not its decentralization.

What then has this story to do with regional policy? The reasons for this apparent paradox are historic. France in the 1960s presented

the spectacle of a country famous for economic planning in which planning was on the wane while regionalism was on the agenda. Indeed,
rather than decline along with economic planning, regional policy, as
Rémy Prud'homme observes, "grew in importance and gained an ever-
increasing recognition in administrative and political circles."[9]

Not only that. Like the War on Poverty in the United States during the same period, regionalism in France came to cover an increasing variety of problems and policies, from the regionalization of the
plan to the reform of territorial administration to the provision of
rural roads and the development of urban planning. For once regionalism had been posed as a politically popular theme, "regional policy
could not be the responsibility of any one particular ministry." Indeed, concludes Prud'homme, it "can hardly be thought of as a policy,
but rather as a necessary component of other policies."[10] Regionalism
had the appeal of policy immediacy, the ideological gloss of enlightened
planning, and the political value of satisfying grassroots demands,
though there is some question of how insistently these demands were
actually couched in regional form.*

But if regionalism was everything, then—much like planning—
it might be nothing, or, at least, it would escape the "rational" mold
of economic planning that had fueled its takeoff in the early 1960s.
Thus, the Planning Commission, whose experts had been the first to
seek the regionalization of the plan, failed utterly to make a mark on
regional policy, except to provide it with a patina of technocracy that
would later cover its more glaring contradictions. The planners
failed in three senses, two of them immediate and one more basic.
First, they failed to wrest control of public investment from the various
spending ministries, which would continue in the future, as in the
past, to follow sectoral priorities in the territorial allocation of their
resources.[11] Second, they failed to shape the ultimate form of the
regional administrative reform; in place of the informal procedures
developed during the Fourth Plan, there arose a rigid panoply of regional structures that would leave practically untouched the traditional
relations between prefectures, ministries, and communes that had
prevented the setting of regional priorities in the past.[12] Third, all
of this was part of the more general decline of planning under a regime,
the Gaullist republic, which cloaked its preference for economic concentration under a technocratic guise.

There was one apparent exception to the decline of planning in
the 1960s: the DATAR (Délégation à l'aménagement du territoire et
à l'action régionale), created in 1963 on a wave of enthusiasm for
planning and reform of the state but, in retrospect, built on the wreck

---

*Again, see Gourevitch, in this volume.

of the Planning Commission's hopes for turning territorial policy
into an arm of planning. It was the DATAR that would be largely responsible for the rigid form of the CODERs, the Regional Economic
Development Committees created after the regional reforms of 1964.
These bodies replaced the older voluntaristic regional expansion
committees with a form of corporatist interest cooptation that ultimately helped only local notables and regional prefects.[13] It was the
DATAR also that would cooperate with the Ministry of Housing and
Public Works to ensure the latter's ability to undertake "a considerable development of its own instruments of intervention in matters of
urban planning," a development that cut deeply into the urban and regional functions of the Planning Commission.[14] Finally, it was the
DATAR that would be the major actor in implementing French industrial policy, through the manipulation of a variety of tools for credit,
subsidy, and tax exemptions to encourage regional decentralization.[15]
As an example, in 1964 it was decided that the agency's approval
would be necessary for all new industrial construction of more than
2,000 square meters.[16]

Behind the DATAR's success, there lay not only a general enthusiasm for regionalism, which, in any case, it had been partly responsible for creating. There was, first of all, the political sagacity
of its founder, Olivier Guichard, an orthodox Gaullist who had made
common cause—as the plan could not—with both the spending ministries and traditional territorial actors.[17] Second, although it tried
in a myriad of small ways to encourage industrial decentralization,
the DATAR increasingly turned to supporting the grandes options of
industrial policy, such as the creation of industrial poles at Dunkerque
and Fos-Marseille. Third, on the flank of its industrial initiatives,
the DATAR's people took growing interest in urban planning, in large
part to help provide the social and physical infrastructure for the
firms it hoped to attract there. The outcome was its ultimate attachment to the Ministry of Equipment, which emerged as the key urban
affairs ministry at the end of the 1960s under Olivier Guichard.

But this anticipates our story. These policy strategies had several results that—along with its special administrative status and talented personnel—would give the DATAR a key position in developing
Gaullist territorial policy. First, its willingness to work with both
mainline ministries and territorial notables removed from the young
agency the potential threat of powerful political enemies. Second, its
involvement in the distributive aspects of industrial policy—minus the
rationalizing zeal of a Commissariat du plan—provided the DATAR
with a network of contacts and with growing legitimacy among French
businessmen,[18] particularly as it tried increasingly to work with big
companies whose market expansion was favored by Gaullist economic
policies. Third, though its initiatives in urban and metropolitan area

planning dated to before 1968, with the shift of the Pompidou government away from the regions and toward local government reform in 1970, the DATAR was in a position to place this experience at the service of the government. [19]

But these characteristics had all the vices of their virtues. Depending on where one sat, the DATAR was an expression of neocapitalism in France, and far from its enemy. Because of its alliance with the major spending ministries and territorial notables, the DATAR was inhibited from setting selective regional priorities. "Regional policy," writes Prud'homme, "was not inspired by a few broad objectives that could be easily stated, and compared with tools or results. . . . DATAR people themselves, however gifted, and despite many efforts, did not succeed in providing an overall framework that could serve as a blueprint for their actions."[20]

Because of both its administrative strategy and its coziness with industry, the DATAR never significantly altered the regional disequilibria in either public or private investment policy. The agency does try to influence the ministries' investment policies, but, as Prud'homme concludes on the basis of a careful analysis, "there are reasons to believe that, on the whole, the spatial distribution of public investments does not follow regional policy prescriptions."[21] Though Lorraine and the north have received higher than average per capita spending from the state, "the goal of favoring the western regions has clearly not been implemented" and "two of the most favored regions were the Paris region and Haute Normandie!"[22] As for the investment subsidy system that is more closely influenced by the DATAR, the findings are mixed, but "on the whole," concludes Prud'homme, "the efficiency of the subsidy system on location decisions does not seem to be very great."[23]

Private investment—the main card played by the DATAR—at first sight appeared to favor the provinces over Paris in the 1960s. But though migration into Paris appears to have slowed, patterns of growth in regional employment were not really reversed. And "although it is true that industrial employment increased more in the underdeveloped west than in the rest of France, it must be noted that it took place primarily in those western regions closest to Paris," where it might have grown even in the absence of a regional policy.[24] Regions further from Paris did not enjoy high growth in industrial employment, and some—like the declining north and Lorraine—continued to lose industrial workers during the decade.[25]

In retrospect, the instruments used to encourage industrial decentralization could hardly have led to radical shifts in regional investment or employment. Despite incentives to invest in backward regions, investment decisions remained largely voluntaristic and—within these regions—policies allocating subsidies were not finely

tuned enough to direct investment toward the most needy areas.* As
for employment, the DATAR's policies subsidized investment rather
than jobs and, in addition, were oriented primarily toward large corporations. Both aspects, of course, tended to favor capital rather
than labor-intensive investment. "In the aggregate," concludes
Prud'homme, "they should result in the creation of fewer—not more—
jobs."[26]

    Finally, though initially following a logic of supporting regional
metropolitan areas as alternatives to Parisian population growth, the
DATAR's commitments in the field of urban planning became open-
ended. In 1967, it began a special effort to attract investment to me-
dium-size cities in the Paris basin; in 1970, to support growth in me-
dium-size towns in the provinces; while within the Paris region and
elsewhere, DATAR was given responsibility, through a Groupe central des villes nouvelles, for the coordination of national policies for
the creation of satellite new towns.[27] One could even eventually read
in a DATAR publication of "the role that Paris had to play in Europe
and the world." The wheel had really come full circle when the agency
charged with correcting the imbalance between Paris and the provinces
observed meekly that "there are two ways of looking at the place of
Paris in regional policy."[28]

    Thus, we see in the DATAR a highly political and flexible agen-
cy, one that succeeded in riding the wave of regionalism into a number of policy arenas, and one that combined the highest Gaullist orth-
odoxy with legitimacy to business and close-working contacts with the
territorial bureaucrats who are responsible for much of French policy
implementation. Though not itself an operating agency, the DATAR
was therefore chosen, almost from the outset, to guide the creation
of the industrial pole at Fos through an interministerial working party,
the Groupe central de Fos, that was lodged in the agency. In addition,
many of the key financing decisions were taken by an interministerial
committee, the Comité interministériel pour l'aménagement du territoire, on which the DATAR's director had a great deal of influence.
Finally, in its later stages, the Groupe central des villes nouvelles
too would play a key role in Paris' efforts to direct the implementation
of the project at Fos.[29] If nothing else, then, the story of Fos-sur-
Mer is part of the story of French regional policy because the DATAR
chose to call whatever it did "regionalism."

---

*For example, in Brittany, the interior of the region has con-
tinued to lose population, while population centers such as Rennes are
finding it hard to produce sufficient revenues to deal with the need for
urban services for their expanding populations.

REGIONALISM AS IDEOLOGY

Why this early and consistent involvement of an agency like the
DATAR in the creation of an industrial pole at Fos-Marseilles? Personality cannot be excluded as a possible explanation. A man with
strong regional ties and an appetite for bold achievements, Olivier
Guichard had provided the first credits to the Marseilles Chamber of
Commerce for the preparatory studies of the port of Fos[30] and was
instrumental in drawing the government's attention back to the project
from time to time, especially when the Ministry of Finance stalled on
part of the funding. Happenstance was also an element; in the early
1960s there were several hundred thousand returnees from Algeria in
the Marseilles area, many of them jobless and some even a threat to
public order. It was natural, if not exactly practical, to imagine a
bold economic project for the region that would ultimately provide jobs
for some of these people. There was also a deeper malaise in the Mar-
seillaise economy; since the collapse of the French empire had deprived
it of much of its function as an entrepôt (warehouse), the city on the
Mediterranean had been losing jobs in industry and transport.[31]

But the region of which Marseilles was the capital, Provence-
Côte d'Azur, was the most thriving in the south of France. For example, it had a positive annual migratory balance between 1954 and
1962 of 1.7 percent—the highest in the country—and, except for a few
isolated zones, it did not even qualify for investment subsidies in the
DATAR's fourfold subvention scheme of 1972.[32] It is true that Marseilles as a city suffered from underequipment and underinvestment,
but its hinterland enjoyed prosperous agriculture and tourism and had
recently become a prime construction site for secondary residences.

Moreover, if regional inequality was conceived as weakness in
employment opportunities, a modern integrated steel plant would
hardly be the best way to promote regional equality. Though the initial
construction of the plant would provide many jobs in construction—
17,000 at one point—these would be temporary and most of them went
to immigrants anyway. The number of permanent jobs created in the
industrial zone of Fos would be 8,270 by the end of 1974, 4,000 fewer
than the target set for 1975 in the Sixth Plan. This was an impressive
increase for the immediate area, but it represented a very low ratio
of jobs created relative to the 10 billion francs that were invested between 1971 and 1975 for land acquisition, dredging, port construction,
loans to the industry, and provision of new urban services for the
communes of the region.[33] Not only that; a large proportion of the
permanent jobs created at Fos would go to people from outside the
region. This was inevitable for highly qualified managerial personnel,
but it was also true for the specialized workers of the SOLMER, the
main steel plant, where only 40 percent of the workers employed by

March 1974 would come from the three-department area of the Gard, the Bouches-du-Rhône, and the Vaucluse.[34] The impact upon unemployment in Marseilles would thus be inconsequential.[35]

It was not only because of the capital-intensive nature of steel that Fos would satisfy few of the regionalists' goals. It was also due to the small number and dimensions of the secondary industries that would locate there. As of 1975, despite an energetic effort on the part of the Port autonome de Marseille and the supreme efforts of regional authorities to provide infrastructure, there would only be two firms employing over 1,000 people in the industrial zone of Fos: the SOLMER, with 6,080 employees, and Ugine-Aciers, with 1,020.[36] The rest were mainly tiny companies serving as subcontractors for the steel industries or using the petrochemical port.

To be fair, part of the problem has been the worldwide depression in the steel industry, but part was the faith in the philosophy of "growth poles," which animated French planners in the 1960s. Part of the theory behind the regional métropoles d'équilibre—of which Marseilles was one—was the notion that they would serve as growth centers for the provinces.[37] However, as Hansen emphasizes, "it is evident that a successful growth center strategy would have to be based on careful analyses of data on employment growth prospects, commuting, migration, and the location preferences of people in the context of actual opportunities available in alternative locations."[38] Not only was there little existing regional market for the steel products to be turned out at Fos; one government planner even confided that no serious studies had been carried out on the secondary employment that would be generated by the production of raw steel in the region. "As far as creating employment is concerned," writes an administrator who was personally involved, "the regional influence of Fos has an ambivalent character."[39] If Fos was to be a growth center, one might legitimately ask "a center of what?"

The answer to the question cannot be found in the domain of regional policy but in more general economic and political goals of the Gaullist regime in the 1960s. France in the mid-1960s faced the prospect of rapidly increased competition from her partners in the European community, with an industrial structure that was, in many respects, still backward. Despite the remarkable recovery of the postwar years, France's industry had neither modernized as fast as her neighbors' nor reached the level of concentration that was considered necessary for international concentration. Even where concentration had taken place, writes J. E. S. Hayward, it "took a financial rather than an industrial form, leading to the creation of larger holding companies but not necessarily to bigger production units."[40]

These problems were particularly acute in steel, whose decision-making structure was not "organized so as to permit the most

rational organization of production units."[41] Its price structure had
been kept down by the governments of the Fourth Republic, thus making it impossible to finance modernization out of profits,[42] and its
location—near the worked-out ore deposits of the north and east—
made access to seaborne transit difficult. A government that saw its
strategic-economic future in terms of the creation and support of large
national economic "champions" could not remain happy for long with
a limping, fragmented, and geographically ill-placed basic industry
such as steel. "Steel on the sea" was thus a watchword of the international economic strategy of the Gaullist policy elite.

The decision to place a major integrated steel mill on the Gulf
of Fos grew out of the planning contracts through which the government
had tried to gain leverage over particular economic sectors in 1964
and the Convention de la sidérurgie, in which it agreed to provide over
3 billion francs to steel in return for a radical concentration in the
structure of ownership and production.[43] Interestingly, the government dealt throughout with the powerful Chambre syndicale de la
sidérurgie française, whose head, Jacques Ferry, negotiated directly
with the ministers concerned.[44] Though the steelmakers grumbled
about the state's heavy-handed dirigisme, steel came out well from
the deal, for the government had put it into the very best position a
large manufacturer can be in: forced to close down uneconomic plants
by government pressures and to move to new, publicly financed ones
that would use less labor and give easier access to raw materials,
with all the physical and social infrastructure (and political costs of
firing workers) to be borne by the government.

National economic considerations were thus the main ones in
the choice of Fos. Insofar as regional considerations came into play,
it was with the goal of getting steel out of Lorraine, where it was not
profitable, and onto seacoast sites, where it was thought to be so.
Indeed, the choice of a site in the Midi was far from predetermined;
an interministerial committee had wavered between Fos and Le Havre,
eventually choosing the latter both for regional balance and to provide
an outlet for French industrial power on the Mediterranean. Pressure
from Guichard and the DATAR were probably responsible for the
choice of Fos, since Le Havre appears to have had the economic edge.
Insofar as there was an indigenous "regional" factor at work, it was
found in the Marseilles Chamber of Commerce and Industry, which
had been lobbying to have a new port facility installed at Fos since
1961[45] to supplement the city's shrinking port revenues.

Why then was the implementation of Fos cast in a regionalist
framework? Why write, as Pierre Durand did on behalf of the DATAR,
that "Fos is radically changing the economy of the Mediterranean lit-
toral, by endowing it with industries of the first rank?"[46] Or declare,
as Olivier Guichard did in 1973: "I personally consider the operation

of Fos to be the most important concerted operation of regional planning . . . and the most exciting?"[47] Or observe, as did one respon-
dent, that "in the future, the Mediterranean will have to set its watch
by Fos?" A massive effort of public relations followed the decision
to construct the industrial pole of Fos, taking as its central theme
the rebirth of a region that had all the resources, and needed only
the will, to achieve economic breakthrough. "If certain conditions
are fulfilled," we read in a pamphlet of Le Documentation française,
"Fos can rival Rotterdam and the great ports of the North," and "If
Fos becomes the Europort of the South, the consequences for the region around it will be considerable."[48]

There are some obvious reasons for these rhapsodies of regional
enthusiasm, for instance, the desire to stimulate the investment in
secondary industries that would make Fos an economic success. But
the basic reason was ideological: public funds were being committed
to an unprecedented degree to finance a vast private merger and relo-
cation in steel. Public authority was being used to close down plants
and liquidate jobs in Lorraine, which needed them greatly, in return
for fewer jobs created at great cost in Provence, which needed them
less. If ever public intervention needed an ideology to justify it, it
was here. As one observer had earlier remarked, steel was to get
unprecedented benefits, but what would the public get in return? "A
shareholding in the firms thus aided and subsidized? No. A seat on
their board of directors, as any bank would require? No. A policy
of factory location and employment in accordance with specific criteria
for the use of geographic and human resources? Again no. All that
the state asks of the steel makers is that they do their duty as em-
ployers."[49]

Regionalism in the case of Fos served the ideological function
of justifying a direct public giveaway on the grounds of broader social
benefits; it diverted attention from Lorraine's economic losses and
toward presumed gains for the Midi; and it provided an entering wedge
for the state's more global intervention in the name of "completing"
the industrial pole with an infrastructure of physical, social, and administrative equipment. Having made a massive commitment to constructing a cathedral to steel, the government was now at pains to
avoid having the cathedral rise up in a desert. For this task it would
require the coordinated efforts of various ministries, territorial
authorities, private actors, and the officials of the numerous municipalities in the area that would "receive" the new residents and infrastructure. To coordinate all these efforts would require planning
skills, administrative and political flexibility, and the best contacts
among both the spending ministries and territorial notables. Given the
history we have outlined above, it was inevitable that the task would
be given to the DATAR and that regionalism would be the ideology used
to unify its efforts.

REGIONALISM AS PERIPHERAL DEFENSE

But would ideology—which, at its heart, is nothing but words oriented toward action—suffice to implement so complex a porject so far from the capital in so short a period of time? Among other things, the Bouches-du-Rhône was not only traditionally hostile to Paris; it was a left-wing region where the Gaullist list had received only 24 percent of the vote in the legislative elections of 1967. The left in 1970 held a majority of places inthe department's legislative delegation, the presidency of its <u>conseil général</u>, and had the largest number of mayors in both the small towns of the interior and in the industrial centers around Fos and the Etang de Berre. Sooner or later a relationship between the government and these local authorities would have to be established. It was at this stage, when housing and urban services would be needed for the new residents, that the cleavage between Paris and the provinces, and the complex relationship between the state, the territorial agencies of <u>tutelle</u>, and the local governments would come into play.

Precedents were few in France for the institutional implementation of a large and complex industrial undertaking at the grassroots, but several models might have suggested themselves:

• First, a model of essentially private development working through traditional territorial administration at the department level
• Second, a model of increased regional authority, with more power for the regional prefect and/or the cooptation of local authorities through the creation of representative organs of policy coordination to cope with the ripple effects of the government's initiative
• Third, a model of development under central government direction, however mediated, short-circuiting both local authorities and traditional administrative agencies so as to achieve rapid policy results

Although elements of the first and second models were present throughout the operation (and ultimately formed part of the solution the government would accept), Paris's first choice was for a model of centrally directed new-town development. There were several reasons for this choice, two of them negative and two more positive:

• First, overcoming the proverbial red tape of traditional administration. Once the key decision was made in 1969 to create the SOLMER at Fos, a number of smaller enterprises quickly followed suit. During 1970, Ugine-Kuhlmann Steel, ICI, Air Liquide, Gaz de Grance, and the Electricité de France, in addition to a number of subcontractors of the steel industry, moved to begin construction. The industrialists were hesitant to begin work until plans were visibly being made for the urban services that they would need to bring in a work force.

- Second, distrust of left-wing local elites, especially those, like Gaston Defferre, who might be tempted to use Fos as a political platform. The decision to leave Defferre out of all the basic planning was the first false step in what was to be a long and tormented history of heated national-local relations.
- Third, the administration's growing interest in urban and regional planning. There was increasing realization among civil servants that the country was retarded in urban-planning institutions, and a number of initiatives were taken at this time to increase the planning capacity of existing local governments.
- Fourth, increasing interest in local government consolidation, especially among national planners contemplating the distribution of increased central government grants for infrastructure to local authorities.

For these and other reasons, the government had decided earlier to encourage the creation of villes nouvelles, of which at least five were to be created in the Paris region and four in the provinces during the Sixth Plan. In addition, a number of provisions made it financially easier for existing communes to consolidate their services, either through outright fusions, the formation of urban districts or urban communities, or the creation of multipurpose special districts.[50] It was a ville nouvelle, however, that the planners decided to set up in the communes surrounding the new industrial zone of Fos.

Two problems had arisen from earlier French ville nouvelle experiences. First, since they were normally planned for the borders of heavily populated metropolitan areas, existing municipalities would have to bear the major burden of the heavy start-up costs of providing new urban equipment for new residents. Second, there would be an inevitable imbalance between communes in which new tax-producing growth took place and those in which the new residents would live and require services. Some way would have to be found both to exempt areas of older settlement from the costs of the new agglomerations and to fuse the fiscal resources of the revenue-generating and revenue-consuming new settlement areas.[51]

The solution proposed was found in a law of 1970, the famous loi Boscher, which was adopted after bitter debate in the national assembly. It proposed that on selected intercommunal territories chosen by the state as centers for new urbanization, an entity would be created whose finances would be detached from those of the participating communes (these would continue to exercise their normal functions on the rest of their territory). It would be governed by community planning syndicates (SCA), which would be made up of members elected by the existing councils of the participating communes.[52] The SCA would offer participating communes many benefits, including fiscal exemptions, higher subsidies for equipment, and accelerated approval of public works applications.[53]

Actual implementation of the new zones or ubanization, including the all-important questions of zoning, land expropriation, and reserving land for specific purposes, would be carried out by a technical planning body, which could take the form of either a mixed development company (the Syndicat d'economie mixte) of the participating communes or an Etablissement public d'aménagement (EPA) under the control of the administration but with a municipal presence on its council of administration.[54] The key powers of the EPAs would be determined by the state and, in practice, their key personnel would probably be drawn from the elite engineering corps of the Ponts et chaussées.

It was clear at the time, and has since become clearer, that, for technical reasons, the ville nouvelle formula was far more adapted to growth on the perimeter of the Paris region than it was for provincial urban areas.[55] First, its financial provisions were geared to a pattern of progressive urbanization like that which typifies the outskirts of Paris. Second, it was designed to create self-sufficient satellite cities to combat the urban sprawl of the metropolis. Third, the law had as its object the creation of "organized agglomerations on a new site" rather than dealing with the multiple interests and traditions of established provincial communities.[56]

These criteria of progressive urbanization, functional balance, and development on a new site were lacking in the case of Fos-Marseilles. Demographic growth related to steel employment would be sudden rather than progressive. Important public and private services were available nearby, and hence the satellite concept was irrelevant. And, due to the existence of well-established, if small, centers of urbanization, a ville nouvelle would not emerge virgin on a new site but would have to struggle for existence among the traditions, the past planning decisions, and the political preoccupations of existing municipalities.

Politics was a second reason why the loi Boscher would not have an easy reception in the Bouches-du-Rhône. Even under its least constraining juridical form, the law would create something approaching a new commune, which could one day escape the control of its constituent municipalities or, worse yet, exacerbate their historic cleavages.[57] Besides, the entire problem of boundaries to be drawn around the new entity—and thus the selection of participating communes—would give the state the power to discriminate between friends and enemies, rich and poor, Communists and non-Communists.

Thus, the most logical technical solution—to include in a single ville nouvelle all the communes whose future would be directly touched

by the project—was never considered at Fos, for it would have left
the administration face-to-face with a Communist majority.   By successive reductions, the planners arrived at the plan of two small
SCAs, one made up of three municipalities sympathetic to the government (Fos, Istres, and Miramas) and one consisting of the three
most manageable Communist towns (Martigues, Port-de-Bouc, and
the village of St. Mitre-les-Remparts).   (A fourth PCF—French Communist Party—commune, Port St. Louis, was excluded, though it was
part of the industrial zone of Fos.)*

As for the technical body that would implement the new zones of
urbanization, there was never any question of creating a locally responsive mixed-development company.   As in the other villes nouvelles, the government turned immediately to the Etablissement public
model in which "the composition of the council . . . its powers, the
method of nomination and the powers of its president, the goals of the
organism" would, by law, be defined by the conseil d'état on the advice of the local authorities. [58]   This body, which would have substantial powers over land use, land condemnation, and building contracts,
would include not only the six communes that would be represented in
the two SCAs, but all 14 communes in the zone around the Etang de
Berre.

The government's planning was, to say the least, optimistic.
Tight central control was chosen over a serious attempt to coopt local
authorities or create a regional authority, both to keep a tight rein
over the Communist municipalities and to meet the fast-approaching
deadline for the completion of the industrial zone.   The basic institut-
tional decisions were made in Paris and were transmitted to the prefecture, which was used as little more than a mail drop.   It was only
at this late stage, and without prior consultation, that "the state
turned to the local authorities and asked them to take the responsibility for an urban development that had been previously defined and decided upon." [59]

Additional complications could be expected from the crossed
lines of authority between the plethora of administrative agencies
that had been working to prepare the ground at Fos.   In addition to
the departmental prefect, who also wore the hat of the préfet de ré-

---

*The reasons for this exclusion were never made clear.   More
than one civil servant, however, described the deputy-mayor of Port
St. Louis, Louis Porelli, as "difficult."   Since it was located to the
west of Fos, Port St. Louis would have been awkward to include in a
"red" SCA with the three other Communist towns, which were found
further to the east.   It was politically unlikely that it could be included
in a "moderate" one with Fos, Istres, and Miramas, its neighbors.

gion, there was, in the ordinary departmental administration, an office of equipment (DDE) whose task was to approve all requests for construction permits. Also depending on the ministry of equipment was the OREAM of Marseilles, a regional planning agency that had produced a master plan for the region several years earlier. Instead of using this agency for the detailed physical planning surrounding Fos, the administration chose to create the embryo of a future Etablissement public d'aménagement, the MAEB, whose young staff of employees immediately got on badly with the administrators of the departmental office of equipment in Marseilles.

Alongside these horizontal tensions, the regional prefect, Jean LaPorte, whose key role in mediating between Paris and the municipalities of the region cannot be overemphasized, made it clear from the beginning that he preferred a more traditional model of administration—if necessary with ceremonial bows toward regionalism, anything but direct Parisian meddling in the affairs of his contentious bailiwick. Ignoring LaPorte's premonitions was another grave error made by the administration.

Finally, there was the potential danger to an extremely fragile environment; the heavily touristed and protected interior of the Bouches-du-Rhône north to the Durance; the extraordinary natural wetlands of the Camargue, one of the last migratory bird refuges in Europe; and even the new seaside tourist meccas established west of the Rhône on the Languedoc-Roussillon coast. It was possible to hear speculation in 1969 about a future "megalopolis, which will go from Toulon . . . all the way to Montpellier and perhaps even to Sète."[60] Such was the technocratic fever for growth in the higher civil service in the late 1960s that the author of these rhapsodies was oblivious to the horror they would evoke among local residents. If nothing else, the prospect of mushrooming industrial growth along the coast would suffice to push up the price of land in the rich agricultural villages of the interior.

Even from Paris it should have been possible to foresee difficulties if the loi Boscher, with its bias toward centrally directed metropolitan area organization, were to be applied mechanically in the politically and environmentally volatile climate of the Bouches-du-Rhône. But national-local conflicts are often the most difficult to foresee, combining as they do the clash of material interests with intangible conflicts between central and peripheral political cultures. But as early as 1969, a warning was sounded by the regional director of equipment in the Marseilles prefecture. At a conference at the Fondation nationale des sciences politiques he said, "The vocabulary of villes nouvelles is not employed in the region of Marseilles. . . . The realizations having not yet begun, it makes more sense to ask 'why' villes nouvelles, rather than 'how.'" He went on to warn that, although technical studies were progressing and getting a fairly good reception, "there is a political-administrative foundation that has yet to be established."[61]

It was in the attempt to establish this "political-administrative foundation" that the government met fiercest resistance, first from the mayor of Marseilles, whose city had been included neither in the SCA that would make decisions on the location of new equipment nor in the planned Etablissement public, which would operate on its borders. Gaston Defferre, recovering from his political wounds in the 1969 presidential election, had much to lose from his exclusion from the decision-making councils regarding Fos. The potential economic losses of his city were more questionable, but these, along with the exclusion of the new regional government of Provence-Côte d'Azur, which he headed, from planning decisions, would constitute the twin prongs of his attack. It certainly looked queer that a project launched in the name of both regionalism and the economic renaissance of Marseilles included neither the city of Marseilles nor the region, both of them headed by Defferre.[62] Could national politics, heating up increasingly as France approached new elections, be responsible?

If so, this was not all; the mayor of the village of Fos—a "left-wing" Gaullist of sorts—entered the fray, using his commune's strategic location and immense tax potential to argue violently, and in one breath, against the environmental threat that the steel mill would pose, and in favor of a more intensive (and more profitable) real estate development on his territory. His voice was joined, successively, by those of his political allies in Miramas and Istres who conspired to try to use the SCA to compensate for the financial weakness of their communes, at the cost of Fos, which promptly took them to court. Finally, the Communist mayors of Martigues, Port de Bouc, and St. Mitre gave battle, refusing to be either enticed or bullied into joining in an SCA.[63]

But the government also met resistance from within its own administration. The attempt to set up a special organ of implementation raised the hackles of mainline agencies like the DDE, whose functionaries saw their role infringed upon by the Mission d'études, the MAEB, which was preparing the groundwork for the future Etablissement public. A paralysis had developed in the relations between these two bodies; the latter was making proposals for zoning and land use, which the former had to approve. The OREAM of Marseilles also saw its functions reduced as the government's priorities shifted from planning for a regional métropole d'équilibre to fashioning an administrative tool for local government consolidation. With the decline of the OREAM, the one regional body with the potential to successfully bring together the municipalities of the metropolitan area was set aside and the raw power of the state exposed.

This placed extraordinary pressures on the prefect, Jean LaPorte. LaPorte, who had a personal commitment to the success of

Fos as an industrial operation,* had none in particular to the concept of a ville nouvelle, which Paris insisted was the only possible way to develop the necessary urban equipment in time to "receive" the industrial zone of Fos. As a regional administrator, LaPorte had to be sensitive to the impact of the project on all the communes of the Marseilles area, most of which would get nothing out of the government's plan. And as the tutelary authority for the communes in the Fos area, it was he who would have to pick up the pieces if a political battle over the ville nouvelle exploded. His task was worsened by Paris, which took the essential decision in favor of a ville nouvelle first in October 1971, and only then instructed the prefect to bring the local authorities into agreement. [64]

It was the mayor of Marseilles who fired the first salvo. At a meeting called by the prefect for the mayors of the region in February 1972, he pointed to the contradiction between the loi Boscher and both regional representation and traditional local autonomy. Defferre argued that "the planning and urbanization of the Marseilles-Fos geographic area forms a whole in time and space. . . . The local government cooperation which follows from it can only proceed through the construction of a communitarian instrument encompassing all of our communes and led by a broad majority of elected officials."[65] If the government used the blackmail of its credits to bludgeon the municipalities into joining a "bastard entity," Defferre warned, the communes could respond by reverse blackmail: unless the mayors were given full responsibility for the urbanization of their own communes, he threatened, the operation might be indefinitely delayed. [66]

Unfortunately for the mayor of Marseilles, his municipality was too far away to be essential to the project. Only those communes whose territories were to be part of the EPA could effectively stall the construction of the services necessary to its completion, and among these there were many whose fear of Marseilles' imperialism was as great as their unwillingness to give over local prerogatives to the administration. But the tone had been established. From then on, opposition to the government's plans, whatever the motive, would be supported on the double ground of regional solidarity and the defense of local liberties.

As the 1973 national elections drew closer and Fos was nowhere near completion, the government, prodded by the prefecture, had to

---

*LaPorte had been a prefect in Lorraine for many years, where he had dealt with the difficult problems of the steel industry and developed close relations with industry leaders. His recruitment to the post of regional prefect of Marseilles coincided with the agreement to construct the SOLMER plant at Fos, 1969.

agree to compromises in its maximum plan so as to win the cooperation of the local authorities. The secretary of the <u>Groupe central de Fos</u>, Philippe Brongniart, began shuttle diplomacy between Paris and Marseilles to work out an accommodation between the director of the DATAR, Jérome Monod, and officials of the prefecture trying to arrange a compromise among the feuding municipalities. To complicate matters, a controversy exploded in the local and national press about the physical and social conditions of the thousands of immigrant workers who had been hired to construct the steel plant.* Though secondary in its political stakes, the issue was volatile enough to make quiet negotiation on basic juridical and financial issues all but impossible.

A first compromise was made in order to win the cooperation of two of the moderate municipalities, Miramas and Istres, whose tax resources were the least adequate for financing the new equipment required for future residents. They were permitted to include their entire territory, not only the new zones of urbanization, in the ville nouvelle, and thus would enjoy special financial concessions even for ordinary projects put up in their older neighborhoods if they joined.[67]

A second compromise was made with the mayor of Fos itself who, despite his ties to the majority, created far more hostile publicity for the government than any of his colleagues. His desire for protection from the environmental impact of the industrial zone was met by a government promise of strict and constant monitoring of emissions. His desire for more real estate was also placated, and to his commune and to none other was reserved the sole right to exploit the maritime taxes from the ships that would be using the industrial zone. Finally, through a complex legal formula worked out by personnel of the prefecture, the relations between Fos and its two "moderate" neighbors were regulated by complex power-sharing formulas in the procedures constituting their SCA.[68]

There remained two major problems: the geographic extent of the perimeter for the EPA, which the government, on the advice of the prefecture, had set to include the entire 14 municipalities of the area around the Etang de Berre,[69] and the problem of the Communist communes contiguous to Fos, whose leaders could not be bought off as easily as their more moderate neighbors.

---

*The problem was partly inevitable, given a high density of mostly male immigrant workers living in trailers on a rural site, but it seems also to have been used as a political football by some of the municipalities, to gain leverage vis-a-vis the administration. So committed was the prefect to completing the project on time, in fact, that organizing the lives of these workers became his primary concern at one time.

As to the first problem, it too was ultimately solved on the initiative of the prefecture. The perimeter of the new Etablissement public (EPAREB) was reduced from the original 14 communes to four; its powers were reduced to land-use operations and would exclude giving out construction contracts—a key function that would remain in the hands of the communes. There would now also be a majority of elected officials on the council, including representatives of the mayor of Marseilles and of the conseil général.[70]

But the evisceration of the Etablissement public left a gap in planning for the region as a whole. To fill this gap without reviving the threat to local autonomy that had sunk the ville nouvelle idea required all the ingenuity of the prefecture and of the prefect's talented young adjoint, Didier Cultiaux, who came up with an almost unique concept, the Interministerial Mission for the Planning of Fos and the Etang de Berre (MIAFEB), to deal with general problems of coordination and planning in the area around the new industrial installations.

With this step, the prefect took control over construction permits away from the departmental office of equipment and vested it in the MIAFEB's director, who would also be responsible for planning new equipment and for channeling financial support to the communes for its construction.[71] This innovation was created totally without reference to the terms of the loi Boscher. It centered extraordinary power in the prefecture—at least for the period of major construction —and it placated the local authorities, who would not now be required to work with technocrats responding directly to Paris. The MIAFEB represented a definite shift from the third model of institutional intervention to the first—coordination and planning within the region on the part of the traditional territorial administration—with elements of the second—limited regional consultation for elected officials, including the mayor of Marseilles.*

As for the second major problem, the Communists, the response was more traditional. The Communist communes of Martigues, Port de Bouc, and St. Mitre all refused to enter an SCA or to have anything to do with the EPAREB, even in the newly modest form in which it had emerged from the prefecture. They demanded the full financial benefits of the loi Boscher but would agree only to enter a traditional inter-

---

*Vieille interprets the innovation of the MIAFEB as the revenge of the prefecture on the communes for the evisceration of the EPAREB. My impression is that LaPorte had always looked upon the Etablissement public as an invasion, while the communes have gotten far more out of the MIAFEB than they would have from participation in a ville nouvelle. In the elections of 1977, the left gained much more influence than it had had on the MIAFEB.

communal multipurpose district. It was ironic, but typical, that the Communist communes made the fullest defense of traditional communal liberties but sought and eventually received those state subsidies that paid the largest share of total expenditures for investments.[72]

The government's first reaction to this retreat was negative. But the Communist communes had two things working for them. First, public opinion, stirred by a year of public debate and traditionally hostile to Paris, was behind them. Second, they could stand pat on the routine administrative prerogative of French local governments to refuse to grant construction permits or to set in motion the construction of new equipment.[73] Their very plausible argument was: how could they be forced to make expenditures for projects for which they lacked the financial resources?

As industrial construction moved along and the electoral campaign of 1973 approached, this stubborn attitude of the Communists began to have an impact. For since the government's primary objective was to create an industrial zone, it could ultimately afford to cede on the question of a ville nouvelle, and this the Communist municipalities well knew. They also had at their disposal the potent if intangible tool of the age-old suspicion of the population of the region for Paris, a suspicion that Paris had done little to assuage by its high-handed tactics.

We can go further. By mobilizing an ideology of regionalism behind an industrial program that had nothing to do with regions and linking it to a plan of local government reorganization that followed Jacobin lines, the government unwittingly provided a unifying theme for the dispersed elements of opposition to its plans: the theme of regionalism as peripheral defense. For in response to the heavy hand of Parisian intervention, a temporary coalition was formed consisting of a big-city machine and its mayor, its smaller Communist allies-cum-antagonists, moderate local notables with their own political interests, environmentalists, trade union leaders, and—subtly and by indirection—the agents of traditional territorial administration. Abused regional ideology stimulated its formation, aroused regional defense held it together, and satisfied local prerogatives would lead to its dissolution soon after.

With the removal of the threat of the ville nouvelle and the reassertion of prefectoral authority, albeit in more modernized form, the traditional circuits of policy allocation and regulation between center and periphery would resume, and political conflict return to its familiar, well-worn paths. Regionalism as peripheral defense had modified the insinuation of the international market—in the form of the SOLMER and as abetted by the French government—on the region. But the battle of Fos was only a "wargame on the Mediterranean," in the words of its most perceptive student, Paul Vieille: no more

than a diversion from the social cleavage that lies at the heart of
capitalist society.

Why then study the case of Fos-sur-Mer? Case studies do not
make theories, nor do they test them, but three lessons can perhaps
be drawn from this exemplary case:

- First, about traditional versus "modern" administration. It was
  de rigeur in the 1960s to vaunt the efficiency of modern civil servants in the capital and to bewail the lumbering traditional bureaucracy in the provinces. But in the case of Fos it was the "innovative"
  DATAR in Paris that failed to take account of the many-faceted political and social needs of the area. In contrast, it was traditional
  territorial administrators who patiently transformed the streamlined
  fantasies of Paris into workable plans for institutional implementation at the grassroots. For the further it gets from the grassroots,
  the easier it is for "modern" administration to forget that the chess
  pieces it wishes to move around the board may want to move in different directions.
- Second, about regionalism and industrial concentration. It is simply
  not possible for a capital-intensive industry like steel to provide a
  large number of jobs, and it will not be possible for some time for
  the region around Marseilles to generate a sufficient mass market
  to attract significant consumer-oriented secondary industries to use
  that steel. Fos will, of course, have regional spinoffs, especially
  in preserving the commercial vocation of the Port of Marseilles.
  But it is not the answer to the region's basic problems, and it was
  a disservice to talk of Fos, as many did in the late 1960s and early
  1970s, as if it were a venture in regional planning.
- Third, about policy synthesis and the concentration of the opposition.
  Where policy is segmented, as in the United States, it tends to segment opposition as well. But the French state, with its capacity to
  fuse, in this example, industrial policy, regional policy, and local
  government reform, caused an opposition front to form linking actors with very different ideological and material interests. Regionalism as peripheral defense reflected the interests of many political
  actors because regionalism as policy and ideology had brought them
  together.

Although the battle of Fos-sur-Mer was little more than a wargame, of such battles is much of politics made up. That is, though
the ultimate stakes in politics reflect the conflict between capital and
labor, politics mediates that conflict in a thousand different ways that,
between them, turn domination into hegemony, understanding the latter, as Gramsci did, to include both domination and consensus. Regionalism as ideology disguised the policy goal of capitalist concentra-

tion, but it also translated the hegemony of big industry through symbols that were thought to be somewhat more acceptable to the people of the region than the bare facts. And although these symbols were in some sense "false," they were in another sense "true," for it was from within their range that regionalism as peripheral defense could extract policy compromises that allowed the project to be completed. It is because such battles can still be fought, and occasionally won, against a centralizing state that the fundamental social cleavage seldom comes to the surface.

NOTES

1. A good example of a Marxist approach to regional policy is Stuart Holland's The Regional Problem (London: MacMillan, 1976).

2. For a "liberal" approach to regional economic policy, see Niles Hansen's "Preliminary Overview," Public Policy and Regional Economic Development, ed. Niles Hansen (Cambridge, Mass.: Ballinger, 1974), pp. 1-32.

3. Manuel Castells and Francis Godard, Monopolville: L'Entreprise, l'état, l'urbain (Paris and The Hague: Mouton, 1974).

4. Andrew Shonfield, Modern Capitalism (New York: Oxford University Press, 1965).

5. Ibid., chap. 4.

6. Danielle Bleitrach and Alain Chenu, "Aménagement: Régulation ou aggravation des contradictions sociales?" Aménagement du territorie et developpement régional, vol. 7 (Institut d'études politiques de l'université des sciences sociales de Grenoble, 1974), pp. 184-214.

7. Pierre Durand, Industrie et régions: l'Aménagement industriel de la France, 2nd ed. (Paris: La Documentation française, 1972), p. 7.

8. Pierre Gremion and Jean-Pierre Worms, "The French Regional Planning Experiments," Planning, Politics and Public Policy: The British, French and Italian Experience, ed. Jack Hayward and Michael Watson (London: Cambridge University Press, 1975), p. 233.

9. Rémy Prud'homme, "Regional Economic Policy in France, 1962-1972," Public Policy and Regional Economic Development, ed. Niles Hansen (Cambridge, Mass.: Ballinger, 1974), p. 39.

10. Ibid.

11. Ibid., p. 40.

12. Grémion and Worms, "The French Regional Planning Experiments," p. 219.

13. Ibid.

14. Ibid., p. 227.

15. An outline of these instruments is provided by Bernard Pouyet in La Délégation à l'aménagement du territoire et à l'action régionale (Paris: Cujas, 1968).

16. Prud'homme, "Regional Economic Policy," pp. 46-55.

17. There is a striking parallelism—but for the ideological affiliation—between Guichard's strategy in constituing the DATAR and David Lilienthal's strategy of cooptation in building up the Tennessee Valley Authority, as described by Philip Selznick in his TVA and the Grassroots (New York: Harper Torchbooks, 1949). Pouyet's largely juridical study does not really deal with the issues of organizational strategy and institutionalization that gave this agency a strikingly powerful role in the Gaullist republic.

18. See Erhard Friedberg (with the collaboration of D. Desjeux), "L'Etat et l'industrie en France" (Rapport d'enquête, Centre national de la recherche scientifique and centre de sociologie des organisations, May 1967), pp. 24-25.

19. Grémion and Worms, "The French Regional Planning Experiments," p. 219.

20. Prud'homme, "Regional Economic Policy," p. 41.

21. Ibid., p. 48. See also his more detailed "La Production d'équipements collectifs en France pendant le Cinquième Plan" (Paris: BETURE, 1972).

22. Prud'homme, "Regional Economic Policy," pp. 48-49.

23. Ibid., p. 54.

24. Ibid., pp. 57-58.

25. Ibid., p. 58.

26. Ibid., p. 59.

27. Ibid., pp. 42-43.

28. Ibid., p. 43.

29. Didier Cultiaux, "L'Aménagement de la région Fos-Etang de Berre," Notes et etudes documentaires, nos. 4, 164-4, 166 (La Documentation française, 1974), p. 49.

30. Ibid., p. 35. For a more detailed development of this lobbying effort, see Chambre de commerce et d'industrie de Marseille, "Le Complexe de Marseille-Fos; historique, situation actuelle et perspectives" (mimeographed, 1974).

31. Cultiaux, "L'Aménagement de la région Fos-Etang de Berre," p. 9.

32. Prud'homme, "Regional Economic Policy," pp. 53-58.

33. Cultiaux, "L'Aménagement de la région Fos-Etang de Berre," pp. 55, 63-64.

34. Ibid., p. 64.

35. Ibid., p. 111.

36. Ibid., p. 62.

37. Hansen, "Preliminary Overview," pp. 22-23.

38. Ibid., p. 24.

39. Cultiaux, "L'Aménagement de la région Fos-Etang de Berre," p. 112.

40. J. E. S. Hayward, "Steel," Big Business and the State, ed. R. Vernon (Cambridge, Mass.: Harvard University Press, 1974), p. 266.

41. Jean-François Besson, Les Groupes industriels et l'Europe: l'Expérience de la C.E.C.A. (Paris: Presses universitaires de la France, 1962), p. 347.

42. John H. McArthur and Bruce R. Scott, Industrial Planning in France (Cambridge, Mass.: Harvard University Press, 1969), pp. 370-72.

43. Ibid., pp. 370-74.

44. Compare Hayward, "Steel," p. 266.

45. Cultiaux, "L'Aménagement de la région Fos-Etang de Berre," p. 33.

46. Durand, Industrie et régions, p. 154.

47. In an interview in Combat in February 1973, quoted in detail in Yves Durrieu, L'Impossible régionalisation capitaliste: Témoignages de Fos et du Languedoc (Paris: Anthropos, 1973), p. 54.

48. "Fos-sur-Mer," La Documentation française, bulletin mensuel, no. 255 (March 1970), p. 29.

49. Michel Bosquet, "Un Cadeau pour les maîtres de forges," Le Nouvel observateur, August 3, 1966, p. 10.

50. For an outline of the alternatives proposed to increase local government consolidations, see Vie publique, March 1972, pp. 56-67, and May 1972, pp. 50-56.

51. Paul Vieille, "Une Séquence de kriegspiel méditerranéen; la bataille des rives de l'Etang de Berre (1972)," Aménagement du territoire et développement régional, vol. 7 (Institut d'études politiques de l'université des sciences sociales de Grenoble, 1972), p. 381. The description that follows leans heavily on Vieille's thorough account of the controversy.

52. Ibid., p. 382.

53. Ibid., p. 373.

54. Ibid., p. 385.

55. Ibid., p. 383.

56. Ibid., p. 380.

57. See René Mayer, "Berre-Est," L'Expérience française des villes nouvelles, ed. Fondation nationale des sciences politiques (Paris: Armand Colin, 1970), p. 114.

58. Vieille, "Une Séquence de kriegspiel méditerranéen," p. 385.

59. Ibid., p. 379.

60. Mayer, "Berre-Est," pp. 112-13.

61. Ibid., pp. 111, 114.

62. The role of Defferre is treated in detail in Bleitrach and Chenu, "Aménagement."

63. These positions and counterpositions are described in detail by Vieille, "Une Séquence de kriegspiel méditerranéen," pp. 389-400. For another view, see Bleitrach and Chenu, "Aménagement."

64. Vieille, "Une Séquence de kriegspiel méditerranéen," pp. 379-80.

65. Ibid., p. 387.

66. Ibid., p. 388.

67. Ibid., p. 401.

68. Ibid., pp. 400-01.

69. Ibid., p. 380.

70. Ibid., p. 397.

71. Cultiaux, "L'Aménagement de la région Fos-Etang de Berre," pp. 49-50.

72. Vieille, "Une Séquence de kriegspiel méditerranéen," p. 399.

73. Ibid., pp. 398-99.

5

CENTER-PERIPHERY RELATIONS
IN A CONSOCIATIONAL DEMOCRACY:
AUSTRIA AND KLEINWALSERTAL
Peter J. Katzenstein

Central European politics, it is widely believed, is marked by a process of political centralization that is both pervasive and enduring. Political centralization is thought to be inevitable because of the growing complexity of modern society and desirable because it facilitates political decisions that are efficient and effective. It is intuitively plausible and accepted by many that the periphery[1] can defend its political autonomy only as long as it succeeds in preserving political institutions and patterns of political behavior that neither resemble those of the center nor interact with them. Since political parties are so important in contemporary European politics, this encapsulation demands, therefore, that party organizations at the periphery be weak and that partisan behavior be avoided. But with increasing centralization, it is believed, such encapsulation becomes less feasible. For as the interaction between center and periphery grows, the center's dominance becomes stronger and stronger and the political institutions and behavior in the periphery will come to resemble, in direct relationship with the level of interactions, political conditions in the center.

I believe that this view is largely misguided, both morally and empirically. It fails to appreciate the intrinsic and instrumental value of political decentralization for adaptable and legitimate democratic institutions. But more important for the purpose of this chapter are

I would like to thank Sidney Tarrow for his helpful comments on several drafts of this chapter. I have also benefited from the criticisms and suggestions of Douglas Ashford, Ron Brickman, Peter Gourevitch, Luigi Graziano, Davyyd Greenwood, David Laitin, Bingham Powell, Thomas Rohlen, Gabriel Sheffer, and Martin Shefter.

the mistaken assumptions about modern politics that this view entails.
For it overlooks the fact that the very process of political centralization establishes conditions that make possible a creative political adaptation of the periphery intent on defending its autonomy. This chapter argues, specifically, that similar political institutions and patterns
of political behavior in center and periphery probably enhance rather
than diminish the prospects of the periphery's political autonomy and
that the interaction between center and periphery offers opportunities
for political entrepreneurship that permit skillful, local leaders to
control, at least partly, the destiny of their communities.

This chapter analyzes the similarity of and the interaction between Austria's center and periphery. For in both political parties
are the main institutions that define and resolve political problems.
In contrast to West Germany and Switzerland, Austria's political parties have three distinctive sources of strength. Political parties are
not only active at election times but also between elections and appear
to shape as much as they reflect the partisan preferences of the Austrian population; they penetrate political interest groups and the state
bureaucracy; and political parties give Austria's political class the
power to be partially autonomous from economic elites. In short,
"local politics must . . . be considered party politics quite similar
to provincial and national politics."[2] At the same time, the literature
on Austrian local government suggests also that the interactions between center and periphery are intimate largely because of the center's
financial strength.

Since the political similarity of Austria's center and periphery
is great and since center-periphery interactions are close, the Austrian experience offers a testing ground that, among the central European states, favors the argument about political centralization. If
that argument is found wanting here, its general claims should become suspect. This chapter will develop a consociational and a federal model useful for an investigation of Austria's center-periphery
relations; justify the selection of one particular commune, Kleinwalsertal, for further analysis; examine the similarity of and the interaction between center and periphery; and conclude with a reflection
on future changes in Austria's center-periphery relations.

CONSOCIATIONALISM, FEDERALISM, AND CENTER-
PERIPHERY RELATIONS IN AUSTRIA

Because they disagree on the central axis of political conflict
in general, consociational and federal models of politics lead to different hypotheses about Austrian politics. The consociational model emphasizes the functional division of society into different classes and

status groups; the federal model underlines the territorial division of
society into different regions as well as the institutionalization of
these divisions at different levels of government. Although both models
accord a crucial role to Austria's political parties, they generate different predictions about the similarity of and the interaction between
center and periphery.

The consociational model underlines the similarity of politics
in center and periphery; politics is segmented into ideological camps
knit together only by the pragmatic bargaining of a handful of party
leaders. The federal model emphasizes instead the uneven strength
of the ideological camps in different parts of the country; this allows
for a greater variation in the political structures and political behavior
that characterizes center and periphery. Political interaction within
each of the different political camps is viewed by the consociational
model as a process by which the center controls the periphery through
the interactions within each of the ideological subcultures. The federal model, on the other hand, predicts a reciprocal bargaining relationship between center and periphery. The predictions derived from
these two models are summarized in Table 5.1.

The recent literature documenting in great detail the critical
role that political parties play in Austrian politics appears to support
the consociational model.[3] The Christian Democratic Austrian Peoples'
Party (ÖVP) and the Austrian Socialist Party (SPÖ) are political manifestations of the deep class and status divisions that make Austrian society; they are supported by a dense network of ancillary associations
organized along partisan lines; and they reflect distinctive mentalities

TABLE 5.1

Two Models for the Analysis of Center-Periphery Relations
in Austria

Defining Variables:	Consociational Model Predicts:	Federal Model Predicts:
Variation	Politics in center and periphery are similar	Politics in center and periphery are different
Interaction	Center controls periphery	Center and periphery in a bargaining relationship

Source: Compiled by the author.

that separate "blacks" from "reds." The mutually reinforcing divisions of political life into these different camps have filtered down from the center to the periphery. Although far-reaching demographic, social, and economic changes since 1945 have led to a partial erosion of these class and status differences, most Austrians continue to view the politics of their country in both center and periphery as being divided into very different political camps.

The existence of these political camps, the consociational model suggests, encourages political bargaining between the leaders of different parties. This bargaining is a political answer to the problems raised by the persistence of deep economic and social differences. Here, though, interpretations vary. Some students of Austrian politics view the process of pragmatic bargaining between party elites as a modern-day adaptation of Austria's traditional penchant for muddling through (durchwursteln). Others interpret elite bargaining as a deliberate response to the destabilizing influences of social fragmentation and political segmentation.[4] On the face of things these two interpretations of bargaining between party elites as either historically determined or as purposefully acquired are both compatible with the main political practices of Austrian politics since 1945: the system of Grand Coalition between 1945 and 1966 in Parliament, the system of proportional representation (proporz) throughout the public sector to this day, and partisan life in Austria's periphery.

The consociational model fails, however, to account for the quality of the political interaction between center and periphery. Recent findings indicate that the top political leadership in each party does not exercise the kind of strict control over all arenas of Austrian politics that the consociational model predicts. Rodney Stiefbold, for example, sought to explain the discernible swings between depoliticization and politicization in Austria in terms of the reliance of top political leaders on technocratic middle-level elites during election campaigns.[5]

But the image of strict control of central political elites over peripheral political leaders is also inappropriate because it neglects the fact that Austria's federal system disperses power territorially. It has been noted frequently that the social and political differences that separate Austria's two large camps have an important territorial dimension. Vienna in the east is "red" while the countryside in the west is "black." At the provincial level Austria is composed of a number of one-party dominant systems. A highly competitive party system at the national level thus conceals great disparities in partisan strength in Austria's provinces. In the eight national elections held between 1945 and 1970 the margin of victory or defeat in each of the nine provinces exceeded the national margin nine times out of ten.[6] Austria is an agglomeration of territorially defined arenas of power that approximates the intensely competitive balance depicted by the consociational model only in the aggregate. Due to the uneven territorial dispersion of political power, center-periphery relations are marked by political bargaining within each of the three most important political institutions in Austria: the state bureaucracy, the interest groups, and the political parties.

Although the political influence of the Austrian provinces is relatively weak, numerous contacts, both formal and informal, link the federal bureaucracy to provincial bureaucracies. Even though it is not required by law, it is customary, for example, that the federal government inform the individual provinces of all federal legislation it intends to enact. This consultation process between different levels of governments occurs in particular on the numerous policies that are administered by the provinces in the name of the federal government.[7] A similar bargaining process also takes place in Austria's chambers, publicly recognized and licensed interest groups that participate in an economic council (Paritätische Kommission). Although closely tied to Austria's political parties, regional and particularistic interests are aired and resolved within these chambers. Austria is thus marked by a lively "group or interest federalism"[8] for territorially based functional interest groups have access to central decision-making bodies. Finally and most important, bargaining relations can be found inside Austria's party system. In terms of leadership recruitment and ideological orientation, Austria's Socialist Party has traditionally been centralized in Vienna. But the gradual extension of the party's electoral base into the western part of the country has attenuated the dominance of Vienna and has introduced at least a moderate amount of bargaining between different layers of the party organization. Such bargaining is more pronounced within the ÖVP since it adheres to a system of proporz not only in the representation of functional groups but also of provinces. The traditional dominance of the central party apparatus, dating back to the interwar years, was greatly undermined by the coming of age of a new generation of party leaders in the early 1960s. The political importance of the provinces thus increased sharply in the 1960s as central control gave way to political bargaining.[9] The continued importance of the territorial dimension in Austrian politics thus encourages within each of these political institutions a bargaining process between center and periphery.

Why, then, is politics in Austria's center and periphery not as dissimilar as is predicted by the federal model? The answer lies in the relative weakness of Austria's federal model, a weakness that has both historic and constitutional roots.[10] For a variety of reasons the Austrians adopted at the end of World War II a constitution that was based not on the constitution of 1920 (in which federal principles had been relatively strong) but on the constitutional amendments of 1929 (which had centralized political power in the national center and, in particular, in the hands of the president). Constitutional developments since 1945 have also favored centralization. The small sphere of legislation accorded to the provinces has been constricted by supreme court rulings that have consistently favored the political prerogatives of the center. In addition, between 1945 and 1966 the Austrian Parliament passed more than 80 constitutional amendments that have infringed further on provincial autonomy. These constitutional developments are reflected politically in the impotence of the upper house (Bundesrat), which merely reflects the partisan alignments in Parliament and which is incomparably weaker than its West German namesake. In short, the institutional barriers shielding politics in the periphery from the center are weak.

The consociational and the federal model offer, then, contrasting predictions about the similarity of and the interaction between center and periphery. This analysis and the sketchy evidence just reviewed suggest the following working hypothesis: Austria's center-periphery relations are a mixed type that express political conflict organized along functional lines depicted by the consociational model and along territorial lines described by the federal model. The consociational model points to the similarity of politics in center and periphery, for the weakness of Austria's federal institutions inhibits the emergence of different political structures and types of political behavior in Austria's periphery. The federal model, on the other hand, underlines the process of political bargaining between center and periphery, for the absence of intense party competition in several of Austria's provinces limits the control that the center can exercise over the periphery.

This mixture of elements drawn from both models is compatible with the fact that important political issues in local politics deal with both national problems (as predicted by the consociational model) and regional or local problems (as predicted by the federal model). National issues such as the protection of the environment, which generate partisan controversy and national legislation, impose new tasks on local governments and have indeed a lasting impact on the politics of the periphery. But it is equally clear that local issues are important on their own terms and are distinct from national issues in their impact on local politics.[11] This finding is compatible with the hypothesis that center-periphery relations in Austria embody in part the logic of the consociational model and in part that of the federal model. Our discussion of the similarity of politics in center and periphery and of the political interactions between center and periphery in the next two sections will try to substantiate and refine this hypothesis.

KLEINWALSERTAL AND CENTER-PERIPHERY
RELATIONS IN AUSTRIA

Among the 3,000 communes that existed in Austria in the early 1970s, Kleinwalsertal is singularly well suited to an analysis of center-periphery relations. Tucked away in Vorarlberg, the most western province of the Austrian Republic, this particular commune is territorially distant from Vienna.[12] In terms of its political institutions and practices the province of Vorarlberg differs considerably from the politics found in Vienna. The reason is partly geographic. Separated from Austria by an imposing mountainous barrier, the Arlberg, Vorarlberg has traditionally been oriented toward Switzerland and Germany. In the aftermath of the dissolution of the Hapsburg Empire in 1919, for example, the province opted virtually unanimously for unification with Switzerland. It is the only province in Austria with a significant portion of the communes (excluding Kleinwalsertal) electing their local representatives not by party lists but by a personality-oriented, nonpartisan procedure (Mehrheitswahlrecht) common in Switzerland. Finally, Vorarlberg perhaps more than any other province in Austria cherishes the institution of federalism, and in pressing its particularistic grievances with all three branches of government it intervenes actively in the political process in Vienna.[13]

Within the province of Vorarlberg, Kleinwalsertal's position also presents a territorial extreme. The valley was settled in the late thirteenth century by emigrants from the Swiss Valise and was conquered by the Hapsburgs in 1453. Geographically, though, it was most easily accessible from Germany, for it was shielded from the rest of Austria by high mountains that were passable only during a few months in the summertime. The defense of the valley against Swedish, French, and Bavarian troops between the seventeenth and nineteenth centuries earned the valley special political prerogatives. With the construction of a road linking Kleinwalsertal with the Bavarian town of Oberstdorf in 1814, the valley's seclusion was increasingly undermined, and it became during the next century more and more integrated with south German markets. As the economic basis of the commune has shifted from agriculture to tourism, these developments have accelerated since the 1930s. Today the valley is one of the biggest tourist centers in Vorarlberg and, indeed, in all of Austria.

In addressing the question of the similarity of politics in center and periphery, this chapter follows the method of crucial case analysis.[14] The method requires the choice of a case, such as Kleinwalsertal, which minimizes the similarity of center and periphery. One might expect, for example, that the dominance of the ÖVP in Kleinwalsertal and the economic prosperity of the valley would make politics in this peripheral commune atypical of politics in Vienna, for both conditions mitigate against the strong party system and overtly partisan behavior characteristic of Austria's center. If politics is partisan in Kleinwalsertal it should be partisan everywhere in Austria's periphery.

Kleinwalsertal is ruled by one party, the ÖVP, which today, as in the past, controls two-thirds of the seats in the communal council. In only about one-third of Austria's communes does the majority party hold such a dominant position.[15] In these communes there is no need for institutional arrangements such as the proporz system, by which power is shared between two competing parties in Austria's center. In a one-party dominant system the organizational strength of the party and partisan behavior should not be manifest and intense but latent and diffuse.

Kleinwalsertal's economic prosperity should also condition the relative weakness of party structures and partisan behavior. The average expenditure per household is higher in Vorarlberg than in any other Austrian province, and among Vorarlberg's communes it is highest in Kleinwalsertal.[16] Due to the strength of its tourist economy, in 1970 the valley ranked ninth among Austria's 3,183 communes in the tax revenues collected per capita, and these revenues have more than tripled during the last two decades.[17] This economic abundance should ameliorate partisan conflict and thus inhibit in this peripheral commune the type of politics that is characteristic of Austria's center.

As is true of the other central European states, political interactions between Austria's center and periphery are widely believed to be increasingly intimate and dominated by the center. In large part this is due to the financial weakness of Austria's communes. They can claim only 12 percent of national revenues as compared to the West German figure of 15 percent and the Swiss figure of 25 percent.[18] For two additional reasons the valley's exposed geographic position leads to the expectation that the periphery succumbs to the center: an Austrian national consciousness is less developed in the valley than in the rest of Austria, and the economic dependence on south German markets far exceeds the dependence on Austrian markets. This divergence between nation and state and between market and state thus makes this a prototypical case, for the geographic position of the valley establishes not the least but the most likely conditions for an interaction process between center and periphery that is dominated by the center. If these political interactions are not fully dominated in this instance, they should be dominated nowhere in Austria.

An independent Austrian national consciousness did not begin to emerge until the mid-1950s, and today that national consciousness is still not fully developed in the western parts of the country.[19] This

is particularly true of Kleinwalsertal, which is geographically accessible only from West Germany. A public opinion survey taken in the
mid-1960s revealed some major differences between respondents living in Kleinwalsertal and Austria on questions that were probing their
national consciousness. In the valley the number of "don't know" responses was much higher than in Vorarlberg and in Austria and, more
important, in Kleinwalsertal "national belonging" was interpreted in
economic—that is, German—terms by perhaps as many as half of
the respondents.[20] Torn between an Austrian and a German national
identity, the inhabitants of the valley often retreat to their local identity. "Whether Austrians or Germans, in the end they are all for-
eigners" is a response frequently heard in the valley. This may help
to explain why the people of Kleinwalsertal have managed, without
any apparent psychological or political problems, to be in their own
assessments both "good Germans" between 1938 and 1945 as well as
"good Austrians" since then.

Political interactions between Kleinwalsertal and Austria should
also be affected by the valley's dependence on West German markets.
Since it traded virtually only on south German markets, Kleinwalsertal has, since the late nineteenth century, formed an economic union
with Germany. Within the valley all economic transactions are conducted in West German currency and 98 percent of all tourists, providing virtually all of the valley's livelihood, are West Germans.[21]
Depending on the particular source and time of estimate, between 30
and 40 percent of the valley's assets are owned by West Germans,
who constitute about one-third of the resident population.[22] And 46
percent of the valley's purchasing power flows to the West German
market, more than ten times the corresponding Austrian figure.[23]
Among the more than 3,000 communes in Austria, Kleinwalsertal is
thus well suited for addressing the two problems of the similarity of
and the interaction between center and periphery.

THE SIMILARITY OF POLITICS IN VIENNA
AND KLEINWALSERTAL

The key similarity between politics in Austria's center and periphery is the institutional strength of political parties in defining and
resolving political problems. This strength is evident in the shape
parties give to the alignment of the Austrian electorate, the institutional penetration of Austria's interest groups and state bureaucracy
by the party system, and the cartel-like character of Austria's political elite. The first part of this section gives evidence for each of
these three propositions. Taking the question of taxation and zoning
as two political problems prominent in Kleinwalsertal as well as many

other Austrian communes, the second section analyzes the implications
that a "strong" party system has for the complex relations between political power and economic interest in Austria's periphery.

The Strength of Political Parties

Partisan Alignments

     Drawing both on his original research and the rich literature
that exists on Austrian public opinion, Stiefbold has recently characterized the Austrian public as partially depolarized, partially depoliticized, and reflecting only limited intergroup partisan hostility.[24] On
the other hand, there is also evidence of the persistence of moderate
psychological divisions of the electorate into distinct groups and a
resulting "mentality" that distinguishes members of the clerical-con-
servative, secular-socialist, and secular-national blocs.[25] Whatever their relative merits, both interpretations agree on the fact that
Austria's political parties have a strong impact on public opinion.
     This description of public opinion at the national level also fits
the conditions in Kleinwalsertal. An opinion survey conducted in the
valley in 1965 revealed that the perceptions of Austria's major political camps in Kleinwalsertal were virtually identical with those of a
control group of respondents in Vorarlberg, and that both sets of responses were very much in line with the results of a nationwide survey.[26]
     The similarity between national and local elections is equally
striking. National elections are highly politicized and characterized
by very high turnout rates and a voting pattern that, despite the growing importance of "switchers," reflects and supports the existing
party structure in Austria.[27] Although Austrian voters tend to distinguish between local and national elections, local elections are also
highly politicized and, in sharp contrast to West Germany, they are
conducted almost exclusively on the basis of national party lists.
Turnout in local elections is only slightly below comparable figures
for national elections and runs normally well above 90 percent. And
as is true of national elections, turnout varies inversely with size.
Generally speaking, the SPÖ and the FPÖ (Austrian Freedom Party)
reach their maximum vote in federal elections in cities and large
towns while the proportion of votes for the ÖVP increases in local
elections and with the declining size of communes. In Hallein, Grömingen, and Watterns, Austrian communes that have been studied in
some depth, the similarity between national and local elections—
measured in terms of turnout, correlation between voting preferences,
and the stability of individual and groups votes cast—was on the whole

striking.[28] And the same pattern can be observed for Kleinwalsertal as well.*

Institutional Penetration

Of the three institutional links between the electorate and the elites—political parties, interest groups, and the bureaucracy—Austria's political parties are most important for they have penetrated the other two. Measured by the ratio of members over voters, the organizational density of the Austrian party system is extremely high in comparison to the rest of Europe. For the two largest parties, the ÖVP and the SPÖ, they lie above 35 percent.[29] Roughly comparable figures can be found at the periphery of Austria's political system. In 1975 Kleinwalsertal's ÖVP organization had 222 members, that is, 23 percent of its electorate. The corresponding figures for the FPÖ and SPÖ were 50 (12 percent) and 22 (22 percent) members, respectively.[30] By this measure Austria's political parties appear to be somewhat weaker in the periphery than in the center, although not drastically so. Furthermore, as is true of the national level, partisan activities in local politics diminishes sharply between elections, in some instances to the point where, in contrast to national politics, party organizations become virtually dormant.

The internal organization of Austria's political parties is also similar in center and periphery. By all accounts the organization of the SPÖ is hierarchical while the decentralized structure of the FPÖ is heavily conditioned by the personality of local and provincial leaders. More interesting and politically important is the internal structure of the ÖVP. It is an umbrella organization of the Austrian Peasant League, the Austrian Business League, and the League of Austrian Workers and Employees, which constitute respectively about 38, 16, and 46 percent of the party's total membership. These leagues are guarantors of a delicate process of coalition politics within the ÖVP at the national level for each is tied to different interest groups and each occupies different ministries whenever the ÖVP is in power.[31] In Austria's consociational system of government, the coalition proporz within the ÖVP is almost as important as the coalition proporz between ÖVP and SPÖ.

Even though the size of the three parts of the ÖVP varies greatly, this "multiparty system" within one party exists also at the Austrian

---

*The majority party, the ÖVP, receives virtually the same number of votes in both local and national elections; but some of the support that the FPÖ gains in local elections is siphoned off by the SPÖ in national elections. Election results are periodically reported in the local newspaper, Der Walser, and in the Vorarlberger Wirtschafts- und Sozialstatistik.

periphery. Kleinwalsertal's business league, headed by the mayor,
is the strongest wing of the party with an active membership of 92;
the peasant league with its 68 members has evidently slipped in terms
of its relative power during the last two decades even though the voice
of its well-respected leader carries considerable weight in the commune's affairs. In sheer size it will soon be surpassed by the league
of employees, which in 1975 counted 62 members representing the
growing service sector in the valley's tourist economy. In both the
center and the periphery the institutionalization of these different interests within the ÖVP assures a large number of citizens that their
particular grievances and economic interests will be heeded in a carefully contrived system of coalition bargaining within the ÖVP.

The strength of Austria's political parties in center and periphery is reinforced by the cohesion that their rivalry in legislative
assemblies imposes. Even though under the Grand Coalition most important decisions were hammered out in an extraparliamentary coalition committee composed of the ÖVP and SPÖ, the three main parties
marshaled their well-organized and disciplined troops for political
battle in Parliament. With the change to a system of one-party government in 1966, vigorous partisan debate in Parliament has naturally
increased.[32] The same is true of Kleinwalsertal. Today votes in
the commune council follow party lines nine times out of ten. Parties
caucus ahead of council meetings and examine every point on the agenda
carefully. Control of the party leadership in the council meetings is
tight, ranging from the preparation of the agenda (a prerogative of
the mayor) to the actual discussion of substantive points and even to
the supervision of voting, which is only formally secret.[33]

Interest groups are the second institutional link between the electorate and the elites. Austria's main occupational groups are sanc-
tioned by public law. Membership in the chambers of commerce and
agriculture, for example, is compulsory, and these chambers are
entitled to tax their members through agencies of the federal government. In addition the chambers are endowed with autonomous and
delegated functions, which they exercise on behalf of the federal government. Despite this formidable array of powers these chambers
are not independent centers of power but are closely aligned with the
two major parties. With monotonous regularity elections confirm that
the chambers of commerce and agriculture are dominated by the ÖVP,
while the SPÖ controls the chamber of labor.[34] These chambers have
federal organizations and provincial branches but lack an organizational presence at the grassroots.

Their place at the periphery is taken instead by voluntary associations. Like occupational groups at the national level, voluntary
associations at the local level are closely allied with the political parties in serving a political function; but in contrast to national politics

that function is latent instead of manifest. Voluntary associations
have political influence in local politics not in their own right but as
extensions of the local party organizations. They serve as a reservoir
for recruiting political leaders; as platforms for dispensing with party
slogans; as channels of information and the airing of citizen grievances;
as a means for party leaders to move in the commune's spotlight and
to acquire a reputation for civic duty and leadership; and, finally,
these associations offer votes for which the parties compete at least
informally.[35] But in their relations with political parties voluntary
associations at the local level, like occupational groups at the national
level, resemble servants rather than masters.

    Group life in Kleinwalsertal accords with this general descrip-
tion. Under the guise of nonpartisanship, key associations such as
the voluntary fire brigade or the singing club serve the political functions just listed. Not unexpectedly, the leadership of these associations rests firmly in the hands of the local ÖVP elite. At the same
time, though, these associations provide a "nonpartisan" guise under
which the opposition can organize more easily than under a party label.
The SPÖ, for example, has recently made its entrance into local politics in the form of a youth organization. Supported initially by the
provincial SPÖ organization with a small grant, a young Socialist has
recognized an area in which the two main parties, the ÖVP and the
FPÖ, have been relatively negligent and has attempted to exploit that
negligence politically. Nobody, to be sure, is fooled by the nonpartisan label of the organization, and in the last local elections this political entrepreneur ran and won as the leading member of the SPÖ list.
But for the purpose of inching his way into local politics (into what
presumably will remain an unimportant position) it was advantageous
to organize political activity under a nonpartisan label.[36]

    The state bureaucracy is the third institutional link between the
electorate and the elite.[37] Like occupational and voluntary associations, the bureaucracy, too, is penetrated by the party system. The
ethic of a "neutral" civil service, which is so distinctive of Britain,
has no place in Austrian thinking. Patronage has always been an important aspect of the Austrian civil service. In the eighteenth and the
first half of the nineteenth century, patronage was mostly of a "social"
kind depending on family, school, and class ties. With the growing
ethnic fragmentation of the Hapsburg Empire came the system of
"ethnic proporz," especially in the provincial bureaucracies. And in
the twentieth century, but particularly since 1945, the Austrian bureaucracy has been governed in part by considerations of a "party
proporz." Although still disproportionately staffed by supporters of
the ÖVP who are largely members of a university-based, ancillary
organization, the Cartell-Verband (CV), an informal system of recruitment coupled with explicit agreements between the two main par-

ties, has resulted in a bureaucracy that is part "black" and part "red."
The proporz system is weaker at the very top of the bureaucracy than
at lower levels, for the Austrian bureaucracy does not know the system of "political civil servants," which can be replaced by an incom-
ing minister. In contrast to Britain or West Germany, the partisan
affiliation of the different branches of the Austrian civil service is
considered legitimate, but in contrast to Italy, the Austrian civil service is not simply a source of patronage for the majority party.

The partisan character of Kleinwalsertal's bureaucracy strongly
resembles that of the central bureaucracy. But in contrast to Vienna,
the predominance of the ÖVP in the valley's politics has caused the
total penetration of the local bureaucracy by ÖVP sympathizers. In
numberous interviews this was widely assumed (by FPÖ and SPÖ
sympathizers) and quietly acknowledged (by ÖVP supporters). According to the most reliable estimate more than 70 percent of the 56
employees of the commune are ÖVP sympathizers. While recruitment
is influenced also by other criteria, at the margin partisan affiliation
does matter. The top civil servant of the commune, an administrative
aide to the mayor (Gemeindesekretär), is actually the chairman of the
ÖVP party organization in Kleinwalsertal, and it is highly probable
that the commune's administrative machinery does much of the organizational work of the party.[38]

In Austria's center and periphery political parties are strong
and penetrate other institutions, such as interest groups and the state
bureaucracy, that link the electorate to the elites. Austria is thus
neither a "chamber state" nor an "administrative state" but rather
a party state.[39]

Elite Cartel

The strength of Austria's political parties in center and periphery is, finally, reflected in the cartel character of Austria's party
elite.[40] Although the cartel is organized somewhat differently at the
national and the local levels, the image the term connotes is appropriate for a description of how political conflicts are managed at both
levels. For in both center and periphery there exists a contrived system of role differentiation and role cumulation among Austria's pivotal
party leaders.

In the center, political elites met before 1966 in a coalition committee, and a spirit of informal checks and consultations has persisted
even after the move to a system of one-party government in 1966.
Austria's economic elites, on the other hand, participate in a system
of "social partnership," an institutionalized procedure of mutual consultation and decision making on all major economic questions. "Thus
the Austrian political system artfully bifurcated 'political' and 'socio-

economic' interest aggregation and decision-making into a 'Coalition' and 'Para-Coalition' then reunited them in an extra-constitutional body whose primary purpose was to mitigate potential, incipient or actual party or group conflict."[41] The top party leaders, numbering not more than two dozen people, are the bracket that holds this system together.

In Austria's periphery one finds a similar pattern of role differentiation and role cumulation. In Kleinwalsertal, as elsewhere in Austria, economic and political elites overlap much less than one might expect.[42] Differentiation also occurs within the political elite. As is true of about two-thirds of the communes in the province of Vorarlberg, Kleinwalsertal's mayor is not the chairman of the local ÖVP.* This permits the mayor, normally the acknowledged unofficial leader of the majority party, to adopt a stance as a nonpartisan spokesman for all local interests, which is indispensable for his electoral success and for an effective political performance. His administrative aide is the leader of the local ÖVP organization. He is actively involved in the internal politics of each of the three leagues that constitute the party and is the president of one of them (the league of employees).

As the valley's two critical political actors, the mayor and his administrative aide also exemplify role cumulation as the second feature of Austria's elite cartel. Apart from his numerous memberships in voluntary associations which, for lack of time, he can no longer pursue actively, the mayor's main position rests in the valley's tourist economy. He continues to be manager of Kleinwalsertal's public system of lifts, a position he has held since the late 1940s, long before he started his political career. He was, in addition, between 1948 and 1970 director of the valley's communal tourist bureau. Kleinwalsertal thus has its own brand of "state capitalism," in which public leadership and public ownership are mutually reinforcing in strengthening elite cohesion at the top. It is thus not surprising that the mayor's tenure in office—two decades at the end of the current legislative period—is long in Austrian local politics.[43] In terms of sheer numbers the cumulation of roles in the hands of his administrative aid is also striking. As the ÖVP chairman he is actively involved in the valley's associational life not only as a member of numerous organizations but as president of two of the most prestigious organizations, the fire brigade and the emergency service. In addition, and not totally atypically of the rest of the province, the administrative aide has, despite his civil service status, pursued his own electoral

*Even though there is no evidence, I suspect that this situation is different in the eastern part of the country.

career energetically. Elected to the council for the first time in
1970, he is now the most important member of the council board and
evidently hopes to eventually succeed the current mayor. This fusion
of power between the executive and legislative branches of government
occurs not only in his person. In fact, 25 percent of the council elected
in 1975 had civil service status, approximately the same proportion
as in the national Parliament. [44]

In both Austria's center and periphery there exists an elite
cartel marked by an intricate pattern of role differentiation and role
cumulation. Kleinwalsertal's mayor and his administrative aide are
the personification of the coalition and paracoalition that manage political conflicts at the federal level. [45] Conflict regulation thus rests
with individual office holders at the Austrian periphery and with an
institutionalized group procedure at the center. Individual leadership
and brokerage skills—"a nose for the stuff of politics"—influence local
politics more than national politics. But the management of political
conflicts in both center and periphery is determined by the strong position of Austria's elite cartel. In summary, in both center and periphery Austria's political parties are the dominant political force in
shaping partisan alignments, penetrating interest groups as well as
the state bureaucracy, and securing the position of Austria's elite cartel.

Political Power and Economic Interest
in Kleinwalsertal

What, concretely, does a "strong" party system mean for the
definition and resolution of political conflicts in Austria's periphery?
This section seeks to address the question by looking at the way in
which two important economic questions confronting the valley—taxation and zoning—are treated politically. To a very considerable extent the split between ÖVP and FPÖ is matched by a bifurcated alignment of economic interests in the valley. The ÖVP is not only the
party of the old, landowning families whose extended kinship systems
assure the party of a substantial vote cast solely on the basis of fa-
milial ties; it is also the party of owners of small guest houses and
homeowners who rent out several rooms to German tourists and are
otherwise active in the sizable service sector of the valley's tourist
economy. The FPÖ, on the other hand, is the party of the newcomers
who, during the last generation, have moved in from West Germany
and have brought with them capital and entrepreneurial skills; it is
the party of commercial enterprises, large hotels, and guesthouses.
The ÖVP stands for an artisanal form of production with small capital requirements while the FPÖ represents an industrial form of pro-

duction requiring large amounts of capital. The political representation of the large landowning families and small guesthouses in the
ÖVP, and thus in the commune council, is to some extent a reflection
of the relatively strong economic position that these classes have enjoyed in the past.

Supporters of the ÖVP and the FPÖ differ also in their views of
the proper role government should play in the management of the valley's economy. On most issues the ÖVP favors public involvement in
economic affairs while the FPÖ prefers a private sector left free of
government interference. This difference in orientation dates back
to the early 1950s when the valley's share of Marshall Aid funds was
used exclusively for the construction of a large, publicly owned and
operated lift. In these years no public investment was channeled into
the private sector. The economic boom of the 1950s legitimized an
active role of the commune in the valley's economy, and a second lift
was built in 1966 also without participation of the private sector. Today this single-handed approach to major improvements of the valley's
infrastructure is becoming increasingly difficult. The private sector
and its political spokesman, the FPÖ, are now actively involved. Only
one-half of the new theater complex to be constructed during the next
five years will be financed by the commune with the private sector and
the federal government sharing in the remainder. These figures indicate, though, that the commune's involvement in the valley's economic
development still remains central even today.

These differences in the underlying economic interests and ideological orientation of the ÖVP and FPÖ help in explaining the political
controversies surrounding questions of taxation. In the 1950s and
1960s fiscal conservatism reigned supreme in Kleinwalsertal, and
the valley's finances were in excellent shape. But the construction of
a new school and of a sewage system for the entire valley has put the
commune's financial resources under increasing pressure. During
the last four years, furthermore, the FPÖ has made a political issue
out of the growing costs of administration and the increasing tax burden. A 30 percent increase in the water tax was adopted in 1974, to
be followed by a similar increase in 1976; the adoption of that second
increase is now being debated intensely in the commune council. Although less dramatically, the tax on beverages has also increased during the last three years. Politically most explosive, however, was
an increase in the guest tax in 1973. Opposition to this tax increase
was strong among both hotel owners and homeowners renting rooms
even though the revenues raised by this tax are restricted in their use
to the strengthening and promotion of the valley's tourist economy.
Although the broad-based opposition among both FPÖ and ÖVP supporters was too weak to stop the tax increase, the ÖVP leadership is
now so aware of the sensitivity of the taxation issue that it proposes

to tie the guest tax to a cost-of-living index that would void the necessity of facing a major political crisis every four or five years. Whether or not the ÖVP leadership will succeed in this effort, it appears likely that its views on questions of taxation will prevail in the future.

The strength of the party leadership is a reflection of the organizational weakness of its political and economic opposition. That weakness exists not for lack of political effort, for the hotel owners of the FPÖ have tried hard to establish a common front with the owners of small guesthouses and private homes who traditionally support the ÖVP. A number of well-publicized meetings were called and the problems faced by the private sector of the valley's tourist economy were discussed at length. Traditional party loyalties, however, stopped large numbers of ÖVP members from attending even though they were sympathetic to some of the economic grievances articulated by the hotel owners and the FPÖ. [46] But the attempt to form an economic coalition cutting across party lines was also undermined by legal restrictions. Austria's economic chambers are given recognition as bodies of public law, and according to the law private homeowners renting rooms to tourists are denied seat and vote in the district organization of the tourist chambers. Afraid of a potentially powerful opposition, the mayor invited representatives of Vorarlberg's tourist chamber to a critically important meeting, organized by the local FPÖ and designed to establish contact with the ÖVP rank-and-file on the issue of taxation; these representatives spoke repeatedly and forcefully about the need to obey the law. Despite the common economic interests uniting the private sector of Kleinwalsertal's tourist economy on questions of taxation, traditional party organizations kept the private sector divided.

But the organizational weakness of the economic opposition to the ÖVP is also a result of economic interests that tie the private sector to policies pursued by the ÖVP. Small guesthouses and private homeowners are in a good position to neutralize increases in the guest tax by cheating, for there is no way in which the commune can supervise the accurate recording of the number of days a guest stays; estimates of underreporting vary between 5 and 15 percent. So far the ÖVP has been remarkably hesitant to increase the effectiveness of raising tax revenues, for the existing system is a workable compromise between the preference of the party leadership for large public revenues and the wishes of the party base for undiminished private incomes. *

---

*The ÖVP leadership has recently organized a lottery for departing guests. To be eligible the guests have to hand their ticket stubs

But the economic interests of the hotel owners are also tied to
the policies pursued by the ÖVP. The outside observer is struck by
the unwillingness of the commercial enterprises and hotel owners
represented by the FPÖ to score political points on the issue of financial inequity. Nobody, for example, raises questions about the fact
that the salary of the commune's civil servants is almost twice as
high as in Vorarlberg[47] and no questions are ever asked in public
about the discretionary annual tax assessments of enterprises profit-
ing from tourism—hotels, lifts, restaurants, tourist shops—even
though it is probable that the lifts owned and operated by the commune
are systematically undervalued at the expense of the private sector.
This reticence can be explained by the fact that the commune, so far,
has foregone the wage tax as its potentially most profitable source
of revenue. Such generosity is atypical, for only 14 of Vorarlberg's
96 communes did not impose a wage tax in 1971, and of these communes all but Kleinwalsertal were economically so backward that the
imposition of a wage tax would have generated virtually no additional
revenue. [48] So far the ÖVP has pointed to the precarious competitive
position of Kleinwalsertal in the tourist economy of southern Germany
as a justification of its policy. At the same time, though, it is clear
that the decision not to collect a wage tax is a subsidy given by the
commune to the large hotels, which would have to carry the greatest
portion of the additional financial burden. [49] The mayor may, therefore, well decide to collect a wage tax in the years ahead. That change
in policy would have two political advantages. It would regain him some
of his former financial autonomy by increasing the share of disposable
revenues in his budget. In addition, such a change in policy would increase the political dependence of the commercial enterprises and
hotel owners on the ÖVP, for subsidies could then be granted on an
annual adjustable cash basis. Indications are that the local ÖVP is
now moving in this direction. [50]

The question of taxation in Kleinwalsertal is instructive, for it
illustrates that underneath the political, economic, and ideological
differences that set the minority party apart from the majority party,
the economic interests of the large hotel owners, who constitute the
core of the FPÖ, are, on the question of the wage tax, intimately tied
to the policies pursued by the ÖVP. At the same time the political
strength of the ÖVP leadership is not infinite, for it has tolerated to
date an informal system of tax evasion practiced largely by its own
rank-and-file.

---

to the commune's tourist office on the day prior to their departure.
It is still too early to assess the effectiveness of this measure in increasing public revenues from the guest tax.

The intricate relations between political and economic interests are also evident in the problem of zoning, which, like the issue of taxation, is also of great importance to the valley's future. Kleinwalsertal's major asset is the beauty of its landscape. Unbridled economic growth during the last decades now threatens to undermine the very foundation of its tourist economy.[51] The adverse consequences of economic growth became a pressing political problem largely because of the actions of the provincial government. In the late 1960s the province of Vorarlberg commissioned a regional development plan that, it was hoped, would provide the data necessary for provincial legislation. But because it became evident very quickly that regional development and local zoning were explosive issues that infringed on property rights and thus touched the core of capitalist society, the provincial government passed only guideline legislation that required all communes to formulate a zoning plan by 1978 and offered some technical and financial assistance in the preparation of these plans.[52]

These external political pressures notwithstanding, some of the political impetus on the question of zoning came also from within the valley. In the early 1960s Kleinwalsertal was, in fact, one of the very first communes in the entire province to move in the direction of imposing zoning requirements. The result of these early efforts was a set of regulations passed by the commune council in 1969 and rejected as inadequate by the provincial government in 1971. One reason for that rejection was a general shift in orientation from growth ("developing the countryside for tourists") to stability ("protecting the environment"). More important, though, were the political compromises that the valley's dominant economic interests imposed on the ÖVP leadership.

These compromises were facilitated by accidental factors. The consultant that the commune had hired was an architect who was inept when confronted with the political horsetrading that the zoning question generated; a politically more skillful consultant might have been less lenient in the fact of economic and political pressures. More important, though, was the fact that the ÖVP leadership tried hard to accommodate all interests. A special commission was set up by the commune council, headed by the mayor himself, which held extensive hearings dragging out over two years. After it had issued a preliminary report for discussion, these hearings were reopened in order to deal with more than 100 complaints that had been filed. When all of these complaints were satisfied, it was inevitable that the original zoning regulations were hopelessly diluted. For more than any other group the valley's large landowning families, the traditional mainstay of the ÖVP, would have had to carry the costs of an effective and strict zoning code. In assessing the results of a decade of fruitless political effort, the mayor was quite explicit about the economic constraints under which he had been operating. "We did not want to create two categories of property owners—consisting of those who could sell their land and those who could not."[53]

Increasingly convinced in the early 1970s of the need for effective zoning regulations, the mayor adopted a dual strategy. He renewed the effort to impose legal restrictions on land use and he tried to attract outside capital for the development of large apartment complexes in Kleinwalsertal. In 1971 the commune council commissioned a development plan for Kleinwalsertal that was to assist it later in the formulation of its zoning regulations. Some of the less important policy prescriptions—the adoption of a five-year financial plan as part of the annual budget meetings and the establishment of a development corporation staffed by both the public and the private sectors—were adopted even before the release of the report to the public.[54] But when faced with the central choice proposed by the report—an immediate stop of all construction until zoning regulations were developed or a policy of muddling through until the adoption of a zoning code in 1977—Kleinwalsertal's political leadership, predictably, opted for the latter.[55] That choice was influenced by both economic and electoral constraints. To abruptly stop the issuing of construction licenses would not only have antagonized the landed interests that had succeeded in diluting the zoning regulations in the 1960s, but it would also have offended business and commercial interests in the ÖVP. With a local election critical to his larger political plans less than two years off, the mayor decided to keep the report secret and adopt a wait-and-see attitude.*

As was pointed out in the report, the mayor's strategy had two critical liabilities: it furthered the disfiguring of the valley's landscape through the haphazard construction of mostly small houses, and it pushed the commune toward investment in infrastructure—roads, canalization, and sewage plants—for which it simply lacked sufficient financial resources. But due to the mayor's second strategy, encouraging the building of large condominia in Kleinwalsertal, these liabilities were less serious than one might have initially thought, for the condominia promised to slow the building boom in single-family dwellings and to generate badly needed financial resources for the investments in infrastructure that the commune was facing during the coming decade. With his active encouragement about 570 apartment units were constructed in Kleinwalsertal between 1970 and 1975. This represented 10 percent of the valley's maximum bed capacity and about one-third of the total growth projected in the commune's development report for the years 1973-77.[56] Two-thirds of these apartments were

---

*This decision was typical of developments throughout Vorarlberg.

concentrated in one large complex tucked away in the far end of the
valley. From the mayor's vantage point this strategy paid off hand-
somely. Construction of single-family dwellings declined from 1972
on and the new apartment complexes contributed to the commune's
investment in infrastructure—from swimming pools to sewage plants
—and thus improved the structure of the valley's tourist economy.[57]

But this strategy had some political costs. While the economic
interests of the large landowners in the ÖVP (who opposed strict zoning
regulations) and of the business and commercial sectors (who opposed
a temporary halt in all construction) were largely left unharmed, the
construction of a number of apartment complexes contradicted the
economic interests of the owners of private houses and small guesthouses. For this additional housing capacity could not help but increase
competitive pressures, exert a downward pressure on prices, and impair their economic prospects in the future. In 1967, for example,
private establishments accounted for 52 percent of overnight stays in
Kleinwalsertal as compared to 42 percent in the province of Vorarlberg. By 1973 the figure for the valley had declined to 40 percent
while that for Vorarlberg had increased slightly to 44 percent.[58] But
even though their economic interests were harmed most directly, the
strongest political opposition did not arise among the ranks of the
ÖVP but among the hotel owners of the FPÖ, who hoped to capitalize
on the muted dissent in the ÖVP. The intensity of that opposition was
revealed in the final vote on the single most important apartment complex. After extended debates the plans were finally approved in the
commune council by a vote of 15 to 9, an uncharacteristically close
vote in the council deliberations between 1970 and 1975.[59]

Some of the most harmful ecological and financial effects of unbridled economic growth were thus mitigated by the mayor's political
strategy. Consensus politics prevented the adoption of strict zoning
regulations, which would have impaired the economic interests of the
large landowners, the traditional core of the ÖVP. The mayor encouraged instead the natural trend toward the concentration of capital
in the market system as a second-best solution. Although this strategy
was opposed to the economic interests of a sizable segment of his own
party as well as the FPÖ, that opposition lacked the political organization to effectively challenge the mayor.[60]

The strength of Kleinwalsertal's political parties, these case
studies illustrate, rests in the fact that they inhibit the organization
of coalitions based on economic interests. To be sure, political
power partly reflects economic interests for the owners of small
guesthouses (on the question of the guest tax), and the interests of the
large landowning families (on the question of zoning) set limits to the
political objectives the mayor could hope to achieve. But of equal importance is the fact that political power is also partly autonomous from

economic interests, for the mayor could pursue policies that, on different questions, were opposed to the economic interests of the owners of hotels, guesthouses, and private homes. The possible introduction of a wage tax in the near future and the encouragement of the construction of condominia in the recent past illustrate that in the distribution of resources "strong" political parties in Austria's periphery can, at times, express the commune's collective interest above and beyond the economic interests of particular classes or groups.

These two case studies provide, then, a concrete illustration of what is meant by a "strong" party system at Austria's periphery. But is the similarity in this key feature of the politics of Austria's center and periphery attributable to the center's domination of the periphery? Or is the center's politics merely the periphery's politics writ large?[61] Both assumptions appear to be unwarranted in the Austrian context. The data we have presented do not permit us to talk in terms of causation but only in terms of congruence. Political patterns that exist in the Austrian center exist also in the Austrian periphery. Only by turning to our second major question, the interaction between center and periphery, can we hope to address more explicitly questions of causation.

POLITICAL INTERACTION BETWEEN CENTER
AND PERIPHERY

In the analysis of the interaction between center and periphery two facts stand out. First, interaction intensified greatly from about 1968 on as federal and provincial legislation imposed enormous new financial burdens upon the commune that far exceeded the valley's capacities. The second notable fact is the successful political career of the valley's mayor in provincial politics since the 1960s. For although it is weak, Austria's system of federalism interjects an intermediate level of government—the province—between center and periphery that, in terms of sheer volume of business, is far more important than the national capital in conditioning center-periphery relations. This is not to say that in extraordinary circumstances individual communes will not seek assistance at the center, but such attempts are costly and time-consuming and will be relied upon only as a measure of last resort. The increasing financial burdens imposed upon the commune and the political involvement of the mayor in provincial politics suggest that the growing economic burdens have led to a political response through which local political leaders have attempted, on the whole successfully, to shape at least in part the valley's future.

Economic Burdens

How great was the economic challenge that Kleinwalsertal faced from the late 1960s on? Before 1968 the valley had incurred no particularly pressing financial burdens. Its tax base was sufficient to cover all ordinary expenses that the commune incurred. In fact, the valley's booming tourist business made the taxation rate in the valley one of the lowest in the entire province. But by 1971 the valley's two major construction projects—a sewage system and a new school complex—had already led to the accumulation of a debt of 30 million Austrian schillings, which since that date has increased to more than 50 million schillings.[62] The valley has been able to finance these projects only by applying for special funds provided either by the federal or, more frequently, the provincial government. Kleinwalsertal's dependence on financial and political forces outside the valley has thus increased enormously.

This picture is by no means atypical of developments on Austria's periphery in general. A vast literature documents the sharp increases in the burden of expenditures that has been imposed by both the federal and the provincial governments on the communes without a corresponding increase in local tax revenues.[63] A complicated system of revenue sharing among the provinces and within each province is designed to neutralize this imbalance. For the communes in particular there exist two allocation mechanisms by which they get allotments of funds from the provincial government. Regular subsidies are granted on the basis of a formula that favors the very poor communes as well as the large urban areas. Special subsidies are granted primarily for major construction projects—schools, hospitals, sewage systems—that surpass the financial capacity of any one commune but may have benefits for a larger region.

Although the law stipulates that communes are eligible for receiving subsidies only after all forms of taxation available to the locality have been exhausted, Kleinwalsertal has successfully applied for special subsidies without collecting a "beverage tax," which, the valley claims, would seriously impair its competitive position vis-a-vis other tourist centers in Bavaria. The fiscal conservatism that is distinctive of Vorarlberg's provincial government has accentuated what is a predictable political consequence of this system of revenue sharing: the enormous political leverage it gives to the majority party in the province in dealing with peripheral political elites. The provincial government, and in particular its treasurer, is in constant conflict with the Association of Communes and the League of Towns, the two local government lobbies; for the subsidies local governments would like to receive are invariably greater than what the provincial government is willing to provide. But such publicized conflicts are

misleading. In the treasurer's negotiations with individual mayors
a spirit of cooperation prevails. Whether that spirit can be translated
into concrete gains for the commune seeking provincial assistance
depends in large measure on the number of political chips that a mayor
has on his side of the table when he sits down with the provincial treasurer to talk things over.

Political Responses at the Provincial Level

Since in Austria's consociational system of government political
parties play a central role, these chips can be accumulated most easily
within the party hierarchy by trying to get elected to the provincial
diet. More than one-quarter of the members of the provincial diet
are mayors, and almost 40 percent are members of a communal executive council. [64] In provinces such as Vorarlberg that are dominated
by the ÖVP electoral success requires adept political maneuvering in
the complex internal party politics that determine the final ranking
of candidates on the ballot presented to the voters. This bargaining
takes place within each of the three leagues that constitute the ÖVP
at the local, district, and provincial level. For an ÖVP mayor to
receive a safe place on the ballot is tantamount to electoral victory,
for the election no more than ratifies the process of candidate selection within the ÖVP.

The geographically exposed position of Kleinwalsertal proved
to be both an asset and a liability in the mayor's political career.
When in 1959 the size of the provincial diet was increased from 32 to
36 members, the preamble to the legislation explicitly mentioned
Kleinwalsertal as one of the province's communes that perhaps deserved a better chance for electing one of its own members to the
diet. [65] Typical of conservative parties throughout Europe, the ÖVP's
favorable orientation toward the political representation of territorial
diversity was also reflected in the revision of the provincial ÖVP
statute in 1968. The executive committee of the party was reorganized
so that two delegates were represented from each of the province's
six court districts. An additional thirteenth member was to be
sent from Kleinwalsertal. This concession to the valley's special
status was made in response to an active lobbying campaign by the
mayor. His main argument was the beneficial effects that this special
recognition would have on the valley's budding Austrian national consciousness. Unknown to the provincial party leadership, though,
the mayor at that time had already decided to move from local into
provincial politics. This stronghold in the party's leadership, he
thought, would be a useful source of power and information not for
the electoral battle he faced in 1969 but, possibly, for future times.

But the valley's geographically exposed position was also a liability in the mayor's political career. In order to win the party's nomination for a safe place on the ballot each candidate must engage in a complicated process of bargaining with candidates from other parts of the province. The geographic isolation of the valley made it, however, virtually impossible for the valley's mayor to assemble an initial core of support from several communes. This liability was reinforced by the fact that the mayor was a member of both the business and the employee leagues of the ÖVP. Both leagues agreed on the fact that he deserved to be ranked very high on the ballot, but due to the proporz thinking within the party they disagreed sharply on whose candidate he should be. These two disadvantages explain why in 1969 and 1975 the mayor failed to get nominated at the district-level meetings of either of the two leagues. His political career might well have ended right then and there. But due to his activity and visibility in the ÖVP's district organization before 1969 and in provincial politics between 1970 and 1975, the special provincial assembly of the party, the final arbiter between the competing claims of the party's three leagues, included his name on the ballot. In 1969, however, the mayor's political influence was insufficient for getting nominated to a safe place on the ballot. To the total surprise of everybody, including himself, the mayor became a member of the provincial diet because one of the members of the elected slate resigned his seat right after the election. In 1975, on the other hand, after five years in office, he was placed in a safe place on the ballot.

This success in 1975 was the result of a two-pronged strategy designed to strengthen the mayor's local political base on the one hand and to increase his political leverage in provincial politics on the other. Kleinwalsertal's politics became intensely political from 1972-73 on. Party leadership, for example, changed hands as the mayor's administrative aide took over from the local notable, who had represented a more traditional style of politics during the preceding two decades. The result of this change was a perceptible tightening of the party organization and an expansion in ÖVP membership. Between 1970 and 1975 membership doubled from 112 to 222 and the number of active party members increased by an even greater margin. In the process of expansion the party managed to rejuvenate itself. Old political notables were pushed out of the inner circle of power. In 1973, for example, the mayor's administrative aide assumed the leadership of the local chapter of the employee league as one of the three corporate groups represented in the party, and the mayor took over the leadership of the business league in 1974. Membership gains in these two groups accounted for 90 percent of the total increase. And through a shrewd maneuver by which the mayor's name was printed on a separate ballot in the local election of 1975 (which gave the voters the impression of voting for the man rather than the party), he reached one of the largest pluralities in the entire province.[66] A more vigorous local party organization was indispensable for gaining political support in provincial politics not because of the few additional votes that a stronger local organization commands in district level meetings but because of the seriousness of political purpose and the image as a good "party man" that a mayor portrays when he is backed by a vigorous local organization.*

But between 1969 and 1975 the mayor also extended and strengthened his influence at the provincial level, for only that influence would help him to shape the political and economic forces impinging on the valley. In his own words, "to be present is all." From 1973 on, for example, his administrative aide filled the position that the valley had been accorded in the provincial party executive since 1968. The committee system of the provincial diet was another arena of power where "presence" counted. The mayor became deputy chairman of the most important committee, the finance committee, and he was also made a member of the important judiciary committee. He was thus placed in an excellent position to scrutinize all budget decisions and to examine all pieces of legislation. "Presence" meant that he could intervene on behalf of the particular needs of his own community early in the political deliberations. Due to Kleinwalsertal's exposed geographic and economic position this occurred frequently on matters of legislation that were drafted without taking into consideration the special position of the valley.

Although the interaction between center and periphery that takes place within the party system is the central element, the role of interest groups and the state bureaucracy cannot be disregarded altogether. Local elites who are trying to fashion a political response to the economic challenges that their communes face can neglect these alternative arenas of power only at their own peril. The mayor of Kleinwalsertal, for one, sought to extend his influence in provincial politics by becoming president of the Vorarlberg tourist lobby. He was elected to this position in 1973 on the basis of his lifelong experience with tourism and the valley's importance for the province's tourist industry as a whole. He has since become the province's representative in the National Association for the Advancement of Tourism. It is difficult to assess the political importance of this position. The economic importance of the tourist industry in this particular province makes it more than a honorific office, for in recent years the tourist

---

*The much greater electoral effort of the FPÖ was related to a change in the party's leadership, which brought a younger generation to the forefront.

association has received more than 7 million schillings in subsidies from the provincial government. But the presence of corporate interest groups within the ÖVP, and in particular of the business league, detracts from the political importance of the tourist lobby. On balance the position appears to give the mayor exposure, additional information, contacts—elements, that is, that are essential to the exercise of power but that in and by themselves do not confer the power, which can only be gained within the ÖVP. Yet it is undeniable that the mayor can now act the role of representing functional interests, which complements and adds to his representation of territorial interests.

Alongside interest groups the state bureaucracy is a third pillar of power that conditions the interaction between center and periphery. As is true of Vienna and Kleinwalsertal, Vorarlberg's bureaucracy is not neutral but partisan. It is a safe assumption, confirmed in interviews with several members of the provincial bureaucracy, that the entire staff of the provincial bureaucracy is supportive of the ÖVP either in its ideological orientation or through party membership. At the level of the section chief (of which there are some 25) the system is overtly political, while at the bureau level the partisan character of the bureaucracy is more disguised. Screening occurs at the time of first employment and is done informally. The overwhelming proportion of the civil servants are members of the CV, the university organization for future civil servants; the annual CV ball in Bregenz is in fact the only social occasion that brings the entire provincial civil service together. Criteria of partisanship are compromised only when the provincial government lacks qualified candidates with the appropriate party identification. In engineering and technical jobs (for which people train primarily in "red" Vienna rather than in "black" Innsbruck) this occurs not altogether infrequently.

Although Vorarlberg's bureaucracy is partisan it lacks the kind of patronage that makes it difficult for an outsider to distinguish between Vienna's city government and the SPÖ headquarters. In Vienna, to get anything done a SPÖ functionary has to operate through the party network. In Vorarlberg the first telephone call of an ÖVP mayor goes almost invariably to the bureau in charge of the particular problem. Yet even in Vorarlberg the difference between partisanship and patronage is small, amounting often to not more than the five feet that separates the office of the treasurer from the office of the financial minister. Of the 250 school principals in Vorarlberg only 4 are reported to be sympathetic toward the SPÖ. The interest group chambers are a preserve of the ÖVP and, due to political machinations at the federal level, all officers of the federal army stationed in the province are ÖVP members.

Because the system is relatively closed to outside political forces party membership in and of itself counts little in getting things

done. For the mayor of Kleinwalsertal to succeed in his economic
and political objectives contact, information, and the ability to express himself well are crucial ingredients. These abilities are found
more often among members of the business league (which the mayor
leads in Kleinwalsertal) than among members of the other two leagues.
By all accounts, then, the structure of Vorarlberg's partisan bureaucracy provides a political arena in which Kleinwalsertal's mayor per-
forms well. Not only does he belong to the right party, but he is a
member of that wing of the party that, in general, does best in internal
bureaucratic politics.

It is easier to assess the character of the political response of
the mayor in meeting the economic challenges of his commune than to
judge the benefits of direct representation at the centers of provincial
power. There is a compelling logic to the argument that "he who
milks the cow first gets the best cream." Yet on closer inspection
of the evidence the advantages of direct political representation are
more subtle. Despite the dominance of the ÖVP in every walk of life,
no scandal of favoritism or corruption has rocked Vorarlberg politics
during the last decade. Even SPÖ functionaries both at the provincial
and at the local level concede that favoritism, should it exist, is not
easily detected from the outside. The system does not work in an
openly partisan way by which, for example, funds for construction
projects are allocated on the basis of partisan criteria. Yet the mayor's
presence has undoubtedly resulted in some benefits. Being on the scene
means being informed—about late appropriations, special funds, altered deadlines, and the like. This knowledge can be translated easily
into small amounts of resources that are useful for shoring up political
support at the grassroots. Thus, when it became clear that the SPÖ
would make its entry into Kleinwalsertal politics by forming a youth
organization, the mayor quickly secured some financial support from
a special youth fund of the provincial government in order to neutralize the partisan character of the new organization and to make the
ÖVP presence felt. Similarly, he got financial support from the provincial government for the construction of a playground that the FPÖ
had demanded for years. And he secured funds for the renovation of
a church graveyard and a fire-engine house, thus strengthening his
political ties with two important voluntary associations in the valley.
These examples illustrate the way the mayor used his newly gained
political leverage to extract financial resources from the province.
Sometimes, though, the economic benefits to the valley were of
greater importance. The mayor succeeded, for example, in lowering
the effective rate of taxation imposed on the valley's tourist economy
not by changing the proposed legislation that was to hold for all of
Vorarlberg but by negotiating inside the bureaucracy an artificially
low exchange rate for the conversion of taxes collected in German

marks and to be rendered in Austrian schillings. And in the major
construction objects of the valley, such as the sewage system, the
advantage conferred by his political office rested on the speed and
quality of the delivery of provincial services and funds.

Political Responses at the Federal Level

To different degrees the political contacts that Kleinwalsertal's
mayor has developed in his political dealings with the provincial party
leaders and bureaucrats are a critical asset in establishing contact
with political institutions in Vienna. To develop these contacts is a
difficult and time-consuming task, and the mayor has tried to do it
only in matters that he considers vital to the future prosperity of the
valley. At times, of course, Vienna is not a key target but a convenient excuse for getting rid of tricky local issues. In 1974, for example, the valley's local skiing club petitioned the mayor to file an application with the federal government for hosting the 1978 world skiing
championships. For everybody but the valley's ski buffs it was perfectly obvious that there was no chance of the application ever being
considered seriously. Austria was going to host the Olympic winter
games in Innsbruck in 1976, the second time in little more than a
decade, and neither the federal government nor the international ski
federation would be interested in holding still another international
meet in this small alpine state. In addition none of the ski runs in the
valley was up to the competitive standards of modern alpine racing.
With this in mind the mayor sat down and wrote the application, mailed
it to Vienna, and never received as much as a letter acknowledging
receipt of the application. But he was perfectly content, for he could
point to the unwieldy and unresponsive federal bureaucracy as a legitimate excuse for not getting a response. Ski club officials in the valley were also satisfied for they had done what they considered their
duty in strengthening the club's and the valley's sport and tourist attraction.

Yet such episodes as these are the exception. On the whole the
federal government is not a political safety valve for hard-pressed
elites on Austria's periphery but rather a center of imposing political
and economic power that has to be dealt with directly on matters of
critical importance to the valley's existence. Bureaucratic irrespon-
siveness, far from being a convenient excuse, is in fact the major
barrier that impedes the flow of information and inhibits the exercise
of whatever political power peripheral elites may have. This is true
in particular for the mayor of an ÖVP-governed commune, for, by the
very logic that enhances his political influence in provincial politics,
he is effectively barred from intruding into the preserve of the SPÖ

in Vienna. In many.cases this pushes the mayor into a position of political ineffectiveness. The construction of Kleinwalsertal's sewage system, for example, depends for half of its funds on federal finances. Although less than half of the work in the valley had been completed by 1975, construction had to be halted until further financing from the federal government was assured. In the case of provincial subsidies the mayor most likely would have tried to see "what could be done," but in the case of federal funds no such attempt was even discussed.

On matters that were vitally important to the commune the mayor attacked the federal bureaucracy not from the bottom but from the top.[67] One such question was the introduction of the Austrian value-added-tax in 1973 and, in particular, the effect that tax had on the amount of beverages sold in the valley. From 1973 on, the total tax imposed on beverages sold in the valley was about 50 percent higher than in the Federal Republic. This had potentially very serious effects on the profitability of Kleinwalsertal's tourist business, for in the first six months of 1973, it turned out, the valley experienced a 30 percent decline in the quantity of beverages sold.[68] The people of Kleinwalsertal had of course foreseen that drop, and the mayor had mapped his political strategy several years earlier.[69] First, he repeatedly approached the federal bureaucracy with his problem in writing. But the finance minister responded either with silence, negatively, or in a noncommittal manner.[70] The mayor therefore decided to apply some pressure via the federal headquarters of the chamber of commerce but to no avail. As his frustration mounted he decided to shift gear again and to approach the finance minister a second time. Using contacts in the Vorarlberg ÖVP organization he succeeded in having a question posed to the finance minister during question hour in the federal Parliament. He then sought and received a personal audience with the finance minister to which he brought along the singing club and the band of the valley. After what amounted to no more than a courtesy call from which he extracted the minister's word that something would be done, the musical performance in the halls of the finance ministry must have left some traces on the minister's mind. To have won the attention of the minister, it turned out, had been well worth the cost of having seriously alienated the lower level bureaucracy.*

A second opportunity for getting a hearing in Vienna arose when, in October 1972, three months before the value-added-tax was to go

---

*In his correspondence with finance minister Androsch the mayor always signed in his capacity of mayor of Kleinwalsertal. But the minister would open his letters with the phrase "Honorable Representative." Being a member of the provincial diet clearly was very important for winning political recognition in Vienna.

into effect, the annual conference of all provincial governors was scheduled to convene in Vorarlberg. [71] Chancellor Kreisky intended to address that meeting, and the mayor used all his influence in provincial politics to convince the state governor that a side trip of the governor's meeting, and of the chancellor, to Kleinwalsertal would be a welcome and inexpensive addition to the program, for the valley promised to cover all costs. This strategy had in fact been a time-honored one, for the argument of strengthening the Austrian identity of the valley's inhabitants had, over the past two decades, brought many ministers, some chancellors, and one president to what still is one of the most picturesque places in Austria. Unfortunately, though, the chancellor canceled his visit because of an important parliamentary debate. But the mayor persisted, and his persistence paid off. Recognizing that Kreisky's overall political strategy required visibility in western Austria, where the SPÖ over the next decade hoped to make its strongest electoral gains, the mayor approached one of the SPÖ members of Parliament elected from Vorarlberg and used him as his conduit both to the finance ministry and to the chancellery. In this fashion he succeeded in arranging for the chancellor and the finance minister, who were planning to travel in western Austria for other purposes, to visit the valley in January 1973. The visit was successful in all respects but one, for the local population gave the "red" chancellor an unusually cold reception. [72] Except for the obligatory and obliged schoolchildren hardly anybody turned up for the ceremonies; it was an affair of the local and provincial political leadership only. As a result of that visit a joint commission staffed by civil servants of the finance ministry on the one hand and representatives of the valley on the other was established to assess the effects of the value-added-tax on the competitive position of Kleinwalsertal. Before the end of the year that commission concluded that the tax on alcoholic beverages should be totally eliminated.

Although that dramatic battle was won to the apparent satisfaction of the entire valley, the war goes on. Austria's value-added-tax will be reexamined in 1978, and the valley is bracing itself for another fight in order to protect its economic interests and to eliminate other areas of economic discrimination. The SPÖ's finance minister has so far refused to change the law for only one commune and has advised Kleinwalsertal's mayor that he intends to press for compensatory financing mechanisms to be established between Austria and the Federal Republic. [73] But the mayor has little hope of this coming to pass in the foreseeable future. No compensatory financing has been involved in Kleinwalsertal's dealing with the Federal Republic since 1945. With the permanent resolution of the taxation question now lodged at the international level, the mayor intends to fight a guerrilla war with the SPÖ government and the federal bureaucracy. He hopes not for a final and decisive victory but for a series of makeshift arrangements that will permit the valley to prosper economically in an atmosphere intermittently clouded by the taxation question. Having established his networks in Vienna, knowing at which doors to knock, the mayor is not pessimistic about the valley's future. For, in his own words, "it is all a matter of personal contact; this is what I am good at; that is the reason why I have succeeded."[74]

Another question of similar importance for the valley's future is the proposed road connection between Kleinwalsertal and Austria. A direct road link to Austria would lead to the most profound economic changes in the valley and would probably be the single most important event in the valley's history. Although the timetable and the financing of such a road make its construction improbable during the coming decade, future developments are inevitably moving in that direction. Kleinwalsertal's mayor and indeed all local political leaders are aware of the explosive character of this issue. During the last five to ten years, when the issue was gradually emerging, the mayor, self-consciously, has never taken a public stand on the question, and during the last election campaign in 1975, when it was very much on everybody's mind, all parties refrained from bringing it into open debate. With questions of this importance, I was repeatedly assured, one does not "play politics."[75]

The mayor has also downplayed the entire question outside the valley, for in both provincial and federal politics he might risk triggering responses that would freeze out the commune at the initial critical stages. Complications arise at the provincial level since the proposed road connection would open up the inner parts of Vorarlberg to an avalanche of German tourists that now stops in Kleinwalsertal. The economic advantages enjoyed by the valley are thus bound to diminish. While this puts the mayor of Kleinwalsertal in direct competition with local leaders from other parts of the province, he can ill afford to engage in confrontation strategies, for he needs their political support for the numerous other political dishes that he is frying. Keeping a low profile has thus appeared to him as the most appropriate strategy. The same is true of politics in Vienna. At all costs, the mayor has argued repeatedly, one must encourage the leaders in Vienna to view this matter in economic terms rather than as a matter of national security.

On this particular problem, then, the valley is playing for high stakes. But in the first phase of what will be a three-phased project it has not done badly. The route of the road has now been chosen, and the magnitude of the valley's victory is readily apparent. When the project was first broached by the Nazis in the late 1930s, the new road was planned to start in the valley's most distant village thus incorporating all of the already existing road. In the federal road act

of 1948 that plan was adopted, but since the Austrian government was
by then committed to eventually link the valley to the rest of Austria,
the valley's main road, which had been local, was reclassified as
federal, thus lifting the burden of maintenance from the commune's
shoulders. The provisions in the 1971 amendment of the 1948 act that
pertain to the valley are identical with one minor terminological
change. * But this change in terminology was of critical importance
to the mayor, for it left undetermined where the new road would eventually begin. The valley could thus hope that the new road would open
up areas inside the valley now inaccessible to tourists and that the
road would lighten the traffic congestion in the valley's three main
villages. For these reasons the mayor lobbied informally but intensively within the provincial bureaucracy to have the province represent
the legitimate interests of the valley in its dealings with the federal
bureaucracy.[†] The highway plans issued in 1974 point to a far-reaching victory of Kleinwalsertal, for they agree with the main objectives
of the mayor. Referring to the road project in a special memorandum,
the mayor wrote in 1975, "questions of whether, when and how are
exclusively federal competence."[76] One might add—not quite. In the
question of "how" the commune intervened and appears to have been
successful in shaping federal policies to fit its own needs.

      These examples illustrate that the periphery is not a helpless
prey of an overbearing central power. Change, to be sure, Kleinwalsertal cannot stop. But in its manner of coping with change the valley's
mayor has revealed resilience and initiative in trying to shape the future. On the question of taxation he has sought to publicize the issue
and to use partisan networks. But on the question of the road construction he has tried to keep the issue depoliticized by working primarily
with lower level bureaucrats. This flexibility in political tactics reveals a political shrewdness that may well be the periphery's main
asset in dealing with the center.

      By and large, Austria's system of revenue sharing, based on
quantitative measures of community need, is fixed by federal law.
But at the margin that can be shaped politically by one commune, the
strength of political parties and the entrepreneurial skills of its mayor
are important factors that condition the distribution of resources between communes. The skills that Kleinwalsertal's mayor displays
are not unique but can be found elsewhere, for political elites on Aus-

_____

      *The 1971 amendment refers to the "commune" instead of the
"village" Mittelberg (until 1975 the official name for Kleinwalsertal).
The result was that planning for the new road was less constricted.

      [†]The mayor did this actually prior to his election to the provin-
cial diet.

tria's periphery are quite successful in gaining some control over the financial, administrative, and political interventions of political forces from the center. In Hallein, for example, contacts inside the provincial and federal bureaucracy were useful for extracting resources that otherwise would not have been forthcoming.[77] Direct representation in provincial assemblies, which is common in both lower Austria and Vorarlberg, gives many mayors some control over center-periphery relations.[78] And short of direct representation there are the numerous informal contacts with provincial legislators and bureaucrats that are apparently widespread in Austria.[79]

The different political tactics that the periphery's elites employ in order to influence central decision making are conditioned by the character of the party to which they belong. The hierarchical structure of the SPÖ, for example, leads to simple interactions between center and periphery that impede local or provincial initiatives encouraged by the more complex internal structure of the ÖVP. The hopelessly weak political position of the SPÖ in Vorarlberg's rural communes leaves the local party organization relatively free from the interference of district or provincial party organizations. But in larger towns and cities where the SPÖ stands on firmer electoral ground, provincial party leaders do intervene in the debates at the local or district level, just as the central party organization intervenes in matters of provincial party politics that have a bearing on national political issues.

But whether they are used by the left or by the right, all the shrewd tactics in the world are ineffective if they are not guided by an overarching strategy. The mayor of Kleinwalsertal has such a strategy, for he has recognized that the only way he can hope to control the growing economic burdens thrust upon the valley by external forces is to extend his political leverage, to form new networks, and to simply be on the scene when important decisions are taken either in Vorarlberg or in Vienna. With limited political resources he has done an astonishing job that belies the notion that peripheral communes are the backwaters of modern Austria.

CHANGE IN CENTER-PERIPHERY RELATIONS

How will center-periphery relations be affected by the economic changes that are currently transforming Austria? Other studies of Austria's local government system suggest that in terms of their economic and social structures Austrian communes fall along a continuum that ranges from small, rural, economic, and culturally backward communes on the one hand to large, urban, economic, and culturally modern ones on the other. Austrian communes such as Grömingen approxi-

mate the first case and cities like Hallein the second. [80] Between
these extremes fall industrial communes, such as Wattens and Kleinburg, or tourist communes, such as Kleinwalsertal. [81] Naturally
each of these four basic economic types exhibit somewhat different
political characteristics. [82] But the technological and economic changes
that are now transforming the face of Austria's countryside and cities
will lead to an even stronger and more competitive party system in
Austria's periphery, for one-party dominance and the overlap of political and economic elites are most prevalent in Austria's rural and
backward communes. The similarity in the political structures and
behavior in Austria's center and periphery is thus bound to increase.

The experience of Kleinwalsertal illustrates the consequences
of these economic changes for politics. The transformation of the
valley's economy from agriculture to tourism during the last generation is mirrored in the changing composition of the commune's council between 1955 and 1975. The proportion of locally born councillors
declined from about 90 percent in 1955 to 60 percent in 1975. And
among ÖVP councillors the relative number of members of the League
of Austrian Workers and Employees has increased threefold while
the share of the Austrian Peasant League has declined sharply. And
in contrast to the 1970s, it was possible, although uncommon, to be
elected to the council in the 1950s without any formal party affiliation. [83]

But the impact of economic change on Kleinwalsertal's politics
is illustrated perhaps most clearly by describing the transformation
of the valley's political leadership. Before the enormous expansion
in its tourist economy in the 1950s, local political leadership was, in
time-honored fashion, almost hereditary, for it was the prerogative
of only a handful of large, landowning families. Old Mayor Fritz, for
example, had presided over the valley's political affairs for several
decades. His son was predestined to become his successor. He enjoyed the high social status conferred upon him as a member of one
of the valley's oldest families. And in addition, his academic title
and legal profession made him something of a modern priest, in contact with many of the valley's citizens and taking care of their secular
(rather than spiritual) needs. [84] By 1960 he had become chairman of
the ÖVP, a member of the provincial diet, and the valley's deputy
mayor. He was, however, not elected mayor, for the year 1960 represented a "historic compromise" between the valley's old landowning
families on the one hand and the new representatives of the tourist
economy on the other. The mayor who was elected in 1960 (and still
holds office today) had been intimately tied to the valley's tourist
economy, for which he had worked since the mid-1930s, first as an
employee of the valley's tourist bureau and later as a director of its
public lifts. Between 1943 and 1955 he served as the commune's top
civil servant, but he relinquished that post when he was elected to the
commune council in 1955.

From 1960 on the delicate political balance between the valley's old and new economic forces, symbolized by the split between the party chairman and the mayor, gradually tilted in favor of the latter. The party leader lost his seat in the provincial diet after only one term, for he proved unable to cope with the work and responsibilities that were conferred upon him. Over the years his personal life deteriorated; he never married and became a heavy drinker who, with the passing of time, treated his clients and his political obligations more and more irresponsibly. In 1973 he was stripped of the ÖVP chairmanship, and he did not get reelected to the commune council in 1975. His death shortly thereafter was the last symbol of the decline of a once-dominant social order. The mayor, on the other hand, through hard work and consummate political skill began his remarkable career in local and provincial politics, which enhanced not only his own power and status but brought advantages to the commune he helped to transform.[85] These two political leaders, in short, symbolized the conflict between a declining and a rising sector of the valley's economy. They stood for the clash between inherited wealth and high social status on the one hand and earned wealth translated into high social status on the other. Most important, they represented two different political eras adhering to different conceptions of politics. In the end the culture of leisure of the political aristocrat succumbed to the habit of work of the political entrepreneur.

What of the future? The man most likely to succeed the present mayor is his chief administrative aide. Like the mayor before him, he has used his civil servant position to start a political career. In 1970 he was elected to the commune council; in 1973 he became the chairman of the ÖVP; and in 1975 he was elected to the executive council of the commune council. But his political prospects are not certain for his recent bid to be elected deputy mayor failed due to strong opposition among the ÖVP rank-and-file. That opposition was directed primarily against his way of conducting political business. For his style of political leadership is not entrepreneurial but technocratic. He thus represents the politics that characterize Austria's center but not yet Austria's periphery. For one of the most valued features of politics in Kleinwalsertal and the Austrian periphery at large is the direct human contact and the sincere gestures that elevate political relations above the level of political manipulation. The people of Kleinwalsertal may well choose to entrust their political fortunes to the hands of a political technocrat. But if they make this choice, it should be viewed not as callous disregard for one of their distinctive political values but as still another attempt to defend the periphery's autonomy with a political weapon furnished by the center.

CONCLUSION

    This analysis has led to two conclusions that confirm the hypothe-
sis, developed in the chapter's first part, of Austria as a mixture of
the consociational and the federal models. For a number of reasons
spelled out in the second part of the chapter, the distinctive experience
of Kleinwalsertal sheds light on two general questions of political importance: the similarity of politics in Austria's center and periphery
and the interaction between center and periphery. The third part confirmed a key prediction derived from the consociational model, for
there exists a great similarity in the strong position that Austria's
political parties occupy in the political life of both center and periphery. Compared to the other states of central Europe this is a striking difference. The fourth part, on the other hand, confirmed an important prediction derived from the federal model: the periphery is
not a passive object of central control but rather develops some influence over the external influences that impinge on it. In short, center-periphery relations in Austria embody in part the logic of the consociational model and in part the logic of the federal model.
    The strong position that Austria's political parties occupy in the
politics of both center and periphery, and the growing interactions
between center and periphery are interdependent. Congruence in the
political structures of center and periphery facilitates the extraction
of resources from the center and improves the control that the periphery has over its own destiny. The similarity of politics in both center and periphery does not, therefore, mean a submission to power
realities at the center but provides political leaders at the periphery
with the opportunity to defend local autonomy. At the same time the
increasingly complex technological and economic requirements of
modern society will lead to more intimate political relations between
center and periphery. Political contacts with the external world more
often than not will lead to a strengthening of local political organizations and thus help to maintain the periphery's political autonomy.[86]
And as was argued in this concluding part, economic changes now under way in Austria work in the same direction. A survey of 50 Austrian communes confirms this expectation and the conclusions drawn
from the experience of Kleinwalsertal. Austria's periphery will probably retain the influence that it can exercise in its bargaining relations with the center.
    Among the central European states, center-periphery relations
in Austria provide a testing ground favorable to the view that stresses
the pervasive and enduring character of political centralization, for
Austria meets two conditions that many believe reflect and strengthen
centralization. Politics in Austria's center and periphery is remarkably similar and the interaction between center and periphery is in-

creasingly intimate. But the overwhelming weight of the evidence presented in this chapter suggests a conclusion that does not confirm a
linear view of ever-increasing centralization. The very process of
centralization, it seems, establishes conditions conducive to the
preservation of political autonomy. This conclusion, I believe, has
important implications for center-periphery relations both within and
between states. For it suggests that the shape of our political future
will resemble the shape of our political past.

NOTES

1. The terms "center" and "periphery" refer in this chapter
to the territorial dimension of politics. For a good overview of the
territorial dimension of European politics, see Gordon Smith, Politics
in Western Europe: A Comparative Analysis (New York: Holmes and
Meier, 1973), pp. 255-96.
2. Peter Gerlich, "Local Government and Local Politics in
Austria" (manuscript, Vienna, June 1970), p. 17. On the Federal
Republic see Linda L. Dolive, "The Non-Function of German Political
Parties," paper prepared for delivery at the Annual Meeting of the
American Political Science Association, Chicago, 1974; Wolfgang
Holler and Karl-Heinz Naßmacher, "Rat und Verwaltung im Prozeß-
kommunalpolitischer Willensbildung," Aus Politik und Zeitgeschichte,
January 24, 1976, pp. 3-31; Dietrich Fürst, Kommunale Entscheidung-
sprozesse (Baden-Baden: Nomos, 1975); Karl-Heinz Naßmacher,
"Parteien im kommunalpolitischen Zielbildungsprozeß," Österreich-
ische Zeitschrift für Politikwissenschaft 1 (April 1972), pp. 39-65.
On Switzerland see Michel Bassand, "Le Systeme politique local
Suisse," paper prepared for the Workshop on the Comparative Study
of Contemporary Switzerland, Geneva, 1972.
3. Important contributions to the literature on consociational
democracy are conveniently summarized in Kenneth D. McRae, ed.,
Consociational Democracy: Political Accommodation in Segmented
Societies (Toronto: McClelland and Stewart, 1974). More recent
contributions include Hans Daalder, "The Consociational Democracy
Theme," World Politics 26, no. 4 (July 1974): 604-22; Brian Berry,
"Political Accommodation and Consociational Democracy," British
Journal of Political Science 5, no. 4 (October 1975): 490-500; and Jeffrey Obler, Jurg Steiner, and Guido Dierick, "The Burden of Conso-
ciationalism: A Review Essay of Austria, Belgium, The Netherlands
and Switzerland" (manuscript, Chapel Hill, N.C., 1975).
4. On the historic evolution of this system see Adam Wandrus-
zka, "Österreichs politische Struktur: Die Entwicklung der Parteien
und politischen Bewegungen," Geschichte der Republik Österreich,

ed. Heinrich Benedikt (Munich: Oldenbourg, 1954), pp. 289-485.
These different interpretations are discussed in Kenneth D. McRae,
"Introduction," in Consociational Democracy, ed. McRae, pp. 2-27.

  5. See in particular Rodney P. Stiefbold, "Segmented Pluralism
and Consociational Democracy in Austria: Problems of Political Stability and Change," Politics in Europe: Structures and Processes in
Some Postindustrial Democracies, ed. Martin O. Heisler (New York:
McKay, 1974), pp. 117-77; Stiefbold, "Elites and Elections in a Fragmented Political System," Sozialwissenschaftliches Jahrbuch für Politik, vol. 4, ed. Rudolf Wildenmann (Munich: Olzog, 1975), pp. 119-
227.

  6. Die Wahlen in den Bundesländern seit 1945: Nationalrat und
Landtage (Vienna: Verbindungsstelle der Bundesländer beim Amt der
Niederösterreichischen Landesregierung, 1971), pp. 20-21. With
the gradual increase of the SPÖ strength in western Austria since the
late 1960s, this picture is beginning to change slowly.

  7. Christa Altenstetter, Der Föderalismus in Österreich (Heidel-
berg: Quelle, 1969), pp. 69-70, 78-80. See also Felix Ermacora,
ed., Föderalismus in Österreich (Salzburg: Pustet, 1970); Friedrich
Koja et al., Bundesstaat auf der Waage (Salzburg: Pustet, 1969); Institut für Österreichkunde, ed., Der österreichische Föderalismus
und seine historischen Grundlagen (Vienna: Hirt, 1969); Kurt Wedl,
Der Gedanke des Föderalismus in Programmen politischer Parteien
Deutschlands und Österreichs (Melk: Wedl, 1969), and Theorie und
Praxis des Bundesstaates (Salzburg: Pustet, 1974).

  8. Joseph H. Kaiser, Die Repräsentation organisierter Interes-
sen (Berlin: Duncker and Humbolt, 1956), p. 18, quoted in Altenstetter, Föderalismus in Österreich, p. 60; on the Socialist Party, pp.
46-56.

  9. Alexander Vodopivec, Wer regiert in Österreich? Die Aera
Gorbach Pittermann (Vienna: Verlag für Geschichte und Politik, 1962),
pp. 214-36, and Wer regiert in Österreich: Ein politisches Panorama
(Vienna: Verlag für Geschichte und Politik, 1960), pp. 123-28.

  10. Altenstetter, Föderalismus in Österreich, pp. 11-28. See
also Dietrich Katzenstein, Die föderale Struktur der Bundesrepublik
Österreich: Mit Vergleichen zum Staatsrecht und zur Staatspraxis
der Bundesrepublik (Hamburg, 1957). Jiří Klabouch, Die Gemeinde-
selbstverwaltung in Österreich, 1848-1918 (Vienna: Verlag für Geschichte und Politik, 1968); Otto Tschadek, Gemeinderecht und Ge-
meindepolitik in Österreich (Vienna: Volksbuchhandlung, 1965);
Klaus Berchthold, Gemeindeaufsicht (Vienna: Springer, 1972); Benno
Hundegger, Die Gemeinde und ihre Wirkungsbereiche: Eine Zwischen-
bilanz der gesetzlichen Anpassung an die Verfassungsnovelle von 1962
(Vienna: Jugend and Volk, 1971); Hans Neuhofer, Handbuch des Ge-
meinderechts: Organisation und Aufgaben der Gemeinden Österreichs

(Vienna: Springer, 1972); Rudolf Petz, Gemeindeverfassung 1962 (Graz: Böhlaus, 1965); Peter Oberndorfer, Gemeinderecht und Gemeindewirklichkeit: Eine verfassungsrechtliche und verwaltungswissenschaftliche Untersuchung zur Problematik der Einheitsgemeinde (Linz: Gutenberg, 1971).

11. G. Bingham Powell, Jr., Social Fragmentation and Political Hostility (Stanford, Calif.: Stanford University Press, 1970), pp. 40-41, 111-15, and "Citizen-Elite Linkages in Austrian Communities," paper prepared for delivery at the Annual Meeting of the American Political Science Association, Chicago, 1974, pp. 4, 6, 10-14, 15-22; Gerlich, "Local Government," pp. 10-12, 28, 33, 38.

12. A breakdown of Austrian communes by size is given in Gerlich, "Local Government," Table 1, and in Christa Altenstetter, "Intergovernmental Profiles of the Federal Systems of Austria and West Germany: A Comparative Perspective," Publius 5, no. 2 (Spring 1975): 89-116.

13. Altenstetter, Föderalismus in Österreich, pp. 70, 74, 118-19. See also Christoph Pan and Gerhard Marinell, eds., Wirtschafts- und Sozialforschung in Tirol und Vorarlberg (Vienna: Braumüller, 1972); Creditanstalt and Bankverein, Die österreichischen Bundesländer: Vorarlberg 1955-1970 (Vienna, 1973).

14. Harry Eckstein, "Case Study and Theory in Political Science," Handbook of Political Science, vol. 7, ed. Fred I. Greenstein and Nelson W. Polsby (Reading, Mass.: Addison-Wesley, 1975), pp. 96-123.

15. G. Bingham Powell, "Anger, Strategy, and Manipulation as Middle Range Theories of Conflict Behavior: Partisan Conflict in Austrian Communities" (manuscript, Rochester, N.Y., 1973), p. 18.

16. Die regionale Kaufkraft der privaten Haushalte in Vorarlberg: Gemeinsame Untersuchung des Amtes der Vorarlberger Landesregierung und der Kammer der gewerblichen Wirtschaft für Vorarlberg (Vienna: Bregenz-Feldkirch, 1974), p. 19.

17. Das Steueraufkommen der Gemeinden im Jahre 1957 (n.p.: Verbindungsstelle der Österreichischen Bundesländer, n.d.); Das Steueraufkommen der Gemeinden im Jahre 1970 (Vienna: Verbindungsstelle der Österreichischen Bundesländer, 1972).

18. Gerlich, "Local Government," p. 14.

19. William T. Bluhm, Building an Austrian Nation: The Political Integration of a Western State (New Haven, Conn.: Yale University Press, 1973); Walter Jambor, ed., Der Anteil der Bundesländer an der Nationwerdung Österreichs (Vienna: Wedl, 1971); Peter J. Katzenstein, "The Last Old Nation: Austrian National Consciousness since 1945," paper prepared for delivery at the Annual Meeting of the American Political Science Association, San Francisco, 1975.

20. Sozialwissenschaftliche Studiengesellschaft, Bericht 39: Meinungsumfragen betreffend das Nationalbewußtsein der Österreicher (Vienna, 1965); Auszählung No. 36 (Kleinwalsertal) (Vienna, 1965).

21. The historic evolution of the valley is described in J. Fink and H. von Klenze, Der Mittelberg: Geschichte, Landes- und Volkskunde des ehemaligen gleichnamigen Gerichtes (Munich: Oldenbourg, 1891); Christoph Krebs, "Der Anschluß der österreichischen Gemeinde Mittelberg an den Duetschen Zollverband," Ph.D. dissertation, Innsbruck University, 1961. Its tourist economy is analyzed in Peter Hermann Höltl, Der Fremdenverkehr im Kleinen Walsertal (Innsbruck: Wager'sche Universitätsbuchhandlung Innsbruck, 1969); "Die Gemeinde Mittelberg und ihre Sonderheiten" (Riezlern: Gemeindesekretariat, 1975); Sozialwissenschaftliche Studiengesellschaft, Bericht 39, pp. 5-6.

22. Heinrich Jäger, Der Kulturgeographische Strukturwandel des Kleinen Walsertales (Regensburg: Kallmünz, 1953), p. 49, and "Die Gemeinde Mittelberg," p. 7.

23. Die regionale Kaufkraft, Table 2.1.

24. Stiefbold, "Elites and Elections," p. 142.

25. Frederick C. Engelmann, "Austria: The Pooling of Opposition," Political Oppositions in Western Democracies, ed. Robert A. Dahl (New Haven, Conn.: Yale University Press, 1966), pp. 260-83; Frederick C. Engelmann and Mildred A. Schwartz, "Austria's Consistent Voters," American Behavioral Scientist 18, no. 1 (September 1974): 97-109; Frederick C. Engelmann and Mildred A. Schwartz, "Partisan Stability and the Continuity of a Segmented Society: The Austrian Case," American Journal of Sociology 79, no. 4 (January 1974): 948-66; Karl-Heinz Naßmacher, "Das Ende der Lagermentalität?" Journal für angewandte Sozialforschung 15, no. 3 (1975): 3-13.

26. Sozialwissenschaftliche Studiengesellschaft, Bericht 39. The only noteworthy difference was a higher proportion of "don't know" answers given in Kleinwalsertal. Because of the politicization of the valley's life during the last years it is probable that the proportion would be smaller today if a similar survey were undertaken now. But like some other peripheral communes in Austria there exists a stratum of the population, amounting perhaps for as much as 20 percent, that is neither able nor interested to identify and to relate to nationwide political alignments.

27. See the literature cited in the two essays by Stiefbold, "Elites and Elections," and Karl Blecha, Rupert Gmoser, and Heinz Kienzl, Der durchleuchtete Wähler: Beiträge zur politische Soziologie in Österreich (Vienna: Europa, 1964). The Journal für angewandte Sozialforschung regularly carries articles on Austria's electoral patterns.

28. Gerlich, "Local Government," pp. 9, 18, Tables 10-14; Powell, Social Fragmentation, pp. 18-19; Werner Pleschberger,

"Vorarbeiten zur theoretisch-politischen und empirischen Kritik herkömmlicher Gemeindepolitologie," Ph.D. dissertation, Salzburg University, 1974, p. 187; Erich Bodzenta, Industriedorf in Wohlstand (Mainz: Matthias Grünewald Verlag, 1962), pp. 47, 196-99.

29. Alfred Stirnemann, Interessengegensätze und Gruppenbildungen innerhalb der Österreichischen Volkspartei: Eine empirische Studie, Forschungsbericht 39 (Vienna: Institut für Höhere Studien und wissenschaftliche Forschung, 1969), p. 8, n. 13.

30. Interviews, Kleinwalsertal, June 1975. The same also appears to be true of Grömingen, a commune that by all measures is economically more backward than Kleinwalsertal. See Pleschberger, "Vorarbeiten zur Gemeindepolitologie," pp. 176-77.

31. A representative of the Austrian peasant league is traditionally assigned the Ministry of Agriculture. The business league and the union of Austrian industrialists traditionally dominate the Ministries of Finance and Commerce. See Stirnemann, Interessengegensätze, and Kurt Steiner, Politics in Austria (Boston: Little, Brown, 1972), pp. 286-318, 373-408.

32. Anton Pelinka and Manfried Welan, Demokratie und Verfassung in Österreich (Vienna: Europa, 1971); Peter Gerlich, Parlamentarische Kontrolle im politischen System: Die Verwaltungsfunktionen des Nationalrates in Recht und Wirklichkeit (Vienna: Springer, 1972).

33. For data on other Austrian communes see Powell, Social Fragmentation, p. 20; Powell, "Citizen-Elite Linkages," p. 10; and G. Bingham Powell, Jr., "Cultural and Strategic Explanations of Conflict Behavior: Partisan Elites in Austrian Communities," paper prepared for delivery at the Annual Meeting of the American Political Science Association, San Francisco, 1975, p. 23. In one of the council meetings that I attended a contested question was decided by secret ballots. Both the majority and minority whips collected the vote cards in a manner that would have made it easy for them to check on the voting of individual councillors.

34. Karl Ucakar, "Die Entwicklung der Interessenorganisationen," Das politische System Österreichs, ed. Heinz Fischer (Vienna: Europa, 1974), pp. 397-428. See also Theodor Pütz, ed., Verbände und Wirtschaftspolitik in Österreich (Berlin: Duncker and Humbolt, 1966).

35. Some of these factors are mentioned in Gerlich, "Local Government," pp. 20-21.

36. Interview, Kleinwalsertal, June 1975. The quality of partisan competition in a particular commune determines whether voluntary associations are explicitly organized along partisan lines, as is true of Kleinburg, or whether they have a disguised political character instead, as is true of Kleinwalsertal. On Kleinburg, see J. Leitner, "Das Untersuchungsgebiet Kleinburg und seine Umgebung," in

Kleinburg: Eine sozialpsychiatrische Feldstudie, ed. Hans Strotzka (Vienna: Österreichischer Bundesverlag, 1969), pp. 37-43.

37. R. Kneucker, "Austria: An Administrative State. The Role of Austrian Bureaucracy," Österreichische Zeitschrift für Politikwissenschaft, 2 (1973/72), pp. 95-127; Steiner, Politics in Austria, pp. 373-408; Eva Kreisky, "Zur Genesis der politischen und sozialen Funktion der Bürokratie," in Das politische System Österreichs, ed. Fischer, pp. 181-232; Heinrich Neisser, "Die Rolle der Bürokratie," in Das politische System Österreichs, ed. Fischer, pp. 233-70; Franz Berner, "Struktur und Träger der Verwaltung," Österreich: Die Zweite Republik, ed. Erika Weinzierl and Kurt Skalnik (Graz: Styria, 1972), pp. 135-61.

38. Other community studies focus on the local bureaucracy only briefly. See, for example, Gerlich, "Local Government," p. 10, and Powell, Social Fragmentation, p. 22.

39. Herbert P. Secher, "Representative Democracy or 'Chamber State': The Ambiguous Role of Interest Groups in Austria Politics," Western Political Quarterly 13 (1960): 890-909; Kneucker, "Austria: An Administrative State."

40. See the literature quoted in notes 3 and 5.

41. Stiefbold, "Elites and Elections," pp. 128, 177-81.

42. Karl Albrecht Kubinzky and Justin Stagl, Kommunale Eliten im Uland: Eine soziologische Untersuchung im Umland von Graz (Graz: Verlag für Recht, Staat und Wirtschaft, 1971), pp. 39-40, 65. See also the following discussion of Kleinwalsertal.

43. See Gerlich, "Local Government," pp. 6-7, 22, Table 6; Kubinzky and Stagl, Kommunale Eliten, pp. 13-15.

44. Heinz Fischer, "Die parlamentarischen Fraktionen," in Das politische System Österreichs, ed. Fischer, pp. 128-33.

45. Gerlich, "Local Government," pp. 6, 22; Kubinzky and Stagl, Kommunale Eliten, pp. 13, 46.

46. Two such meetings are reported in Der Walser, no. 15 (April 12, 1974), p. 2, and no. 42 (October 17, 1975), pp. 2-3.

47. Dieter Brechmann and Ulrich Jäger, "Der wirtschafts- und steuerpolitische Sonderstatus des Kleinen Walsertales: Versuch einer Analyse der Einkommenswirkungen auf die verschiedenen Haushalte," Ph.D. dissertation, Innsbruck University, 1973, pp. 105-06.

48. Gemeindefinanzstatistik 1971 (Bregenz: Amt der Vorarlberger Landesregierung, Landesstelle für Statistik, 1971), pp. 16-17.

49. Brechmann and Jäger, "Sonderstatus des Kleinen Walsertales," p. 109.

50. Der Walser, March 26, 1976, p. 4. The mayor's strategy is to diminish the political visibility of tax increases by tying taxes to a cost-of-living indicator and to enhance the visibility of subsidies by changing to a system of cash grants. The relationship between con-

flict intensity and resource availability is discussed at length in Powell's study of Hallein.

51. For quantitative estimates of these adverse changes, see J.
Edinger and Robert Wyss, Entwicklungsleitbild der Gemeinde Mittelberg: Grundlagenstudie zur wirtschaftlich-touristischen Weiteren-
twicklung (Innsbruchk/Bern, 1973), p. 34.

52. Rudolf Wurzer, ed., Raumordnung Vorarlberg: Strukturanal-
yse des Landesgebietes; Entwurf des Landesentwicklungsprogrammes
(Vienna: Springer, 1971); Heinz Rill, Die Stellung der Gemeinden
gegenüber Bund und Ländern im Raumordnungsrecht (Vienna: Jugend
and Volk, 1974); Österreichisches Institut für Raumplanung, Der
Planungsspielraum der Gemeinden in der Raumordnung (Vienna:
Jugend and Volk, 1974). A brief description of progress is contained
in Der Walser, no. 21 (1972), p. 3.

53. Vorarlberger Nachrichten, January 15, 1972.

54. Der Walser, no. 32 (1975), p. 2.

55. Edinger and Wyss, Entwicklungsleitbild, pp. 47-54.

56. Der Walser, no. 34 (1970), p. 12; no. 33 (1972), p. 1; no.
42 (1973), pp. 2-3; no. 29 (1976), pp. 2-3.

57. The economic recession after 1973, however, makes the picture more complicated. Der Walser, no. 22 (1971), p. 1; no. 42
(1973), pp. 2-3.

58. Höltl, Der Fremdenverkehr, p. 33; Strukturdaten der Alpen-
länder (Munich: Bayrisches Statistisches Landesamt, 1974), pp. 84-
87; Der Walser, no. 18 (1976), p. 1.

59. Der Walser, no. 16 (1971), pp. 3-4; no. 23 (1976), p. 2.

60. Within a few years the mayor spoke up in public against the
further growth of apartment buildings in the valley, for he had regarded
them as a temporarily useful tool but not the panacea for a modern
tourist economy. See Der Walser, April 26, 1974, p. 3. For an analysis of the relation between political and economic power in a Swiss
village see Ellen Wiegandt, "The Politics of Control: Power and
Wealth in a Swiss Alpine Village," paper presented at the Workshop
on the Comparative Study of Contemporary Switzerland, Geneva,
June 1975.

61. The literature on consociational democracy and Gerlich in
his article "Local Government" subscribe to the former view; Philip
Goldman, "The Periphery as a Model for National Politics," unpublished paper, argues for the latter.

62. Brechmann and Jäger, "Sonderstatus des Kleinen Walsertals,"
p. 108; Der Walser, no. 12 (1976), p. 1.

63. On local government finances see Ernst Kubin, Die Gemein-
deaufgaben und ihre Finanzierung: Das zentrale Problem der Kom-
munen (Linz: Gutenberg, 1972); Elisabeth Langer, Kommunale Auf-
tragsvergabe in Österreich (Vienna: Schendl, 1973); Erwin Weissel,

Möglichkeiten und Grenzen der Kommunalverschuldung in Österreich
(Vienna: Gutenberg, 1971); Erwin Lanc, "Die Gemeinden und der
Kapitalmarkt," Informationszentrum für kommunale Finanzierungen,
no. 3 (Vienna, 1967); Rudolf Wilhelm and Eduard Mayrhofer, Gemein-
definanzen im Wiederaufbau (Vienna: Hollinek, 1950); Ludwig Fröhler,
Die Gemeinde im Spannungsfeld des Sozialstaates: Ein Beitrag zur
Kommunalen Planungs- und Finanzhoheit (Linz: Gutenberg, 1970);
Karl Saindl, Der Gemeindehaushalt: Voranschlag, Rechnungsabschluss,
Rechnungswesen (Vienna: Verlag Jugend, 1972); Erwin Melichar,
"Die Finanzaustattung der Gemeinden Österreichs," Archiv für Kom-
munalwissenschaften 5, no. 2 (1966): 285-302.

64. Interviews, Bregenz, June 1975.

65. There existed a historic precedent to this arrangement in
1848. It is briefly described in Krebs, "Der Anschluß," p. 342.

66. Der Walser, no. 50 (1974), p. 3. The mayor's electoral
campaign included contacting all voters living in southern Germany and
encouraging them to return to the valley to vote; speculations of electoral fraud have lingered on after the district's electoral commission
voided a number of ballots that had been contested by the FPÖ.

67. Der Walser, no. 28 (1972), pp. 1-2; no. 47 (1972), p. 2; no.
52 (1972), p. 3.

68. Brechmann and Jäger, "Sonderstatus des Kleinen Walsertals,"
pp. 56, 75, 111.

69. Der Walser, no. 48 (1967), p. 3; no. 50 (1967), p. 2. A
documentation of the history of the entire affair is printed in Der Walser, no. 51 (1972), pp. 2-3.

70. The obstinacy of the federal bureaucracy united the valley
and resulted in a statement signed by all; see Der Walser, no. 28
(1972), pp. 1-2.

71. Ibid., no. 42 (1972), pp. 1-2.

72. For a comparison with the visit of former ÖVP chancellor
Klaus, see ibid., no. 14 (1967), pp. 2-3.

73. Ibid., no. 8 (1975), p. 1; no. 6 (1976), p. 1.

74. Interview, Kleinwalsertal, June 1975.

75. For a statement of the problem by the mayor after the election, see "Expose," Riezlenn, June 1975.

76. Ibid., p. 7.

77. Powell, Social Fragmentation, pp. 72-73.

78. On Lower Austria, see W. Crane, The Legislature of Lower
Austria (London: Hansard Society, 1961), p. 16, quoted in Gerlich,
"Local Government," pp. 35-36.

79. Gerlich, "Local Government," p. 36.

80. Powell, Social Fragmentation; Pleschberger, "Vorarbeiten
zur Gemeindepolitologie." Vienna is a case all of its own. See Peter
Gerlich and Helmut Kramer, Abgeordnete in der Parteiendemokratie
(Vienna: Verlag für Geschichte und Politik, 1969).

81. Bodzenta, Industriedorf im Wohlstand; and Strotzka et al.,
Kleinburg. G. Bingham Powell and Rodney Stiefbold have collected
a data set on 50 Austrian communes. Some of their results are presented in Powell's papers cited in note 11.

82. See the description in Bodzenta, Industriedorf im Wohlstand,
pp. 47-49; Pleschberger, "Vorarbeiten zur Gemeindepolitologie," pp.
175-77, 203, 211, 220-21; Gerlich, "Local Government," pp. 19-20.

83. Interviews, Kleinwalsertal, June 1975.

84. For a historic analog, see the discussion of the role of the
priest in Charles Tilly, The Vendee (Cambridge, Mass.: Harvard
University Press, 1964).

85. Der Walser, May 22, 1970, pp. 1-2.

86. Powell, "Anger," p. 21.

6

**LOCAL POLITICS, STATE LEGISLATURES,
AND THE URBAN FISCAL CRISIS:
NEW YORK CITY AND BOSTON**
Martin Shefter

In 1975 New York City experienced a fiscal crisis that was more
severe than the financial difficulties any major American city has
faced since the Great Depression of the 1930s. The city was unable
to find buyers for its notes and bonds, and consequently faced the prospect of being unable to meet its payroll, service its debt, and pay its
bills as they fell due. In an effort to keep the city from defaulting,
the state government imposed upon it a series of increasingly stringent
controls, which culminated in the creation of the Emergency Financial
Control Board.

The creation of the Emergency Financial Control Board severely
curtailed New York City's fiscal autonomy. The board was granted
ultimate authority over the city's finances, and a majority of its members were state officials or gubernatorial appointees. Shortly after
it was created the board instructed the mayor of New York City to
freeze the wages of city employees, cut municipal expenditures, and
develop a financial plan that would enable the city to balance its expense budget within three years.

Despite these drastic measures, financial markets remained
closed to the city, and New York State found that the very commitment of its resources to shoring up the city's finances made investors
unwilling to buy state bonds and notes. As the alternatives open to
New York City were reduced, city and state officials asked the federal

I would like to thank Sidney Tarrow for his detailed comments
on successive drafts of this essay. I also have profited from the suggestions of Peter Katzenstein and Susan Harris Shefter, and from a
discussion of this essay with Peter Gourevitch, Luigi Graziano, and
Theodore Lowi.

government to guarantee New York City's bonds. President Ford refused to endorse this course of action, but he ultimately directed the
U.S. Treasury to lend the city the funds it needed to avoid a default.
The president insisted that the city, as a condition of receiving these
loans, adhere strictly to its budget-cutting plan.

STATE LEGISLATURES AND THE URBAN
FISCAL CRISIS

How did New York City get into this difficult situation? The recession of 1973-75 certainly played a role in precipitating these difficulties—just as the Great Depression had led to a wave of municipal
defaults and near-defaults in the 1930s—and the decline of the north-
eastern regional economy made New York City more vulnerable in the
face of a national recession than the major cities in more prosperous
regions of the country. But why did the impact of a sluggish national
economy and a stagnant regional economy hit first and hardest in New
York City rather than in some other declining city in the northeast,
such as Boston? In this chapter I will provide at least a partial answer
to this question by analyzing the fiscal consequences of the interaction
between the state legislature and municipal government in New York
City and Boston.

The sources of the New York City fiscal crisis are many and
complex. But a clue to at least one of those sources can be found in
an incident that occurred in 1976, in the wake of the events outlined
above. The financial plan and the budget prepared by the mayor in
1976 did not propose that expenditures be reduced equally in all areas
of municipal activity. Rather, the mayor proposed that expenditures
for "life-support services"—namely, fire protection, policing, and
sanitation—be spared crippling cuts. Consequently, expenditures for
other services—such as education, social services, parks and recreation—were to be disproportionately reduced.

In order to prevent the implementation of such major reductions
in the area of education, the New York City Board of Education, the
city's United Federation of Teachers (UFT), and the United Parents
Association (UPA) called upon the state legislature to pass a bill (the
so-called Stavisky Bill) that required the city to allocate to education
a proportion of its budget no smaller than what had been allocated
prior to the fiscal crisis. The mayor of New York City strenuously
opposed the Stavisky Bill, claiming its passage would compel the city
either to increase its budget by $115 million or to institute draconian
cuts in other municipal services. Further, he feared that it would
encourage other service-demanding groups to seek to have their claims
upon the city's budget entrenched in state law and, consequently, that
it would utterly disrupt the city's three-year financial plan.

The mayor's arguments had little effect upon the legislature. Both the assembly and the senate passed the Stavisky Bill. Governor Carey did, however, veto it. Thereupon the UFT, the UPA, and the board of education redoubled their lobbying efforts, and though a gubernatorial veto had not been overridden by the New York State legislature in more than a century, both chambers of the legislature voted by comfortable majorities to overturn the veto and to enact the Stavisky Bill into law.

Two aspects of this case are especially worthy of note. In the first place, it illustrates, as much as the creation of the Emergency Financial Control Board, how intimately state legislatures in the United States are involved in municipal affairs. When it became evident that the mayor's budget-cutting plans would work to their special disadvantage, the New York City Board of Education and its clientele groups sought to reverse the mayor's decision by appealing over his head to the state legislature. In the second place, the case of the Stavisky Bill illustrates one of the major sources of inflationary pressure upon New York City's budget. Even when the city faced serious financial problems, the state legislature was prepared to compel the mayor to increase expenditures on education by $115 million.

The case of the Stavisky Bill is by no means unusual. As I will argue below, the state legislature characteristically exerts inflationary pressures on New York City's budget. These pressures contributed heavily to the New York City fiscal crisis of 1975. One reason that the financial problems of a city such as Boston are not as serious as those of New York is that the interaction between Boston and its state legislature does not take such an inflationary form.

State Legislatures and City Government:
Some General Considerations

In order to understand events such as the New York City fiscal crisis, as these examples suggest, one must understand the forces that shape the interaction between different levels of government in the American federal system. Generally speaking, the distribution of power between higher and lower levels of government within political systems is a function of two conditions. The first of these is formal and constitutional: the extent to which legal authority is concentrated toward the peak of the political system or is dispersed among governmental units at the periphery. The second is political and institutional: the degree to which the political institutions linking the center and the periphery—especially political parties and public bureaucracies—are strong and are themselves centralized.[1]

FIGURE 6.1

Political Systems: A Typology of Power Distribution

Political Institutions
(parties and bureaucracies)

		Centralized	Decentralized
Distribu- tion of authority	Centralized (unitary)	Italy France	?
	Decentral- ized (federal)	Germany Austria	United States Switzerland

These two conditions are independent of one another, and hence it is possible to locate political systems in one of the four cells of Figure 6.1. In systems where legal authority is concentrated and linking institutions are centralized, political forces at the center are in the strongest position relative to those at the periphery.[2] In systems where legal authority is dispersed and political parties and public bureaucracies are fragmented, intergovernmental relations are shaped to a much greater extent by local political forces.[3]

In systems where these two conditions work against one another —namely, those located in the lower-left and upper-right cells of Figure 6.1—the situation is somewhat more complex. A large body of literature exists dealing with nations in the lower-left category— nations that are federal in constitutional form but that have strong, centralized political parties. These studies generally find that political forces at the center prevail over those at the periphery, and hence they conclude that as a general rule intergovernmental relations are influenced more by political arrangements than by constitutional forms.[4]

But what of cases that fall in the upper-right cell of Figure 6.1? There are few studies of intergovernmental relations in this category because there are few nations in the Western world in which legal authority is highly concentrated and political parties and public bureaucracies are weak and fragmented. State-local legislative relations in the United States, however, fall squarely within this category. As the two New York City examples cited above show, state legislatures (under the legal doctrine known as Dillon's rule) have virtually unlimited authority over municipalities in the United States.[5] And in the American states, political parties—if they have any organizational existence at all—are effectively organized at the local and not at the state level. What forces shape intergovernmental relations in such a setting? Do statewide majorities composed of rural and suburban interests hostile to the city use the legislature to dominate and exploit the city, draining it of resources and depriving it of the authority it needs to cope with its problems? This is the common complaint of American mayors and a number of political scientists have echoed their charge.[6] Alternately, are interests from the city itself the chief beneficiaries of Dillon's rule because they are able to use the state legislature to overturn local policies that threaten their interests?[7] The example of the Stavisky Bill is consistent with this second possibility, although any single example leaves open the question of which local interests benefit the most from state legislative involvement in local affairs. An understanding of events such as the New York City fiscal crisis depends upon the answer to these questions.

State Legislatures and City Government:
New York City and Boston

This chapter seeks to answer these questions through an analysis of state-local legislative relationships in New York City and Boston.* These cases are similar in a number of important aspects. The state legislatures in both Massachusetts and New York during the

---

*The conclusions of this chapter are based upon a series of 200 interviews with state legislators, local officials, and interest group leaders in New York City, Albany, and Boston conducted in 1968 and 1969. Quotations that otherwise are unidentified are drawn from those interviews. Unless otherwise noted, statements about local politics and intergovernmental relations in New York City and Boston refer to the period of the last Wagner administration and the first Lindsay administration in New York (1962-69) and the two Collins administrations in Boston (1960-68).

period that concerns us had plenary authority over municipal affairs,[8] and political party organizations in both states are fairly weak and quite fragmented.* Moreover, the economic situation and the objective problems faced by the two cities are quite similar. Boston and New York City are the major commercial and financial centers of their respective regions—New England and the Middle Atlantic states —and both experienced booms in office construction and white-collar employment in the 1960s. Further, both cities lost a significant proportion of their manufacturing bases and their middle-class populations in the postwar decades and have experienced a large (though not overwhelming) influx of poor blacks and Puerto Ricans (in 1970, 21 percent of New York City's population and 16 percent of Boston's was nonwhite).

There are, however, some important differences between these cities, differences that make a comparison between the two potentially interesting. As I have already indicated, although the municipal budget and municipal tax rates have increased significantly in both cities over the past two or three decades, New York City's financial problems in the mid-1970s were far more critical than Boston's. In addition, there are major differences in the character of the prevailing political coalitions in New York City and Boston, and in the strategies that are pursued by candidates for public office in these two cities.

An analysis and comparison of these two cases, then, should shed light upon the two questions posed above. First, why has New York City experienced financial problems greater in magnitude than those faced by comparable American cities? Or, stated more narrowly, why did the interaction between the state legislature and local government have a more inflationary impact in the New York City case than in the case of a comparable city, Boston? Second, and more generally, where legal authority is concentrated and political parties are weak (as in both New York and Massachusetts), what forces shape the relationship between higher and lower levels of government?

---

*The attentive reader will recall that I noted above that public bureaucracies provide the institutional means through which authorities at the peak of the political system can dominate the relations between central and local governments. State bureaucracies, however, play little role in the relationship between city governments and state legislatures, and hence cases being analyzed in this chapter—state-local legislative relations in New York City and Boston—fall squarely within the upper-right cell of Figure 6.1.

TABLE 6.1

State Legislation Pertaining to the Affairs of New York City and
Boston

New York City		Boston	
Policy	Bills	Policy	Bills
Civil service	570	Neighborhood	52
Courts	172	Education	8
Education	145	Parks, culture, and	
Housing	82	recreation	7
Independent activities	50	Government organization	
Lands under water	46	and procedure	6
Elections	44	Housing	5
Government organizations		Independent authorities	5
and procedure	32	Business	5
Taxation and finance	32	Civil service	5
Labor	30	Public safety	3
Liquor law	30	Health	3
State aid	23	Welfare	3
Neighborhood	23	Taxation and finance	3
Business	21	Commuter transit	3
Water supply	20	Traffic	2
Health	19	Citizens' grievances	2
Parks, recreation, and		Property and homeowners	1
culture	16	Race relations	1
Miscellaneous	15	Sanitation and pollution	1
Welfare	14	Miscellaneous	1
Traffic	14		
Property and homeown-			
ers	12		
Nonprofit organizations	12		
Public safety	11		
Commuter tax	10		
Commuter transit	9		
Race relations	7		
Consumer protection	7		
Sanitation and pollution	4		
Citizens' grievances	2		
Total	1,473	Total	116

Source: Compiled by the author.

STATE LEGISLATIVE INTERVENTION, THE
RULE OF RECIPROCITY, AND THE
STRUCTURE OF LOCAL POLITICS

Table 6.1 provides some basic data from which one can begin fashioning an answer to these questions; it enumerates by subject all the legislation pertaining explicitly to the affairs of New York City and Boston that was introduced in a single legislative session in each state in the late 1960s.* As the data reported in Table 6.1 indicate, the total number of New York City bills is far greater than the total number of Boston bills—1,473 in the one case as against 116 in the other. Evidently, the state intervenes through legislation far more frequently in New York City than in Boston.

Not only is there a large difference in the frequency of state legislative intervention in the two cases, there also is a difference in the focus of such intervention. As Table 6.1 indicates, by far the greatest number of Boston bills—almost half the total—deal with individual neighborhoods in the city. (An example of such a bill would be one directing the city to construct a playground in a particular neighborhood.) Fewer than 2 percent of the New York City bills could be classified as neighborhood legislation. Rather, the great majority of New York City bills deal with the concerns of functional groups within the city. Legislation that increases the benefits (especially the pensions) of municipal employees in the city is particularly prevalent in New York City. Almost 40 percent of the New York City bills are of this character. By contrast, fewer than 4 percent of the Boston bills fall under this heading, and interestingly most civil service legislation in Boston deals not with broad categories of municipal employees—policemen, teachers, firemen—but rather with individual civil servants or with categories that include only a handful of city employees.

---

*I use the number of bills that are introduced in each legislature rather than the number of statutes that are enacted by each legislature as my indicator of legislative intervention for three reasons. First, the introduction of a bill in the state legislature is often used as a bargaining ploy in urban politics. Second, by relying upon bills rather than statutes, it is possible to increase the size of one's data base without running into the analytical problems that would be introduced if one summed the statutes passed over a number of legislative sessions. Third and finally, the ratio of bills introduced to statutes enacted is roughly identical both between the two cities and across various policy areas within each city.

TABLE 6.2

The Sponsorship of Municipal Legislation in New York City
and Boston

Legislator	New York City Bills		Boston Bills	
	Number	Percent	Number	Percent
From the city	1,384	94	105	91
Not from the city	89	6	11	9
Total	1,476	100	116	100

Source: Compiled by the author.

If Table 6.1 indicates what the legislatures do with regard to
the two cities, Table 6.2 indicates who calls upon the legislature to
intervene in these ways: this table records the sponsorship of municipal legislation in the two states. Here what is most striking is the
similarity between the two cases. In both states, the great majority
of all municipal bills—94 percent of the New York City bills and 91
percent of the Boston bills—were introduced by legislators who represented districts within the city itself rather than legislators whose
constituencies lay outside the city.

In both states members of the city's legislative delegation are
primarily responsible for drawing the legislature into municipal affairs
because both state legislatures observe what might be termed a "rule
of local reciprocity" when they deal with municipal legislation. In
New York and Massachusetts (and in many other states)[9] the legislature will pass a bill that bears upon a single locality if and only if
the legislators from that locality support the bill in question.* The

---

*I do not display any analyses of roll-call votes to confirm this
point because the requisite data are unavailable in the case of Massachusetts and meaningless in the case of New York. The Massachusetts
legislature did not conduct any recorded votes on Boston bills during
the sessions I studied; these bills were either buried in committee or
passed by voice vote. And the New York legislature relies too commonly upon the "short roll call" to make statistical analysis meaning-
ful. On "short roll calls" the clerk rapidly calls the first and last
names of the majority and minority floor leaders, and records everyone in the affirmative who does not explicitly ask to be recorded otherwise. The public records do not distinguish between bills passed un-

conditions under which such a legislative norm will be observed can
easily be specified. When legislators can contribute to their prospects
for reelection by securing benefits for their constituencies;[10] when
the desire of politicians to make a career out of service in the legislature exceeds their ability to squeeze out members of the opposition;[11]
and when a bill has no spillover effects for other districts and is not
regarded as having any broader (and questionable) ideological implications*—in this context and on such pieces of legislation, each representative has a stronger interest in controlling what the legislature
does with regard to his own constituency than he has in sharing control over what it does with regard to other constituencies. In this
situation, logrolling arrangements characteristically emerge and become endowed with normative significance in legislative bodies just
as in other collegial groupings (for example, political parties, universities, balance-of-power systems) patterns of mutual indulgence and
forbearance (ticket balancing, departmental autonomy, recognition
of the internal sovereignty of member states) characteristically emerge
when the domination of others is not feasible and each member finds
it is most prudent simply to protect and enhance his position within
his own domain.

The rule of local reciprocity has important consequences for
state-local relations. It makes members of the city's legislative
delegation the pivotal actors in the relationship between the state legislature and the municipal government. For this reason if one is to
account for the differences among cities in the frequency and the content of state legislative involvement in municipal affairs (such as those
indicated in Table 6.1) one must analyze the forces that influence the
behavior of the city's legislative delegation.

In cities where an old-style political machine is able to dominate the electoral process, the state assemblymen and senators who
are beholden to the machine will not find it necessary to be active
legislatively in order to build a political following for themselves.
The support of the machine is necessary and sufficient to guarantee
their reelection, and the machine itself is not likely to rely significantly upon legislation to win votes.[12]

In cities where such a dominant party organization does not
exist—as is true in most major American cities today—state assemblymen and senators find it necessary to put together their own political
followings in order to win elections, especially primary elections. It

---

der this procedure—which equates absence, inattention, and tacit consent with affirmative support—and those subject to genuine roll-call
votes.

*As it did to the Jacksonians.

is possible to distinguish broadly between two electoral strategies legislators might pursue in this situation. They can seek to win the support of organizations and groups by introducing legislation favored by those organizations, or they can attempt to build a personal following by intervening before public bureaucracies on behalf of individual constituents. Assemblymen and senators who pursue the former strategy are far more likely to introduce legislation that draws the state into municipal affairs than are those who pursue the latter strategy.

Which one of these election strategies state legislators will adopt is a function, in turn, of the local political environment in which they operate. If legislators are to win elections by focusing upon their "ombudsman" role, the volume of personal requests they process must be large enough and the number of votes needed to win elections must be small enough so that the personal following that can be built by responding to these requests is sufficient to guarantee their reelection. Moreover, if legislators are to be able to do favors for individual constituents, they must enjoy access to the agencies that dispense municipal services, and this will only be possible if the interest groups and public employee unions that might defend the autonomy of these agencies are too weak to prevent such intervention. On the other hand, where interest groups and public employee unions are powerful, they will not only be able to prevent legislators from pursuing a constituent service strategy but will also be able to reward legislators who introduce municipal legislation that these organizations favor.

In the final analysis, then, it is the structure of local politics that ultimately determines how often, on whose behalf, and in what way the state legislature will intervene in municipal affairs. In the sections below I will indicate how this understanding of state-local relations can account for the frequency and the focus of legislative involvement in the affairs of Boston and New York City. I will argue that the structure of local politics in Boston encourages state legislators from the city to confine themselves chiefly to intervening in the local administrative process on behalf of individual constituents, whereas the structure of local politics in New York City encourages assemblymen and senators from the city to be far more active legislatively. I then will discuss the consequences of these two patterns of state-local interaction for policy making in the city and for the urban fiscal crisis.

LOCAL POLITICS AND LEGISLATIVE
INTERVENTION: BOSTON

The rule of local reciprocity implies that the way a state legislature relates to a city is a function of the behavior of legislators from that city. What forces shape the behavior of state legislators from Boston? Why, in particular, do they introduce much less municipal legislation than their counterparts from New York City?*

The City Delegation and Legislative Intervention

It is not the case that state legislators from Boston are able to take their legislative functions less seriously than their New York City counterparts because they face less serious difficulties at the polls and hence find it less necessary to exploit every opportunity they have of mobilizing political support. State representatives from Boston tend, if anything, to be more insecure than the state assemblymen from New York City. Although few legislators from either city face serious competition in the general election, state representatives from Boston are more likely than New York City assemblymen to face such competition in primary elections. Of the state representatives from Boston in 1968, 70 percent were challenged by opponents who received 40 percent as many votes as they did in either the primary that immediately preceded or the one that followed that legislative ses-

---

*It might be suggested, of course, that New York City's population is more than ten times that of Boston's and hence if one normalized for population—if one spoke of city bills per capita—the differences between the two cities would disappear. It is not clear, however, how sensible such an exercise would be and what meaning might be attached to such a per capita figure. There is no question but that there are more occasions for legislative intervention in the case of large cities than there are in the case of small cities. Considerations of scale alone are sufficient, for example, to explain why a city that simply is too small to operate an independent water supply system will not be faced with state legislation regulating the operations of that system. But there is no reason whatever to assume that a one-to-one relationship exists between the population of a city and the "occasions for legislative intervention," especially when one is dealing with cities each of which is very large and socially heterogeneous and is situated at the core of its respective metropolitan area. Most of the New York City bills listed in Table 6.1 would make sense if applied to Boston: bills increasing the benefits of categories of civil servants that both cities employ, bills enacting programs to deal with problems that both cities confront, and so forth. That legislation of this character is far more common in one case than in the other is a reflection much more of political differences between the two cities than it is of differences in their size.

TABLE 6.3

Electoral Security and the Introduction of City Bills: Boston
Legislators, 1968*

Bills Introduced	Electorally Insecure	Electorally Secure
More than median number of Boston bills	13	12
Less than median number of Boston bills	12	5

*The median number of city bills introduced by Boston legisla-
tors in 1968 was two. A Democrat is considered to be electorally insecure if in either the primary preceding or following the 1968 session his top opponent received 75 percent as many votes as he. A
Republican is deemed insecure if his top opponent did this well in
either the primary or general election.

Note: .30 < p < .50.

Source: Compiled by the author.

sion.   The comparable figure for New York City assemblymen was
48 percent.   Moreover, as the data reported in Table 6.3 reveal,
those legislators from Boston who are most insecure electorally are
no more likely than those who are less insecure to introduce greater
than the median number of city bills.

The differences in the behavior of members of the Boston and
New York City legislative delegations are a function of the different
strategies they adopt to deal with the political problems that they both
face.   In their quest for electoral support the great majority of Boston legislators adopt a constituent service strategy rather than a legislative strategy.   Instead of attempting to win the endorsement of
organizations by working to pass legislation that would benefit the
groups these organizations represent (or claim to represent), Boston
legislators seek to win the support of individuals by intervening on
their behalf before municipal and state agencies.   The range of services that state representatives from Boston perform for their constituents is suggested by the data reported in Table 6.4.   This table reports the subjects of the letters written to municipal departments in
Boston by one state representative during a five-month period in response to letters he received from his constituents.   These letters
are by no means indicative of the total number of requests for ser-

TABLE 6.4

Letters from One Legislator to Boston Municipal Departments,
January-May 1968

Request	Number
Park maintenance	7
Board-up or raze building	6
Traffic regulations, crosswalks	4
Building inspections	4
Sidewalk repairs	2
Street lights	2
Apartments in public housing	2
Civil service interventions	2
Other	4
Total	33

Source: Compiled by the author.

vices handled by this legislator, since most such requests come to
legislators by telephone or in personal conversation, and are conveyed to municipal agencies in a like manner.*

State legislators from Boston build personal followings by doing
favors not only for ordinary citizens but also for individual civil servants. Legislators appear before the civil service commission on
behalf of city employees to ask that a particular requirement for promotion be waived. They use whatever leverage they have with city
commissioners to place "friends" in temporary positions—positions
that tend to endure for very long periods of time. In addition, they
are able to help city employees secure better job assignments, such
as a transfer from one public works yard to another closer to the employee's home.

A majority of the 105 city bills that state representatives from
Boston did introduce follow this same general pattern: they are efforts to reallocate public benefits to the advantage of the district represented by the legislator who sponsored the bill in question (52 neigh-

---

*While sitting for a half-hour in the office of the legislator whose
files contained the letters classified in Table 6.4, I overheard telephone conversations that obtained larger apartments in public projects
for two of his constituents and a new refrigerator for a third.

borhood bills) or to the advantage of one individual or a handful of individuals (the two bills in the "citizens' grievances" category and three
of the five bills in the "civil service" category). To be sure, the
beneficiaries of the neighborhood bills that Boston legislators so commonly introduce are groups rather than single individuals, but legislation that directs a public agency to build a skating rink or playground
in a particular neighborhood is an effort less to change public policy
than to secure special treatment for a legislator's district. In this
situation, no organization—no labor union or interest group—is involved in the exchange between the provider of the benefits in question
(the legislator) and the recipients of those benefits (his constituents).

Local Politics and the Constituent Service
Strategy

What is it about the politics of Boston that encourages state
legislators from that city to pursue a constituent service strategy
rather than a legislative strategy? The answer to this question is to
be found by analyzing those aspects of the Boston political environment that make it politically profitable and administratively feasible
for state representatives to pursue the former course of action and
profitless for them to pursue the latter.

Political Profitability

In order for it to be politically profitable for legislators to focus
their efforts upon their constituent service role, the size of the following that incumbents are able to acquire by doing favors for individual constituents must be large relative to whatever is required to
win a legislative election. This is more likely to be true the larger
the number of requests for favors that legislators receive from their
constituents and the smaller the number of votes that are necessary
to win a legislative election.

In Boston state representatives receive an enormous number
of requests for assistance in dealing with city bureaucracies because
they are the only public officials from the city who are elected on a
neighborhood level. All elections for municipal offices in Boston—
mayor, school committeeman, city councillor—are conducted on an
at-large basis, and consequently voters tend to contact their state
representatives when they have an individual grievance, even when
the difficulty they wish to remedy falls within the jurisdiction of a
municipal department. There is an additional reason why requests
for favors of this sort are funneled to state legislators. Since James
Michael Curley waged war upon Boston's ward bosses in the early

twentieth century, party organizations have been so weak as to be virtually nonexistent, and hence local political clubs and ward committees are not in a position to perform this function.

State representatives from Boston have an incentive to respond
to these requests because by doing so they can significantly further
their reelection efforts. To be sure, there are just so many demands
that a single politician, who has no staff assistance, can process over
his two-year term—even if he handles ten to fifteen calls a day, as
many Boston legislators contend they do. And the proportion of citizens receiving such assistance who will express their gratitude by
turning out to vote on primary day—let alone by working in the campaign of the politician who helped them—is not large, which further
limits the political payoff a state legislator can receive from taking
his constituent service function seriously. Nonetheless, three aspects
of Boston's political structure make it worthwhile for legislators to
stress this role.

First, legislative districts are small: single-member constituencies average 18,000 in population, two-member constituencies
average 36,000. Second, Boston has a one-party system—in the past
15 years only the Beacon Hill-Back Bay area has sent Republicans to
the legislature—and consequently state representatives need only
worry about amassing enough votes to win in the Democratic primary.
Third, as I already have noted, party organizations are extremely
weak in Boston: in Boston as in the American South, a one-party
politics has issued in a no-party politics. [13] Because party organizations are weak, no candidate in primary elections has an insurmountable advantage over his rivals, and hence numerous candidates are
encouraged to enter the primary. (In 1966, 104 candidates contested
for the 36 house seats in the Democratic primary.) This proliferation
of candidacies fragments the primary vote and further reduces the
number of votes a legislator must receive to secure renomination and
hence reelection. In 1966, the median vote received by the winning
candidates in the Democratic primary for state representative in Boston was only 3,530 votes.

State legislators in Boston, then, find it politically rewarding
to act as ombudsmen because they receive a large number of requests
for personal assistance and because they need win so few votes in order to be assured of renomination and reelection.

Administrative Feasibility

If legislators are to pursue a constituent service strategy they
must be able to influence the distribution of municipal services.
State representatives in Boston gain access to municipal service bureaucracies by dealing with the administrators of municipal agencies
and by entering into alliances with lower-level civil servants.

In Boston the administrators of municipal agencies are prepared
to allocate public services according to political demand because they
generally are not professionally oriented and their departments are
not bureaucratically structured. Municipal agencies in Boston are
of this character because the social forces—particularly the upper
middle classes and their civic associations—that in other cities support the professionalization and bureaucratization of municipal agencies are politically weak in Boston. Because these groups are weak
they are unable to provide effective political backing to municipal department heads who might wish to resist the demands of favor-seeking
politicians.[14] And because of the weakness of these groups, it has
not been politically useful for Boston's mayors to appoint officials
with professional credentials and identifications to high administrative
positions.* Rather than seeking the support of civic associations and
the upper middle classes, Mayors Hynes and Collins, in particular,
won election by constructing a coalition of downtown business leaders
and politicians who had followings in the city's working- and lower-
middle-class neighborhoods. Hynes and Collins won the support of
the city's business elite by sponsoring an ambitious program of downtown redevelopment, and they won the support of these politicians by
appointing them to positions in their administrations and by granting
them access to municipal departments.

The case of two municipal agencies can be cited to illustrate
the implications that the electoral and governing strategies of Boston's
mayors have for administrative behavior in the city. The first involves the Boston Housing Authority (BHA), which supervises the fed-
erally financed public housing program in Boston. The BHA is run
by a three-member board. Mayors have treated positions on the board
as part of their patronage, appointing to these positions local politicians, the leaders of building trades unions, and so forth. The members of the board, in turn, have used their authority to benefit their
friends and allies. Jobs in the BHA, supplies, and apartments in desirable housing projects were distributed to individuals who had political contacts. As one state representative from Boston remarked:

> You have to know a politician if you want to get into one of
> the better housing projects, like the ones in Brighton or
> Roslindate [two middle-class Boston neighborhoods]. If

---

*To cite an admittedly extreme example, the first three men ap-
pointed as parks commissioner by Mayor Collins were respectively
a parks department groundskeeper who had contributed to his campaign, his chauffeur, and the personal aide responsible for pushing
his wheelchair.

you've ever been to one of the good housing projects for
the elderly you'll notice that there are an awful lot of
Pontiac Catalinas and Oldsmobiles parked outside. They
belong to retired fire lieutenants and police captains who
are friends of state reps.

For three years in the 1960s the BHA operated without a chief
executive officer, because the members of the board found it easier
that way to delve into matters of administrative detail. The board
turned a deaf ear to demands by the press, civic associations, univer-
sity-connected activists, and civil rights groups that a professionally
competent administrator be appointed until it became clear that it
would be necessary to do so if Boston were to receive any additional
funds from Washington. The new administrator, however, found himself to be powerless. His nominal subordinates refused to attend
meetings that he called or to follow his directives. The managers of
individual housing projects often would simply refuse to give apartments to tenants sent to them by the Central Office of Tenant Selection he had established, and they continued to be assigned apartments
in the old way. When the administrator attempted to call his subordinates to account, they simply would appeal over his head to the
board.[15] This effort to reform the BHA foundered because the groups
responsible for the hiring of a professional administrator were not
strong enough to provide him with the backing he would have needed
to insulate the BHA from "political interference."
       The Boston Redevelopment Authority (BRA) stands as an excep-
tion to this pattern—but it is an exception that proves the rule. Mayor
Collins, as I have noted, sought to win the support of the downtown
business community by sponsoring an extensive urban renewal program. To accomplish this end, Collins hired Edward Logue, the man
chiefly responsible for the success of Mayor Richard Lee's urban renewal program in New Haven, as Boston's Redevelopment Administrator. Logue insisted as a condition of coming to Boston that he be
given complete authority to hire his own subordinates and to run his
own shop. Collins acceded, and the old employees of the BRA, who
were connected with the other element of Collins' constituency, were
shunted off to a separate division of the authority. During Logue's
tenure, state representatives and other local politicians were unable
to influence the administration of his redevelopment program because
Logue was able to turn a deaf ear to the entreaties of favor-seeking
politicians because he (and they) well knew that the mayor would support him in any conflict with such politicians. Collins, in turn, would
back Logue because doing so was a condition of his retaining the support of the downtown business community. Business interests in Boston, however, were not deeply concerned with the way municipal agen-

cies other than the BRA were administered, and consequently during
the Collins administration local politicians continued to enjoy access
to these departments.

State representatives are able to gain access to municipal departments in Boston not only by contacting the heads of these agencies
but also by dealing directly with lower-level civil servants. By channeling their requests directly to "street level bureaucrats"[16] legislators often are able to get speedier and more reliable service than
by beginning at the top. As one of Mayor Collins' lobbyists at the
state house noted:

> If a guy has been in the legislature for a number of years,
> he can establish pretty extensive contacts in the depart-
> ments. Why, Jim Kelly and John Tynan [two long-time
> state representatives] knew more people in the municipal
> service than I did.

Civil servants respond to these requests because they find it
useful to enter into alliances as individuals with local politicians.
Such alliances are feasible because local politicians are able to help
individual city employees secure jobs, promotions, and better assignments, and this is possible because the political forces that defend
the integrity of the civil service system in other cities either do not
attempt to do so or are too weak to do so in Boston. In particular,
civil service unions, which in a city such as New York serve as the
chief organizational defenders of the autonomy of the civil service,
did not, at least through the mid-1960s, serve this function in Boston.
City employee organizations, to be sure, did exist in Boston, but
they took on a character rather different from that of their New York
City counterparts.

Civil service unions in New York City are characterized in
Max Weber's terminology by a "legal-rational" administrative style.[17]
They seek to advance the interests of their members collectively and
to prevent politicians from intervening in the civil service on a case-
by-case basis. City employee organizations in Boston, through the
1960s at least, were, by contrast, characterized by a "patrimonial"
administrative style. Rather than seeking to insulate the civil service from case-by-case intervention and to "collectivize" the relationship between civil servants and politicians, city employee organizations in Boston served as intermediaries or brokers in the transactions between individual civil servants and individual politicians. The
leader of a city employee organization might, for example, put one
of his members who had a grievance against his supervisor in contact
with a politician who could use his influence to remedy that grievance.
The civil servant, in turn, will heed requests for favors the politician

funnels his way. An official of one major city employee union in Boston, the Building Service Employees International Union (BSEIU), explained what he did for his members in these terms:

> Of course political connections can get you a promotion or
> a better assignment. Why not? It's human nature to try
> to help your friends: you'd do it too. I tell my members
> that I know more politicians than any of them do, so I can
> get things for them that they couldn't get for themselves.

Civil service unions in Boston, then, do not stand in the way of state legislators' pursuing a constituent service strategy. Indeed, they facilitate such a strategy.

The alliances that state legislators enter into with city employees in Boston not only facilitate the adoption by legislators of a constituent service strategy; they also discourage the introduction of civil service legislation of the type that is so prevalent in New York City. Civil service unions in Boston cannot get their members to campaign for legislators who introduce such legislation—for to do so would involve forgoing the opportunity to reap individual credit for one's campaigning. Hence state representatives have little incentive to sponsor bills that would benefit large numbers of city employees. Indeed, when one speaks to Boston legislators of "civil service bills," they interpret this to mean bills that would reclassify a single civil servant or that would increase the compensation grade of a civil service title occupied by a few city employees. Such bills, which simply are not to be found in New York City, represent the efforts of individual city employees to improve their position relative to that of their co-workers through political connections.

LOCAL POLITICS AND LEGISLATIVE
INTERVENTION: NEW YORK CITY

The state legislature in Albany intervenes into the affairs of New York City much more frequently than the Massachusetts legislature involves itself in the affairs of Boston. It does so because state assemblymen and senators from New York City introduce a much larger volume of municipal legislation than do their Boston counterparts. In this section I will analyze the forces that influence the behavior of the members of New York City's legislative delegation.

FIGURE 6.2

Legislation Introduced and Primary Elections

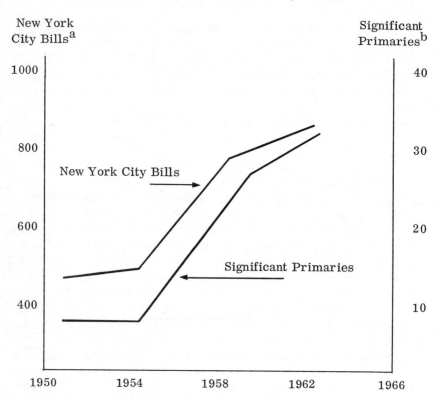

New York
City Bills[a]

Significant
Primaries[b]

[a]Excludes duplicate senate and assembly bills.
[b]As defined in text.

The City Delegation and Legislative Intervention

Figure 6.2 suggests why assemblymen and senators from New York City introduce so much municipal legislation. This figure records the changes through time in two indicators: the number of New York City bills considered by the state legislature and the number of legislative primary elections in New York City in which the losing candidate received at least 40 percent as many votes as the winning candidate. The first of these is the indicator we have been using for state legislative involvement in the city's affairs, while the second is an indicator of the strength of the local Democratic Party organizations in New York City.[18] Evidently, as increasing numbers of state legislators have found the endorsement of the local party organization insufficient to guarantee their return to office, they have searched for other sources of support by introducing legislation that would appeal to other groups. The case of one veteran assemblyman illustrates the adjustment that legislators from New York City have made as party organizations in the city have declined in strength:

> Until a couple of years ago I never had to worry about being
> reelected. My club would handle everything. But I guess
> that people are just not interested in politics anymore:
> they don't come down to the club like they used to. . . .
> My opponent this time is an attractive kid whose wife has
> a lot of money and they're trying to buy him a seat in the
> assembly. They're handing out free shopping bags at all
> the supermarkets, putting two, three signs on every street
> light, shaking hands at the subway stations while I'm up
> here attending to legislative business. But I'm not worried:
> he won't be able to match my troops. In the last few years
> I've passed some bills for the line organizations [that is,
> civil service unions]. I've never had to ask for help be-
> fore, but now they're being good to me. They'll pour in
> by the hundreds.

If assemblymen and senators from New York City introduce city bills in the state legislature as a means of coping with electoral insecurity, one would expect that the legislators who are least insecure would find it least necessary to pursue such a strategy. Party organizations in New York City have not decayed at the same rate and to the same extent in all sections of the city. Legislators who come from districts—mostly in Brooklyn, Queens, and the Bronx—where old-line political clubs are still able to control the primaries should find it unnecessary to do more than toe the party line in Albany in order to be renominated and to win reelection.

The data reported in Table 6.5 confirm this hypothesis. In classifying legislators for the purposes of this table, I have labeled as "insecure" those regular Democrats who faced "significant" challenges (as defined above) in their party's primary, Republicans who faced such opposition in either their primary or general election, and all Reform Democrats. (Reform Democratic clubs, unlike the old-line party organizations, are characterized by an intense concern for issues.[19] A legislator who depends upon the support of such a club has reason to fear that unless he proves himself to be an active and liberal lawmaker he may be stripped of his designation; all reformers

TABLE 6.5

Electoral Insecurity and the "Legislative Strategy": New York City
Assemblymen and Senators, 1965*

| | Assemblymen | | Senators | |
Bills Introduced	Insecure	Secure	Insecure	Secure
More than median number	25	9	8	5
Fewer than median number	10	21	3	9

*During the 1965 legislative session the median number of city
bills introduced by New York City assemblymen was seven and the
median number introduced by senators from New York City was thir-
teen. A Democrat is considered to be electorally insecure if he is a
reformer or if his top opponent in either the 1964 or 1965 primary
received 40 percent as many votes as he did. Republican legislators
are considered to be insecure if they fared this poorly in either the
1964 or 1965 primary or in the 1965 general election. Republicans
who did not win by such a large margin in the 1964 general elections
were not thereby deemed electorally insecure because in that election
Republican candidates had to overcome the negative coattail effect of
Barry Goldwater's presidential candidacy.

Note: For assemblymen, $p < .01$; for senators, $.02 < p < .05$.

Source: Compiled by the author.

are in this sense insecure.) The data reported in Table 6.5 show that
the members of New York City's legislative delegation who are the
most insecure electorally tend to introduce more than the median number of city bills; those who are least insecure introduce fewer city
bills.

In their effort to establish a record for themselves by sponsoring legislation, assemblymen and senators from New York City solicit
various interest groups in the city, inquiring whether they have any
bills they want introduced. Especially prominent in this regard are
the city's prestigious civic associations (such as the Citizens Union,
Community Service Society, Citizens Housing and Planning Association)
and municipal employee unions (such as the Uniformed Sanitationmen's
Association, UFT, Patrolmen's Benevolent Association). As an official of one major civic association observed:

Many legislators from the city are desperate for bills.
They come to us begging for the opportunity to sponsor one

of ours: "Do you have a bill for me? . . . Please." Assemblyman Abrams got a lot of mileage out of our child
abuse bill. He appeared on a radio program with me
where we discussed the problem. We can also ask a legislator to speak at one of our press conferences. They
know we can get a story in the Times, and that several
of our people have close ties with the Americans for
Democratic Action, the Reformers, and the Citizens
Union.

One reason that legislators turn to these organizations is that
they have neither the time nor the resources to generate legislation
on their own. The job of a state legislator, unlike that of a congress-
man, is not a full-time one: it occupies three or four days of the
week for five or six months of the year. And rank-and-file legislators
(that is, those who are not committee chairmen) do not have access
to staff assistance. A second and more important reason they turn
to such organizations is that the benefits they can obtain by so doing
are considerable. Because civic associations have access to the
press, they can provide legislators with valuable publicity. And civil
service unions are able to provide legislators with direct campaign
assistance: they print campaign literature, make campaign contributions, and, most valuable of all, provide friendly legislators with campaign workers. Legislators claim that the policemen's, firemen's,
and teachers' unions will provide their allies with 20 to 30 campaign
workers. The politically most active civil service union, the Uniformed Sanitationmen's Association, is able to place as many as 150
to 200 men in the campaigns of its major legislative allies and, in
addition, it lends one of the six soundtrucks the union owns to friendly
politicians. The Democratic and Republican clubs in most areas of
New York City cannot mobilize resources of this magnitude and, consequently, as the major party organizations in the city have decayed,
many assemblymen and senators from New York City have grounded
their political careers upon an alliance with the civil service unions.
    An alliance of this sort is especially valuable to legislators with
higher political ambitions because it enables an assemblyman or sena-
tor to build a campaign organization outside his legislative district.
In recent years a number of assemblymen and senators have sought
in this way to make the leap from the state legislature to such borough-
level offices as district attorney, city councilman-at-large, and
borough president. An extreme example of such a strategy—so extreme that it was unsuccessful—involved Assemblyman Leonard Stavisky, the sponsor of the Stavisky Bill mentioned earlier. During the
1969 legislative session, Stavisky steered a bill through the legislature
authorizing New York City to rehire 16 ferryboat officers who had

been dismissed for having participated in a strike. Stavisky was running for the borough presidency of Queens that year, and the union that represented the officers, the Marine Engineers Beneficial Association, contributed $40,000 of the $40,020 he spent in his campaign![20]

Local Politics and the City Delegation

Why do assemblymen and senators from New York City not pursue a constituent service strategy as do their counterparts from Boston? Why, rather, do they cope with electoral insecurity by seeking to build a legislative record for themselves? The answer to these questions is to be found by analyzing the structure of local politics in New York City, for in New York City as in Boston the local political structure determines which reelection strategies legislators from the city will find possible and impossible, profitable and unprofitable, to pursue.

One reason why legislators from New York City do not commonly adopt a constituent service strategy is that, even if it were possible to respond to all the requests they received, they would find it difficult to win elections simply by focusing their energies upon their ombudsman's role. In the first place, state legislators from New York City do not receive a large number of requests for such services. City councilmen in New York City are elected on a district basis rather than at-large, and hence demands for administrative intervention tend to be channeled to councilmen rather than to state legislators. Moreover, party organizations retain a measure of vitality in some areas of the city, and in those neighborhoods voters are more likely to visit the local political club than to speak to their state legislator when they face some difficulty with the city government.

In the second place, the size of the following a politician must amass to win a state legislative election is much larger in New York City than in Boston. The population of state legislative districts is far greater in New York City than in Boston—120,000 versus 30,000 (in a two-member district). In addition, the vote in primary elections tends to be less fragmented in New York City than in Boston. Because the Republicans are somewhat stronger in New York City than in Boston, fewer novices are tempted to enter primary elections in the hope that they may win the primary and hence the general election by mobilizing their friends and neighbors. This very fact raises the threshold of victory in New York City—the median vote received by the victors in the 1966 Democratic primary for assemblyman in New York City was 5,120 as opposed to 3,530 in Boston. This makes it more difficult for legislators to win elections simply by doing personal favors for individual constituents.

These considerations, however, are not fully sufficient to explain why New York City assemblymen and senators pursue a legislative strategy. Even where councilmen as well as legislators are
elected on a district basis (rather than at-large) and where legislative
constituencies are large, it is possible for politicians to win elections
by intervening on behalf of individual voters if these politicians are af-
filiated with a party organization and if they are able to obtain access
to the resources necessary to fuel such an organization. This indeed
was precisely how elections were won in New York City when party
organizations were stronger than they are today, and in the past, as
Figure 6.2 indicates, assemblymen and senators from the city introduced far less municipal legislation than they do currently. The primary reason for this change in their behavior is that today politicians
in New York City find it quite difficult to secure access to administrative agencies and quite profitable to pursue a legislative strategy. The
sources of this development lie ultimately in the increasingly prominent role that civic associations and civil service unions have come to
play in electoral and administrative politics in New York City.

Civic associations—and their allies in the press—play a much
more prominent role in New York City than in Boston politics. In
running for the mayoralty in New York City, candidates are compelled
to appeal far more to what Sayre and Kaufman term "service-demanding" than to "money-providing" groups, whereas in Boston the municipal tax rate is an overriding issue in mayoral campaigns.[21] New York
City mayors annually submit a large package of bills to the state legislature and a lengthy set of proposals to the city council (in 1967, for
example, the mayor's state legislative package included 177 bills)
and the administration turns to its allies in the civic associations to
provide much of this material. By contrast, Mayor Collins of Boston
submitted a program of only 36 bills to the state legislature in 1967,
and in an interview he stated that civic associations were the source
of "a bunch of screwy ideas." Even more important, New York City
mayors, in appointing members to their cabinet, have been compelled
increasingly to select individuals whose professional skills and affilia-
tions meet with the approval of civic associations and the press.[22]

The data reported in Table 6.6 provide an indication of differences between prevailing alliance patterns in New York City and Boston politics. These data record the positions taken by the mayor and/or
city departments in New York City and Boston, on the one hand, and
by civic associations and business organizations on the other hand, on
municipal legislation during the 1966 sessions of the New York and
Massachusetts legislatures. (Memoranda submitted by the Home and
School Association [HSA]in Boston are listed separately, for in contrast to the standard Boston pattern, the HSA is a clientele group that
enjoys very good relations with its "parent" agency, the Boston School
Department.)

TABLE 6.6

Civic and Business Association Activity on City Bills Relative to the
Positions Taken by Municipal Agencies, 1966

	(1)	(2)	(3)	(4)	(5)	(6)	(7) Total
Position of city	Yea	Nay	Yea	Nay	—	—	—
Position of organization	Yea	Nay	Nay	Yea	Yea	Nay	—
New York City*							
Civic associations	44	16	2	3	41	42	148
Business associations	5	6	17	1	1	7	36
Boston							
Civic associations	0	1	2	8	0	0	11
Business associations	2	1	0	0	4	1	8
Home and school associations	1	2	0	0	1	0	4

*The New York City data were compiled from the files of the
minority leader of the New York State Senate in the archives of the
Syracuse University Library. The Boston data were compiled from
the records of the Joint Committee on Cities of the Massachusetts
General Court, the committee that had jurisdiction over most municipal legislation.

Source: Compiled by the author.

The data summarized in columns (1) through (4) are especially
relevant to us because they indicate the stands taken by civic and business associations in the two cities on bills that municipal agencies
either supported or opposed. Civic associations in New York City
took the same position as the city government on 60 occasions [col-
umns (1) plus (2)] and opposed the city only five times [columns (3)
plus (4)]. The balance of business association activity in New York
City was in the other direction: business associations supported the
city's position 10 times and opposed it 18 times. In Boston the patterns of support and opposition were exactly reversed: civic associations supported a municipal agency only once while they clashed with
municipal agencies on 10 occasions. (The HSA, on the other hand,

fought at the side of the Boston School Department three times, and on no occasion in 1966 did it tackle the department head-on in the legislative arena.) Business associations in Boston, in contrast to its civic associations, supported the city's position on three bills and did not oppose any bill the city introduced or support a bill the city opposed.

The pattern of alliances suggested by these data has some important consequences for politics in New York City. Administrators whose credentials meet with the approval of civic associations are inclined to resist the efforts of local politicians to intervene in the administration of their agencies and to influence the allocation of its outputs. (Edward Logue, who was atypical in Boston politics, would feel at home in New York City.) These department heads, moreover, are able to call upon their allies in the city's civic associations and the press to denounce such efforts at "political interference" as they occur. To avoid being embarrassed by such charges, New York City mayors instruct their commissioners to pay no heed to the requests that legislators and other politicians transmit to them. In order to indicate the policy of the Wagner administration on this score an aide of the former mayor recounted the following incident:

> We asked some assemblymen to meet with a few people
> from the Housing Authority to discuss the housing bills in
> the city's legislative package. One of the old-timers pres-
> ent told the Authority people that he'd do his best to pass
> the bills if they'd give him carte blanche on a half dozen
> apartments—let him select the tenants. Of course they
> said no. After the meeting one of the guys from the Au-
> thority came over to me and shook his head in amaze-
> ment: "This guy is supposed to be a lawmaker—and here
> he was asking me to break the law."

Such resistance by housing authority officials in New York City to the demands of state legislators contrasts sharply with the responsiveness of their Boston counterparts and explains why members of New York City's legislative delegation are not in a position to pursue a constituent service strategy.

The practices of the departments responsible for housing inspection in the two cities provide another example of differences in the behavior of municipal agencies in Boston and New York City. The Boston Housing Inspection Department will only inspect a building for violations of the housing code if it receives a complaint regarding that building from a tenant or public official. The New York City Buildings Department, by contrast, runs a "cyclical" inspection program: in designated sections of the city the department conducts periodic inspections of all buildings, whether or not complaints about particular buildings have been received. This program was instituted at the urging of New York City's Community Service Society, the Citizens Housing and Planning Association, and the housing committee of the New York City Bar Association.

There are, additionally, important differences between civil service unions in New York City and Boston that reinforce these tendencies, making it less feasible for legislators in New York City than in Boston to obtain benefits for individual constituents and more profitable for them to pursue a legislative strategy. In Boston, as I have noted, state legislators are able to secure access to administrative agencies by establishing alliances with individual city employees, and civil service unions make no effort to put an end to such behavior. In New York City, by contrast, city employee unions work assiduously to make it impossible for individual civil servants to benefit from relationships with local politicians. For example, District Council 37 of the American Federation of State, County and Municipal Employees strenuously supported legislation to establish an independent health and hospitals corporation, a reform that would further insulate and "depoliticize" the administration of New York City's public hospitals. City employee unions in Boston, by contrast, resisted the passage of such legislation because they feared that such a reform would interfere with the relationships their members had cultivated with local politicians. Or, to cite another direct contrast with Boston, when an officer of New York City's United City Employees Union, Teamster Local 237—whose jurisdiction is similar to that of the Boston BESIU official quoted above—was asked if a member of his union could benefit in any way from political contacts, he exploded:

> An employee in one of the titles we represent could only
> get away with something like that over my dead body! If
> you permit that sort of thing to go on you just don't have
> a union. That's the first thing you have to establish when
> you're organizing: the purpose of a union is to help every-
> one by putting an end to favoritism. . . . Once one of my
> members tried to arrange a transfer from the Bronx to
> Staten Island by getting the two borough presidents to
> write to the commissioner asking for the transfer. The
> commissioner turned it down flat. He knew he'd have
> hell to pay if he tried to pull something like that on me.

The civil service unions managed to reorient public employee relations in New York City during the 1960s by staging a series of strikes, which demonstrated their ability to cripple the city, and by becoming major forces in the city's electoral politics. Mayor Wagner was renominated and reelected in 1961 by switching his base of support from the old-line party organizations to the civil service unions. Mayor Lindsay won election in a three-way contest in 1965 without such support (indeed he denounced the leaders of the public employee unions as "power brokers") but it became increasingly difficult for him to govern the city while maintaining this stance, and he found it necessary to come to terms with the unions—especially the UFT, with which he had been at war—in order to secure reelection in 1969.

City employee unions in New York City do not only make it difficult for state legislators to intervene in the municipal bureaucracy and to obtain benefits for their constituents; they also make it profitable for them to pursue a legislative strategy. The unions have interposed themselves between politicians and city employees, but they have not put an end to all relations between the two; rather, they have "collectivized" those relations. In return for securing the passage of legislation that benefits all the members of a civil service union, legislators now receive campaign assistance from that union, and thus, unlike their Boston counterparts, they have an incentive to introduce such legislation. The rise of the city employee unions in New York City, then, has had implications not only for the conduct of the elections and the behavior of public officials in the municipal arena but also for the behavior of officials in the state legislative arena.

THE FISCAL CONSEQUENCES OF LEGISLATIVE INTERVENTION

The two patterns of state-local interaction that I have analyzed in this chapter have significant consequences for the level of municipal expenditure, taxation, and debt in New York City and Boston. The first of these consequences is a direct one: the very way that the local political structure in Boston encourages state legislators to handle their constituents' requests for assistance leads citizens, in effect, to compete with one another for a larger share of a fixed municipal budget when they seek to improve the services they receive from the city government. In New York City, by contrast, the political configurations described above lead legislators to reformulate the demands of their constituents into requests for the enactment of new and potentially costly municipal programs.

The second consequence is somewhat less direct. The different patterns of state-local interaction in the two cities present groups and interests that wish to see new public services performed in the cities with different opportunities and constraints. The Boston pattern encourages these interests to seek to have the responsibility for administering and financing new urban programs placed in the hands of the

state government, while the New York City pattern encourages reformers to press for the enactment of state legislation that directs
the city itself to administer—and finance—new programs.

In the following sections I will discuss these two consequences
in turn, providing examples from the field of housing policy. I then
will discuss state-local interaction in the area of municipal taxation
and the relationship of taxation to the question of municipal expenditure and debt.

Responding to Citizen Grievances

State legislators in Boston and New York City respond in rather
different ways to the requests for assistance they receive from their
constituents. In Boston, as I have indicated, state representatives
generally find it possible to secure redress for individual complain-
ants by channeling their requests to administrators or civil servants
in municipal agencies. Civil servants respond to state representatives'
requests because legislators are able to help them advance their careers, and municipal administrators respond because they thereby
build support for themselves and for the mayor within the community
of local politicians. State legislators from Boston thus play a crucial
role—a role as brokers between citizens and bureaucrats—in the operation of a system of municipal service delivery that allocates public benefits (for example, visits from city building inspectors or
apartments in desirable public housing projects) according to individual political demand. Since legislators profit politically by performing this brokerage function, they have every incentive to respond to
all expressions of grievance as requests for individual redress rather
than as data indicating the advisability of increasing the volume of
municipal services or reforming their performance. State legislators
from Boston, in other words, play a crucial role in the maintenance
of a system that deals with grievances by making marginal realloca-
tions in the delivery of municipal services rather than in ways that
are potentially far more costly.

In New York City state legislators find it much more difficult
to help individual constituents in this way. If they are to build a personal base of support, they must work through the legislative process
rather than through case-by-case intervention in the administrative
arena. For this reason state legislators from New York City are inclined to interpret and to reformulate the complaints they hear as demands for the enactment of a new law or a new program to remedy
the problems that are called to their attention.

One legislator from New York City, for example, reported in
an interview that the most common complaint he heard from his con-

stituents concerned the difficulties they had in dealing with their landlords and with the city's buildings department. He responded to these
complaints not by contacting the buildings department on behalf of
individual constituents but rather by working to secure passage of a
law establishing the cyclical inspection program described above.
The legislator in question found it easy to acquire allies in this endeavor; indeed, the bill he introduced was drafted by members of the
housing committee of the Community Service Society and was supported
by the city's building commissioner. In short, the political system
on both the state and local levels in New York City encourages state
legislators to formulate general responses to particular problems.
Such responses are likely to be far more costly than the ones characteristic of Boston.

The Process of Reform and the Domain
of City Government

The two patterns of state-local interaction I have described in
this chapter have a second important consequence for city finances.
They present different opportunities and constraints to groups and interests that wish to increase the range of public services in the city.
In the case of Boston, programmatic reformers have strong
reasons to prevent their proposals from being identified as "Boston
bills." Legislation that pertains only to the city of Boston must receive the support of the city's legislative delegation if it is to pass but,
as I have indicated, state representatives and senators from Boston
do not invest their energies in passing such legislation. For this
reason, reformers in Boston have an incentive to search elsewhere
in the legislature for support and hence to propose programs that will
apply throughout the commonwealth rather than just to Boston and be
administered by state agencies rather than by municipal departments.*
The process of policy reform in Boston thus tends to increase the

---

*It is possible for legislation to be of general application and yet
be administered by municipal governments; a law requiring schools
throughout the state to provide special classes to handicapped children
would be an example. However, as I noted above, with the important
exception of the relationship between business groups and the BRA,
the relationships between civic associations and municipal agencies
in Boston are not close. To the extent that they enjoy better access
to state agencies, civic associations in Boston have reason to prefer
that the state administer any new urban programs the legislature
enacts.

powers of the state government rather than adding to the functions
performed by the municipal government; consequently in Boston, in
contrast to New York City, many fewer public programs that operate
in the city are administered—and financed—by the city.

In the field of housing policy, for example, the city of Boston
in the 1950s and early 1960s administered only one program that was
designed to improve its existing housing stock—a program of housing
code enforcement that had been enacted a half-century before. The
city of New York, by contrast, administered more than half a dozen
such programs. In 1966 a group of liberals from the Boston area
sought to catch up with New York City and they successfully pressed
the Massachusetts legislature to enact a package of housing bills that
were modeled on the New York legislation. There was, however, one
significant difference between the Massachusetts and the New York
legislation. In Massachusetts, unlike New York, the bills were
drafted to apply throughout the commonwealth, and the programs they
established were to be administered by the state, not the city. The
process of policy innovation in the field of housing, then, increased
the powers—and the budget—of state government, not of city government.

In New York, by contrast, the process of policy innovation focuses upon the city government. Civic associations in New York as
a rule enjoy better access to municipal than to state agencies, and
hence they wish to have the city administer new programs. Legislators from the city are anxious to sponsor bills providing for such programs, and the state legislature is prepared to pass them so long as
they impose no financial burdens on the rest of the state.

There is an additional reason why the state legislature in New
York passes so many new programs for the city to administer. Policy reformers find it easier to get the state legislature to enact new
programs than to overcome the resistance that old programs run into
while being implemented. The groups whose interests are threatened
by new programs usually are better able to mount protests in their
neighborhoods or to stage noisy demonstrations before the City Council or the Board of Estimate than they are to undertake lobbying campaigns in Albany. Rather than fighting their opponents in the local
arena, reformers often seek to outmaneuver them by securing the
enactment of yet another program. For this reason the state legislature piles program on top of program, and the burden of financing
them all is placed upon the city.

The field of housing policy provides a clear illustration of this
cumulative process. When the city's housing inspection program
failed to solve the problem of housing dilapidation, reformers induced
the legislature to authorize the city to take substandard buildings into
receivership, to collect the rents, and make necessary repairs before

returning these buildings to the control of their owners. The legislature subsequently authorized the city to make emergency repairs in
buildings and to bill the owners for the expense it thereby incurred,
to grant tax abatements to landlords to encourage them to renovate
their buildings, and to grant loans to landlords to encourage them to
make renovations. This list could be continued at greater length,
but it should suffice to reveal how the pyramiding of new programs on
top of old contributed to the city's expenditures upon housing programs
more than doubling (from $216 million to $485 million) between 1962
and 1972.

Municipal Taxation, Expenditures, and Debt

The control that state legislatures are constitutionally authorized to exercise over municipal taxation is even greater than their
authority over municipal expenditures. Nonetheless, the formation
of municipal tax policy in New York City and Boston conforms broadly
to the rather decentralized patterns of state-local interaction that
have been described in this chapter; in both cases the state legislature's interactions with the city are conditioned by the domestic politics of the city. And the interaction between the state legislature and
the city in this field of policy, as in other policy areas, has contributed to the development in New York City of fiscal problems that are
more severe than those of Boston.

New York City

Each December the mayor of New York presents to Albany a
"Christmas list" of requests for new legislation, increased state financial aid, and additional municipal taxing authority. The leaders
of the state legislature and the governor never give the mayor all that
he requests, but after extended negotiations they have agreed almost
every year in the past 15 years to approve additional taxing authority
for the city on the condition that every member of the city's legislative delegation vote for the authorizing legislation.

The mayor employs a number of means to round up the necessary votes. The leadership of both parties—the legislative leaders,
the leaders of the county party organizations, and the governor—generally are willing to put pressure upon their fellow party members
to support the mayor's tax legislation. The mayor regularly an-
nounces that unless the necessary taxing authority is forthcoming he
will be compelled to cut municipal services drastically, and he thereby
is able to mobilize service-demanding groups to pressure members
of the city delegation. And finally, the mayor appeals directly to a

legislative norm of "responsibility"—a norm that New York City legislators always cite when asked to explain their votes on tax legislation ("you can't vote for bills that spend money and then not for the taxes to pay for them—that would be irresponsible").

Through this process the state legislature has voted to give New York City authority to levy an enormous variety of taxes. By 1975 New York City had acquired the authority to tax the incomes of corporations and unincorporated businesses; the stock of financial corporations; certain assets of conduit companies and utility companies; the gross receipts of businesses; admissions to places of amusement and race tracks; cigarettes, plastic containers, and commercial vehicles; the transfer of real property, stocks, and bonds; sales within the city; purchases outside the city by city residents; the income of city residents; and, finally, the wages and salaries of nonresident commuters. The range of municipal taxation in New York City is broader and the rate higher than in any other city in the United States.

The state legislature has increased the taxing authority of New York City so regularly because the process through which it does this, in conjunction with the expenditure process outlined above, is self-reinforcing. On the one hand, the rule of reciprocity has effectively limited the city's taxing authority either to taxes that are inelastic (that is, their proceeds to not increase commensurately with inflation or with economic growth) or to transactions that are mobile (that is, they can be moved beyond the taxing authority of the city). The one exception to this pattern is the tax on the salaries and wages of commuters, a tax whose enactment was the occasion of enormous conflict. It was able to pass only because Governor Rockefeller, who supported it, was at the height of his power and because its rate was set so low by the legislature that it yields only minimal revenues.

On the other hand, the expenditures that the enactment of these taxes make it possible to finance are highly elastic. The establishment of each new program creates a clientele that presses for increasing the expenditures on that program or for the establishment of yet another program to overcome the administrative and political obstacles encountered by the first one. The expenditures upon these programs necessitate an increase in taxes because the revenues from earlier taxes have remained relatively stable. This tax increase both finances service-demanding clientele groups for yet another year and encourages some of the persons or transactions being taxed to move beyond the city's boundaries, thus leading to another round of expenditures and tax increases.

As municipal taxes have increased regularly in this way, the costs of further increases to all the political actors involved have also risen. The mayor cannot but be concerned with the effect of this spiral upon what is termed the "business climate" and the "plight of the middle-income homeowner" in the city—that is, upon the level of investment and employment in the city, and the class and racial composition of its population. If his concern for these values does flag, they can be called forcefully to his attention by the political actors who speak for them—the city's major commercial and investment bankers in the one instance, and politicians who represent lower-middle-class constituencies in the other. The mayor depends upon bankers to market and purchase municipal securities, and their level of confidence in his administration determines the interest the city must pay on its notes and bonds. The mayor must be concerned with the city's marginal homeowners because they are a significant force in municipal elections. This interest, indeed, has become the looming omnipresence of New York City politics: it is not organized for regular action in the city's (or the state's) policy-making institutions, but its spokesmen have recently been able to win elections often enough (for example, the 1969 Democratic and Republican mayoral primary elections and the 1972 Republican mayoral primary) that its presence can no longer be ignored by policy makers.

As for state legislators, they may be willing under pressure to vote for tax increases, but they are well aware that they make few friends in doing so. It is for this reason that members of the city's legislative delegation engage in collusive behavior when the time for voting on tax legislation arrives—why each member of the delegation will agree to vote for a tax bill only if he can be assured that all members (including members of the other party) will vote for the tax increase. With the organization of the Conservative Party, however, which speaks for tax-conscious homeowners, outsiders in recent years have been able to win legislative elections on antitax platforms despite such collusion.

Both municipal and state officials from New York City have thus increasingly faced strong temptations to evade the necessity of raising taxes sufficiently to cover increases in municipal expenditures. The city began to do this in a major way in 1965 when Mayor Wagner requested, and the legislature granted the city, authority to issue short-term notes in anticipation of revenues the city would receive the next year if the electorate in a referendum approved a constitutional amendment increasing the revenues the city could raise through its property tax. The amendment was defeated and the city the next year borrowed additional funds to redeem those notes. Between 1965 and 1975 each of the budgets hammered out in negotiations between city and state officials included some such fiscal "gimmick"—the deferral until the following fiscal year of payments for expenses incurred the previous year and the issuance of short-term notes to cover the difference between current expenditures and current revenues.

In this way the city acquired a large floating short-term debt. The city also, with the assent of the legislature, placed in its capital

budget (the budget financed by the sale of long-term bonds) many expenditures that more prudent hands would have placed in the expense
budget (the budget financed by current revenues). The legislature,
for example, in response to all the pressures described in this chapter, authorized the city to finance through its capital budget some of
its contributions to municipal employee pension funds. It was the
adoption of these financial practices that led to the growth of the city's
short- and long-term debt, and thence to the closing in 1975 of financial markets to the city—that is, which led to the New York City fiscal
crisis of 1975.

Boston

The Massachusetts legislature has not contributed to the development of such an expenditure-taxation-debt cycle in Boston because
it does not regularly enact new programs for the city to administer
and finance, and because it does not authorize the city to levy new
forms of taxation, taxation that finances—or almost finances—further
expenditures. The reason it does not do either of these things is that
legislators from Boston will not unite behind such legislation, and
they will not do so because the political organizations that can pressure state legislators to support tax increase legislation (service-
demanding groups and party organizations) have little political leverage with Boston legislators.

This argument cannot be confirmed directly because proposals
for new forms of municipal taxation in Boston fall so far outside the
realm of political feasibility that they never get drafted in legislative
form. It is, however, possible to provide indirect support for this
argument by citing a stronger case: legislation that ties increases
in state aid to Boston to state tax increases. Even when such legislation provides disproportionate increases in state aid to Boston, members of the city's legislative delegation fail to unite behind it.

A dramatic example of this phenomenon is the Massachusetts
welfare reform bill of 1967. This bill provided for the state to assume the administration and costs of the public assistance program,
and it provided for an increase in state taxes to finance this reform.
Boston's proportion of the total welfare expenditures in the state in
1967 was far higher than the proportion of state tax receipts collected
in the city; hence if this bill were to pass there would be a net inflow
of cash into the city. This consideration, however, was not sufficient
to induce members of the Boston legislative delegation to unite behind
the bill. Their refusal to do so is a reflection of the absence of any
strong linkage between Boston legislators and either the mayor or
service-demanding groups.

The mayor of Boston, unlike his New York City counterpart,
is unable to mobilize the leaders of county or district party organiza-

tions to put pressure upon (at least some) members of the city's delegation because these organizations are too weak to be of any consequence to the state representatives. Nor is the mayor able to get service-demanding groups to pressure legislators because members of the Boston delegation do not seek to build a base of support for themselves by allying with such groups. And, finally, the mayor of Boston is unable to appeal directly to the legislators on the basis of an accepted norm of responsibility or of a sense among members of the Boston delegation that the budgetary difficulties of the municipal government are a matter of concern to them—that his problems are their problems. In interviews members of the Boston delegation do not express any attachment to norms akin to the ones that are spontaneously mentioned by their New York City counterparts. This reflects the fact that the mayor and the members of the delegation do not share a common base of organizational or group support. The structural foundations for a legislative norm of responsibility or for a sense of collective identification between legislative and executive officials such as exists in New York City simply does not exist in Boston.[23]

Indicative of the weakness of the structural links between the mayor and legislators in Boston are the tactics that Mayor-elect White was compelled to employ to pressure members of the Boston delegation to support the welfare reform bill. This bill finally received the support of a majority of the Boston delegation and was able to pass after White pulled an extremely clever political maneuver. At the time he was elected mayor, White was serving as secretary of state, and there is no constitutional or statutory provision in Massachusetts that prevents officials from serving concurrently in state and local office; he was therefore able to threaten not to resign as secretary of state unless the welfare reform bill passed. This would have prevented the speaker of the house from fulfilling his ambition of becoming secretary of state. White's threat induced the speaker and his heir-apparent, the house majority leader (who was from Boston), to call in all their political debts with the Boston delegation. That the mayor-elect had to rely upon such an extreme (and unrepeatable) maneuver to gain the votes of Boston legislators for a bill he strongly supported is a reflection of the fact that the mayor and the members of the city delegation are not responsible to any common set of political organizations or political forces, and that the ties between the mayor and the Boston legislators are not institutionalized. The weakness of these ties means that one of the crucial local political linkages that encourages the New York City delegation and state legislature to contribute to a reinforcing cycle of municipal taxation, expenditure, and debt has not been present in the Boston case.

CONCLUSION

The financial difficulties faced by New York City in the 1970s, as was noted at the outset of this chapter, were more severe than those faced by any other major American city in recent decades. These difficulties were caused by an explosion in New York City's expenditures, taxation, and debt. A few simple statistics indicate what happened to the city's budget in the 1960s. Between 1962 and 1972 municipal expenditures in New York City grew from $2.6 billion to $9.1 billion. This increase in expenditures was financed in part by increases in the grants the city received from the federal and the state government, but the remainder of the increase had to be financed by local taxation and by borrowing. Between 1962 and 1972 the revenues raised by municipal taxation grew from $1.7 billion to $3.8 billion, the city's outstanding long-term debt grew from $5.9 billion to $8.4 billion, and its short-term debt grew from $470 million to $2.9 billion. During this same period the amount of wealth and economic activity in the city—the resources that might be tapped to finance current expenditures and to meet debt service payments—did not grow at a comparable pace, and hence during this period municipal expenditures as a percentage of the value of real estate more than doubled, and municipal tax revenues as a percentage of the value of real estate increased by a factor of more than 1.5. The ratio of the city's outstanding long-term indebtedness to the value of real estate did remain stable over this period, but the ratio of outstanding short-term indebtedness to the value of real estate in 1972 was 1.5 times what it had been in 1962.

In Boston expenditures, taxation, and debt also increased significantly between 1962 and 1972, but the rate at which at least the first two of these figures increased was not as great as it was in New York City. Between 1962 and 1972 municipal expenditures in Boston grew by 127 percent whereas in New York City during this period they increased by 250 percent; and revenues from municipal taxation grew by 88 percent in Boston as compared to 124 percent in New York City. During this decade Boston's outstanding debt did increase more rapidly than New York City's—chiefly as a consequence of the city's ambitious urban renewal program—but relative to the value of real property in the city, the rate of borrowing in Boston remained well below that in New York City. In 1972 Boston's outstanding short-term debt was 1.9 percent of the equalized value of real estate in the city as compared to New York City's 3.7 percent, and its outstanding long-term debt was 6.5 percent of the value of real estate in the city as compared to New York City's 10.7 percent.

There are numerous reasons why American cities—New York City and Boston among them—spent more in the 1970s than in the early

1960s, why they taxed their citizens more heavily, and why over the decade they accumulated far more debt than they managed to retire. Indeed, one can say without exaggeration that the entire structure of American urban politics was transformed in the 1960s by a set of related developments that had major fiscal implications for large cities. First, the relationship between the federal government and local government in the United States was altered fundamentally by the grant-in-aid programs of the Great Society. Second, the rates of political participation among urban blacks increased and the forms of that participation multiplied. And, finally, a coalition between elements of the upper middle class and elements of the urban black population emerged and became a major political force in most large cities. These developments manifested themselves in somewhat different ways in Boston and New York City—Boston did not succumb to these political forces quite so completely as did New York City—and these differences between the two cities can account for some of the differences between their respective budgetary curves.

A full understanding, however, of the background of the New York City fiscal crisis of 1975 requires an understanding of the interaction between the state legislature and the city. As I have argued in this chapter, the involvement of the state legislature in urban affairs over the past decade-and-a-half has contributed, in the case of New York City far more than Boston, to a municipal budgetary explosion. The New York City legislature has passed a large number of new programs for the city to administer and finance, and it has played a role in the emergence of a self-reinforcing spiral of taxation, expenditure, and debt in the city. The Massachusetts legislature, by contrast, has tended to place the responsibility for administering and financing new programs in the hands of the state rather than the city, and it has not authorized the city to levy new municipal taxes or encouraged it to amass more debt.

To say that the state legislature plays a major role in urban affairs is not to say, however, that external forces are responsible for whatever difficulties cities face. As I have argued in this chapter, where the institutions that link higher and lower levels of government are weak or fragmented, political forces at the base of the political system determine the form that the interaction between these two levels of government will take. If one were to assign the responsibility for New York City's fiscal crisis to any set of individuals—assuming that the attribution of responsibility is called for—one could confine one's search to the city itself. But the question of causality is all that has concerned us in this chapter; the question of responsibility must be left to others.

NOTES

1. William Riker, Federalism: Origins, Operation, Significance (Boston: Little, Brown, 1964), chaps. 3-5.

2. For a discussion of the Italian, French, and British cases see the chapters by Peter Gourevitch and Douglas Ashford in this volume. These chapters belong to the growing body of literature that argues that even in systems where both legal authority and political institutions are centralized, local officials are not entirely without bargaining resources in dealing with the central government. The seminal work in this literature is Jean-Pierre Worms, "Le Préfet et ses notables," Sociologie du travail 3 (June–September 1966): 249-75.

3. Morton Grodzins, The American System (Chicago: Rand McNally, 1970).

4. This is the central conclusion of Riker's survey. Riker, Federalism, pp. 123-36. See also Ivo Duchacek, Comparative Federalism (New York: Holt, Rinehart and Winston, 1970), chap. 10. Peter Katzenstein's contribution to this volume discusses the bargaining resources local officials are able to bring to bear upon the central government in one such system, Austria.

5. The movement for municipal home rule has not substantially changed this situation. On the limited significance of constitutional home rule in New York, see W. Bernard Richland, "Constitutional City Home Rule in New York," Columbia Law Review 54 (March 1954): 311-37, and 50 (May 1955): 598-629; and "Statutory and Practical Limitations on New York City's Legislative Powers," Fordham Law Review 24 (Autumn 1955); 326-37.

6. Murray Stedman, "American Political Parties as a Conservative Force," Western Political Quarterly 10 (1957): 395. See, for example, Gordon Baker, Rural versus Urban Political Power (Garden City, N.Y.: Doubleday, 1955).

7. Wallace Sayre and Herbert Kaufman, Governing New York City (New York: Norton, 1965), p. 563; Edward Banfield and James Q. Wilson, City Politics (Cambridge, Mass.: Harvard University Press, 1963), chap. 5.

8. Even the 1965 revision, and purported strengthening, of the constitutional home rule article in New York did not fundamentally alter the situation analyzed by Richland, "Constitutional City Home Rule." Reuben Lazarus, "Constitutional Amendment and Home Rule in New York State," New York Law Journal, October 13, 1964, p. 4; and Frank Grad, "The New York Home Rule Amendment—A Bill of Rights for Local Government?" Local Government Law Service Letter 24 (June 1964): 6. In 1970 Massachusetts adopted a home rule amendment to its constitution. On the consequences of this amendment, see James Spady, "The State Legislature and Boston under Home Rule," unpublished seminar paper, Harvard University, 1973.

9. J. Wahlke, H. Eulau, W. Buchanan, and L. Ferguson, The Legislative System (New York: Wiley, 1962), pp. 144, 145; David R. Derge, "Metropolitan and Outstate Alignments in Illinois and Missouri Legislative Delegations," American Political Science Review 52 (September 1958): 1061, 1065; V. O. Key, Jr., Southern Politics (New York: Knopf, 1950), p. 151.

10. Compare David Mayhew, Congress: The Electoral Connection (New Haven, Conn.: Yale University Press, 1974), chap. 1.

11. Compare H. D. Price, "The Electoral Arena," The Congress and America's Future, ed. David Truman, 2nd ed. (Englewood Cliffs, N.J.: Prentice-Hall, 1973).

12. For a case study of the legislative behavior of machine and nonmachine congressmen from metropolitan Chicago, see Leo Snowiss, "Congressional Recruitment and Representation," American Political Science Review 60 (September 1966): 627-39.

13. Key, Jr., Southern Politics, p. 300.

14. See the discussion of the concept of a "constituency for universalism" in my "Patronage and Its Opponents: A Theory and Some European Cases," Western Societies Program Occasional Paper, no. 8 (Ithaca, N.Y.: Cornell University Center for International Studies, 1976), sec. I.

15. Lewis Popper, "The Boston Housing Authority: A Study of Conflict in Bureaucracy," unpublished senior thesis, Harvard University, 1968.

16. Michael Lipsky, "A Theory of Street Level Bureaucracy," Theoretical Perspectives in Urban Politics, ed. Willis Hawley and Michael Lipsky (Englewood Cliffs, N.J.: Prentice-Hall, 1976).

17. For an analysis of the internal governance of voluntary associations, including labor unions, which draws upon Weber's typology of regimes, see James Q. Wilson, Political Organizations (New York: Basic Books, 1973), p. 221.

18. David Greenstone and Paul Peterson, "Reformers, Machines, and the War on Poverty," City Politics and Public Policy, ed. James Q. Wilson (New York: Wiley, 1968), p. 280.

19. James Q. Wilson, The Amateur Democrat (Chicago: University of Chicago Press, 1962).

20. New York Times, July 24, 1969, p. 40.

21. Sayre and Kaufman, Governing New York City, p. 514.

22. Theodore Lowi, At the Pleasure of the Mayor (New York: The Free Press, 1964). Mayors Wagner and Lindsay, to be sure, did not rely upon precisely the same organizations and social groups for political support. In the social welfare field, for example, the Wagner administration was closely allied with the established voluntary agencies and organizations (for example, the community council, the citizens committee for children) while the Lindsay administration

drew personnel and policies from institutions that considered themselves to be opposed to this establishment (for example, the Ford Foundation, the Columbia School of Social Work). Both administrations, however, were allied with forces that wished to insulate the bureaucracy against intervention by party politicians and public officials who spoke for working- and middle-class constituencies.

23. That legislative norms have such structural roots is an insight that appears to have escaped students of American legislative behavior. Such norms can best be analyzed as the way legislators go about understanding and justifying the political and organizational imperatives that confront them, and as a means by which powerful members of the legislative system justify and exercise their rule in a body that ostensibly is collegial. Such an understanding of legislative norms is far better able than the "system maintenance" perspective of Fenno (even as modified in his more recent work) to account for variations across political systems—such as those described in this chapter—in the character of legislative norms and for the changes through time in these norms. The materials for such an analysis of the development (and decay) of congressional norms lies just under the surface, though unrecognized by its authors, in the writings of David Mayhew, Nelson Polsby, H. Douglas Price, and James S. Young. See, respectively, Richard Fenno, "The House Appropriations Committee as a Political System: The Problem of Integration," American Political Science Review 56 (June 1962): 310-24, and Congressmen in Committees (Boston: Little, Brown, 1973); Mayhew, Congress: The Electoral Connection; Nelson Polsby, "The Institutionalization of the U.S. House of Representatives," American Political Science Review 62 (March 1968): 144-68; Price, "The Electoral Arena"; and James S. Young, The Washington Community (New York: Columbia University Press, 1966).

LOCAL INFLUENCES IN A CENTRALIZED SYSTEM: RESOURCES, LOCAL LEADERSHIP, AND HORIZONTAL INTEGRATION IN POLAND

Jacek Tarkowski

The growing importance of governmental centralization has led students of local power to shift their attention from the problems of the internal organization and functioning of local units to the relationships between local communities and the central government and between local communities and intermediate levels of government. Factors external to the local scene (hereafter referred to as extralocal factors) decisively influence the future of local communities. A high degree of centralization in the organizational system of a society and its system of central economic planning—as in Poland—causes local communities to become highly dependent upon decisions made by external centers.

Terry Clark has observed that "a major variable—or, more precisely, cluster of variables—to be dealt with when considering factors related to community inputs is the characteristics of the national society."[1] This applies especially to Poland and to countries with similar sociopolitical systems. Any analysis of a system of local power should take as its starting point the characteristics of the political, social, economic, and spatial organization of society. It should include the society's principles of political leadership and economic management as well as its basic systemic values. All of these factors should be viewed, of course, from a specifically "local" perspective.

Such an analysis should attempt to determine the location of local subsystems within nationally based social, political, and economic systems. When studying the functioning and the development of local communities, the national system can be treated as an independent variable. Indeed, a full description of the national system would demand a separate study. For our purposes, it is sufficient to isolate a "subcluster" of extralocal variables that determine both the autonomy of local communities and their dependence upon the centers of power. It is the character of the national system that determines the range of duties assigned to all communities and the maximum scope of their independence. Within these boundaries, there is some freedom of action that can be used by various communities to different degrees.

This chapter highlights the ways in which local communities in Poland, acting within the same national system and having the same degree of formal autonomy, can influence decisions of prime concern to them. Hence, the characteristics of the national system are treated as an independent variable and policy decisions as a dependent variable. At the same time, it is assumed that the extent to which local communities can influence decisions within a given system depends on local resources, the structure and quality of local leadership, and the degree of horizontal integration among local organizations. These three factors comprise the intervening variables of the proposed model.

CENTRAL CONTROL AND LOCAL AUTONOMY

The Polish system of local government is characterized by a high degree of uniformity. The structures of local government at a given level are identical throughout the country. Political parties and voluntary associations also have uniform structures. To better understand the model, it seems appropriate to begin with a short description of the organizational structure of Polish local government.

Prior to June 1975, Poland had a three-tiered administrative system. The first tier was composed of 17 voivodships (provinces) and 5 cities with voivodship rights. The second included 314 rural-municipal poviats (districts) and 76 towns with poviat rights. The third level consisted of 4,313 gromadas (communes), each comprising several neighboring villages. The local government at each level was composed of a people's council acting as a legislative body with the council presidium acting as the executive. The chairman of the presidium was also the chief of the local administration.

This chapter focuses on the lower unit of the administrative division, what after 1973 came to be known as the gmina, and, in particular, on the municipal gmina. Knowledge of the municipal system before the reform and some exploratory research done after June 1975, along with the professional interests and experiences of the author, have influenced this choice. The town will undoubtedly be the more interesting object of the study since its political and economic system is more complicated and functionally differentiated than that of the rural gmina. An analysis of the town system will better reveal the mechanisms through which local power operates. For the remainder

of the chapter, the terms "local community" and "gmina" will refer
to towns rather than to rural communities.

As the first stage of a reform of local government and territorial
divisions at the beginning of 1973, gromadas were replaced by gminas.
Each gmina incorporated several gromadas. On June 1, 1975 this
reform was completed. The poviat level was abolished and a two-
tiered administrative system was introduced. Poland is now divided
into 49 voivodships and over 2,700 gminas. The majority of the
gminas, over 2,300, are rural communes that comprise several villages. The rest are municipal gminas and rural-municipal gminas.
The latter comprise a town and its surrounding rural area.

Another important change introduced by the reform was a division between legislative and executive power. An elected council of
the voivodship or gmina, generally headed by the first secretary of
the local committee of the Polish United Workers Party (PUWP),
continues to perform legislative functions. The administration of the
voivodship is headed by a voivode who is nominated by the prime minister. The administrative head of the gmina is nominated by the voivode.
These administrative officials are endowed with a wide range of prerogatives. They are responsible both to the higher level administration and to the people's councils of their communities. People's
councils at the gmina level are subordinated to the voivodship council.
The latter, according to the People's Councils Act, "establishes the
general direction of the activity of the people's councils in the territory of the voivodship and also coordinates their activities."[2] Thus,
there is a uniform, hierarchical system of local government in which
all units at the same level have identical structures, rights, and
duties, and are subordinated to the units at the next highest level.

The local party organizations also have a uniform structure.
The basic unit of the PUWP is the voivodship or town committee, elected at the party conference every two years. The committee elects
an executive and four to five secretaries. The other two parties,
the United Peasant Party and the Democratic Party, have similar
structures. According to the principle of democratic centralism,
town committees are vertically subordinated to the voivodship committees.

Local communities in Poland are not independent political and
economic units. Rather, they are treated as integral parts of the
wider system. The People's Councils Act clearly states that councils
"directing economic, social, and cultural activities bind local needs
to nationwide tasks." They also "aim at the development of their
communities as a coherent, socialist organism, whose existing and
potential resources should be utilized for the further development of
the country."[3] Many important consequences result from these general provisions of the act.

The basic operational and developmental orientations of the
community are defined by its economic plan. This plan determines
the tasks of all the economic organizations located in the territory of
the community over a given period of time. These organizations include communal services, cultural and educational institutions, as
well as the local government. In a centralized, planned economy,
the economic plans of the local community as well as the plans of economic organizations are not merely the sum of the plans made in each
constituent unit of the system. Rather, they are treated as mutually
coordinated and balanced elements of the wider national scheme. The
local budget is part of the voivodship budget and, through the voivodship, part of the national budget. Local communities, to a very limited degree, finance their activities directly from their own income.
However, almost all money raised in a community is remitted to a
higher level of the government or to agencies of the central government. Redistribution of these funds is not made in proportion to the
financial contribution of each unit; rather, it is made according to
priorities established at the central or the voivodship level.

Extralocal factors thus exert considerable influence over decisions concerning the development of local communities. All decisions
connected with sizable investments are made by the voivodship government or by the central ministries acting in consultation with voivodship authorities. Towns have only a limited capacity to invest in
projects. Almost all investments undertaken by the gminas must be
ratified at the voivodship or the central level. In general, relations
between the local community at the lower level and the community at
a higher level, and between the higher level community and the central government, resemble models of industrial organization.

Within the framework of this hierarchical, uniform system,
local communities are highly dependent upon extralocal decisional
centers. Gminas are not autonomous communities, capable of independently determining their own futures. On the contrary, decisions
at the central level can determine the future of all local units, as was
the case in the 1975 reform. Extralocal actors can also determine
the future of individual communities by deciding where to build a factory, a railway line, or a dam. The routine functioning of towns
depends upon the amount of money redistributed by the voivodship government as well as upon decisions made by agencies of the central or
the voivodship government.

There are additional limitations on the freedom of operation of
local governments. In a system of central planning and hierarchical
management of the economy, the local government loses control over
its own economic system. The majority of economic organizations
located within the community are vertically subordinated to extralocal
units and indirectly subordinated to the central ministries. Local

economic organizations are directed from the outside and their activities are externally oriented. Their earnings are remitted to the
voivodship and to higher level economic organizations.

But it would be a mistake to overemphasize the centralization
of the political-economic system of Poland and its influence on the
structure and functioning of local authorities to the point of overlook-
ing the self-reliance and differentiation of the communities. Bearing
in mind the profound role played by extralocal decisional centers in
the life of the gminas, more attention should be given to the influence
of local factors. For instance, the freedom of action of local authorities, their effective autonomy, and their capacity to influence higher
level decisions affecting the communities should also be considered.
Some students of local power in the American tradition have treated
local communities as closed, autonomous systems. Others, concentrating on characteristic features of the Polish system, have been
exclusively concerned with the subordination of local communities to
the central and voivodship governments and their agencies. This latter approach is undoubtedly the more correct of the two. At the same
time, it protrays local communities as the passive objects of central
and voivodship government policy rather than active participants in
the political process.

The domination of the gminas by extralocal actors is by no means
total. To a limited degree, these communities are also arenas of
local politics. Even in the most centralized of systems, centralization has some limits. Those limits are determined, in party, by the
diversity of the constituent units of the system. This diversity forces
higher governments to differentiate the ways in which they deal with
subordinate communities and compels them to leave local communities
with some measure of independence, thus allowing some tasks to be
performed according to local needs and capabilities. A further restriction on centralization is the limited capacity of channels of communication. These limitations make it impossible for central actors
to regulate every activity undertaken at the local level. Finally,
higher authorities are interested in mobilizing local energies and resources. This is impossible to achieve without allowing some local
autonomy.

Unfortunately, it is not possible to specify, at the present time,
the degree to which local autonomy exists in Poland. This is particularly the case in view of the short period of time that has elapsed
since the local government reform of 1973-75. An analysis of local
bylaws would be of only limited value, as they are formulated in such
general terms that interpretation is difficult. For instance, article
4 of the People's Councils Act states that "the people's councils determine the economic plans for the development of their communities
according to directives concerning local autonomy issued by Parlia-

ment and the Council of Ministers."[4] One cannot estimate precisely
the extent to which these plans are mere mechanical transpositions
of the central plan to the local level and to what extent they are the
result of directives from above and of needs articulated from below.

Similarly, article 13 of the above-mentioned act, which gives
the voivodship council the right to direct and coordinate activities
of the gmina councils, is difficult to interpret in practice. Actual
political life rarely conforms fully to the letter of the law. In some
cases, higher authorities might allow less local autonomy than granted
by law. In other cases, the efforts of local leaders or decisions by
the higher authorities themselves might lead to a degree of local
autonomy in excess of that specified in the act or in other regulations.

In trying to establish the extent to which local communities can
influence central decisions, I will not try to analyze all decisions
concerning local issues. The discussion will center around developmental decisions that shape both the future prospects of the community
and the satisfaction of its inhabitants' needs. The importance of
these decisions is not the only criterion on which this choice is based.
Developmental decisions are usually made outside the community.
Hence, an analysis of the decision-making processes leading to them
provides insight into the functioning of the system of center-local
relations and the place of the community in this system. An attempt
will be made to explain to what extent differences in developmental
perspectives and in the levels of economic development and the provision of local services are due to local efforts rather than to the activities of extralocal actors.

THE DETERMINANTS OF LOCAL INFLUENCE

Three elements are of particular importance in attempting to
understand why some communities are passive objects, dependent on
the decisions of extralocal actors, while others are active subjects,
influencing decisions of concern to them. These are local resources,
the structure of local leadership, and leadership role performance.

Local Resources

The analysis of local politics in terms of the use and exchange
of resources does not, as yet, have many adherents in the scholarly
community. To understand the importance of this aspect of local politics, we must not overlook the fact that "influencing the outcome of
decision making, or, more generally, achieving results in interaction,
. . . in all cases is based on access to some form of resources."[5]
What is to be understood by "resources?" Gamson writes:

> In any decision, there exists some thing or weight such that
> if enough of this weight is applied to the decision-maker
> the probability of an alternative being accepted or rejected
> will be changed. This thing must satisfy two important
> conditions to be considered a resource. First, it must be
> possessed by, or more accurately controlled by, the influ-
> encer. He must be able to determine its use. Second, he
> must be able to bring it to bear on decision-makers in in-
> teraction with them.[6]

It seems useful to define "resources" broadly as material means and
objects as well as situations and relations that, when used by an actor
in the decision-making process, allow him to influence the behavior
of other actors participating in this process.

An analysis of the decision-making processes in terms of the
mobilization and utilization of resources allows us to answer the questions of who and what has influenced the outcome of the process. The
answer to the "who" question provides an insight into both the structure of power and influence in the community and wider, interlevel
structures. Determining "what" influences decisions helps to understand what decides the power of particular actors in the local system
and in the community as a whole.

This last problem is very important. The Polish system of
local power has been shown to have a high institutionalized structure. Interlevel relations as well as the relations inside the community are stable. Decisional processes rarely result in changes of the
structure of power and influence or in the formation of new, stable
coalitions. The substance of these processes rests upon the movement of resources in a stable structure of power. Hence, their outcome is more of a "technical" nature (new investments, the distribution of funds, changes in economic plans) than of a "political" character (changes in the power structure). If we were to add to this the
narrow range of local autonomy, without employing the concept of resources, it would not be possible to understand why some communities
are at times able to exert more control over decision-making processes than is allowed by law.

Making use of the data gathered before the 1975 reform and the
results of some preliminary studies conducted in a few towns since
the reform, an attempt shall be made to characterize the main resources available to local leaders in their effort to influence the outcome
of decisional processes. No attempt will be made, however, to evaluate their respective strength or to construct a hierarchy of their importance. The lack of empirical material makes such an endeavor
meaningless. In "The Concept of Power," Clark constructed a "general applicability index" of types of resources, allocating the highest

scores for credit, knowledge, and control of the mass media.[7] Partly
as a result of the wide variety of criteria employed in the decision-
making process, it is not possible to construct a similar index for
Poland.

Consider, for example, the location of an industrial plant.
Sometimes it is the economic effectiveness of the investment that determines where such a plant will be located. In this case, a town
with desirable natural conditions, rich raw materials, and skilled
manpower is most likely to be chosen as the plant site. In other cases,
economic criteria give way to social criteria. Despite unfavorable
economic conditions, an investment could be granted to activate a lag-
ging local economy and to provide employment for the local inhabitants.
In yet other cases, the preferences of the final decision maker cannot
be so clearly defined. Here, the decision is a result of the interaction
of various tendencies taken together with the personal preferences of
individual actors. This is not to say that rigid preferences on the part
of the central or the voivodship government prevent local leaders from
influencing the decision-making process. Rather, it indicates that
local leaders must adjust their actions and the resources they choose
to employ to each specific decisional situation. This section, therefore, will be limited to a brief description of the most commonly employed local resources and their uses.[8]

Economic conditions include a well-developed infrastructure
(water supply and power installations, sewage, transportation and
communication facilities, and so on), skilled manpower, and the existence of industrial plants and service workshops. These resources
are particularly useful when choosing a location for an industrial
plant and when the basic criterion for the decision is economic effectiveness. An industry already located in the town strengthens the
bargaining position of the community. The mechanisms of horizontal
coordination enable town authorities to exploit the resources of these
plants for the benefit of the community. We shall return to these problems later in the chapter.

Natural conditions, such as raw materials, suitable land for
construction, and climate or topographical features, play a role similar to that of economic conditions. Such conditions are favored when
investments are contemplated for the territory of the town.

Money and credit are usually considered universal resources
with "general applicability." In a centralized, planned economy, however, they do not have a universal quality. As has been explained
above, Polish towns finance their needs directly from their incomes
to only a very limited degree. Money granted for local budgets does
not form a pool for free disposal by local authorities. Rather, each
sum in a town budget is destined to finance a specific item in the economic plan. The local government is highly restricted in making

changes within the budget and in using money according to its own
preferences. In a planned economy, there is no free market where
local leaders can freely buy necessary commodities. Goods and services, as well as funds, must be allocated to the community. Ap-
proving an investment for a town means granting a building site and
construction materials, introducing the investment into the plan of
local construction enterprises, and, in the final stage, granting money
to purchase these goods and services. This does not mean, of course,
that the disposal of money is of no importance to local communities.
Money is an important decisional resource, but without any special,
privileged position among many others.

Unsatisfied needs are often a very effective resource. This is
particularly true in a situation where the level of satisfaction of a
given need is significantly below that of other towns. Poor teaching
conditions in the local schools, a shortage of working places, or a
scarcity of drinking water can be important and effective arguments
in favor of building a new school, factory, or water supply plant.
There is always the possibility that a low level of local services will
induce the voivodship government to grant the desired object, even
where the economic effectiveness of the investment is low in comparison to its possible effectiveness in some other place. In summary,
weakness is sometimes a resource.

Support of public opinion is especially effective in cases of
sharp deficits and unsatisfied needs. Demands of the citizens are
not only a signal but also a confirmation that a given need is not satisfied. When the means for the satisfaction of needs lie outside the
community, as is usually the case, local leaders often mobilize public opinion in order to exert additional pressure on extralocal decisional centers. Town leaders use a number of public opinion devices
to promote decisions favorable to their community. These include
proposals set forth in the course of election campaigns and delegations of citizens to the voivodship administration or to the voivodship
party committees.

Resolutions by citizens' meetings, voluntary associations, people's councils, and local party organizations are also useful in influencing extralocal opinion. In one village, permission had been given
to build a school and this project had been incorporated into the poviat
investment plan. The voivodship authorities, however, decided to
postpone the construction of the school for several years. The local
leaders undertook several activities designed to reverse this decision. As one step in this process, the secretary of the poviat party
committee advised the gromada council chairman to form a delegation of villagers to petition the voivodship council to reinstate the
school-building project. In addition, the secretary suggested that
the delegation remind the council that construction of the school had

been announced twice in the election platform of the Front of National Unity. He also advised the delegation to point out that the school had been demanded at many meetings of villagers and local voluntary associations. Thanks to various pressures exerted by the local people and their leaders, to the personal support of the deputy chairman of the voivodship council, and to the mobilization of the local construction enterprise, the school was finally built. [9]

Information is one of the resources that plays a decisive role at the beginning of the decision-making process. Sometimes the decisions concerning the initiation of that process or participation in it depend upon readily available information. Obviously, in the course of the process, information remains an important and desired resource. There are at least four kinds of information of particular importance to local leaders. The first is information about existing possibilities. This gives local leaders the chance to mobilize their resources and to initiate their demands at an early stage in the process. The second category includes information about the priorities of the final decision makers. This enables local leaders to mobilize the resources appropriate to a given priority. The third is early information concerning plans, particularly when economic plans and budget allotments are unfavorable to the local community. This sort of information gives the local leaders time to mobilize resources and make countermoves before plans are finalized by the voivodship. Finally, it is necessary to secure information concerning the workings of the decision process. Included in this category are changes in the structure of support and opposition in coalition patterns and so on.

Access to decisional centers is a particularly important resource. It is necessary if local resources are to reach the final decision makers. It offers the opportunity to present arguments for solutions favorable to the town, to carry on negotiations and present offers of support for various projects using local resources. No less important is the possibility of gaining information through contacts with extralocal officials. As a general rule, the organizational principles of the local government guarantee local leaders access to all governmental and party agencies on a higher level, and to other organizations that have an influence on the life of the community. But, in practice, local leaders experience many difficulties in dealing with some of these organizations. Groups at the center, such as ministries, central industrial associations, and large industrial corporations, can be particularly troublesome.

Sometimes the support of an influential person suffices to gain the attention of representatives of key organizations in the decision-making process. The character of these contacts is also important. They can be highly formalized and conform to bureaucratic routine. Alternatively, they can have an "intimate character," marked by benevolence on the part of representatives of extralocal organizations. This was evident in one town's attempt to get approval to build a school. The key person in the decision-making process was the head of the education department of the voivodship government. This man had previously lived in the town for many years. He arranged for the minister of education to visit the town during a tour of the voivodship. This enabled the town leaders to demonstrate to the minister the inadequacy of existing teaching facilities. As a result, the minister promised to grant some funds for the construction of a new school from the ministry budget.

The right to enact formal decisions gives local leaders considerable potential for regulating the routine functioning of their community. Decisions made by the local council and the head of the town, together with the decisions of the local party committee, mold the functions of the town administration and the operation of economic and service institutions that satisfy the everyday needs of the population. In developmental decisions, this resource is much less important because of the limitations of local autonomy. Nevertheless, in some cases it can be effectively used by the local leadership in order to change disadvantageous decisions made by extralocal actors.

All essential changes involving local enterprise production must be approved by the administrative head of the town.[10] If he finds the change unfavorable to the interests of the town, he can veto it. While the decisions of local leaders can always be abrogated by the voivodship government, there are many examples that show that the veto right is an efficient tool in the hands of local leaders. J. Borkowski offers a typical example of this use of the veto power by local authorities. A local cooperative that provided services for the population of a particular town decided to start production for extralocal customers. A presidium of the people's council ordered this production to stop. Despite numerous interventions by the cooperative, the final decision of the voivodship central of cooperatives and the voivodship administration upheld the decision of the town authorities.[11]

The support of extralocal decisional centers very often results from the application of all the other resources. Gaining this support is usually a decisive factor in determining the final outcome of the decisional process. At the same time, this support can be an independent resource, for at least two subtypes can be distinguished:

- The case in which general policies of the government, though not addressed directly to the community, can be exploited in favor of local objectives.
- The case in which the criteria governing the distribution of desired goods is not clearly defined by higher level actors, or where several communities meet required conditions to the same degree. In such

cases, an appeal to the allegiance of extralocal officials can be very
effective.

An example of the first subtype—the exploitation of government
policies for local objectives—was found when one small town, with
no sewage-cleaning system and no funds to build one, took advantage
of a central government policy recommending the concentration of investment funds and the construction of communal facilities. Two local
industrial plants were proposing to build their own sewage facilities.
After consultation with the factory directors, who proved willing to
provide the bulk of the funding necessary for a common sewage system, local leaders approached the voivodship council. They reminded
the council of the central government's recommendations. The voivodship council was able to obtain funds from the central government
to support this sort of initiative and the sewage system was built.
Many other towns were able to take advantage of this same central
government policy to facilitate the construction of water supply and
sewage treatment systems, boiler houses, and so on.

The second subtype of the use of extralocal decisional centers—
the appeal to the allegiance of higher officials—most frequently occurs when local representatives to Parliament or to the voivodship
council simultaneously hold important posts in the government, in the
party apparatus, or in economic organizations. For example, the
director of a big local machine plant along with its supervising ministry wanted to extend his factory. They proposed to locate the new
branch in a neighboring town. This initiative had the full support of
that town's leaders. It was strongly opposed, however, by the voivodship planning commission, which coordinates investments in the territory of the voivodship. The commission proposed to locate the new
branch in an underdeveloped part of the voivodship. In the face of
this opposition, the town leaders turned for support to the vice-chairman of the voivodship council and to the deputy prime minister. The
former had been elected to Parliament from the town; the latter had
been born there and had previously supported many local initiatives.
From the point of view of economic criteria, the town was in a strong
bargaining position. At the same time, it is doubtful that the branch
would have been located there without the support of these two influential leaders.

Clearly, local communities differ from each other according to
the resources they possess. Some have a wide variety of resources
at their disposal. Others are almost devoid of resources. The well-
endowed communities have, of course, a privileged position in the processes of distribution of finances and other means for various local
undertakings, though it is not always the case that poorer communities
lose out. Only a few resources, such as unsatisfied needs, economic

and natural conditions, exist independently of the activities of leaders, and their possession improves some communities' bargaining position. Application of the other resources demands additional activities, such as the mobilization of intermediary resources, the transformation of mobilized resources into resources appropriate for a given process, and the formulation of tactics for their use. The sole fact that a given resource is in the possession of a local community does not indicate anything about the actual influence that the community can exert on a decision. To understand how local leadership is exerted, one has to analyze the factors that organize, mobilize, and introduce resources into the decisional process. In this analysis, attention will be focused first on the formal structure of local leadership and then on leadership role performance.

Formal Leadership Structure

Before analyzing the problems of leadership role performance, it is necessary to outline the structure of the local political system. This system consists of the pattern of formal roles derived from the occupation of positions in local organizations. According to the results of all the studies of local power carried out in Poland,

> it is highly unlikely that a person who does not hold an institutionally defined position of leader will either be chosen by other leaders as having influence over the decisions made by the local system or be identified by a researcher as one who was influential in a sample of examined decisions. . . . Local leadership was, therefore, defined as a group of people performing roles institutionally defined within the framework of the local political system as leadership roles.[12]

What is the formal structure of the town system and who are the members of the local leadership? The results of the studies done before the reform were, again, generally consistent. Summing up the results of a study of the poviat (the unit later abolished by the reform), Ostrowski and Przeworski concluded that "the local political system should be viewed as a pattern of interaction between the Council, the political parties, and the social and economic institutions located at the territory of the poviat."[13] This observation is also true for municipal gminas, with the provision that a new position in the system of local power should be added, that of the town head.

In a study of the gromada, the lowest administrative unit before the reform, Narojek found that the

> basic consolidating mechanism of the gromadas' political
> system was a personal union between the local people's
> council and political and social organizations, at the level
> of their executives. . . . The local leaders occupying the
> key positions in the local council and in the political par-
> ties also hold managerial functions in the other local or-
> ganizations.[14]

Narojek came to similar conclusions in his study of a small town in
Poland. The primary method of integrating local organizations was
through the membership of their management staff in other organizations that played the role of "local integrators." Table 7.1 shows
the number of managerial positions open to the leaders of this town.[15]

Before describing the functional differentiation of local leadership roles resulting from the diverse tasks and aims of the actors in
the system, another distinction should be introduced: the horizontal
and vertical orientation of the actors. As noted above, in a centralized, hierarchically organized system, every organization and hence
every formal role is subordinated to an organization at a higher rung
of the hierarchical ladder. But the activities of an organization can
be primarily oriented toward the realization of tasks and goals of a
superior organization (vertical orientation) or toward the tasks and
goals of the local community (horizontal orientation).

Typical "vertical organizations" are the large industrial plants
located in the territory of the local community. Their functions are
regulated by extralocal, superior organizations. The local council
and administration are, however, horizontally oriented. Although
they should, in their activities, "unite local needs with nationwide
tasks,"[16] there is no doubt that they act primarily in a horizontal
dimension. The third organizational level with a horizontal orientation
is composed of the town committees of the PUWP and of the other
two parties. One Polish student of local power has pointed out that
"the general agreement of the party leadership and the leadership of
the central [governmental] organs does not yet mean full agreement
in approach to local objectives. . . . In practice party leadership is
exercised rather in the horizontal dimension."[17]

The "horizontal orientation" of local party committees does
not contravene the principle of the hierarchical subordination of the
committees at the lower level of the party hierarchy to committees
at higher levels. According to the party statute, the actions of local
committees cannot contradict the general line of the party or the resolutions of its higher organs. In addition, resolutions and directives
of the party's higher organs must be executed by local committees.
At the same time, within the framework of the general party line,
local committees have "a right to determine independently resolutions
on issues regarding their community."[18] According to Dobieszewski:

TABLE 7.1

Managerial Positions in a Polish Town, by Political and Public Offices Held

Office	Total Members	Heads of Organiza- tions	Other Managerial Staff	Total Managerial Staff
Town people's council	40	15	8	23
Town PUWP committee	15	9	4	13
Town united peasant party committee	5	2	2	4
Town Democratic party committee	3	2	—	2
Town committee of the Front of National Unity	24	19	4	23
Voluntary committee of the activization of the town	37	18	10	28
Other voluntary committees	35	19	11	30
Total	159	84	39	123

Note: The figures in the table indicate the number of positions, not individuals. A single individual may occupy several positions.

Source: W. Narojek, "Organizacje w układzie miasta" [Organizations in an urban community], Studia so-cjologiczno-polityczne [Sociological and political studies] 17 (1964): 41–61.

> Formulating guidelines . . . is not the property of the [na-
> tional] party congresses and the plenary sessions of the
> Central Committee only. In the framework of these general
> resolutions, each party organization lays out the program
> for its territory, taking into account its specific conditions
> and social and economic problems.[19]

In each town, there are numerous formal roles that can be characterized as horizontally or vertically oriented, according to the organization in which the role is performed. The first group of roles
are those performed in the people's council of a town, the local organizations of the political parties, voluntary associations, and some
economic organizations directly connected with service delivery to
the community and its inhabitants. It is from this circle that the local
leadership, narrowly defined, is recruited. The roles they perform
include those connected with the management of the horizontally oriented organizations, the coordination of their activities, and the external representation of town interests. Two roles are of particular importance. The first is that of town head; the second, that of first secretary of the PUWP town committee. The leaders performing these
roles preside over the three basic "horizontal organizations" in a
town.* From this, they derive important prerogatives and the potential to influence all spheres of community life.
    The local leadership is not limited to horizontally limited roles.
In each community, local leaders can also be seen performing vertically oriented roles. This is most evident in the case of directors of
industrial plants. To understand this phenomenon, it will be helpful
to examine the horizontal integration of the local economic and political systems.
    The basic problem confronting local organizations and systems
structured and functioning horizontally is to counterbalance the vertical subordination of local units. The system of horizontally organized
local power cuts across the hierarchical lines of vertical subordination. While the whole institutionalized structure of Polish society is
integrated vertically, the local system demands horizontal integration.
This dilemma is very familiar to organization theorists.

> The principle that the unit of organization should have only
> one superior [the structure of the line dependencies] con-
> tradicts the principle of functional coordination, demand-
> ing the subordination of particular activities to general ob-
> jectives.[20]

---

*As noted previously, the first secretary of the local PUWP com-
mittee is, as a rule, also the chairman of the local people's council.

The integration of the economic-political system of the gmina
is achieved by a complicated system of interorganizational links, special integrational schemes, and existing informal and semiformal
contacts of local organization representatives. The most popular and
most highly effective tool of integration is for the managing staff of
"vertical organizations" to participate actively in horizontally oriented
organizations. Economic leaders of a town are usually members of
the local council and its presidium, as well as of local committees of
the political parties and their executives and secretariats. They also
function in the local committee of the Front of National Unity. In addition to their vertically oriented roles resulting from their positions
in economic organizations, these leaders perform horizontally oriented roles at the local level. The extent of multiple-role performance
can be estimated from the results of a study conducted by the Institute
of Legal Sciences of the Polish Academy of Sciences in 1969. After
surveying 862 gromada leaders, it was concluded that

> just over 20 percent of the leaders hold one position in so-
> cial and political organizations. Nearly half of them (45.8
> percent) hold three, four or even more such positions.
> Nearly one-fourth of the leaders (24.9 percent) perform
> four or more functions.[21]

It seems likely that a study of current gmina leaders would yield similar results. The inclusion of economic leaders in the local political
leadership roster ensures the integration of vertically oriented organizations into the local political system.

Of course, these connections would not be effective if they did
not have "systemic sanction" or were organized entirely through local
initiative in contradiction to the structure of the national system.
The framework of the system of horizontal integration is a systemic
solution. Various ordinances, party guidelines, and governmental
decrees define the rights and duties of local governments, local economic organizations, and their mutual relations. They also define
the principles by which local roles are entrusted to the representatives
of vertically oriented organizations.

All these arrangements are an attempt to resolve a contradiction between the vertically organized structure of the economy and
the operational and developmental imperatives of local communities
viewed as the places where people work and satisfy their needs. As
noted above, the structure of vertical subordination is such that economic organizations are primarily oriented toward their superior organizations and not toward the communities in which they operate.
The problem is not one of the domination of communities by economic
organizations. Rather, it is one of inducing these organizations to

act, at least partially, on behalf of the communities' interests. Since the vertical orientation of the economic organizations is a result of the structure of the national system, it is clear that local communities cannot break away from the system of vertical subordination by themselves. Modification of the system requires a systemic solution.

Coordinative authority vested in the heads of towns and in secretaries of local party committees is an important integrative mechanism. These actors, primarily oriented toward the realization of local interests and endowed with formal prerogatives, can exert influence over organizations not formally subordinate to the local council or to the local administration. At the same time, economic organizations are obliged by law to take part in some local undertakings.[22] As these economic organizations are limited in their autonomy and cannot freely determine the use of their resources, the integration rules make it possible for them to take part legally in activities on behalf of the town.

The organizational system of the PUWP also plays an important role in the integrative system of local communities. A party member, irrespective of his place of employment, is a member of the local party organization and is thus subordinate to the town party committee. The party committee is therefore able to influence economic leaders through the latter's role as party members. This is one way in which local economic organizations come to consider the interests of the town. In addition, the nomenklatura system allows party committees to influence the assignment of important posts in local organizations. No important position in the town can be filled without the consent of the party committee.[23]

Leadership Roles and Role Performance

The local political system of the town, as well as the broader system of local power, will be defined in Almond's terms as "a set of interacting roles."[24] A role will be defined as "an organized sector of an actor's orientation which constitutes and defines his participation in an interactive process."[25] By stressing interaction, a dynamic analysis of the system is encouraged. Of primary concern will be activities connected with mobilization and application of local resources. At the same time, the stress on roles fits our model, in which a role, along with local resources, constitutes one of the two main intervening variables.

According to studies carried out before the 1975 reform, the composition of leadership groups in different poviats and towns was quite similar. It can be assumed that the local leadership groups of different towns have retained their similarity following the reform.

These groups consist of the town heads, the secretaries of the PUWP town committees, and the managers of the largest local economic organizations.

The concept of local leadership is not mere analytic concept. Local leaders usually do form a group, and a vast network of mutual contacts links the key role incumbents of the town. The first secretaries of party committees are the chairmen of town councils. The presidents of the local committees of the two other parties usually occupy the posts of vice-chairmen. The town heads are, as a rule, members of the executives of the party committee, as are managers of local economic organizations.

In many towns, local coordinating committees, or "councils of directors," have been established. They typically consist of the town heads, the secretaries of the party committees, the directors and secretaries of the party cells, and the chairmen of the trade union councils of the larger plants. These bodies coordinate current activities relating to community interests or to the common interests of the staffs of the economic organizations.

All of these institutionalized contacts are reinforced by a network of informal and semiformal contacts among local leaders. Permanent and diversified contacts stemming from multiple-role performance foster the consolidation of the local leadership. This occurs irrespective of the vertical dependencies of the various leaders. All these arrangements facilitate activity on the functional plane, which is much more effective in solving local problems, than on the structural plane, which is dominated by vertical dependencies and rigid institutional divisions.

As has been pointed out in the discussion on local autonomy, the network of formal roles can be treated as a common institutional framework constructed at the central level for all local communities. Hence, the uniformity of institutional solutions is not limited to the formal structure of local government, political parties, or voluntary associations. Macrosystemic factors also standardize the real power structure of a town and its general pattern of interactions.

This tendency toward uniformity is counteracted by numerous factors that cause the same formal roles to be performed differently in various towns. While the common features of the municipal political-economic systems are relatively easy to describe, an analysis of leadership differentiation demands empirical studies of a wide variety of communities.* Having no such research at hand, we can only point

---

*Extensive research on the political system of municipal gminas is planned at the Institute of Sociology at Warsaw University under the direction of Professor J. Wiatr. The research will cover a representative sample of 30 towns that were formerly the seats of poviats.

to some factors that influence the actual role performance of local
leaders. Unfortunately, we cannot go further and show the relationships between these factors and the behavior of the leaders.

Individual factors that form the background characteristics of
leaders certainly influence leadership role performance. Four important background factors are age, education, type of career and political experience, and personality traits. Of course, these factors
do not operate independently. They influence each other and tend to
group themselves into syndromes, forming different types of leaders
and differentiating their behavior. These well-known phenomena have
been analyzed by Jasinska in her study of the sociopsychological characteristics of the leaders of four Polish towns.[26] She identified two
categories of leaders. The first is composed of younger, better educated, and more mobile individuals. Leaders in the second group are
older and usually without higher education. They have lived in the same
town since birth. These findings have been confirmed within the
framework of the International Study of Values in Politics.[27] They
are well known to psychologists and are corroborated by many studies
of local leadership. In Poland, as in other countries, individual
characteristics influence the ability of leaders to evaluate, both professionally and politically, the alternatives open to them. Also influenced by these factors are the selection of objectives, the propensity
for risk taking, the style of power performance, and the perception
of roles.

Another group of factors influencing leadership role performance
consists of specific features of the community. Of primary importance
here is the character of the town economy or, more precisely, the
type and size of the economic organizations operating in its territory.
This feature has a profound impact on the composition of the local
leadership. In towns where industrial plants are small and weak,
with activities primarily directed toward local need satisfaction, the
local government and party committee are involved in a vast network
of interorganizational contacts. They can easily influence and coordinate the functioning of these units. Leadership groups in such towns
are probably numerous but dominated by government and party leaders. In contrast, in towns with a few, large industrial plants, the
total life of the community can be dominated by the plants. The basic
problem of integration in this situation is one of the relations between
local authorities and factory management. There are probably few
leadership groups in these towns and "horizontally oriented leaders"
play less important roles.

The character of a town's economy usually has an impact on the
sociopsychological characteristics of the local leadership. Modern,
technologically advanced industries attract younger, better educated
people with innovative personalities. According to Jasinska's findings,

> This group approves of self–dependence, initiative, and
> decisions based on individual convictions rather than di-
> rectives from superior authorities, as well as of bold
> and ambitious decisions which contain an element of risk.
> . . . Sociometric analysis shows that these people enjoy
> a considerable popularity and are highly liked by the other
> leaders. The analysis also shows that they constitute a co-
> hesive group from the point of view of personal connec-
> tions.[28]

In towns where economic change, usually caused by rapid industrialization, brings about a sudden influx of "modern" leaders, sharp conflicts often arise between the well-settled, more conservative local
leaders and the newcomers. Sometimes, such conflicts can undermine
the integrative system of the community and postpone the consolidation
of the local leadership.

Strong, well-grounded traditions, especially traditions of local
initiative and activities, can also have an impact on the involvement
of economic leaders in community issues and on the consolidation of
local leadership. A similar impact can result from unsatisfied needs
common to the town as a whole and to the local organizations. The
necessity of solving common problems is usually a factor that creates
strong links between community leaders. Organized cooperation on
one issue often provides the incentive to organize cooperation on other
issues as well.

"Centrally defined" formal roles can be modified locally depending upon the configuration and strength of all the above factors. Leaders who occupy identical roles in various towns perform those roles
differently. Local political systems are differentiated according to
variations in role performance and in the solidarity of the local leadership. According to our hypotheses, differentiation between communities in terms of the amount of local resources possessed and leadership role performance determines the influence that communities
can exert on extralocal decisions concerning their development. Despite these differences, the decision–making processes have many
common features. This similarity stems from the fact that they operate within the framework of the same, uniform system of local
power. A simple description of such processes will provide a further
understanding of the ways in which towns can influence the outcomes
of these processes.

DECISION-MAKING PROCESSES

The system of vertical subordination described above practically
excludes competition between the town and its organizations, on the

one hand, and higher level governmental and economic bodies, on the
other. Interlevel relations have no political character in the sense
that the actors do not sanction each other or exchange resources on
equal terms. The majority of funds received by local organizations
are granted according to a well-defined routine. Local organizations
initiate the decision-making process and exert pressures on the distributional centers only when grants are insufficient, do not satisfy
local needs, or do not insure the realization of assigned functions.
The high degree of dependence of local organizations on extralocal
decisional centers and the "distributional" rather than "exchange"
character of vertical relations determine the decisional mechanisms
of the system of local power. Demands by local organizations must
be formulated in such a way, and supported by such actions, as to
set in motion binding rules of distribution.

As has been noted above, there are two basic criteria that determine the distribution of funds at the local level in Poland. One is
the tendency to try to meet unsatisfied needs. The other is the economic efficiency of an investment. The choice between efficiency and
the systemic postulate of social equality is, as Narojek correctly
states, an important political dilemma constantly faced by leaders at
all levels:

A dilemma of choice between equality and efficiency always
appears when planning decisions are made. When it comes
to the question of "where to produce," the principle of balanced development of all regions, which leads to a preference for economically underdeveloped regions, confronts
the principle of technically and economically optimal location.[29]

The choice of distributive criteria by the center not only determines a community's chances of obtaining desired goods; it also determines the choice of resources to be applied in the decisional processes. In cases where the social equality criterion is binding, local
leaders will lean toward calling for public support, manipulating information, and making references to "systemic" values. In cases
where economic efficiency has priority, they will lean toward using
material resources to enhance the economic attractiveness of their
community. Thus, for example, they can develop local infrastructure,
grant investors construction sites or a building owned by the town, or
change the curriculum of the local vocational school to supply specialists for a new factory.

It often happens, however, that distributional criteria are not
clearly defined and, in controversial situations, conflicting parties
appeal to different rules of distribution. The final result of such a

controversy is usually dependent upon which resources are mobilized
and the skill with which they are applied. Generally speaking, in order to influence extralocal centers of decision making, local leaders
must develop effective actions on two levels: on the horizontal plane,
there is a need for the mobilization and concentration of resources;
on the vertical plane, the representation of local interests and the
application of resources are important.

Developmental decisions are usually very costly, demanding
large outlays of money, materials, and manpower. Hence, a maximum concentration of local resources is needed in order to influence
the final decision maker. The situation is made easier by the existence of the town's integrative system. A well-developed network of
interorganizational contacts, as well as multiple-role performance
and concentration of important roles in the hands of a few local leaders, help to mobilize all the important resources possessed by local
organizations. A key role in this process of resource mobilization
is frequently played by the local party committee. Because of the
central position of the party in the national system and, consequently,
at the local level, party committees have undisputed rights to procure
information about activities undertaken by each organization and to intervene in these activities. This is particularly the case when the
activities are related to issues of importance to the community as a
whole.[30]

Local actors accordingly seek the support of party committees.
Because of the vertical subordination of local organizations to various
extralocal centers, party committees and, to some extent, the heads
of towns effectively coordinate the activities of local organizations on
the horizontal plane. The entrance of the committee into the process
usually broadens the circle of actors involved. The committees mobilize and coordinate the support of other local organizations.

Even though the party committees and the local administration
play crucial roles in the process of mobilizing local resources, the
role of other leaders should not be overlooked.

All evidence indicates that the formal borders of local institutions are, to a great extent, fictitious, since leaders
simultaneously perform roles belonging to distinct institutions. What is particularly important from the point of
view of local decision-making is that multiple role performance results in a situation in which any major decision
made within the framework of the local political system
cannot be treated as a decision of any single institution,
but a collective output of the local leadership.[31]

Once local resources have been mobilized and the tactics for
their use worked out, the process moves from the horizontal to the

vertical plane. Representation of local interests and resource application follow a double track. On the one hand, each local organization involved in a project tries to persuade its superior unit to support
its initiative or to make a favorable final decision if the unit is entitled to do so. On the other hand, the local leadership undertakes
collective action. Party secretaries and town heads contact the superior units of local organizations. These contacts can take the form
of collective visits by local leaders to the extralocal organizations.
Alternatively, invitations may be extended to extralocal agents to attend sessions of the party committee's executive, the council presidium, or special conferences devoted to the local project. Representatives of these organizations bargain with the voivodship administration and other organizations at the voivodship and central levels.
This is the crucial point at which the power of vertical subordination
can be balanced or modified by the local community's integrated system. Local leaders are able to pool the resources of various local
organizations either to support local undertakings or to modify decisions unfavorable to the community. This point is best illustrated by
two examples concerning the town of Wadowice.

In the first case, the local cooperative sought to expand its factory in order to provide additional jobs for the local work force. The
voivodship central of cooperatives, the superior unit of the local cooperative, did not have sufficient funds to finance this investment. A
further obstacle was presented by the limited capacity of construction
enterprises in the voivodship. The director of the local factory asked
the local council presidium and the party committee for assistance.
They, in turn, approached the voivodship council presidium and offered
to help finance the investment. The chairman of the local presidium
ordered the local department of architecture to design a new workshop.
At the same time, the first secretary of the party recommended that
the local construction enterprise treat the investment as a priority and
assist the department of architecture in the preparation of the project.
One year later, the new workshop for the cooperative was erected.

In the second case, the central issue confronting the town was
the inadequacy of its water supply system. A small river, the main
source of water, could no longer meet the needs of the population and
the town's expanding industry. Construction of a reservoir was planned
for 1969-70. In 1968, the Ministry of Communal Affairs dropped this
project from its plans. The organizations in the town undertook collective action. The council presidium and the party committee appealed
to the voivodship presidium. They received a promise of intervention
at the central level in the Central Planning Commission and in the
Ministry of Communal Affairs. The directors of the town's largest
enterprises appealed to their superior units, the Ministry of Light Industry and the Ministry of Machine Industry. These ministries, in

turn, intervened in the Planning Commission and in the Ministry of Communal Affairs on behalf of the town. A delegation was formed by the town's presidium chairman, the secretary of the local party committee, the directors of enterprises, and the representatives of the voivodship council and the party committee. It visited one of the vice-prime ministers. As a result of all these efforts, funds were granted for immediate construction of an emergency water supply installation. Furthermore, it was promised that the reservoir would be constructed in 1971.

It is extremely important for town representatives to maintain good relations with voivodship authorities. This is necessary to ensure routine services as well as the funding of investment from the voivodship budget. If investment is financed from other sources— for example, a central ministry—the coordinating authority of the voivodship is such that its support is usually indispensable for the success of the project. Also, contacts with the central government and its agencies are usually realized via the voivodship government. In fact, town leaders rarely come into direct contact with central authorities. Their interests are represented instead by the voivodship government.

The same type of relationship is reproduced at the various levels of local power, that is, coordination on the horizontal plane and representation on the vertical level. There are, however, many exceptions to this general rule. Some local projects, especially those concerning large industrial plants, are dealt with directly by their superior units at the central level. Various kinds of coalitions can thus be formed. Sometimes, local authorities unite with the central organization. In other cases, common interests unite local and voivodship leaders against a central organization. An example will make this easier to understand. Let us assume that the central ministry wants to expand a factory located in the territory of town X. Economic criteria clearly show that it is more practical to expand the existing facility than to build a new one. At the same time, voivodship authorities would prefer to gain ministry funds for the construction of a new factory in town Y, where there is a surplus of manpower. In this situation, the leaders of town X would support the ministry. The leaders of town Y would form a coalition with voivodship authorities.

The final outcome of the decision-making process is a result of the interaction of many factors. Skillfully mobilized local resources can enhance the attractiveness of a town as an investment center. The town can support the initiative with local money, manpower, and materials. Local leaders can mobilize public opinion for mass participation in local undertakings. They can also secure the support of extralocal decision makers. Finally, local authorities can manipulate the decision-making process by injecting information, by changing

other actors' perceptions of the situation, or by using their right to
issue formal resolutions. The system of horizontal integration provides facilities for the mobilization of local resources and fosters
the consolidation of the local leadership. The following two cases
from a small town in the Warsaw Voivodship are good examples of
such successful local initiatives.

In the first case, a bridge was needed to join two parts of the
town divided by a river. Although there already was a bridge, it was
situated outside the town. A doctor, a well-known, popular figure in
the town, proposed at a meeting of the town council that a Citizens'
Committee for Bridge Construction be organized. The committee
was formed under the leadership of the chairman of the town council,
the secretary of the town PUWP committee, the doctor, and the local
chief forester. In response to an appeal from the committee, many
citizens volunteered both time and money for the project. These activities, however, were not sufficient to solve the problem. The doctor therefore turned to a graduate of the town's college, at that time
a high official in the Ministry of Transportation, for support.

As a result of this official's intervention, the minister received
the Bridge Committee. The minister subsequently granted half of
the necessary funding and ordered the ministry's designing office to
work out the technical aspects of the project. After receiving this
money from the ministry, the town council chairman and the party secretary visited the vice-chairman of the Voivodship Council. They suggested that the voivodship government should also contribute to the
project. They pointed to the generous attitude of the ministry, to the
difficult situation in the town, and to the enthusiasm of the town's
citizens who had offered their time and money for the project. In
the end, the Voivodship Council provided one-quarter of the necessary
funding. The remainder was obtained from local sources. These included labor and money provided by citizens of the town and a contribution from the town council. In addition, in response to an appeal
from the local party committee, local enterprises contributed free
transportation and manpower.

In the second case, central government policy during the mid-
and late 1960s favored industrial decentralization. Large factories
in cities were encouraged to locate new branches outside urban centers. This policy was designed to relieve pressure on urban infrastructure and to encourage industrial development of smaller towns.
The local leaders of the town in question learned through contacts in
the Voivodship Planning Commission that a big electronics factory
planned to locate a new branch in the voivodship. The town, along
with three others, was under consideration as a site for this expansion.

Town and poviat leaders immediately visited the factory management. They offered the factory free buildings for the new branch as

well as a supply of skilled labor. The buildings offered were, in fact, old, ruined army barracks owned by the local council. Following an appeal by the town council and the town party committee, local citizens and enterprises offered to help renovate the barracks free of charge. Financial support from the poviat council enabled the work to be completed on schedule. Simultaneously with these activities, the town and poviat leaders asked the Education Department of the Voivodship Council for permission to change the curriculum of the local vocational school. During the next year, classes for electronic engineers were instituted and the new factory began its operations.

The scope of resources mobilized and their effectiveness depends greatly on the quality of the local leadership. Poorer communities not endowed with material resources can nevertheless have decisions go in their favor as a result of the eagerness, experience, and efficiency of their leaders. A number of factors can help these towns secure better results than those obtained by communities with rich but ineffectively utilized resources. These include an appreciation of the distributional criteria being employed and the support of extralocal decisional centers. Also important tools are mobilization of public opinion and mass participation on the part of citizens. The efficient mobilization of even modest material resources can provide the backing necessary for these activities.

Of course, because of the limitations on local autonomy, even communities with efficient leadership and ample resources have no guarantee of success in every decisional process. This is true not only because their freedom to employ local resources is limited, but also because higher level organizations dominate local ones through the hierarchical system of local power and the centralized organization of the economy. Where the preferences of the higher units are rigid and strictly defined, local freedom to maneuver is strictly limited. In such cases, the decision ceases to be the object of political bargaining. Rather, the technical and executive aspects of the decision form the basis of the process.

AFTER THE LOCAL GOVERNMENT REFORMS?

Throughout this chapter, the objective has been to describe the Polish system of local power as it functions today. However, the effects of the 1975 reform cannot yet be fully evaluated. The lack of data is the most important, but not the only, reason for this. New territorial units and their governments are still in the process of being formed. A complicated new network of interlevel and interorganizational relations is still to be "broken in." Bearing in mind that it will take quite some time for the recent changes to become routinized, a few cautious observations can nevertheless be made.

Generally, it can be assumed that the scope of voivodship autonomy and the opportunities of exerting local pressures will be more limited as a result of the reform. This is a matter of simple arithmetic. Before June 1975, the central government dealt with 22 voivodships, each with an average of 1.5 million people in a territory of 14,500 square kilometers. Since the reform, the number of voivodships has doubled. The average voivodship now has 600,000 inhabitants and an area of 6,000 square kilometers. This may very well limit the ability of the voivodship to intervene at the central level.

Similar changes have taken place at the lower levels of the system. A pre-1975 voivodship, much larger than the present one, was divided into 23 poviats with an average poviat population of 90,000 in a territory of 800 square kilometers. A new voivodship is divided into 55 gminas populated on the average by 12,000 people in an area of 150 square kilometers. Poviats, the intermediary level between the gmina (until the end of 1972, gromada) and the voivodship, were abolished. Before 1975, the domination of gminas by poviats was often criticized. At the same time, poviat authorities, representing the interests of their gminas, could mobilize considerable resources to support these interests. They could also reinforce these resources with the relatively strong power of the poviat government and party committee.

The disappearance of the "poviat cap" has given the gminas more freedom in their everyday functioning. This, indeed, was one of the aims of the reform. Gebert maintains that "the substance of the reform lies first of all in the abolition of the poviat . . . and the handing over of the majority of tasks and rights of the abolished poviats to gminas, the basic units of the new system of administrative division."[32] At the same time, the position of the gminas vis-a-vis the voivodship has probably been weakened. The strength of poviat resources and the broad range of the formal authorities of the poviat government and party organization resulted in a situation in which the outcomes of decisional processes often depended upon the free play of mobilized resources. In this way, elements alien to the logic of a planned economy were introduced into the process. Abolition of the intermediary level between the gmina and the voivodship, together with the unchanged authorities of the latter, will undoubtedly weaken these spontaneous, uncontrolled processes. Confirmation of this tendency can be found in the pronouncement of E. Gierek, the first secretary of the PUWP, who has stated:

> One of the aims of the reform is to create conditions conducive to stronger connections between local initiatives and national undertakings. Shortening the route from central nuclei of disposition to the basic units should reinforce and strengthen this connection.[33]

At the same time, local integrative systems have been left almost intact by the reform. In addition, systemic principles still give local leaders tools for mobilizing resources and exerting pressure on extralocal decisional centers. The difference is one of quantity, not of quality. Writing about local autonomy, Wiatr and Ostrowski have observed that

> local decisions . . . are only in part autonomous solutions to problems facing a given community. In their essential part, they are a concrete expression of decisions made on higher rungs of the ladder of power, which are carried into practice via incompletely autonomous decisions of local authorities. This is why the social role of the political leader consists not only of his role as a decision maker, but also as a decision executor.[34]

Wiatr and Ostrowski might also have mentioned the third role of the local leader: that of influencer, a role that is still underestimated in the scholarly literature on Poland. This chapter has sought to fill this gap by showing how local resources, local leadership, and horizontal integration serve to condition the working of even such a centralized system.

NOTES

1. T. N. Clark, "Who Governs, Where, When and with What Effects?" Community Structure and Decision-Making: A Comparative Analysis, ed. T. N. Clark (San Francisco: Chandler, 1968), p. 19.

2. "Ustawa o radach narodowych" [The People's Councils Act], Dziennik ustaw [Journal of laws], no. 26, chap. 139 (1975), art. 13.

3. Ibid., art. 4.

4. Ibid.

5. R. Nuttal, E. Scheuch, and C. Gordon, "On the Structure of Influence," in Clark, Community Structure, p. 354.

6. W. Gamson, "Reputation and Resources in Community Politics," in Clark, Community Structure, p. 355.

7. T. N. Clark, "The Concept of Power," in Clark, Community Structure, p. 64.

8. Rich empirical material on resources used by the local authorities in the decisional processes is found in J. Wroblewski, ed., Problemy rad narodowych [Problems of the people's councils], vol. 30 (1974). This volume is a collection of monographs on factors and processes shaping decisions of the towns' people's councils. This volume contains numerous examples based on 51 decisions in 17 towns.

9. J. Tarkowski, "A Study of the Decisional Process in Rolnowo Poviat," The Polish Sociological Bulletin 2 (1967): 89–96.

10. "Rozporzadzenie rady ministrów nr 278: [Decree of the Council of Ministers No. 278], Dziennik ustaw [Journal of laws], no. 47 (1973), sec. 6.1.

11. J. Borkowski, "Determinanty decyzji miejskich rad narodowych" [Determinants of the decisions of the towns' people's councils], Problemy rad narodowych [Problems of the people's councils], vol. 30 (1974).

12. K. Ostrowski and A. Przeworski, "Local Leadership in Poland," The Polish Sociological Bulletin 2 (1967): 55.

13. Ibid.

14. W. Narojek, "Demokracja lokalna w gromadzie w swietle badan empirycznych" [Local democracy in gromadas in the light of empirical research], Problemy rad narodowych [Problems of the people's councils], vol. 21 (1971): 123–25.

15. W. Narojek, "Organizacje w ukladzie miasta" [Organizations in an urban community], Studia socjologiczno-polityczne [Sociological and political studies] 17 (1964): 41–61. See also W. Jakubowski, "Rola partii w miescie powiatowym" [The role of the party in a poviat town], Studia socjologiczno-politiyczne [Sociological and political studies] 15 (1963): 199–209; and E. Machocki, "Schemat zinstytucjonalizowania zycia w miescie" [The pattern of institutionalization of the life in a town], Studia socjologiczno-polityczne [Sociological and political studies] 14 (1963): 203–22.

16. "Ustawa o radach narodowych" [People's Councils Act], art. 4.

17. Z. Rybicki, "Niektore problemy partyjnego kierownictwa radami narodowymi" [Some problems of the party leadership in the people's councils], Gospodarka i administracja terenowa [Local economy and administration] 7–8 (1966): 3.

18. Statut polskiej zjednoczonej partii robotniczej [Statute of the Polish United Workers' Party] (Warsaw: Ksiazka i Wiedza, 1976), art. 19, p. 56.

19. A. Dobieszewski, "Kierownicza rola PZPR w procesie budownictwa socjalistycznego" [The leading role of the PUWP in the process of construction of socialism], Wybrane problemy teorii i funkcjonowania partii [Selected problems of the theory and functioning of the party], ed. A. Dobieszewski (Warsaw: Ksiazka i Wiedza, 1971), p. 221. The horizontal dimension of party leadership produces important practical consequences: "As a result of research, one can formulate a principle of uniformity regarding the position adopted by town councils and town committees on important local issues. In case of controversies between the council and a council at the higher level, local party committees take the same stand as the town coun-

cil." E. Smoktunowicz, "Wplyw partii na decyzje miejskich rad
narodowych" [The party influence on the decisions of the towns' coun-
cils], Problemy rad narodowych [Problems of the people's councils],
vol. 30 (1974): 155-95.

20. M. Hirszowicz, Wstep do socjologii organizacji [Introduction
to the sociology of organization] (Warsaw: Państwowe Wydawnictwo
Naukowe, 1967), p. 201.

21. S. Zawadzki, "GRN w systemie spoleczno-politycznym gro-
mady" [Gromada's people's council in the socio-political system of
the gromada], Gromadzkie rady narodowe w świetle badań empirycznych [Gromadas' people's councils in the light of empirical re-
search], ed. S. Zawadzki (Warsaw: Państwowe Wydawnictwo Naukowe,
1973), p. 45.

22. For example, Decree No. 118 of the councils of ministers
obliges enterprises investing in the territory of a community to help
fund construction of electrical, water, and sewage facilities and construction of roads and streets. They must also reimburse the local
government 15 to 20 percent of the amount spent on housing constructed for enterprise employees. These funds are intended for construction of local service, cultural, and social institutions. "Decree
No. 118 of the Council of Ministers on the Local Coordination of Investments and Realization of Supplementary and Common Investments,"
Monitor polski 31 (1969).

23. One can find a good description of the nomenklatura system
in I. Dryll-Gutkowska's paper on the activities of the district party
committee in a large industrial town: "By 'nomenklatura' we mean a
certain way of filling the posts in the district laid down by the instruc-
tions of the [PUWP] Central Committee. The most important element
here is that the candidate for a given post be accepted by the executive
of the DC [District Committee]. Acceptance of a candidate by the
DC is by no means the same thing as saying that the DC seeks and
molds suitable people. It only means that the DC has no objections to
a given candidate. . . . The majority of the more important management jobs, as well as the higher echelons of the district party apparatus, and some jobs in social organizations . . . are found in the
nomenklatura of the DC. A small group of the top jobs in the district,
in industry and in the local authorities . . . are listed in the nomenklatura of a higher level of the party." I. Dryll-Gutkowska, "The
PUWP District Committee's Directive Role with Regard to Industry,"
The Polish Sociological Bulletin 2 (1967): 101-02.

24. G. A. Almond, "Comparative Political Systems," Comparative Politics, Notes and Readings, ed. R. C. Macridis and B. E.
Brown (Homewood, Ill.: Dorsey Press, 1964), p. 52.

25. T. Parsons and E. A. Shils, eds., Toward a General Theory
of Action (Cambridge, Mass.: Harvard University Press, 1951), p. 23.

26. A. Jasinska, "Socio-Psychological Characteristics of Local Leaders," Studies in the Polish Political System, ed. J. Wiatr (Wroclaw: Ossolineum, 1967), pp. 215-42.

27. International Study of Values in Politics, Values and the Active Community: A Cross-National Study of the Influence of Local Leadership (New York: The Free Press, 1971), pp. 107-35.

28. A. Jasinska, "Socio-Psychological Characteristics of Local Leaders," pp. 232-33.

29. W. Narojek, Spoleczenstwo planujace: Proba socjologii gospodarki socjalistycznej [A planning society: an attempt of sociology of the socialist economic system] (Warsaw: Państwowe Wydawnictwo Naukowe, 1973), pp. 83-84.

30. J. Wiatr and K. Ostrowski characterize the role of the PUWP as follows: "The party and not the formal, legal, hierarchized system of the state administration is the constitutive political institution determining the entire political mechanism. . . . What is needed, and indeed constitutes the essential element in the research procedure, is the analysis of the role of party leadership in the whole process of making political decisions." J. Wiatr and K. Ostrowski, "Political Leadership: What Kind of Professionalism?" in Wiatr, Polish Political System, p. 144.

31. K. Ostrowski and A. Przeworski, "Local Leadership in Poland," p. 58.

32. S. Gebert, Wladze i administracja terenowa po reformie [Local authorities and administration after the reform] (Warsaw: Ksiazka i Wiedza, 1976), p. 37. At the seventeenth plenary session of the central committee of the PUWP, Prime Minister P. Jaroszewicz said that "lately the gminas have been reinforced and have developed many-faceted activities. The poviats were constantly losing their organizational-managerial functions, thus becoming an apparatus of transmission between voivodship and gmina. The poviat administration tends to replace the gminas in decision making, which restrains the gminas' self-reliance and weakens their responsibility for the task entrusted to them." Trybuna ludu [People's tribune], no. 109 (May 13, 1975).

33. Ibid.

34. Wiatr and Ostrowski, "Political Leadership," p. 145.

8

THE LIMITS OF CONSENSUS: THE REORGANIZATION OF BRITISH LOCAL GOVERNMENT AND THE FRENCH CONTRAST

Douglas E. Ashford

The most striking characteristic of center-periphery relations in Britain has been the frontal attack of the central government on local government structure. Legislation comparable to the Local Government Act of 1972 would probably not survive the decision-making process in any of the other industrial democracies. It most likely would not even be attempted. From about 1966 to the implementation of the law in 1974, the spatial and functional organization of the entire substructure of British government was changed. These changes involved administrative relations between center and periphery, the level of party influence in local governments, the organization of local services and councils, and the boundaries of the entire local government system. The reorganization was global in the sense that nearly all key relationships were affected, yet the British political system as a whole was virtually unaffected by these changes.

A much longer study would be needed to analyze the variety of changes that were made.[1] The aim of this chapter is to place the reorganization in the context of British politics by asking how an apparently radical reorganization could take place without seriously dislocating the larger pattern of British political life. The essence of such a system is no doubt what Beer and Eckstein have termed "consensual" politics,[2] but it is consensus purchased at a very high price. Consensual politics depends on the moderation and compromise of contending forces in the formation and implementation of policy. At-

I wish to express my thanks for the thoughtful and detailed criticism my colleagues have given in the preparation of this chapter. They are Professors Luigi Graziano, Davydd Greenwood, Peter Gourevitch, Peter Katzenstein, and Sidney Tarrow.

titudes of deference and acquiescence support such a structure. This provides the British system with a decision-making capacity that is probably unequaled among the industrial democracies. To be able to agree on legislation of the scope and importance of the Local Government Act of 1972 is only further testimony to the ingenuity and stability of the strongest of parliamentary systems.

But consensual politics also places severe limitations on the system; these can best be uncovered by examining the shortcomings of actual decisions. Though the Local Government Act is of historic importance and probably unique in its effort to reorganize local politics and administration, the issue was formulated in a way that was amenable to consideration and eventual determination within the limits of consensual politics. Agreement on reorganization was reached, but only by defining the problem in relatively narrow terms, thereby excluding a variety of problems at the local level. An act of Parliament has great force in terms of the compliance that can be extracted from the population and the uniformity of its execution and implementation, probably more than in any other parliamentary system. But the power of Whitehall is also limited by the way in which the center formulates major policy decisions and the nature of the compromises that must be made in order to make consensual politics possible.

ISOLATING THE PERIPHERY

The Local Government Act of 1972 has been subjected to many criticisms by British scholars.[3] But these criticisms seem to me to miss the most important point, for they view policy as a result rather than a vehicle for consensual politics.[4] From a comparative perspective, policies can be analyzed as a characteristic of how decisions are formulated, agreed upon, and executed within systemic constraints rather than tests of the efficiency, effectiveness, or rationality of politics. There is no perfectly rational or totally effective solution to any problem as complex as a country's subnational structure. Important as it may be to improve the level of performance of the industrial democracies, it appears to me equally important to understand how policy is shaped within the institutional limitations of every political system. Under a system of consensual politics these constraints have taken a particular form, and they have had very specific implications for local reorganization.

Complexities of Local Reorganization

My aim is to describe the constraints imposed on the formation of local reorganization policy by the national political system. These

constraints are mostly based on the strength of Parliament and the institutional arrangements that have provided parliamentary stability in
Britain. The contrast with the French Fifth Republic should be immediately apparent, where the parliamentary constraints on policy, especially local reorganization, have been those of a weak, unstable Parliament. Perhaps the most important requirements of British parliamentary stability have been the power of the cabinet and ministers,
resting on a disciplined two-party system. Closely related to this
need is the anonymity and subordination of the bureaucracy. Nearly
all modern parliaments are hard-pressed to sustain these conditions,
and Britain is no exception. For present purposes it need only be acknowledged that relative to most Western democracies Britain has had
considerable success.

In this section I am especially concerned with establishing the
rapid emergence of Parliament in the nineteenth century as a source
of local government policy, the early reliance on administratively centralized agencies to oversee local government, and the disinclination
of the parties to make local affairs partisan issues at the national
level. This is not to say that local politics and policy were not highly
controversial, even ideological, but these disputes did not permeate
parliamentary politics and could only momentarily obstruct parliamentary decision making. [5] Local partisan differences appear to be as
strong as those in France and other European countries, but they did
not become a means of structuring national political conflict and were
not able to paralyze central administration.

The major nineteenth century attempt to directly impose strong
urban interests on national party politics was Josseph Chamberlain's
Birmingham caucus, but it, too, failed to generate close ties between
local and national parties. Nor did the British state provide the integrated administrative structure that might have become an avenue for
local interference with central government business such as we find
in France. The wave of legislation affecting localities continued
throughout the nineteenth century, but execution and implementation
were in the hands of centrally appointed boards, linked closely to the
central power structure and protected from local partisan interests.

The consensual requirements placed on local reorganization are
discussed in the section, "Consensual Needs and Local Reorganization."
Again, the purpose of this section is not to analyze the Local Government Act in terms of its efficiency or effectiveness, but to delineate
the institutional constraints that shape whatever policy might emerge
as the best possible outcome. Seen in this context, a variety of evidence underscores the isolation of the periphery from the center.
Only six instances can be dealt with in this chapter. First, the Royal
Commission on London (Herber Commission) provides a precedent
for the Royal Commission on Local Government (Redcliffe-Maud Com-

mission). The complexity of the subnational structure delayed overall reorganization, but the problems of the capital city could not be
delayed. The central decision-making process was set in motion despite local forces rather than because of them. Agreement was forged
within Parliament, often with intense partisan debate, but it nonetheless produced a law that became the agreed and accepted framework
for Greater London. The power of the center appears again in the appointment of the Royal Commission on Local Government, a decision
made in an arbitrary way, virtually ignoring local and national partisan interests and the major local government interest groups. The
event testified to the unusual power of Parliament in the consensual
system, but the terms of the commission also reveal the limitations
on power within a consensual system. The commission was not to
consider central-local administrative relations and was to be concerned with only England and Wales.[6] In one stroke the most partisan
issues of local reorganization were simply divorced from the investigation.

In all countries local governments are basically housekeeping
bodies, but the British system goes farther toward isolating the local
distribution of services and benefits from partisan consideration,
either local or national, than any other system.[7] The statistical analysis in the section, "Consensual Needs and Local Reorganization,"
demonstrates the extent to which equity considerations, for the most
part centrally defined, govern the actual performance of the subnational structure. The statistical analysis also shows how minimal
were disagreements over the spatial division of local government, although clear partisan emphases may be detected. In the following
part of the section, I consider the problem of boundary determination
in more detail because it was clearly the most hotly debated element
of the new legislation. The debate is significant because of the small
scale of the partisan infractions on impartial boundary determination.
This can be attributed to the neutrality of high-level politics, but a
more persuasive explanation is that in Britain, unlike nearly every
other democracy, the determination of local boundaries has very little relevance to national politics. There is neither local nor national
political advantage to gerrymandering because such abuses would cast
a shadow over the structure of consensual politics itself.

The last two parts of the aforementioned section deal with potentially disruptive forces in the British pattern of center-periphery
relations. The first is the dispersive effect that strong neighborhood
or community associations might have if they were to place new pressures directly on local, maybe even national, government. The negative response of both local and national governments to community-
level organizations is a function of consensual politics, which requires
that the center be protected from local political issues. The power

of the national parties and their discipline rests on keeping decisions
within the central parliamentary machinery. The extraordinarily
nonpartisan character of local councils in relation to national parties
also works in this direction. There are heated partisan differences
at the local level on such topics as housing, but somehow these questions remain disconnected from parliamentary differences. In some
instances, the local councils even reject assistance or advice from
the local member of Parliament. [8] The survey data from both councillor and local elector samples also demonstrate the remarkable
distance between local and national politics.

Perhaps the strongest European contrast to British isolation of
the periphery is found in France (discussed in the section, "The
French Comparison: A Center with Too Much Periphery?"). The
political links between localities and the center have been kept remarkably indirect in Britain; such links are very direct in France. Deputies, senators, and ministers hold and even seek local office to buttress their national status. The consideration of local reorganization
has been protracted, intensely debated at all stages, and for the
most part a failure. But the French failure to consolidate the 37,000
communes and to create the regional bodies imagined by the Gaullists
may in some respects also be a success. Again, one must see the
relevance of systemic factors to local reorganization to perceive this
and treat policy as a representation of the system rather than as an
objective with uniform standards across political systems. Oddly
enough, the French are among the first to lament the failure to reorganize local government in their country. [9] In fact, they have experienced a move to the cities and an industrial growth that is hardly par-
alleled in Europe. Given the complications of French policy formation,
a remarkable number of decisions appear to have been made and implemented.

Nor should one be too quick to condemn the policies the French
government has been able to make. The laborious history of forging
the communautés urbaines, the villes nouvelles, the métropoles
d'équilibre, and, most recently, policies favoring fusions et regroupe-
ments (even now shifting their goals) reveals a center-periphery relation that permits redefinition of objectives that can achieve a good
deal with incremental change and that may even design a better policy
by virtue of the disjointed and intricate policy process. France may
have been much more successful than Britain in relating policies for
local development and change to national goals. There may be some
advantages in being confronted with the uncertainties and complexities
of French politics and administration. [10] British single-mindedness
would be both inappropriate and impossible in France, where proposals must be more carefully thought out and have more specific objectives. The government must be more ingenious in using resources

and incentives to build new local structures. [11] The more intricate
and diverse relationship between local and national leadership may
not only convey local needs and preferences more accurately than
the indirect links of the British system, but it may also contribute to
finding workable solutions in a way that is precluded in consensual
politics.

This argument may be clearer on reading the section, "The
Limits of Functional Control," which outlines the major weaknesses
of the British reorganization, all of which stem from the difficulty of
achieving coordination within the system. Local government was no
sooner reorganized, largely in spatial terms, than government was
forced to turn to more substantive problems: planning at the local
level; the internal organization of local governments; the monumental
problems of local taxation and finance; the integration of national objectives with local government decisions; and the perennial dilemma
of capitalist systems, land use. It is consistent with my interpretation of consensual politics that the approach of the center has in all
these cases been to isolate the problem from local politics. The central administration formulates problems, immune from the ministerial
rivalry and competition seen in France, and a strong parliament and
cabinet produce laws free of local partisan intervention. In specific
and narrowly defined ways, the consensual system is remarkably effective, but in dealing with complex problems it has distinct limitations. Important as these limitations are, it should not be forgotten
that devising policy in this way has also enabled Britain to enjoy a
form of parliamentary stability that is rare among industrial democracies. The final calculus must be the nature of the state itself, and
this is a normative problem that each society must somehow decide for
itself.

Confining Local Politics to the Periphery

Why has the highly politicized character of British local authorities failed to generate some form of direct conflict with the center?
Even with the strongly pluralist tendencies of British government, it
was possible that the subunits would have developed a political organization and style that would inhibit, if not conflict with, the increasing
activities of the center. The counties and, after 1888, the boroughs
had strong political leadership. There was strong partisan leadership
locally and these same men often had influence at Westminster. An
account of how partisan relations became manageable within the British context is needed to indicate why these forces were not able to
intrude on politics at the center.

The historic circumstances in Britain were such that partisan
politics at the periphery, though extremely intense, never competed

with politics at the national level. The nineteenth century was one of
great ferment at the local level, and the illustrations below make it
clear that party alignments might have emerged in a form that would
pit local authorities against the center. But the notion that counties
and boroughs were "small republics" in the French fashion never appeared despite the presence of very strong partisan feelings in the
localities. There are a number of historic reasons for this. First,
the representative machinery at the center was continually expanding
in terms of franchise and scope of legislation throughout the nineteenth century. Second, the growth of social legislation in the nineteenth century paved the way for an alternative way to link center to
periphery.[12] Partisan forces, both locally and nationally, had specific issues and major programs around which differences were cry-
stallized, thereby preventing a crisis of authority in center-periphery
relations. Third, the rural subunits remained very much in the hands
of the rural gentry and new industrial elite, which were linked together in Britain to provide a very different class structure than that
found in France.[13] Fourth, the new urban centers were the site of
considerable agitation and even violence that brought the plight of the
worker to the attention of the elite fairly early compared to France,
and, of course, a workers' party emerged well before the end of the
century. Thus, the strong partisan differences that were taking shape
in the new industrial towns and that still controlled the rural areas
were channeled toward the center from a very early date in the development of local government. More than this, the center was responding with both political and social concessions to the periphery that
made this seem a plausible, effective alternative to the more hostile,
defensive posture that emerged in a stormy, unsettled France.

The history of Lincoln provides a rural illustration. The county
remained under the control of the rural gentry. As Sir Francis Hill
writes, "The class could not be precisely defined, but there was little doubt who was within it; the rest of the world was outside."[14] The
stability of county government bordered on lethargy. Lord Brownlow
was lord-lieutenant for most of the first half of the century, and the
third Earl Brownlow continued from 1867 to 1921. The rural elite was
mainly concerned with the privileges of land ownership, either in the
form of sales for the growing road and rail network from which they
profited or in the more trivial concerns of horse and hound that appear
to have distracted them from the true proportions of the changes taking place. The rural elite had strong claims on parliamentary representation and national issues clearly penetrated their rustic plea-
sures.[15] They had strong feelings, even prejudices in modern eyes,
but Westminster remained a stronghold for the elite, making room
for the new industrial tycoons and railroad magnates of Victorian
England.

The Municipal Corporation Act of 1835 did little to change the style of politics. Because only the town's major landlords were listed as ratepayers, the limited franchise extended early in the century had little effect until the Local Government Act of 1858 terminated such manipulation of voting rights. A local conservative caucus managed to control local government for much of the century, and borough rates (taxes) were resisted until market fees no longer would support necessary improvements. Local elections reflected the dangers attributed to the Whig reforms. Throughout the century, Lincoln like the rest of England saw new services organized outside the realm of local government: assistance to the poor in 1834, courts and prisons in 1835, police in 1836, roads in 1866, education in 1870, and health in 1875.[16] These came under functionally organized committees. Differences over the development of the town were severe, leading the town clerk to reflect that the council "hankered after affairs over which it had no legitimate control."[17]

Though the pattern of partisan politics varied a great deal among the growing industrial cities of the provinces, there is no doubt that political views and differences having national implications were strongly felt and influential in urban politics, too. Liverpool, for example, remained a Conservative stronghold during most of the nineteenth century. Proposals to build schools were resisted[18] but more paternalistic services, like public baths, were provided to placate the working class. The brief period from 1835 to 1841, when the Whigs took control of the council, was marked by fierce partisan intervention; the Liberals seized all public offices to press the reforms of the Whig government in London.

The grip of partisan interests on the local government system is no less evident in the evolution of London government. In early Victorian England, the city remained under the control of the bankers, merchants, and industrialists who dominated the corporation of the city. When Peel's Metropolitan Police District was established in 1829, the corporation managed to have the central district exempt and continued to resist central police subsidies until 1919 in order to maintain its autonomy.[19] A few years after the corporation successfully evaded the terms of the 1835 Municipal Corporations Act. A separate report was made in 1837, but the declining strength of the Whigs made it impossible to obtain legislation. Subsequent attempts were made by Lord Grey in 1856 and again in 1858, 1867 (by John Stuart Mill no less), 1870, 1875, 1880, and 1884.[20] Under Conservative influence London remained a strange collection of 7 boards of sewer commissioners; about 100 boards for paving, lighting, and street cleaning; 172 parish vestries and poor-law unions; and numerous commissions superimposed to oversee roads, bridges, turnpikes, lighting, and so on.

A frequent complaint of local authorities today is that the center is constantly imposing new requirements and functions on them with very little consultation.[21] In fact, this tendency can be traced to the lively debate over policy reform that Peel initiated in 1829.[22] The central contribution to the new Metropolitan Police, which the city corporation so carefully avoided, was extended to boroughs by the Municipal Corporations Act of 1835. The counties generally refused to participate in police reform until an act of 1856 extending similar subsidies to them where their forces met the standards of Home Office inspectors. Closely associated with the pressing need for a unified and efficient police force was the reorganization of the judicial system. In 1835 the central government agreed to pay half the cost of criminal prosecution in local courts and a portion of prison expenses. These grants were increased in 1846. Thus, the object of the first imposition of central supervision and support of potentially local functions was, not too surprisingly, the preservation of law and order.

In addition to the poor-law amendment, the major legislation setting forth the functionalist pattern for center-periphery relations was mid-Victorian health legislation. Again, industrialization overtakes the ability of government to deal with its consequences, and the local authorities prove themselves inadequate to the task. The cholera epidemics, later complicated by paratyphoid, in 1831-32, 1848-49, 1854, and 1867, "attacked all, notably the middle classes with their better water supplies and struck fear into the hearts of the governors, local and national."[23] Death rates soared from about 19 per 1,000 in 1830 to 25 per 1,000 in urban areas, reaching an unknown height of over 30 per 1,000 in Glasgow and Liverpool slums in 1841. While the poverty problem bewildered utilitarians, the physical destruction of the new industrial towns positively threatened them. For the first time the English realized "they were living on a dung heap."[24] The poor-law commissioners were relieved to release the rather testy, arrogant Chadwick to conduct a study on the request of the House of Lords. Assuring his friends that this was only another problem that the "science of engineering" could readily resolve, he began the famous Report on the Sanitary Condition of the Labouring Population of Great Britain. Published in 1842, it became the basis for a new round of decisions directing local governments to meet central standards. Indeed, the history of Victorian local government has been characterized as a problem in sanitation.

In mid-nineteenth century England, the center intervened forcefully, though often both Tories and Liberals were reluctant to see more state action. But the transformation was relentless. In 1830 payments from central to local governments were less than £100,000; by 1870 the center was providing £1.5 million.[25] In the same time period, local rates (taxes) had doubled from £8 million to £16 million. As both the inadequacies and the costs of housing, police, roads, education, and health increased, local taxing power was extended, but at a much slower rate than the center's contribution to local needs and services.

In nineteenth century Britain, new services were superimposed on British local authorities, a trend that neither major party seriously resisted. Of course, the periphery could not be expected to withstand all the forces of centralization unleashed by rapid industrialization. The periphery's leverage over the center is always relative, but the structures used to establish central influence also affect center-local political relationships and define the scope of partisan politics in center-local relations. In France centrally designated and supported services grew much slower than in Britain. Industrialization in France came much more slowly but, in addition, resistance to central power has been more intense and strongly rooted in the territorial integrity and legal powers that constitutionally rest with the commune. The reversal of this trend began very early in Britain. The Local Government Act of 1888 established two forms of local government: a unified urban government in the borough and (from 1894) a two-tiered rural government in the county. The "dual system of local government,"[26] which persisted to 1974, makes political alignment and coalition of the peripheral units of government difficult.

Not unlike the 1972 law, the Local Government Act of 1888 incorporated the balance between country and city into its provisions for organization. With the major parties reaching a compromise at the center, territorially based conflict with the center was minimized. Each major party had its territorial base more or less intact and there was no national requirement to deal with local initiative or local political complications. No such happy geographic circumstance intervened in France, partly because of the multiparty system itself, but also because territorial and legal integrity were constitutionally linked and could become a focal point for central-local conflict. The commune was protected from the center, in part by its legal and political claim on the Republic itself, and in part by capturing the prefect and providing high status for mayors. The territorial base for resisting, even obstructing, central government remains in France today, while it has virtually disappeared in Britain. The disjointed array of local authorities established in 1888 was better suited to meet the national needs of the parties than to provide a channel for advocating local needs and protecting local interests. Local autonomy was sacrificed to national stability, an exchange that French society is still considering.

CONSENSUAL NEEDS AND LOCAL REORGANIZATION

The argument to this point has consisted of three historic gen-
eralizations about the emergence of center-periphery relations in
Britain. First, in Victorian England highly politicized activity took
place in the provincial industrial cities, the counties, and London.
Second, the expanding role of local government was largely the product
of new requirements and services superimposed, often unwillingly,
on the boroughs and counties. These two trends took place more or
less independently of each other. Whitehall tried to respond to the
misery and dislocation of the new industrial towns and cities on a
piecemeal basis, the legislation often being very unevenly enforced
or accepted and the local power structures remaining relatively intact. Third, the Tories had neither an incentive nor a workable alternative.

The aim of this section is to note the subdued but pervasive
character of consensual politics on the center-periphery link. To
demonstrate the elusive but pervasive quality of partisan activity in
the relationship to the periphery, I shall discuss five aspects of local
organization and reorganization in Britain: the London reorganization
of 1963, the decision to appoint the Royal Commission on Local Government, resource and budgetary control, boundary determination,
and center-local partisan links.

London: A Rehearsal for Global Change

Although most British scholars and citizens see their local government system as relatively immune to partisan politics, this
claim is rarely, if ever, made about the reorganization of London.
Conservative vestrymen controlled the London parishes and the corporation until the Local Government Act of 1888 when the London
County Council was formed. Conservative control persisted well past
the 1888 act. When the Local Government Act of 1894 created urban
and district councils for the rest of the English counties, they managed to exclude London and thereby further delay grassroots control
of the city. A royal commission reported shortly afterward that new
local councils were needed as part of a merger of the county and city,
but its views were condemned by Conservatives. The Liberal leader,
Lord Roseberry, withdrew his support for amalgamation even though
he had been a Progressive (Liberal) member of the council and had
advocated reform.[27] The Liberals organized a special reform committee, while the Conservatives consolidated their ranks within the
London Municipal Society. With the war nothing was accomplished
until the Conservative minister, Neville Chamberlain, was confronted
with London's problems after a second Royal Commission (1923).

The 1923 report of the Royal Commission on London (Ullswater report) was in many ways bipartisan, though Conservatives opposed it in Parliament as "part of a plan for the establishment of socialism."[28] Nonetheless, Chamberlain did organize a Greater London Planning Committee in 1927, and the Local Government Act of 1929, which he sponsored, distributed powers to the metropolitan boroughs. The leader of the London Labour Party, Herbert Morrison, immediately issued a statement that the boroughs would be abolished in 20 years.[29] These delays did not deter the Labour Party, which finally took control of a majority of the boroughs and the County Council in 1934. After the war the Conservative position on London softened, though their 1945 platform still favored restoring functions to smaller authorities. When the Conservatives returned to power in 1951, Enoch Powell presented a new Conservative solution for London's problems, advocating a suitably weak areawide body.[30] He proposed 7 enlarged boroughs of about 400,000 persons with as much autonomy as existing counties. It was an ingenious combination of Conservative views —meeting the need for coordination but keeping the subunits independent.

The Conservatives were, nonetheless, concerned with local reform, and a Ministry of Local Government and Housing had been formed in 1952. Henry Brooke, its first minister, surprised Parliament by announcing the formation of another Royal Commission on Local Government in Greater London in 1957 under Sir Edwin Herbert. The Herbert report, released in 1960, argued for a directly elected Council for Greater London, strong local councils, and a division of functions between tiers. The clear option for "localism" over centralization drew bitter protest from the London Labour Party.[31] Deeply partisan feelings were fully exposed in the parliamentary debates leading up to the London Government Act of 1963;[32] Hugh Gaitskell, Labour's shadow minister for health, vowed to fight the bill "clause by clause, line by line." After over a thousand attempts to amend the bill and the invocation of the "guillotine" to reduce debate, London finally received a new government in 1963.

The London reorganization is important because it reveals the essentials of the Conservative strategy for local reorganization that continues to the present time. First, it shows the Tories' reservations about large units with concentrated powers. The 1961 government White Paper[33] placed education solely in the hands of the second-tier units, the boroughs, though this was compromised later to preserve the highly successful Inner London Educational Authority, which Labour had built. Also, the size of London was reduced from the commission's recommendation of over 800 square miles to just over 600 square miles. Second, partisan emphasis was muted so as not to outrage Labour sensitivities, even though the boroughs preserved much more local rule (and many more Conservative councillors) than Labour would have preferred. Nonetheless, in the first elections under the new system Labour won handily with 64 of the 100 seats on the council and holding 20 of the 32 boroughs. Thus, London is a model of consensual politics in the British context, leaving final political decision to Parliament, exercising partisan influence with moderation, and making evenhanded compromises in the distribution of powers between center and subunits. As we shall see, London provides the scenario for the Local Government Act of 1972.

The Royal Commission: An Exercise
in Reducing Complexity

The appointment and setting of the Royal Commission on Local Government provides the second illustration of the constraints governing center-periphery relations. The appointment of the commission is itself the object of some interest because Britain had steadily worked toward local reorganization since the war. While it would be an exaggeration to say that the decision to find a global solution was inspired by Labour interests at the expense of the Conservatives, it is true that Labour decided to push much harder than Conservatives. In this respect, Labour departed from the "rules of the game" about local legislation, though by the late 1960s both parties felt that major changes were needed. In 1945 the Local Government (Boundary Commission) Act set in motion a review confined to boundary problems. Its chairman, Sir Malcolm Eve, resigned in 1949 and its work was abruptly terminated by Aneurin Bevan. But the main issue had surfaced, for it had become clear that territorial changes without functional changes would be senseless, that further central control would totally debilitate local democracy, and that the central departments were incapable of agreeing on the best system.[34] In 1954 the Conservative government asked the local government associations for suggestions for a major reorganization, which led to an inconclusive White Paper (1956) and the Local Government Act of 1958.

The new Boundary Commission renewed hopes that a solution to this complex question could be found outside direct political channels, that is, without parliamentary legislation. In this respect, the reliance on administrative decision and intricate local consultation is akin to the French approach to communal reorganization. The terms of reference for the commission are relevant for they disclose the Conservative orientation to such change. Functional powers were omitted, denoting the Conservative bias toward ad hoc, departmental solutions and the party's aversion to massive increases in central government administration. The large metropolitan regions, conurba-

tions, were omitted; this neatly avoided the areas of concentrated
Labour strength and placed emphasis on adjusting the old boroughs.
Appropriate comments were included, of course, to safeguard the
counties, many of which were Conservative strongholds.[35] The entire process was designed to maximize the influence of the localities
and thus conformed to the historic position of the Conservatives on
local matters.

The work of the commission has been neatly summarized by
Stanyer.[36] Despite the slow procedures imposed by the requirement
for complete, public hearings and the consequent legal action against
boundary adjustments, it appears that a good deal was accomplished.
Nine general area reports were completed before the commission was
dissolved and changes had begun, each change requiring consent by
the Minister of Housing and Local Government. It is at this point
that partisan concerns enter into the work of the commission. The
most blatant was a Conservative minister's (Sir Keith Joseph) refusal
to dissolve the tiny county of Rutland, a geographic and historic an-
achronism north of London. Further confusion was added in 1965
when the Labour minister accepted the creation of the Tyneside County
Council and then reversed himself in favor of an enlarged borough.
In the final months of the Conservative government, resistance to
change was stiffening in the House of Lords,[37] and implementation
was increasingly bogged down in the courts.

Over the first year of the new Labour government in 1964, the
Minister of Housing and Local Government, Richard Crossman, seemed
satisfied with the work of the commission. In the last months of the
Conservative government, the Mallaby and Maud committees had been
appointed to review local government personnel problems.[38] Crossman left these groups at work and repeatedly stated before the press
and local government associations there was no chance that the government would make a frontal assault on local government reorganization.[39] Unlike Sir Keith, who felt that larger planning regions were
of doubtful value, Crossman had reservations about the 150 planning
authorities (the first tier of the entire system) but saw no need for
immediate change in the basic structure. His views changed radically
in late 1965, and before the Association of Municipal Corporations
Conference (AMC) he announced "that the whole structure of local
government is out of date and that our county boroughs and county
councils as at present organised are archaic institutions."[40] Clearly,
the work of the Boundary Commission was entering delicate territory.
Labour had rejected the Tyneside proposal. Under the Conservatives,
a proposal easing the commission's work by amalgamating the Merseyside and East Lancashire reviews had also been turned down by
Sir Keith. Whether the possibility of affecting local political bases
had anything to do with Crossman's reversal is impossible to tell,

but one member of the commission resigned and its chairman died
before its work was complete. In February 1966, Crossman announced the formation of the Royal Commission.

Crossman's action reveals another aspect of the partisan behavior in a consensual system. In his view, the endless public inquiry might bring democracy into contempt, though an advocate of locally generated reform might well have concluded the reverse. He
also appears to have become exasperated with the local government
pressure groups, which were divided along urban-rural lines, with
the AMC and CCA (County Councils Association) at loggerheads on
nearly every proposed change. The Labour solution, then, was to
impose reform from the top, a strategy that Conservatives had resisted over the past decade. This change of heart is suggested by a
police reorganization at this time, which the Home Secretary approved
without consulting local authorities or local government associations. [41]
In any event, the choice of a strong, centrally devised solution was
consistent with Labour's approach to change, though political fortunes
were to bring about outcomes very different from the plans that Labour
had prepared.

Policy: Generating Central Domination

The third major point where partisan differences could enter
into the subsystem is through the distribution of functions, population,
and resources to the subunits. To some extent these choices are predetermined by urbanization and industrialization, and all parties must
respond to new needs and demands. However, even the demographic
and physical constraints leave a variety of alternatives for the center.
Each system, of course, operates within an institutional and constitutional matrix that shapes how such decisions are made. For example,
the decision to move from the taxe locale to the tax sur le salaire in
France was influenced by the need to increase local revenues but was
largely worked out by the Ministry of Finance. In Britain, the local
authorities also operated with assigned revenues, basically the local
property tax, but this tax has a very different history and can be
traced back to the poor rates of Elizabethan England. A reorganization of the British tax structure as fundamental as the French changes
would be virtually impossible.

The examination of the more detailed policy evidence shows
both the narrow scope for partisan differences within the consensual
system and the enormous shift to a functional formulation of central
control since the war. As I have argued above, I see these two trends
as interdependent. To understand the more detailed information, it
is important to note the magnitude of change in the formation of center-

periphery policy immediately after the war. Like many structural reforms within the British system, the postwar changes came from both Labour and Conservative ideas. The initial law affecting localities was the Education Act of 1944, designed by rapidly rising Conservative leader Rab Butler.[42] The aim of the law was to make the county councils a unified educational authority, reducing the duplication of school planning and organization under the district-based structure established in 1902. Beneath this issue lay not only the nineteenth century problem of religious and state schools, but the Conservatives' interest in finding a way to enable the counties to improve their educational system and to enable the deteriorating church schools to benefit from state aid. Under this law the Ministry of Education was established and became the functional focus for educational planning and standards for the entire system.

Another major step toward a functional structure was the enactment of the National Assistance Act of 1948 and the National Insurance Act of 1946. This battery of social welfare legislation brought a major shift of power to the center organized around the Ministry of Health, which remained responsible for local authority affairs as well. The radical Labour figure, Aneurin Bevan, faced a difficult problem in organizing the new service, for the doctors did not want health services to remain under local control.[43] Thus, finance, procedures, and standards became wholly central concerns, with the localities' health functions reduced to those services that could only be delivered in a personal way, such as school medical inspections, maternity care, home nursing, and ambulance service. The major shift was to place all hospitals, which had been operated by the counties and boroughs, under national direction through area health boards.

Thus, the trend to larger authorities began, responding to individual functions and creating what Smellie has called "an imperative mood"[44] in the rapidly growing central departments. The array of legislation was formidable: fire services were elevated to county and borough level in 1947; the borough and county police forces were merged in 1946; town and country planning became a major central activity in 1948, leading to the formation of a new Ministry of Local Government and Planning in 1951. Under the Conservatives, who came to power on a platform promising more housing, it became the Ministry of Housing and Local Government in 1952. These changes were surface manifestations of the restructuring of center-periphery relations: building strong, specialized ministries at the center and moving the decisional authority of the subunits to larger units. For policy purposes, the tension that develops around this choice became the focus for center-periphery relations over the next generation.

Until the Crossman decision to attack center-periphery relations frontally, the partisan link between the center and the subunits was subdued and moderated largely by administrative means. The important exception was the Housing Act of 1957, which adhered to the Conservative principle of encouraging housing construction through private means rather than through public housing under local authorities. Most of the controversies were minor—over such matters as the specific benefits of health services, benefits for less privileged children to be distributed through schools, and the like. Partisan feelings can still become inflamed over school milk programs, but the basic structure remains. The Local Government Act of 1958 made no structural changes, but it did amalgamate numerous specific grants to localities into an "equalization grant." The aim was to provide the localities with more choice in using the accumulation of subsidies provided from the center, though the increasing supervision and control from departments may well have made this a pyrrhic victory for local control.

The evidence to be extracted from the empirical study of policy confirms these trends within the narrow range of partisan influence but does not show large differences between Conservative- and Labour-controlled councils. Oliver and Stanyer[45] conclude that socioeconomic differences explain more about expenditure decisions than party differences. Boaden and Alford and Davies[46] control statistically for the level of resources and needs, coming to the conclusion that Labour is more responsive to social problems. A later analysis of Boaden's (1971) confirms this result, using similar controls in the analysis of borough spending. When budgetary data from boroughs and counties are compared, it appears that the more rural, conservative counties have in fact made larger increases in spending since the war and that competitive politics in the counties (not boroughs) is weakly related to increases in spending.[47] More detailed analysis will be needed to resolve this issue, and one study had appeared showing that services for the elderly and children's services are more strongly supported by Labour.[48]

The empirical analysis of spending patterns shows that central decisions do not differentiate subunits very clearly. The most obvious way to study this is to analyze the central support for the subunits. When changes in central governmental subsidies are analyzed in terms of per capita spending and the rates of change in spending from 1949 to 1969, few marked differences appear between parties or types of authority. Much the same result is obtained using paired comparisons and controlling for the size of the local resource base.[49] Thus, there is little reason to think that the large part the center plays in the providing of local funds, now roughly 60 percent of local spending, is strongly influenced by partisan interests at the center. The center has immense power but does not use it.

However, this evidence, combined with the proliferation of central control over local services outlined above, provides a key insight into the workings of a functionally determined subsystem. The link between local and national parties is weak, and the partisan voice at the center concerning local policy is similarly weak. The most interesting result is precisely that no clear political direction emerges in analyzing policy data for the system as a whole. Nonetheless, the system seems to operate relatively smoothly and neither party appears particularly concerned that political relationships do not link the periphery to the center. This is a major difference from the French system, one to which I shall return.

If the partisan difference is only one of emphasis, such differences might appear in the overall pattern of resources (tax base) and population distribution revealed in the major proposals for reorganization. Tables 8.1 and 8.2 compare the direction of change under the pre-Maud organization, the Redcliffe-Maud report, and the actual division made by the Local Government Act of 1972. In this context, partisan emphasis appears rather more clearly. The old system had both smaller authorities and more internal variation in size (Table 8.1) and also placed preponderant financial power in the hands of the counties.

The population distribution, like resource distribution, suggests an important dimension of partisan difference. The royal commission would have placed about two-thirds of the tax base in the newly proposed unitary authorities. The dispersion that occurred would have been to second-tier units within the metropolitan areas, not to the second-tier units of counties which were to be abolished. The Conservative law retains much of this distribution of population and resources, but it clearly moves toward more dispersion and smaller scale in all respects. Both the ranges of difference and the per capita figures indicate the Conservative preference for more local autonomy and a more diverse system, a preference stemming from the historic roots of their local government policy.

Boundary Determination: A Test of Consensual Politics

The fourth dimension of consensual politics within the British system is the problem of boundary determination. This is one of the major differences from the French system, where territorial identities are much more closely tied to representation as well as to the administrative structure of the state. Even in so consensual a system as Britain, the territorial adjustments have generated fierce debate and a remarkable amount of strongly partisan decision making. When the

TABLE 8.1

Comparison of Property Values in Proposed Local Government Units, England
(to nearest £100,000)

Unit	Total	Average	Per Capita	Per Capita Range
Local government, mid–1968				
Administrative counties (45)	953.4	21.2	38.3	60.2–28.4
County boroughs (79)	612.2	7.7	43.7	72.3–29.6
Royal commission				
Unitary authorities (58)	1,226.7	21.1	40.4	65.8–28.4
Metropolitan areas (3)	333.1	113.0	39.0	44.5–38.5
Metropolitan districts (20)	339.1	16.9	39.0	48.1–30.8
Local Government Act of 1972				
Metropolitan counties (6)	505.7	84.3	42.4	49.1–36.1
Metropolitan districts (34)*	505.7	14.8	42.4	56.9–32.5
Nonmetropolitan counties (39)	1,206.1	30.9	45.4	59.9–35.2
Nonmetropolitan districts (296)	1,206.1	4.1	45.4	—

*Only 34 districts indicated in 1971.

Sources: 1968 figures from Annex 4, Royal Commission (1969), pp. 331–40; recommended figures from Royal Commission (1969), The New Units, Table 1, pp. 304–07; 1972 figures from Department of the Environment, Circ. 84/71.

TABLE 8.2

Population Size in the Different Proposed Local Government Units, England
(to nearest 1,000 inhabitants)

Unit	Total Population	Average Population	Maximum Size	Minimum Size
Local government, mid-1968				
Administrative counties (45)	24,404	542	2,428 (Lancashire)	30 (Rutland)
County boroughs (79)	13,564	172	1,074 (Birmingham)	33 (Canterbury)
Royal commission				
Unitary authorities (58)	29,800	514	1,081 (Sheffield)	195 (Halifax)
Metropolitan areas (3)	8,309	2,770	3,232 (Selnec)	2,250 (Mersey)
Metropolitan districts (20)	8,309	415	1,314 (Birmingham)	176 (Warrington)
Local Government Act of 1972				
Metropolitan counties (6)	11,906	1,959	2,791 (West Midlands)	1,249 (Tyneside)
Metropolitan districts (35)	11,906	336	1,096 (Birmingham)	174
Nonmetropolitan counties (39)	26,585	709	1,466 (Hampshire)	272 (Northumberland)
Nonmetropolitan districts (296)	26,585	93	—	—

Sources: 1968 figures from Annex 4, Royal Commission (1969), pp. 331–40; recommended figures from Royal Commission (1969), The New Units, Table 1, pp. 304–07; 1972 figures from Department of the Environment, Circ. 84/71 and Norton and Mawhood, "British Local Government: The Reform of 1974 and Their Background," unpublished paper, 1975, p. 22.

Labour government responded in a White Paper[50] to the Redcliffe-Maud
report, some restoration of territorial dispersion was already con-
ceded. Two metropolitan (two-tiered) units were added—South Hampshire and West Yorkshire—reducing the proposed unitary authorities
from 58 to 51 and increasing the number of districts from 20 to 28.
Labour's preference for larger functional units, however, was revealed by moving the key local function of education to the top tier
in the two-tiered authorities. The government fell before legislation
could be passed, and the Conservative White Paper[51] went even further toward dispersing functions and authority. The direction was
clearly stated in Heath's desire to see representation take precedence
over administrative efficiency. The law that finally emerged was
more like the Local Government Act of 1888 than the proposed streamlined unitary local governments of Lord Redcliffe-Maud and Harold
Wilson.

In the Conservative law, the initial two-tiered metropolitan units
were increased to six, dropping South Hampshire (Southampton being
a Conservative borough) and adding South Yorkshire and Tyneside.
The "metropolitan counties" were to be divided into 38 districts and
given important control in education, social services, and planning.
The remainder of England and Wales was to be divided into 39 "nonmetropolitan counties" having 278 districts each with a population of
about 100,000 persons and retaining most of the power of the old
boroughs and the new district level. Some of the more rural districts
might have a population as low as 40,000, while one metropolitan district (Birmingham) had over a million persons. The Conservatives
also wanted to preserve the historic parishes, which had become advisory local councils under Labour designs, and simply postponed
consideration of the problem of provincial authorities, which had been
proposed as a consistent addition to Labour's long interest in developing stronger regional authorities.

The debate over the county boundaries was fierce even within
the outspoken tradition of British parliamentary debate. No sooner
had the Conservative plans been announced than cries of "carve up"
began.[52] Peter Walker, the minister shepherding the bill through
Parliament, faced stiff resistance from his own party, and the parliamentary committee to review the bill was carefully selected to exclude such potential dissidents.[53] Some changes were made that had
unmistakable partisan intent. An adjustment was made along the
Hampshire-Dorset boundary to protect a Conservative stronghold.
Newmarket, a strong Conservative constituency, was left within a
more conservatively oriented West Suffolk county rather than placed
in the stronger Labour county of Cambridgeshire. Though the strange
appendage that Coventry now makes to Birmingham has some justification given overspill (housing) needs, it also helps protect the Con-

servative influence in Warwickshire. Perhaps by way of compensation, the upper-class northern tip of Berkshire was included in Oxfordshire, almost certain to be a Labour county. The most blatant change was to exclude Stokesley-Whitby from North Yorkshire on the alleged request of Timothy Kitson, who had been Heath's private secretary.[54]

Nonpartisanship: Local Councillors and
National Politics

Compared to French mayors and municipal departmental councillors, British local politicians are extraordinarily complacent. The Committee on the Management of Local Government attributed this to several causes, though it is interesting that they did not consider national links as a way of invigorating local democracy.[55] They were impressed by the age of many councillors and aldermen and the tendency for local representatives to be reelected without opposition for many years. They also saw that the endless municipal committee meetings and investigations were a deterrent to balanced social representation on local councils. The complex local election system was also seen as a deterrent to both voters and candidates.[56] But the central issue of increased partisanship at the local level has never been directly confronted, nor does it seem a potential way of strengthening local-level democracy.

How increased local partisanship might change the system goes beyond the aim of this chapter, but the widespread agreement that partisanship has little or no place at the local level unmistakably confirms the indirect nature of center-periphery relations in Britain. Until the late 1960s, avowedly nonpartisan candidates prevailed in local elections.[57] Councillors steadfastly resisted the intrusion of doctrinaire ideas at the local level and saw their jobs as commonsense housekeeping roles for the locality. These views were repeatedly expressed in the survey for the Committee on the Management of Local Government (Maud Committee). In another survey, 75 percent of the local councillors claimed they never aspired to national office regardless of party and 40 percent said they were more interested in local than national politics.[58] These results go far toward explaining the indirect linkage between local and national politics in Britain.

In the Maud report approximately half of the councillors in all types of subunits except the most rural (rural districts) defended local party organization. But just under half of all councillors also felt that local government work could be done better without parties.[59] If rural units are included, nearly two-thirds reject parties. Only in the most urban areas (boroughs, London boroughs) did more than half support parties as "essential" to the work of local councils. Sixty-two percent of those believing the party to be essential (361) gave as their reason the belief that work gets done more quickly. Of those feeling work would be better without parties (775), explanations were about evenly divided between the views that party policies are followed regardless of the individual (48 percent) and that party politics has no relevance to local government (47 percent). These ambivalent and divided views on party politics within councils should be assessed knowing that nearly all councillors belong to a national party[60] and that within a year of the local government reorganization in 1974 nearly all councils had been aligned with national parties.[61]

The data relating central politicians to their localities are scattered but are indicative of the disassociation of local and national politics within the British system. First, of those feeling the party system essential, very few (17 percent) felt that this was because parties stood for definite things. In even the highly politicized London boroughs, only 20 percent felt that parties had a defined, policy relevance to local government. Second, the councillors' views of central government display divergent attitudes. In the most politically active types of subunits (London boroughs), nearly 40 percent felt that the council did not make full use of its power, though about half the members in all types of councils felt more power was needed and that the center placed unnecessary limitations on the freedom of the council.[62] It is interesting to compare these results with attitudes toward parties. Nearly half the councillors of all types resent central control, but few see the party link as a means of adjusting such control. Local government policies and politics are divorced from national party politics and the center is seen as exercising excessive control. These attitudes represent a limitation on the scope of local politics that few French mayors would understand.

These attitudes are entirely consistent with those of another battery of local activists, the local agents of the national parties, whose views have been carefully studied in four Merseyside boroughs by Parkinson.[63] The most remarkable finding related to this inquiry is how little direct relationship local agents see between council and national politics. In addition, they view the relation of local and national party organizations in much the same context as the local councillors see their relationship to Whitehall. The local party is essentially the servant of the national party and is largely divorced from local level politics for such purposes. Thus, 47 percent of Conservative party agents and 53 percent of Labour agents see their organization as having little or no influence over the national party. Both view their main contribution to the national party as attending to community needs. No Conservatives and only 3 percent of Labour party agents see the local organization as an agent of national policy promotion.

For the party agent reelecting local council members occupies a much lower and secondary priority to electing members of Parliament. Less than a fourth of the agents see local elections as the most important part of their work compared to 20 percent of those who have not served in local elected office. The results confirm the general detachment of local from central political activity. Partisan politics appears as neatly compartmentalized within the local government system.

An important deterrent to the association of local elections with national politics was the complex electoral system in effect until the Local Government Law of 1972. The Royal Commission proposed and Parliament agreed to abolish the indirectly elected aldermen. But the recommendation to have a uniform local election system was not fully accepted. The nonmetropolitan counties, Greater London, and its boroughs have a general election every four years. The Conservatives decided to permit the nonmetropolitan districts to choose between an election of the entire council of a third of its membership every three years, while the metropolitan districts all elect a third each year. The system is slightly different in Scotland. Whatever partisan meaning might have penetrated local elections remains confused by a variety of local electoral procedures. Furthermore, the reorganization fails to bring together district and parliamentary boundaries that might have further encouraged local political action at the national level.[64] Whether from design or disinterest, the new election system, though clearly much fairer than the old system on the local level, provides little incentive for local politicians to change the pattern of detachment from the center that has characterized local politics.

THE FRENCH COMPARISON: A CENTER WITH
TOO MUCH PERIPHERY?

In France, most of the conditions described in Britain are reversed. Local and national politics are more closely linked and the integrated administration reaches down to the local level. The direct political links between center and periphery are readily apparent: an electoral system that imprints the center with local partisan differences; a splintering of parties around regional, occupational, and ideological differences; party organizations that are difficult to control from the center; and the intermingling of political roles at the various levels of government. The communes are not functionally isolated but are "small republics" with a political and legal status that reinforces their integral relationship to the society as a whole.[65] Consistent with the intricate penetration of local politics at the national level is the functional organization of the state. Paris tries to reach to the grassroots of the society through its own administrative apparatus. Policy is not the fortuitous product of detached local governments but the accumulation of local decisions made and executed under careful scrutiny by prefects and inspectors from the center. Since the state cannot readily dominate the periphery, it extends itself to the periphery.[66] Once this is done, it becomes virtually impossible to achieve a major reorganization without provoking a state crisis of unmanageable proportions.

In comparing the French effort to reorganize the periphery with the British effort, it is important to consider the exertion required in both systems for the visible results. Even with the powerful administrative apparatus attached to the center, France has made little progress. In the early years of the Gaullist regime a concentrated effort was made to reduce the complexity of the system by increasing the powers of prefects and organizing regional governments.[67] The distinguishing feature of these devices was their strategy of circumventing the political complexity of the locality by enlarging the units of local government surreptitiously and by avoiding the intense debate that legislative change creates in the national assembly.[68] Increasing the ability of the state to aggregate decision making at the lower levels of government did nothing to remove resistance to change. After more than a decade of political debate and administrative manipulation, the loi Marcellin of 1971 was only a feeble approach to communal consolidation. In fact, it appears that the French system could create neither the political nor administrative conditions that made reorganization possible in Britain. Political forces at the periphery could not be isolated and central control could not be simplified.

The British solution to the complexities of local reorganization has concentrated on the delivery of services, while the French treatment of local reorganization remains heavily concentrated on the territorial problems of the subunits. This is not to deny that the French proposals for local reorganization have not had functional objectives, but in relation to Britain the redistribution and reorganization of services has been remarkably limited. The Syndicat à vocation unique (SVU) was created in 1890 to entice communes to enter voluntarily into very limited functional agreements. No major reforms appeared until 1959, with the Syndicat à vocation multiple (SVM), the first of several Gaullist efforts to provide incentives for further cooperation among communes. But even this highly permissive step toward change was couched in voluntary terms and made few legal inroads into the authority of the commune. By the end of 1973 this weak solution had been used only 1,772 times, affecting 17,233 communes and about 23 million Frenchmen.[69] Of course, the reorganization of the French state did not await the reorganization of the subunits of government and the administrative machinery steadily worked to advance both public and private interests in a variety of ways. But the transformation of the communes has been steadily resisted and achieved largely by directly superimposing the center's administrative apparatus on the subunits through the office of the prefect.

As Médard has stated, for the French state the "slow death of communes [was] preferred to a brutal death."[70] Certainly the center would have welcomed a more decisive result, but French local government has managed to cling tenaciously to its territorial identity. That the French state has found ways to bypass the territorial complexity of local government by no means eliminates territorial complications in the French center-periphery relationship. Lacking Britain's strong functional link between the subunits and the center, France has had to depend on the prefect to moderate partisan differences at the local level and to coordinate policy. This structure, in turn, diminishes the influence of both local and national representation. There is ample evidence of the political behavior of French mayors within the administrative system, but aligning these differences with parliamentary decision making has proved an insurmountable task. As a result, the prefect remains the political and administrative cornerstone for center-periphery relations. Local reorganization in France becomes an exercise in legal ingenuity, relying heavily on the Etablissement publique[71] in order to circumvent the influence of the collectivités locales and their constitutional powers. A decade of intensive effort to reorganize French communes and departments has made only a dent in the basic structure. The defeat of the regional proposal in the 1969 referendum is only the most dramatic evidence of the suspicion and controversy surrounding local reorganization in France.

If Britain is the consensual state par excellence, France is the organizational state without constraint.[72] The organization of decision making and the center-local linkage of parties both work to make a global solution impossible. France cannot find a solution by simplifying the decision-making process or by isolating local-level politics from the center. Even the strongest single party of France, the Communists, which has the best coordination between national and local organizations, succumbs to the intricacies of local political influence and resists reorganization.[73] Though a more severe problem for the Gaullists, there has been little correspondence between the major party's national and local strength. For example, the Gaullists received over 40 percent of the vote in the 1967 national elections but only 9 percent in the 1965 local elections. Parties suspect changes that might affect their local power, while the system cannot provide the mandate for change at the national level.[74]

The partisan link between communes and the center is indeed so intermeshed with administrative politics that the two processes cannot be disentangled.[75] The territorial claims of the mayors are conveyed through the representative machinery, buttressed by the influential Association of French Mayors. Proposals for change may come from ministerial initiatives such as the Fouchet plan, launched by circular in 1964 (not published in the Journal officiel) but the state still depends on the prefect in his political role to assess possibilities for change.[76] Open political debate is postponed to the last moment when the avant-project is considered by the relatively weak committees of the National Assembly. There can be no reliance on strong consensus as in the British system, not only because of the assembly's divisions, but also because the territorial conflict remains at the heart of reorganization in France.

The territorial complexity of the French system has made the collection of comparable data difficult, but there is evidence that the diversity in the provision of services and benefits through French local government is greater than in Britain, probably even greater than that of the unreformed British local government. Studies of Nîmes and Montpellier indicate that partisan characteristics of the two cities indeed are associated with very different patterns of budgetary choice.[77] Similar studies of a sample of 20 large cities reveal more variation than found in budgetary analysis of British boroughs.[78] Further policy studies of the French system may well persuade us that the common interpretation of administrative power in France has exaggerated its influence, a question already raised at the national level by Suleiman.[79] Efforts to pursue urbanization policies outside the local government framework have been severely handicapped rather than enhanced by administrative politics.[80] The intricate financial controls exercised over spending and investment subsidies have been criticized by the Cour des comptes and other interministerial planning bodies.[81] A closer examination may indicate that the French administrative system has not prevailed in any coherent policy sense. On the contrary, it is surprising that it has been able to produce the programs and policies, given local political and administrative complexities.

Faced with these difficulties, it is remarkable that France has adjusted to her urban problems as well as she has. The strategy appears very different from that of Britain. France has depended more heavily on solutions involving the private sector, calling into play economic influence to do what the public sector finds difficult. Most of the major urban policies, such as the villes nouvelles and métropoles d'équilibre, have been qualified successes, but they have permitted the state to adjust to new industrial needs where localities could not act. The Sociétés d'économie mixte are used as a tool to combine private and public sector interests for urban development.[82] The effect has been to concentrate resources and services more heavily in areas favoring industrial development, reinforcing the strong capitalist emphasis that has characterized much French planning and development since the war. Unable to work with the communes and unwilling to sacrifice its historic power, the French administration has found support by turning to the private sector to solve local development problems. These solutions only circumvent the issue of local reorganization. While such a strategy may meet the needs for economic growth and industrial development, it may also increase the disparities among communes and departments and exacerbate partisan differences, making a solution to France's center-periphery problem even more remote.[83]

THE LIMITS OF FUNCTIONAL CONTROL

The center-periphery link has been conceived in this chapter as an aspect of national and local institutions, involving the link between partisan activity at national and local levels and the nature of administrative intervention at both levels. As has been argued, it is not the growth of functionally organized departments that is surprising about the transformation of this relationship over the past generation. All industrial nations have had to provide a vastly greater array of benefits and services to organize burgeoning cities, to combat growing poverty problems, and to find effective ways to relate territorial and population problems to industrial development. The functional problem of modern government is not in itself very interesting as a comparative question, for all systems have accommodated this immense growth of governmental activity, some more gracefully than others. What makes comparative analysis interesting and essential is how this transformation relates to key political relationships in the system, of which the center-periphery link is one of the most important.

The British have devised a way of handling this problem that, as I have tried to show in the section, "Consensual Needs and Local Reorganization," permitted partisan concerns to enter into policy formation at all levels but still maintained the supremacy of central political institutions. This enabled Britain to maintain a degree of political stability that the French might envy, as several of their scholars have envied the ease with which Redcliffe-Maud and Parliament made their frontal attack on the local government system. The contrast is important for, if the administrative apparatus of the French state is as powerful as often surmised, why has it been so unsuccessful in reorganizing the local government structure? A brief answer, to which I shall return, is that not changing the communes was indeed an assertion of the individual and collective concept of democratic representation within France,[84] while not changing the local structure of Britain would have implied the weakness of central institutions that few British citizens or officials could imagine. Each system derives a certain vitality from its conception of democratic government. It is no paradox that opposite experiences—that is, major reorganization in Britain and incremental reorganization in France—might hold the same meaning in relation to fundamental questions of legitimacy of the state.

Nonetheless, it is important to ask whether the unrestrained functional solution of Britain, coupled with the necessary ease of transforming the local structure, may bring with it other disadvantages. The purpose of this section is to underscore some of the major shortcomings of the British reorganization, and it should not be surprising to find that these are in several instances precisely the strengths of the French system. The first of these is the difficulty of achieving coordinated local planning within the British system of local government. This is in part a result of the growth of the functionalist state where many more activities of a specialized nature must be coordinated. But it has not emerged as a basic problem in French local government where the prefect serves as the coordinator of local budgets and development plans, working with the representatives of central departments, mayors, and regional officials. His overall planning role at the local level appears to have survived relatively unscathed by the various attempts to change local government in France. [85] The British, in decided contrast, are just beginning to devise a way of achieving some integration of decision making at the local level.

The Redcliffe-Maud report placed great emphasis on the necessity of increasing the efficiency of local authorities, though it was later criticized for failing to deal with precisely those organizational problems that integrated planning requires. [86] In the period between the report and effective date for reorganization (April 1974), there was a flurry of publication and discussion of how planning would be improved in the new counties. [87] The partisan dimension appears to have been neturalized in this discussion; the Conservatives set much of this research into motion because of their belief that government suffered from not adopting private management techniques; Labour was interested because they hoped that improved planning would increase efficiency and, thereby, the amount of services and benefits local government could deliver. In any event, the result was the formation of a group known as the Bains Committee, whose report on management and structure for the new authorities appeared in 1972.

Its aim was not to introduce sophisticated forms of performance budgeting, but only to achieve a degree of common definition of goals and program needs in a context known as "corporate planning." Though the change was presented in many guises, Stewart, one of its most sensitive critics and supporters, felt that it "should be to assist the political process not to assist retreat from politics." He fears what France has done, noting how "local and central government functional departments buttress each other in an apolitical alliance."[88] The new local-planning process presumably will build responsiveness and vitality by bringing politics into a more coherent framework and enabling elected officials to grasp overall objectives that may be obfuscated in detailed departmental plans. Most new authorities have indeed adopted some variation of the corporate planning model, but in a wide variety of organizational forms.[89] Most authorities have followed the Royal Commission's recommendation that the local governments have a chief executive, most often without departmental responsibility. Whether this office represents a nascent prefect remains to be seen, but the contrast with France in sequence or organizing locally is perfectly clear.

A second weakness of the disjointed character of British local government in relation to the center has been resource planning and control. In sharp contrast to the French system, the issue of local finance was postponed until after the reorganization. This happened in part because the economic deterioration of the cities became more acute, but the center-periphery link has never had the integrated structure found in France. Over 80 percent of local investment was raised on the private market and public loans were not integrated with budgets at either the national or local level.[90] Individual central departments might impose conditions on capital spending, such as the Department of Education's condition that all new schools be designed for comprehensive use, but neither the macro- or micro-level implications of investment were reviewed as a whole. At the root of this issue were no doubt the clear lines drawn between the private and public sectors in Britain. Twenty years of Labour rule notwithstanding, Britain has never had the interlocking relation between private and public sector activity that is common in France.[91]

The functional pattern of center-periphery relations makes the collective choice over investment difficult. As Green has noted, the local authorities became "virtual agents of the central departments, each acting independently in its own affairs."[92] The resource problem was not unknown to central government. The Conservative government issued the Green Paper in 1971, promising a review of local taxes and subsidies. The Royal Commission was free to study the problem, but decided to concentrate on the efficiency-local democracy issue. The British system did not receive even the partial relief that the new tax sur le salaire provided in France, nor has there ever been anything comparable to the department-level coordination provided by the prefect. The result has been that in a financial crisis there is no alternative but arbitrary, and often ambiguous, central decision making, placing overall limits on local budgets and borrowing. For example,

in the recent economic crisis the Department of the Environment has
decided to "monitor" local taxes and to establish a watch committee
to limit personnel increases.[93]

A mechanism for mutual consideration of local resource problems was more or less forced on Britain by the most recent wave of
economic problems. The Layfield Committee was appointed to review
the entire issue. In mid-1975, the Department of the Environment
announced that a Consultative Committee on Local Finance would be
instituted, bringing representatives of departments, local government
associations, and the various local professional groups into a single
body for the first time.[94] The historic importance of this move is
hard to exaggerate, for it provides the first trial of collective decision making between center and periphery to be found in British local
government. Nonetheless, the effort has not prevented impatient and
angry exchanges, such as Anthony Crosland's outburst charging the
local authorities with reckless spending even though 80 percent of
their costs are mandated by central legislation.[95] Not only has the
interplay of public and private resources been less compartmentalized
in France, but the communal system has been encouraged to enter
into arrangements with private developers.[96] The Société d'économie
mixte provides a vehicle for business cooperation with local governments, not without its pitfalls, but clearly bringing a dimension to
local financial operations that has barely appeared in Britain.

A third weakness of the extreme functionalist model for center-
periphery relations is the severe problems encountered in coordination between the city or county and the central government. Lacking
the political penetration of the center provided by the locally and de-
partmentally elected officials in France as well as the coordination
provided by the prefect, the British system leaves little alternative
but to superimpose intermediate authorities in an arbitrary way.
France has, of course, experienced the same problem with regional
authorities, but the Gaullist efforts to regionalize were politically
blocked by the notables. Gaullist manipulations achieved the power
assigned to the British departments and ministries. In effect, the
functionalist model permits decentralization without political resistance, something that is virtually impossible in the French system.
This is not to argue that the administrative state may not be more
advanced in France, but only that in relation to center-periphery
problems the British can move with greater ease and authority than
their French counterparts, who must deal with the territorially based
political power. The intricacy of French administration may be a
demonstration of weakness rather than strength.

The direct and forceful intervention of British departments has
been repeatedly demonstrated in the past decade. The Transport Act
of 1968 gave Whitehall the authority to organize regional passenger

transport areas having a passenger transport executive to develop integrated public transport plans and financial schemes. Despite a plea in the Royal Commission's report that the localities' role in health might be expanded, the National Health Service Reorganization Act of 1973 took away many of the few remaining health responsibilities of local government. The Water Act of 1973, also a Conservative bill, set up area water authorities, leaving the localities to test water purity and to oversee sewerage within their specific areas. Under the Local Authorities Social Services Act and the Social Services Reorganization Act of 1970, the localities are required to unify all personal health services and appoint a director of social services subject to ministerial approval. The police and road functions of local government had been substantially amended well before this wave of legislation.

When the cumulative impact of these changes is added to the existing powers of the central departments to approve most key local officials (social services, education, police, fire), the British system may in fact operate in a more highly centralized fashion than the French. The significant difference is that the British have little of the fascinating competition among the grands corps to moderate administrative ambitions at the center.[97] Nor do they have the interlocking of representation and administration found in the communal and departmental structures. The influence of Whitehall arrives at the periphery untouched by local complications and backed by the unswerving strength of a strong parliament. Each function has in effect been nationalized and policies for each function rest unequivocally with the central administration. The departments, in turn, deal with the subunits individually for the most part, and, where collective needs appear, the arrangements are most often defined by the center and suited to the needs perceived by the center. Like most industrial societies, both France and Britain have moved toward the functionalist model, but Britain differs by giving its administrators dependable and strong representative support.

A final weakness of the extreme functionalist model of center-periphery relations is the difficulty of local planning. Indeed, it has been argued by one analyst of the British reorganization that the justification of the entire exercise was to improve planning.[98] If this is so, British planners must be very disappointed because they now find themselves confronted with about 500 local-planning authorities rather than the approximately 150 formerly constituted by the boroughs and counties. Under the Town and Country Planning Act of 1968 and subsequent amendments, the counties were directed to construct "structure plans," which were to be general, strategic plans for the development of the area. The progress of the structure plans is a story in itself, but under the 1972 law the districts were given responsibility for development plans. Thus, Britain now has a seriously divided planning process that is vastly more complex than the old system. At the local level the procedure has become almost unmanageable: some 623,000 development decisions have been funneled through the new structure in 1973 alone.[99] Before the Conservative government fell, a special committee was appointed to try to disentangle the growing snarl.[100]

At the root of the local planning problem is the question of land use. The British solution to this problem is testimony to both the strength of Parliament and to the disadvantages of a functionally compartmentalized relationship between the center and the periphery. In 1947 Labour approached the problem with legislation by imposing a "betterment levy" on developed land, intended to provide local authorities with some of the capital gains from rising land values within their areas. When the Conservatives came to power in 1951, the law was repealed. Labour renewed its efforts to redistribute the product of land speculation when it returned to power in 1964 and finally in 1975 passed a community land act nationalizing all development land within urban areas.[101] The new law came at a difficult time for British local governments, already burdened with reorganizational requirements and severe financial difficulties. More important, it placed even greater stress on effective lateral relationships among the districts, which has been one of the notable shortcomings of the functionalist structure oriented largely to central departmental demands and requirements.

Both France and Britain have had their share of land scandals in recent years, but the French system is further along toward a solution to land-use problems. The ability of the municipalities to form sociétés d'économie mixte provides them with a device involving land use and overall development of the area. The French system, of course, takes a more relaxed view of the interpenetration of private and public interest. The French device also leaves room for local initiative in consultation with administrative officials locally and nationally. In contrast, the British nationalization of local development land began, like so many other local reforms, by placing a centrally designed, uniform solution on all subunits. Like the local planning activity generally, it also lacks any organizational substructure to assure that bordering districts will indeed coordinate their implementation of the law and cooperate in order to extract the full benefit of its product. The functionalist model is preserved in the British Land Act by default if not by intent, for the central departments remain detached from local disputes and local political conflict.

CONCLUSION: PRAGMATIC FUNCTIONALISM
AND FUNCTIONAL PRAGMATISM

The purpose of this chapter has been to show that a major reorganization of British local government was possible only because the decision conformed to the underlying structure of authority in the society. The British system is a strong partisan system, but partisan choice is confined to a relatively narrow range of policy making. Were strong partisan influence exercised at all levels of political activity, as in France or the United States, central political institutions would be compromised. At the very least, France and the United States could not have undertaken such a massive reorganization of local government. The British system has been able to attack other fundamental problems in the same way, not always with success, but in a way impossible in more intricate decision-making structures. The Labour Relations Act of 1972 would be unimaginable in the more complicated industrial democracies. For all the intrigue and influence concentrated in the French Ministry of Finance or the American Office of Management and Budget, these institutions cannot achieve the degree of financial and fiscal control typical of the British treasury. This degree of central control is not due to simply the administrative and technocratic dominance of decision making but to the ability of partisan control to work within the limits of a strong, national parliament.

There are, of course, costs in maintaining strong central institutions and an effective two-party system. Some decisions have been patently wrong and some problems have been sadly neglected. Nonetheless, the partisan structure has intervened in its limited but decisive fashion in every major decision regarding local reorganization: the London Act of 1963, the formation of the Royal Commission, the allocation of resources and benefits through the subnational structures, the determination of boundaries and the setting for local political activity, and, most recently, the role to be assigned to community and parish level organization. As I have tried to show, the French government and probably most other industrial democracies have been unable to influence the center-periphery relationship with anything approaching the decisiveness and finality of the British Parliament. This is, of course, a reciprocal relationship. Were Westminster and Whitehall unable to do this, the foundations of British parliamentary government would be threatened.

The power of Parliament has meant that Britain remains closer to the classical liberal state than any other state of Europe. Consensual politics are still practiced over a greater range of subjects and issues than in any other European government. In other states extra-governmental institutions have become increasingly common in order to compensate for weak parliaments. True, the British system may be a form of "stagnant pluralism," as Beer has suggested,[102] but it has provided political stability through upheavals and crises that are certainly as severe as those faced by France. Even the Algerian crisis has its parallel in Northern Ireland. Despite the terror tactics and concessions to the Stormont Assembly, the status of Parliament remains relatively untouched. This is not an insignificant achievement, given the stresses and strains that modern democracies are undergoing.

My explanation for Britain's ability to sustain parliamentary rule is the conversion to a functional state, where policy formation is concentrated at the center and sheltered from partisan politics. The emergence of a functional state is not unique to Britain for it has followed with rapid urbanization and industrial growth in all the modern democracies. The difference for Britain is that functional control was achieved because Parliament was strong, not weak as in several continental states. The centralization of the British state represents pragmatic functional control. New activities are linked to the center as they fit within the requirements of a partisan but consensual Parliament. For France and much of Europe the process is reversed. New functions are assembled around the center as it appears possible to work out agreement outside the central machinery of government and Parliament.

Space prohibits illustrating how this relationship has worked in other areas, but the evidence indicates similar solutions to regional government, economic planning, labor relations (with some difficulty), and industrial development. The roots of the functional centralization for British local government can be traced back to the early nineteenth century. It is not that other states, such as France, have not achieved similar degrees of functional organization, but this has been done in many instances by going outside the formal democratic institutions of the society. This strategy has often been strongly resisted, if not totally rejected, by the local government system. The British local politician, though linked to parties at the local level, does not see his role as one of extracting benefits from the center; much less are his basic skills those of working his way through a complex decision-making process and leading to ministerial favors. The local links of members of Parliament are probably as well developed as those of French deputies and senators, but mutual dependence is carefully circumscribed in Britain. One does not get elected to Parliament in order to do favors for a local authority, even though roughly a third of the members of Parliament have local government experience and, of those, about two-fifths are in parliamentary constituencies corresponding to local authority areas.[103]

The functional state has prospered in Britain because intricate political links between center and periphery have never been developed, either by members of Parliament or by local politicians. The transformation of the subnational structure into primarily a set of service agencies subordinated to central ministerial circulars and standards is, of course, only one part of the full manifestation of functional pragmatism. The French ministries, of course, do not lack administrative devices to subordinate communes, but the formal institutions are carefully circumscribed by legal codes and definitions of compétence, while the informal links are infinitely more complex. Even the formidable power of the administration, meshed with Gaullist determination, was unable to convert the communes to the uniform, standardized structure we see in Britain. The British local governments still operate under only a slightly amended rule of ultra vires, though chief executives are known for their skill, like French mayors, in circumventing legal requirements. The crucial difference, of course, is that French mayors seek to penetrate the center in every way possible, while British councils accept their detachment and their subordination.

The capacity of the British system to change is achieved at a price. Thus, it is quite consistent with this pattern of authority that strong planning beyond parliamentary supervision is unwelcome. The result has been one of the most confused and ineffective planning structures in Europe today, both nationally and locally. Likewise, Britain is unable to achieve the overall direction of investment found in French industrial and urban programs. Though pressure groups operate in all modern systems, in Britain it is predominantly the professional groups that are consulted in making changes, each consulted for its expertise rather than to achieve an integrated policy. The functional links to the periphery are virtually captured by a professional group whether it be in social services, health, or education. The consensual system requires that political bargaining and favoritism be excluded from such decisions. Last, but by no means least, the regional pattern emerging in Britain is largely accidental. Each central function is linked to different areas and uses different institutional procedures. The dissent of Crowtherhunt and Peacock to the Royal Commission on the Constitution is a rare national voice suggesting that this confusion can be eliminated.

The center-periphery link in Britain takes its present form, I would argue, in order to sustain an effective, two-party system at the center. This means excluding those subjects from partisan discussion that might irreparably damage the consensual machinery of Parliament. Protecting Parliament from local political forces also maximizes central control of policy. Functional organization increases the strength of the center, but the moderated form of partisanship, pervasive as it is, implies that many problems are neglected. The centrifugal forces operating on the modern democratic state are immense. Despite the failures and weaknesses of the British system of linking center to periphery, it may still appear that political effectiveness and stability at the center will prevail as the most important quality of the modern democratic state.

NOTES

1. These changes are a similar assessment of the French approach to reorganization and are the subject of a longer manuscript under way by the author, "British Idealism and French Pragmatism: The Politics of Decentralization."

2. Beer's classic statement is British Politics in the Collectivist Age (New York: Knopf, 1965); Eckstein, A Theory of Stable Democracy (Princeton, N.J.: Center for International Studies, 1961). They are by no means the only writers of the period who concentrate on parties, pressure groups, and Parliament as a way of characterizing political systems. Even more policy-oriented writing of the period, such as David Easton, continued to look upon "inputs" and "outputs" as easily separated. The general theoretical position of this chapter is that a closer examination of decisions indicated that this distribution is not only difficult to make, but may also be misleading. How demands and performance interlock may even be conceived as a way of comparing systems themselves.

3. G. W. Jones, "The Local Government Act of 1972 and the Redcliffe-Maud Commission," Political Quarterly 44 (April-June 1973): 154-66; W. Hampton, "Political Attitudes to Change in City Council Administration," Local Government Studies 5 (April 1972): 23-35; S. L. Bristow, "The Criteria for Local Government Reorganization and Local Authority Autonomy," Policy and Politics 1 (December 1972): 143-62; C. J. Davies, "The Reform of Local Government with Special Reference to England," Studies in Comparative Local Government 7 (Winter 1973): 35-45; J. Stanyer in The Role of Commissions in Policy-Making, ed. R. Chapman (London: Allen and Unwin, 1974), pp. 105-42; R. Rhodes, "Local Government Reform: Three Questions—What Is Reorganization? What Are the Effects of Reorganization? Why Reorganization?" Social and Economic Administration 8 (Spring 1974): 6-21.

4. This point is made very clearly by H. Eckstein in his reconstruction of the consensual model, "Authority Patterns: A Structural Basis for Political Inquiry," American Political Science Review, December 1973, pp. 1142-61.

5. Not surprisingly, the most effective locally based resistance to central reform came from the most powerful city, London, which did have a strong lobby in Parliament and did resist the major reforms of 1888 for a time. For an excellent account, see K. Young, Local Politics and the Rise of Party (Leicester: University of Leicester Press, 1975).

6. Scotland's local organization was reviewed by the Royal Commission on Local Government in Scotland (Wheatley Commission), Report (London: HSMO, 1973, cmnd. 5460). See especially vol. 1, chap. 4, pp. 21–32 and vol. 2, chap. 6, pp. 84–108, for the conflicting views on regional devolution, which at the time of writing are still before Parliament.

7. There is an important group of countries where local policy escapes partisan treatment at the local level because of the force of national-level agreement. Thus, the Netherlands version of consociational democracy tends to centralize policy decisions in order to evade conflict over fundamental social cleavages, though this may be breaking down. See A. Lijphart, The Politics of Accommodation: Pluralism and Democracy in the Netherlands, 2nd ed. (Berkeley: University of California Press, 1975). Sweden appears to be a case where center-local links are so closely governed through a peculiar way of formulating policy that again local partisan forces may have little impact. See T. Anton, Governing Greater Stockholm: A Study of Policy Development and System Change (Berkeley: University of California Press, 1975). Thus, there may be several ways in which the locality may be relieved of significant policy choice, thereby foreclosing this channel for partisan expression.

8. A number of excellent community-level studies convey this detachment. See J. Dearlove, The Politics of Policy in Local Government (Cambridge, England: Cambridge University Press, 1973); W. Hampton, Democracy and Community: A Study of Politics in Sheffield (London: Oxford University Press, 1963); The Scope of Local Initiative: A Study of Cheshire County Council, 1961–1974, ed. J. M. Lee (London: Martin Robinson, 1974); A. H. Birch, Small Town Politics (London: Oxford University Press, 1959); A. M. Rees and T. A. Smith, Town Councillors: A Study of Barking (London: Action Society Trust, 1964); Kenneth Newton, Second City Politics (London: Oxford University Press, 1976). For similar evidence on London, see P. Kantor and D. Lawrence, "Policy-Making and the Role of the Representative: An Analysis of Local Politics in London," paper prepared for meeting of the American Political Science Association, September 1975.

9. A number of French local government analysts have looked with favor upon the Redcliffe-Maud formula for city-centered subunits of government. See J. F. Médard, "Les Communautés urbaines:

Renforcement ou declin de l'autonomie locale?" Revue de droit publique, vol. 84 (July–October 1968); H. Roussillon, Les Structures
térritoriales des communes: Réformes et perspectives d'avenir
(Paris: Librairie Générale de Droit et de Jurisprudence, 1972), pp.
354–57.

10. The excellent studies of the Crozier group have established
this point, though I shall put a rather different interpretation on their
findings. See Jean-Pierre Worms, "Le Préfet et ses notables,"
Sociologie du travail 3 (1966): 249–75; P. Grémion, "Résistance au
changement de l'administration térritorial: Le cas des institutions
régionales," Sociologie du travail 3 (1966): 276–95; and also J. Milch,
"Influence as Power: French Local Government Reconsidered,"
British Journal of Political Science 4 (1974): 139–62.

11. One of the most dramatic illustrations is the very different
handling of national subsidies for local investment. See D. Ashford,
"Financial Incentives for Local Reorganization in Britain and France,"
paper prepared for the Meeting of the International Political Science
Association, Edinburgh, August 1976.

12. D. Fraser, The Evolution of the British Welfare State (London: MacMillan, 1973).

13. B. Moore, Jr., The Social Origins of Dictatorship and
Democracy (Boston: Beacon Press, 1966), especially pp. 3–39.

14. Sir Francis Hill, Victorian Lincoln (Cambridge, England:
Cambridge University Press, 1974), p. 63.

15. Ibid., pp. 189–200.

16. Ibid., pp. 60–61.

17. Ibid., p. 39.

18. R. Muir, A History of Liverpool (Liverpool: University
Press of Liverpool, 1907), p. 327.

19. A. T. Patterson, Radical Leicester (Leicester: University
College of Leicester, 1954), p. 220.

20. W. A. Robson, The Government and Misgovernment of London (London: Allen and Unwin, 1939), pp. 50–53.

21. For example, see the protest of the organ of the local authorities association when cuts in local spending were announced,
Municipal Review, January 1975.

22. K. B. Smellie, History of Local Government, 4th ed. (Cambridge, England: Cambridge University Press, 1974), p. 52.

23. Fraser, British Welfare State, p. 30.

24. A superb account of how central influence was shaped is
contained in S. E. Finer's The Life and Times of Sir Edwin Chadwick
(London: Methuen, 1957), p. 213.

25. Smellie, History of Local Government, p. 48.

26. Ibid., p. 39.

27. K. Young, "The Conservative Party Strategy for London
1855–1975," The London Journal, Spring 1975, pp. 56–81. See also

his "The Politics of London Government 1880-1889," Public Administration (United Kingdom) 51 (Spring 1973): 91-108.

28. Young, "Conservative Party Strategy," p. 73.

29. Robson, Government and Misgovernment, pp. 358-64.

30. Young, "Conservative Party Strategy," p. 77, and Local
Politics and the Rise of Party.

31. See the protest by P. Self, Whither Local Government?
Fabian Society Tract No. 279 (January 1950). An almost identical position was taken 20 years earlier in reaction to first efforts to provide
large-scale local assistance. See S. Webb, The Local Government
Act, 1929, Fabian Society Tract No. 231 (November 1929).

32. F. Smallwood, Greater London: The Politics of Metropolitan Reform (New York: Bobbs-Merrill, 1965); and Gerald Rhodes,
The Government of London: The Struggle for Reform (Toronto: University of Toronto Press, 1970).

33. Royal Commission on Local Government in Greater London,
1957-60 (Herbert Commission), Report (London: HMSO, 1960, cmnd.
1164).

34. Smellie, History of Local Government, pp. 115-16.

35. J. Stanyer, "The Local Government Commissions," Local
Government in England, 1958-69, ed. H. Wiseman (London: Routledge and Kegan Paul, 1970), pp. 25-28.

36. Ibid., pp. 36-40.

37. G. W. Jones, "A Forgotten Right Discovered," Parliamentary Affairs 19, 3 (1966): 363-72.

38. These two committees should not be confused with the Redcliffe-Maud Royal Commission. Maud was knighted between chairing
the earlier committee and the royal commission. The Mallaby report
is on staffing. See W. S. Steer and D. Lofts, "The Mallaby Committee," Local Government in England, ed. Wiseman, pp. 71-95.

39. G. W. Jones, "Mr. Crossman and the Reform of Local Government," Parliamentary Affairs 20 (Winter 1966): 77-89.

40. Municipal Review, November 1965, pp. 655-60.

41. This view is expressed in Jones' interpretation of the decision. See his "The Local Government Act."

42. Fraser, British Welfare State, p. 207.

43. Ibid., pp. 215-16.

44. Smellie, History of Local Government, p. 108.

45. F. R. Oliver and R. Stanyer, "Some Aspects of the Financial Behaviour of County Boroughs," Public Administration (United
Kingdom) 47 (Summer 1969): 169-84.

46. N. T. Boaden and R. Alford, "Sources of Diversity in Eng-
lish Local Government Decisions," Public Administration (United
Kingdom) 47 (Summer 1969): 203-23; B. Davies, Social Needs and
Resources in Local Services (London: Michael Joseph, 1968).

47. D. Ashford, "Parties and Participation in British Local Government and Some American Parallels," Urban Affairs Quarterly 11 (September 1975): 58-81; and his "Resources, Spending and Party Politics in British Local Government," Administration and Society 7 (November 1975): 286-311.

48. B. Davies et al., Variations in Services for the Aged (London: Bell, 1971); and B. Davies et al., Variations in Children's Services among British Urban Authorities (London: Bell, 1972).

49. Ashford, "Resources, Spending and Party Politics," and "The Effects of Central Finance on the British Local Government Systems," British Journal of Political Science 7 (July 1974): 305-22.

50. Reform of Local Government in England (London: HMSO, cmnd. 4276, 1970).

51. Local Government in England: Proposals for Reorganization (London: HMSO, cmnd. 4584, 1971).

52. New Society, February 18, 1971.

53. Ibid., December 9, 1971.

54. The Economist, January 29, 1972.

55. Committee on the Management of Local Government, Report, vol. 1 (London: HMSO, 1967). This was the initial Maud inquiry that became the basis for the royal commission that he chaired.

56. For details, see P. G. Richards, The "Reformed" Local Government System (London: Allen and Unwin, 1973), pp. 65-67. The aim of having standard elections in London, England, Wales, and Scotland has not been achieved, nor do the parliamentary constituencies conform to local election district boundaries except for some cities.

57. W. Grant, "Local Parties in British Local Politics: A Framework for Analysis," Political Studies 19 (June 1971): 201-12, and "Nonpartisanship in British Local Politics," Policy and Politics 1 (March 1973): 241-54; and Ashford, "Parties and Participation." A fascinating essay on conservative resistance to partisan local government is K. Young's "Values in Urban Politics: The Case of 'Localism,'" unpublished paper, 1975.

58. Committee on the Management of Local Government, The Local Councillor, vol. 3 (London: HMSO, 1967).

59. Ibid., p. 206.

60. Ibid., p. 188.

61. R. Rhodes, "The Changing Political Management System of Local Government," unpublished paper, 1975.

62. Committee on the Management of Local Government, The Local Councillor, p. 162.

63. M. Parkinson, "Central-Local Relations in British Parties: A Local View," Political Studies 19 (December 1971): 440-46.

64. The failure to achieve codeterminous boundaries has a long history, starting with the failure of Labour to alter parliamentary constituencies to reflect population shifts in 1969; see The Economist, July 12, 1969 and July 19, 1969. When the new counties were laid out in 1971, the country was then on the brink of another parliamentary adjustment. Parliamentary districting is compulsory under the Representation of the People's Act of 1948, and under the new Local Government Law, but identical boundaries will not be drawn until the next decennial census in 1981.

65. For ample documentation of the direct link between local and national politics, see J. E. S. Hayward and V. Wright, "The 37,708 Microcosms of an Indivisible Republic: The French Local Elections of March 1971," Parliamentary Affairs 24 (Autumn 1971): 284-311.

66. This observation does not necessarily run counter to the long tradition of literature on the administrative power of the French state, for example, Brian Chapman, The Prefects and Provincial France (London: Allen and Unwin, 1955); and F. Ridley and J. Blondel, Public Administration in France (London: Routledge and Kegan Paul, 1964). It is only to suggest that every state must formulate a way to link the periphery to the center. Where political links are unstable, weakly associated with policy direction, and working within a small-scale structure, the state requires a mechanism to reach the hinterland. Put slightly differently, the conventional view does not answer the question of what might have happened to France in the absence of a strong administration.

67. For an account of this effort and its poor results see H. Machin, "Local Government Change in France—The Case of the 1964 Reforms," Policy and Politics 2 (March 1974): 249-65, and "The French Prefects and Local Administration," Parliamentary Affairs 27 (Spring 1974): 237-50. The general interpretation of administration and politics advanced here has been argued by V. Wright, "Politics and Administration under the French Fifth Republic," Political Studies 22 (March 1972): 44-65; and is reflected in J. E. S. Hayward, The One and Indivisible French Republic (London: Weidenfeld and Nicholson, 1973).

68. The inability of the French system to separate politics and local reorganization is admirably documented by Y. Mény in Centralisation et décentralisation dans le débat politique français (1945-1969) (Paris: Librairie générale de droit et de jurisprudence, 1974).

69. Institut national de la statistique et des études economiques, Statistiques et indicateurs des régions françaises, Collections de l'INSEE, Series R., no. 19-20 (November 1975), pp. 345-46.

70. Médard, "Les communautés urbaines," p. 709.

71. The essential distinction here is that the établissement publique can be created by administrative order and operates as part of

the central state machinery. For example, the 1971 regional changes were accomplished in this way. The collectivité locale is a constitutionally defined body, having a political and representative role and a definite administrative competence apart from the state administration. See Ridley and Blondel, Public Administration, pp. 55-61.

72. This point is common in the literature on French politics and has been most forcefully argued by Mark Kesselman in "Overinstitutionalization and Political Constraint: The Case of France," Comparative Politics 3 (October 1970): 21-44; and M. Crozier, The Bureaucratic Phenomenon (London: Tavistock, 1965).

73. Mény, Centralisation, pp. 89-118. The importance of mutual dependence, which, in turn, resists change, is suggested by J. E. S. Hayward and V. Wright in "The 37,708 Microcosms," where they note that among the local candidates were 36 of 41 ministers, 379 of 487 deputies, and 191 of 283 senators.

74. For an excellent account of the struggle in territorial terms, see Roussillon, Les structures térritoriales.

75. See P. Grémion, "L'Administration térritoriale," in Collections Sociologie des Organisations, Où va l'administration française? (Paris: Editions d'organisation, 1974), pp. 75-100; also P. Grémion and J. P. Worms, Les Institutions régionales et la société locale (Paris: CNRS, 1968), and P. Grémion, La Structuration du pouvoir au niveau départmental (Paris: CNSR, 1969).

76. For details, see Roussillon, Les structures, pp. 75-85.

77. Milch, "Influence as Power"; also M. Laget, "Données financières de la gestion communale," Revue de l'économie méridionale (Etudes et enquêtes) 18, 73 (1971): 1-15; M. Laget and J. Rouzier, "Equipements urbains en Languedoc-Rousillon," Revue de l'économie méridionale 13, 49 (1965): 1-28.

78. Yves Fréville, "L'Evolution des finances des grandes villes depuis 1967," Revue de science financière, 1973, pp. 725-58; J. Kobielski, "L'Influence des structures des communes urbaines sur leurs dépenses de fonctionnement" (thesis, University of Rennes, 1974).

79. E. Suleiman, Politics, Power, and Bureaucracy in France (Princeton, N.J.: Princeton University Press, 1974).

80. J. M. de Préneuf, "Finances locales: Les projects Pompidou," Revue politique et parliamentaire 818 (1971): 46-55. Similar doubts are raised about policy confusion by F. D'Arcy, Structures administratives et urbanisation (Paris: Editions Berger Levrault, 1968); and by Henri Coing, "La Ville en plan," Revue français de science politique 23 (1973): 250-303.

81. Commisariat générale du plan, Rapport de l'intergroupe d'études des finances locales (Paris: Documentation francaise, 1971).

82. D'Arcy, Structures administratives.

83. Grémion, L'Administration térritoriale, p. 84. Clear evidence exists at the regional level. See R. Prud'homme, "Regional Economic Policy in France, 1962-1972," Public Policy and Regional Economic Development, ed. N. Hansen (Cambridge, England: Ballinger, 1974), pp. 33-63.

84. This is essentially the argument of Hayward and Wright, "The 37,708 Microcosms." See also P. Mawhood, "Melting an Iceberg: The Struggle to Reform Communal Government in France," British Journal of Political Science 2 (April 1972): 501-15.

85. H. Machin, "The French Prefects and Local Administration," Parliamentary Affairs 27 (Spring 1974): 237-50.

86. W. Hampton, "Political Attitudes to Change in City Council Administration," Local Government Studies 5 (April 1972): 23-35.

87. J. D. Stewart, The Responsive Local Authority (London: Knight, 1974); J. D. Stewart, Management in Local Government: A Viewpoint (London: Knight, 1972); J. K. Friend and W. N. Jessop, Local Government and Strategic Choice (London: Tavistock, 1969); J. Cullingworth, ed., Planning for Change (London: Allen and Unwin, 1973); R. Greenwood and J. D. Stewart, "Towards a Typology of English Local Authorities," Political Studies 21 (March 1972): 64-69; A. H. Marshall, Financial Management and Local Government (London: MacMillan, 1970).

88. Stewart, Responsive Local Authority, pp. 137-38.

89. R. Greenwood, C. R. Hinings, and S. Hinings, "Contingency Theory and the Organization of Local Authorities: Part I. Differentiation and Integration," Public Administration (United Kingdom) 53 (Spring 1975): 1-23, and "Part II. Contingencies and Structure," Public Administration (United Kingdom) 53 (Summer 1975): 169-90.

90. N. P. Hepworth, The Finance of Local Government, 2nd ed. (London: Allen and Unwin, 1971), p. 20.

91. For similar conclusions in the area of planning policy see J. Hayward, "Introduction," Planning, Politics and Public Policy: The British, French and Italian Cases, ed. J. Hayward and M. Watson (Cambridge, England: Cambridge University Press, 1975) and in industrial relations, his "State Intervention in France: The Changing Style of Government-Industry Relations," Political Studies 20 (September 1972): 287-98.

92. L. P. Green, Provincial Metropolis: The Future of Local Government in South East Lancashire (London: Allen and Unwin, 1959), p. 156.

93. Department of the Environment, Rate Fund Expenditure and Rate Calls in 1975-76, Circular 171/54 (London: HMSO, December 23, 1974).

94. Department of the Environment, Local Authority Expenditure, Circular 51/75 (London: HMSO, May 2, 1975).

95. The Economist, March 22, 1975.

96. See D'Arcy, Structures administratives.

97. For example, see the study of the ponts et chausées administrative elite by J. C. Thoenig, L'Ere des technocrats (Paris: Editions d'Organisation, 1973). Part of the internal struggle over local reorganization involved this grands corps, who felt their technical talents might even compete with prefectoral control. The key step in their bureaucratic power struggle was establishing a direction d'équipement at the prefecture in 1966, which would be staffed, of course, by a member of the ponts et chausées.

98. J. Brand, Local Government Reform in England (London: Croom Helm, 1974).

99. The Economist, February 22, 1975.

100. Department of the Environment, Review of the Development Control System (Dobry report) (London: HMSO, February 1975).

101. R. Barras, A. Broadbent, and D. Massey, "Planning and the Public Ownership of Land," New Society, June 21, 1973. For a discussion of the results in the 1975 Community Land Act, see M. Eyers, "The Land Bill: A Recipe for Its Own Repeal?" New Society, October 16, 1975.

102. Beer, British Politics in the Collectivist Age, postscript to 2nd ed.

103. See C. Mellors, "Local Government in Parliament—Twenty Years Later," Public Administration (United Kingdom) 52 (Summer 1974): 223-29. The view from the bottom underscores this detachment. For example, few local councillors aspire to national office and see national parties having little effect on local policy. See M. Parkinson, "Central-Local Relations in British Parties: A Local View," Political Studies 19 (December 1971): 440-46.

9

CENTER-PERIPHERY RELATIONS
AND THE ITALIAN CRISIS:
THE PROBLEM OF CLIENTELISM
Luigi Graziano

Although in Italy, as elsewhere, there are many "peripheries," depending on the definition of the term, one historic cleavage characterizes the center-periphery dimension more than any other, that is, the north-south cleavage. In terms of social and economic structure as well as in terms of values, the perception "of being in the center or at the margin of historical progress," to use Pizzorno's words,[1] the south has remained at the margin of Italian development. It is not only underdeveloped; it is also "different," objectively different and negatively viewed as such by southerners themselves.[2]

The persistence of territorial dualism a century after unification calls attention to the peculiarity of the southern question as a problem in center-periphery relations within an industrialized country. Historians generally refer to Italy's development as "dual development." This term is defined not only as regional diversity but also as the capacity of the south to condition the overall course of Italian history. As a noted historian of the Mezzogiorno, Rosario Villari, remarked, "The Southern question has influenced, sometimes in a decisive manner, the political and economic development of Italy, unlike other cases of 'backwardness' which have only had an imperceptible impact on the general process of development" in other societies.[3] In this national dimension of the southern question lies, then, the peculiarity of the Italian periphery.

When applied to the problem of the south and to its persistence and resistance to change, most models of center-periphery relations are not very helpful. Sidney Tarrow has conveniently grouped such

*I would like to thank Peter Katzenstein and Sidney Tarrow for their helpful comments on earlier drafts of this essay.

models into three categories: models of cultural diffusion, models centered on the market and economic marginality, and models based on the role of state bureaucracies in center-periphery relations.[4]

The "diffusionists" define the center in terms of modernizing values and see development as a process whereby such values reach into the periphery. It seems evident that a century-old problem like that of southern Italy cannot be viewed in purely normative terms. Clearly more than values are involved in the mechanisms that have produced and preserved southern inferiority. To the extent that the problem is one of values, it is not clear which of the "two nations," north or south, has had the greatest impact on national development.[5] In the field of bureaucratic behavior, to cite just one crucial example, the state has less modernized the south than the south has "meridionalized" the state. I shall return to this point later in the chapter.

The notion of market-induced marginality has greater plausibility. The commercialization of an economy both integrates society through the market and generates new differentiations. Included here are forms of uneven territorial development such as the concentration of industry due to considerations of scale and the localization of infrastructure. Furthermore, economic marginality may be accentuated by the action of the state. In trying to spur development, the state may divert resources from one region to another. It thus joins the market as a potential factor in the unbalanced development of society. But, although the market has greatly contributed to the perpetuation of southern inferiority, the market hypothesis can explain neither the genesis of that inferiority nor the persistent characterization of the south as a largely precapitalist, precontractual society.[6] As I have said, the market sets in motion processes both of exploitation and integration. In the Mezzogiorno, however, deprivation occurs without integration. If such deprivation had been the product of capitalist exploitation, its counterpart would have been a degree of similarity to the north in terms of structures, behavior, and so on, far superior to what is witnessed today.

The economic marginality model is inadequate simply because a national market developed very late in Italy. A number of studies, especially by Marxian scholars,[7] have shown how slow and limited has been the penetration of the market into nineteenth century southern Italy. These works seriously weaken the "internal colonialism" hypothesis that underlies the work of so many meridionalisti (southern experts) (Salvemini, Fortunato, Nitti, and many others). The truth of the matter seems to be that the south has suffered less from capitalist exploitation than from the lack of it; that is, from the lack of a truly capitalist revolution that, along with exploitation, would have effected the sweeping changes the market carries with it. The south suffered enormously after 1860 in terms of people (emigration) and material resources. But it suffered less for what was taken from it through the market and fiscal oppression than for what it was prevented from producing due to the survival of its semifeudal social relations. [8]

The next question is then: why did a liberal bourgeoisie that brought to Italy the basic agents of modernity, the national state and capitalism, so conspicuously fail to bring them to bear on the south? To answer this question we must turn to the role of the state. The bureaucratic model worked out by Crozier and his associates is a step in the right direction, but with one exception. It is more helpful in explaining the functioning of center-periphery relations than either their genesis or the systemic constraints within which they operate. Before looking at the functioning of the Italian state and the network of informal arrangements between its officials and local notables, it is necessary to look at the social basis of the state, that is, at the classes in the population whose consent was needed at given points in history, and at how they constrained government policy.

If the south has been cut off from the mainstream of Italian development, this was originally due to the political alliances that made the new state viable. The basic alliance was between the northern bourgeoisie and the southern landed middle class, whose property came mainly from the usurpation of exbaronial and common land. [9] The capitalist modernization of the south, especially the dismantling of the _feodo_ economy, would have penalized a large section of the southern ruling class and disrupted the social basis of the new state. The result was that the Italian revolution was limited to a purely political one. As Fortunato once bitterly remarked, "it is easier to make a political revolution than a social reform, . . . to change regime than conscience." [10]

In short, to understand the southern question, the Italian version of the center-periphery problem, it requires a model that is more than purely normative, that goes beyond the market as the exclusive factor in territorial marginality, and that views the state both in its functional and its structural dimension. One way of meeting these analytical requirements is to look at the problem of the south from the viewpoint of clientelism, a social pattern that has characterized southern politics since unification. The problem of clientelism enters into the study of center-periphery relations in at least two ways. Traditional clientelism manifests itself in highly stratified societies. The patrons control crucial resources, including the knowledge and skill that is necessary for interacting with the world that is external to the local community. From this evolves the role of patrons as mediators between the periphery and the center. This is a role that has been intensively studied, especially by anthropologists. [11] In more modern settings, patron-client ties may be seen either as a device by which local elites gain access to the bureaucracy (see the section, "Some Current Interpretations of the Italian Crisis") or as the center's strategy for controlling the periphery through particularistic methods of resource allocation. [12]

More important, the study of clientelism in its systemic dimension, and not simply as a mode of behavior, allows one to work out a structural model of politics that is also very useful in the study of center-periphery relations. That is, political clientelism, based as it is on direct relations between social actors and public officials, signals the defective development of generalized structures of social regulation such as the market, the party system, and the state bureaucracy. Since these structures are also basic to the shaping and regulation of center-periphery relations, the analysis of clientelism has important implications for the problem under consideration.

In this chapter, the section "Clientelism and the Political System" will delineate a structural model of the political system. The political system will be viewed as a historic formation, not merely as an analytical construct as in systems theory. Political development will be defined as a process whereby the political system emancipates itself from a backward society, especially from the point of view of efficiency and legitimacy. It develops legitimacy through the political mediation of the most important cleavages in society, including regional cleavages. Clientelism, implying as it does a sort of "confusion" of state and society, will be defined as a case of structural emancipation manqué.

The second section, "Clientelism as Political Emancipation Manqué: National Integration and Political Development in Italy," will investigate some of the factors and processes that hindered the political emancipation of the south in nineteenth century Italy. Of particular concern will be the pattern of unification, the structure of the political class, and the role of the south in the politics of trasformismo. Finally, the section "Some Current Interpretations of the Italian Crisis" will illustrate some contemporary manifestations of clientelism as they affect center-periphery integration and the role of the middle classes, especially in southern Italy.

CLIENTELISM AND THE POLITICAL SYSTEM

Clientelism has been studied mainly from a behavioral perspective, and far less in its relation to the political system. [13] Much is known about clientelistic forms of association, but relatively little about the systemic implications of patron-client ties. First, I shall briefly criticize what I take to be a serious shortcoming in the literature on patronage: its exclusive concern with consensus. Second, I

shall offer a conceptualization of the political system that I believe
provides a better paradigm for the study of clientelism and, more
generally, of political development.

Some Observations on the Literature on Patronage:
Emphasis on Consensus and the Notion
of the Political System

In the specialized literature, clientelism has been seen essentially as a consensus formation mechanism. The following quotation
from René Lemarchand is fairly representative of the prevailing attitude in the field:

> Insofar as it implies a normative commitment to certain
> "instrumentalities and procedures for the achievement
> of goals and resolving conflicts" (Weiner), clientelism
> may provide at least some of the ingredients which enter
> into processes of consensus formation at the national
> level.[14]

This may or may not be the case, as will be shown later in this chapter with respect to the Italian experience. In the case studied by Lemarchand (ethnicity in Africa), patronage seems rather to have exacerbated ethnic conflict. "The irony is that the same forces that encouraged the birth of political machines also helped activate the ethnic
solidarities which in many instances destroyed the machine."[15]
     Although important, this is not my basic critique of clientelism
as a mode of acquiring consensus through particularistic incentives.
My main point is that even when clientelism encourages consensus,
it generates support, never legitimation. It may help "get out the
vote," but it does not help to develop the kind of commitment that is
associated with the idea of legitimacy. The distinction is crucial.
Support is consensus engineered by the political class and granted by
an aggregate of single individuals (the "public," the electorate, and
so on) to the same political class. It is manifested typically through
the vote. Legitimation is consensus granted "spontaneously" by organized groups and institutions in society (families, schools, the church,
intellectuals, trade unions, the press, and the like). It is consensus
granted to the regime and its official representatives rather than to
the ruling class as such. Legitimation is expressed less by the vote
than by supportive values and attitudes.[16]
     While not all supportive actions are clientelistic, by nature all
clientelistic incentives aim at generating support. This is evident,
for instance, in Sorauf's characterization of patronage as an "incen-

tive system—a political currency with which to purchase political activity and political responses," that is, votes.[17] While one can buy
votes, one cannot buy legitimacy. Weber defines legitimacy as "the
belief that a regime (and the government entitled according to certain
rules in it to make decisions) has the right to the obedience of its
citizens . . . even when its decisions do not coincide with the subject's
personal interests (or his understanding of those interests)."[18] If
one agrees with this definition, then one cannot have legitimacy and
individually acquired consensus at the same time.

Yet, as Linz points out, "the main and essential function of any
political system . . . [is] the establishment of a legitimate system
of authority capable of mediating . . . conflicts of interest in a society
without frequent and intense disturbance of public order."[19] What is
needed, then, is a definition of the political system as the locus of
legitimate power.

The Political System: Politics as a Process of Emancipation from Civil Society

To introduce a complicated matter, let me start with a simple
illustration. In southern Italy, as in other underdeveloped countries,
one has often the impression of being cheated. One takes a taxicab
or buys some goods. After exhaustive bargaining, one is never sure
if the price agreed upon is a fair one. If the same price is paid for
the same service in Milan, one feels reassured. Why? Because in
Milan there are standardized tariffs. In the south, as a rule, either
such tariffs do not exist or, when they do exist, they cannot be enforced (the taxi meter is unavailable, and so on).

The sociological reason for these different reactions is that
bargaining for each new transaction leaves the two parties, so to speak,
at the mercy of each other. Unmediated relationships create uncer-
tainty and tension. This produces the need for social regulatory mechanisms, the most important of which are the state and the market.
Patron-client ties and the elaborate ritual that accompanies them, especially in traditional settings,[20] is one way to mitigate interpersonal
tension in the absence of such mechanisms.

Although a remedy, clientelism is no substitute for more generalized mechanisms of social regulation. The point has been argued
at length by Durkheim in his discussion on contractual solidarity. He
writes:

> The greater part of our relations with others is of a con-
> tractual nature. If, then, it were necessary each time to
> begin the struggles anew, to again go through the confer-

ences necessary to establish firmly all the conditions of
agreement for the present and the future, we would be put
to rout. . . . But contract-law is that which determines
the juridical consequences of our acts that we have not determined. It expresses the normal conditions of equilibrium, as they arise from themselves.[21]

The market is, then, an important regulatory device. Yet for
the very reasons mentioned by Durkheim it is an inadequate one,
since it simply reflects the balance of forces in civil society. What
is needed is a political mechanism capable of emancipating the actors
from the power structure of civil society. The state and other political
associations, such as unions and parties, are the agents that historically have performed such a function. The state has done so by extending formal rights of participation and by treating the citizen-voter
as equal units "in abstraction from (their) particular roles in the
. . . structure of society."[22] Unions and parties, especially class
parties, have done so by trying to redress the inequalities that survive the formal equalization of the citizens through political action.
In Rokkan's apt phrase, class parties develop "countervailing powers"
to the power of the economic elite.

This said, the political system may be defined as follows:

The political system may be regarded from a developmental perspective as a historical formation which emancipates
itself from civil society, particularly from the point of
view of legitimacy and efficiency. . . . [The] political system emancipates itself to the extent that it succeeds in
developing its own resource base of legitimacy, that is, it
is capable of integrating its subjects politically (nation-
building) . . . and to the extent that it succeeds in developing its own resource base of efficiency, primarily a bureaucracy capable of carrying out the policy of the "centre" into the "periphery" of the political system and of
civil society (state-building).[23]

For a number of reasons, this notion of the political system provided
by the Italian scholar Paolo Farneti seems more useful than that provided by systems theory in which the political system is viewed as a
purely analytical construct.

The first point to be stressed is that the political system is conceived here as a historic formation whose legitimacy depends on the
"autonomous" and effective mediation of cleavages in society. Generally speaking, the deeper the cleavages, the greater the role of the
state, and of politics in general. A crucial element that affects the

role of the state is the timing of national unification. It is no coincidence that the theory of the ruling class developed in two countries
(Italy and Germany) that were, politically speaking, "latecomers."
The essence of such theories is that the state is constitutive of civil
society, not just an aspect of social activity.[24] This contrasts sharply
with the tradition of American pluralism, which is summarized in
Bentley's dictum: "The state is an intellectual amusement of the past."

Such a view of the state implies that the development of the political system has a structural aspect that differentiates this process
from any other in society. To "the extent that the political dimension
is viewed as constitutive of civil society, emancipation is a proble-
matic process and . . . calls attention to a number of contradictions
and tensions [it is not a process merely to be described empirically].
That is, in such a case, emancipation is structural . . . and not
functional, in the sense that, unlike any other sector in society . . . ,
it has a global impact on the constitution of civil society."[25] This
notion provides an order of theoretical priority that is totally lacking,
for example, in Almond's functional theory.

The development of a polity consists, then, of two distinct processes. The first is a process of structural emancipation. It is sig-
nified by the emergence of such institutions as the army, the bureaucracy, political parties, and a class of professional politicians. The
second is a process of institutional emancipation whereby the system
creates the resources necessary for coping with the various crises in
development. This process affects the status of individuals and groups
in their roles as citizens (electoral systems, the right of association,
and so on), as producers (the level of employment, social security,
and so on), as consumers (the distribution of income), and as units
of support and legitimation (the school system, mass media, and so
on).[26]

CLIENTELISM AS POLITICAL EMANCIPATION
MANQUÉ: NATIONAL INTEGRATION AND
POLITICAL DEVELOPMENT IN ITALY

In terms of Farneti's model, clientelism emerges as a problem
of boundary maintenance between polity and society. Clientelism may
take one of two forms: the "privatization" of politics or the "colonization" of civil society. Politics is "privatized" when groups have direct,
unmediated access to political authority, which they treat as a tool
for their private aims. "Colonization of society" is the opposite process. It occurs when formerly autonomous social institutions come
to be regulated by the parties in power. Its aim is to restrict the
scope of action of nongovernmental groups by "occupying" key centers

of power in civil society such as banks, hospitals, and so on. In either case, a sort of confusion of state and society occurs. When such a situation persists over time, as in the case of clientelism in Italy, it points to structural weaknesses in the political system. Clientelism may then be considered a case of structural emancipation manqué.

The notion of structural emancipation is helpful in that it calls attention to a number of problems in nation building and state building. These include the pattern of national unification, the emergence of a professional bureaucracy and organized parties, and the like. This section will deal with three such problems in the case of nineteenth century Italy: the pattern of national unification, the structure of the political class after 1860, and the role of the south in the politics of trasformismo.

North and South and the Pattern of National Unification

The Lipset-Rokkan model of cleavage structures and party systems provides a convenient starting point.[27] The model is centered around the social bases of political parties, which are conceived both as agents of conflict and as instruments of integration. By giving organized expression to social cleavages, parties both structure and regulate social conflict. They also help to solve a central problem in the functioning of societies, the conflict-integration dialectic. The rule here is summarized by E. A. Ross's well-known aphorism: "Society is sewn together by its inner conflicts."

From this point of view, parties may be conceived as "alliances in conflict over policies and value commitments within the larger body politic."[28] As Lipset and Rokkan remark, there is "a hierarchy [of conflicts] in each system and these orders of political primacy not only vary among politics, but also tend to undergo changes over time."[29] From a developmental perspective, according to Lipset and Rokkan, there are two basic dimensions of cleavage, the territorial-cultural and the functional. They roughly correspond to the problems created by the national and the industrial revolution.

In terms of this model, what is remarkable about Italy is that there never were organized forms of territorial opposition of the kind experienced by other European countries (for example, the left counterculture in the south and west of Norway, the support for the Liberals in Wales, and so on).[30] Extensive conflicts did break out in the south in the wake of unification. They took the form of widespread peasant brigandage, followed by emigration of biblical proportions. But no "southern party" gave organized expression to such conflicts.

If anything, southern elites advocated the sternest repression of peasant rebellions and carried them out themselves when they came into
power (Crispi and the fasci siciliani, 1894). From this point of view,
the success of the northern ruling elite was complete.

For the country as a whole, it was success bought at a heavy
price. The south was less integrated into the nation than "absorbed"
into a system dominated by the north. Whatever "integration" did
occur, it occurred in such a way as to violate the conflict-integration
dialectic that is basic for successful nation building. Without organized conflict, there can be no national integration. This point can
be argued on two levels. On the social level, the "integration" of
north and south was less a merging of broad regional interests than
the imposition of northern interests on the rest of Italy. On the political level, the encounter of north and south resulted in trasformismo, a system of government that used the "availability" of southern
deputies to strengthen the class rule of northern elites. Let us consider these two points in order.

The idea that the Risorgimento was a national revolution manqué is the central theme in the works of Guido Dorso, a meridionalista
of the progressive school.[31] For Dorso, the Risorgimento was not a
national movement because it meant the "conquest" of the south by the
north. It was not a revolution because it did not express any ideal
capable of appealing to the masses. Far from mobilizing the country, it devitalized Italian society. For Dorso, the "essential characteristic of the Risorgimento lies in the dissolution of all the ideological movements which fought for leadership in the revolution, as a
result of the . . . spread of the Piedmontese conquest."[32]

The conquest was not merely military, it was also moral and
political. The mechanism that made it possible was a style of politics
based on "political transactions" and the cooptation of the southern
elites. Cavour was the great master in this process of "castration of
the revolution through personal transactions with the leaders."[33] The
result was the quelling of any moral and ideological rigor among southern elites and the repression of those leaders who refused to be coopted into the system.

All this had been possible because of the "profound political im-
maturity of the Italian masses."[34] Even more important was the attitude of southern elites vis-a-vis national unification. The classe
dirigente (ruling class) in the south was the rural bourgeoisie. Control of the land was the basis of their power and indeed their raison
d'être. As a rule, southern elites rented out their land. Had they
cultivated the land themselves, their involvement in the economy
"would have . . . led them to [a greater] understanding of the national life of the country."[35] Instead, as rentiers, their interests
and political ambitions were greatly limited.

What the southern bourgeoisie asked from the new regime was essentially a recognition of their landholding to protect themselves against both the old barons, whose land they had usurped, and the peasants. To achieve this, they needed local freedom and local power, not national influence. Here was the essence and main limitation of their liberalism. They tended to reduce "the general problem of Italian unity to the necessities of their regional domination."[36] They did get control of local government, but at a "very high cost. They renounced any claim to control of the state and unconditionally accepted the policy of the dominant classes in the north."[37] The mechanism by which the southern elites were coopted into the national system of power as subordinate partners was called trasformismo.

The Structure of the Political Class after 1860

A discussion of trasformismo may usefully start with a description of the political class that came into power in 1876. That year marks the end of the rule of the Destra (Cavour's conservative party) and the beginning of the rule of the Sinistra. It also marked a radical change in the social composition of parliamentary and governmental personnel.

By 1876, the Destra had realized most of its historic aims. With the conquest of Rome (1870), national unification had been completed. The problem of the church had been temporarily solved through a law that guaranteed the independence of the Vatican. Above all, the new state had established a solid financial basis. Just before resigning as prime minister (1876), Minghetti, the last of the historic Destra's great leaders, could proudly announce that the budget was no longer in deficit. This had perhaps been the Destra's chief goal.

Though the state was now on firmer ground, large sections of the nation continued to feel alienated from the new political entity. For one thing, only 2 percent of the population had the right to vote. Even within the body of the pays légal, resentment against the Destra was widespread. It is significant that the Destra fell in Parliament by the joint opposition of two groups, which were largely regional in character. These were the Tuscan moderates, who had been antagonized by the railroad policy of the government, and the Sinistra, which represented mainly the southern electorate, until then largely excluded from power.*

---

*Here is the regional distribution of votes in the 1874 general elections:

The change in government in March 1876 was massively sanc-
tioned by the electorate in the November 1876 general elections.
Depretis's government set in motion a sweeping purge of unfriendly
prefects.[38] This action had beneficial electoral effects. Four hundred and fourteen members of Parliament were returned for the Sinistra against only 94 for the Destra. The result was a drastic change
in parliamentary personnel, with one-third of the deputies elected
for the first time. Equally drastic was the change in its social composition. Table 9.1 shows the magnitude of the changes in members
of the government. (Data on the composition of Parliament are not
available from before 1892.)

Four points need to be emphasized with reference to Table 9.1.
First, the Destra was the party of the military and landowners. The
Sinistra was represented mainly by lawyers and public servants. It
can be inferred from the change that after 1876 the basic underpinning
of the political elite was no longer land but professional skill. The
skill in greatest demand was familiarity with the bureaucratic machinery of the state. Second, industry and commerce continued to play
little role in the recruitment of political personnel. This was equally
the case for deputies (see Table 9.2) and for ministers. This was
all the more surprising given the very rapid development of finance
and industry after 1880. It suggests that the capitalist bourgeoisie
had access to the government through noninstitutional channels.
Third, the smaller proportion of members of Parliament among the
Sinistra who had participated in the Risorgimento meant the decline
of that sense of the state that was the hallmark of the statesmen of
the Destra. The smaller role of the aristocracy is a sign of the declining influence of the court. Finally, after 1876, the structure of
governmental personnel changed very little. Even under Giolitti
(1903-13), an increasingly industrialized country continued to be governed by a class in which lawyers were all-important and entrepreneurs practically absent.

Deputies Elected in:	Destra (percent)	Sinistra (percent)
The north	56.5	28.5
The center	23.2	8.2
The south	15.6	43.5
Sicily and Sardinia	4.7	19.8

Source: Compendio delle statistiche elettorali itali-
ane dal 1848 al 1934, vol. 2 (Rome: Failli, 1946-47), p.
102.

TABLE 9.1

Governmental Personnel, by Profession, Aristocratic Birth, and
Involvement in the Risorgimento, 1860–1913
(in percent)

Profession	Destra (1860–76)	Sinistra (1876–1903)	Giolittian Period (1903–13)
Lawyers	15	29	27
Public servants	11	22	16
Intellectuals*	19	16	18
Military	23	15	16
Men of letters and artists	10	10	10
Landowners	21	3	4
Industrialists and merchants	0.6	1	1
Other professions	0.4	4	7
Aristocracy	43	16	28
Percent involved in the Risorgimento	51	37	—

*University teachers, doctors, experts in law and finance.

Source: Adapted from Paolo Farneti, Sistema politico e società civile (Turin: Giappichelli, 1971), pp. 170, 180, 182.

Another feature that is particularly relevant to the topic under
consideration was the regional distribution of governmental personnel.
The Sinistra had its electoral stronghold in the Mezzogiorno. Yet
Table 9.3 clearly illustrates that it did little to change the traditional
predominance of the northern leadership in the government. These
data confirm the subordinate role of the south in the national system
and help to explain why the Italian state acted in such a way as to
deepen the north–south contrast rather than to promote the emancipation of the south.[39] As Nitti remarked in commenting upon these
data, if the southern regions (26.5 percent of the Italian population
in 1900) had had the same proportion of ministers as Liguria (3 percent of the total population), the continental south should have had 119
ministers in the same period instead of 41.

Turning now to the social composition of Parliament, the situation was substantially the same as in the government. If anything,
the role of lawyers and other professional men was even more exalted.
They represented some 50 percent of the parliamentary class in 1892
and increased steadily after that to over 60 percent in 1913.

TABLE 9.2

Parliamentary Personnel in Italy, 1892-1913, by Profession
(in percent)

Profession	1892-97	1900-09	1913
Lawyers	38.6	41.3	48
Other professional men	11	12.6	13
Landowners	20.3	14.3	10
Public servants and military	9.6	7.6	7
Industry and finance	6.6	7.6	7
Teachers	6	6.6	5
Professional politicians	5	5.3	7
Other professions	2.3	4	3

Source: Adapted from Paolo Farneti, Sistema politico e società civile (Turin: Giappichelli, 1971), p. 243.

To summarize and conclude, the data on the composition of government and Parliament in liberal Italy show that the political class underwent a radical change in 1876. So did the nature of its relationship with the electorate. The change was from what may be called the "organic representation" of the Destra to the "contractual representation" of the Sinistra. As Gramsci wrote, the men of the Destra were an "organic . . . vanguard of the upper classes because eco-

TABLE 9.3

Regional Distribution of Ministers in Italy,* 1859-1900

Region	Number = 74
Piedmont	47
Lombardy	19
Liguria	14
Sicily	14
Continental south	41
Other regions	39

*Politicians who held the position of minister at least once between 1859 and 1900.

Source: Francesco S. Nitti, "Nord e Sud," Scritti sulla questione meridionale, vol. 2 (Bari: Laterza, 1958), p. 453.

nomically they themselves belonged to the upper classes: they were
. . . political organizers and at the same time factory directors,
large farmers or farm administrators, commercial and industrial
entrepreneurs, etc."[40] The Destra exerted a "powerful" and "spontaneous" leadership vis-a-vis broad strata of the population because
it was part of a class that performed a progressive function in the
political field and in the economy.

The Sinistra was in a very different position. It represented
strata of middle and petite bourgeoisie, mainly from the south, whose
chief ambition was to share in the opportunities of the new state.
They were especially interested in job opportunities in the expanding
state bureaucracy. Vis-a-vis such strata, the Sinistra did not exert
any "spontaneous" attraction. Rather, consensus had to be engineered
through the provision of political services. It is in this sense that
one may speak of "contractual" representation in the case of the Sinistra.

The modern instrument that helps to aggregate a heterogeneous
electorate is the political party run by professional politicians. In
Italy there was, instead, the prevalence of a type of political personnel, mainly lawyers, who neither represented broad private and institutional interests (case of landowners, capitalists, and so on) nor
could be easily organized into an autonomous body of professional politicians. The result was a system of representation in which deputies
acted not as party men but as political brokers. The development of
the political system, especially the political emancipation of the most
backward part of Italian civil society, the south, suffered accordingly.

Trasformismo and the South

We are a progressive government and if somebody wants
to transform himself . . . and accept my very moderate
program, can I reject him? [Depretis, 1882]

Especially after 1880, the south came to play an increasingly
important political role in the new structure of power. At the same
time, it remained cut off from the mainstream of Italian development.
To understand this paradox, it is necessary to turn to trasformismo,
the system of power that emerged at the time of Depretis's premier-
ship (1876-87).

In the literature, trasformismo has meant one of three things.
First of all, the term has been used to describe a pattern of political
behavior characterized by the devitalization of political conflicts, in
both society and Parliament, through personal transactions. Second,
it has also been defined as the end of organized parties. Depretis's

politics favored the "transformation" of the old parties, Destra and
Sinistra, into a single parliamentary majority, while preventing the
formation of a modern bourgeois party.[41] Finally, in terms of policy,
it has stood for the conservative reaction of the Italian ruling class
vis-a-vis the newly enfranchised masses.[42]

While trasformismo is generally associated with the Mezzogiorno, it did not start there. It began in the north as a reaction against
a distinctively northern phenomenon: urban and, above all, peasant
radicalism. Thus, out of 30 deputies of the so-called Estrema (radicals, Republicans, Socialists) elected in 1882, almost none were
elected in the south. The center-north was the site of all "bipartisan"
tickets and the other transformist tactics that characterized the 1882
elections such as the merging of local newspapers through subsidies
from the state. There was hardly any need for such arrangements
in the south because, in the south, the Destra had all but disappeared
after the 1874 elections (see above). Finally, the two main architects
of trasformismo were both from the north: Minghetti from Emilia,
Depretis from Piedmont.

Yet it is true that if trasformismo started in the north, it was
the south that made it possible. The Mezzogiorno quickly became the
reservoir of votes for all of Depretis's governmental majorities as
well as those of Crispi and Giolitti later on.[43] To understand this,
it must be remembered that trasformismo embodied a project of government that did not go unopposed. Opposition came mainly from three
sectors, all of them from the north: the industrial bourgeoisie, the
old left—both objecting to Depretis's collusion with high finance—and
the radicals. The southern elite also opposed it for some time, but
for different reasons. They were opposed essentially because the
south did not get its share of public works and because the government
continued to be directed by northern leaders.

Once these demands were satisfied, southern opposition would
quickly die out, as the history of Pentarchia group testifies. (The
Pentarchia was the name of a predominantly southern opposition group
to Depretis.[44]) In fact, as a bastion of conservatism,[45] the south
was to become the keystone in any conservative front, acting as a
counterbalance to the pressures from the radicals in the north. One
must add that traditional clientelistic politics in the Mezzogiorno made
that region very receptive to Depretis's method of government based
on the devitalization of conflict through cooptation.

Carocci, the best student of trasformismo, puts the matter
this way:

In the Mezzogiorno Depretis found . . . in a natural state,
so to speak, the kind of situation which he . . . was trying
to bring about throughout [Italy], that is, the devitalization

of any popular pressure from below, . . . the elimination
of any political conflict by reducing it to the level of a
personal conflict. [In the south] there existed no radical
"danger" to be opposed by the united front of trasformismo. But there was, to a degree unknown in other regions,
. . . a tendency for personalism and compromise, which
were necessary conditions, as well as the instrument,
for the implementation of trasformismo. Precisely because in the South there did not exist the conditions which
originally caused . . . [the politics of] trasformismo,
the Southern bourgeoisie was the decisive element which
made the full realization of that politics possible. [46]

The increasing weight of the south can be illustrated by recall-
ing some of the most crucial political decisions of the 1880s, all of
them made under pressure from southern deputies. These include
the postponement of important social reforms, such as old-age pensions and accident insurance, and the imposition of high customs barriers. The latter served the interests of southern absentee landlords
particularly well. What I would like to stress here is the role that
trasformismo assigned to the south. The Mezzogiorno became important not because governmental elites recognized the political primacy of the "southern question" and the need for emancipation of the
south. It became important because it was backward and because organized social conflict had hardly developed there. At a time when
the rule of the bourgeoisie was beginning to be threatened by peasant
and urban movements (the 1880s saw the first massive peasant strikes
in the Po Valley), the south was, so to speak, "safe" for bourgeois
rule. From this came its decisive and increasing importance for social stability. Thus, trasformismo enormously increased the role
of the south without in the least helping its modernization. The Mezzogiorno became important to the extent that it remained premodern.
The "political emancipation" of the country as a whole suffered accordingly.

SOME CURRENT INTERPRETATIONS OF THE
ITALIAN CRISIS

Italian politics has suffered from the most contradictory evils.
Sometimes called the land of trasformismo, Italy is also supposed
to be a prime example of the excessive "ideologization" of politics
that, according to one author, Almond, is mainly the result of the
ineptitude of Italians for "political market behavior."[47] Another
scholar blames Italy's problems upon Italians' all-too-pragmatic de-

sire to share in the benefits of patronage.[48] It seems, therefore, appropriate to start our discussion on clientelism and the Italian crisis by investigating the nature of partisanship in Italy.

Partisanship and Political Exchange: Clientelism as a Mode of Center-Periphery Integration

Clientelistic politics would conceivably affect the nature of partisanship of both leaders and party members in a political system. In a patronage party, the politician would be typically linked to his party by instrumental ties rather than by an ideological commitment. Furthermore, in a "clientelistic state," the bureaucracy would be run according to partisan rather than bureaucratic criteria.* What would be the impact of such a state on the nature of partisan involvement?

Questions concerning the nature of partisanship and the role of the Italian state have been raised recently by Sidney Tarrow in a comparative study on French and Italian local elites.[49] Tarrow's findings confirm first of all a fact observed by other scholars. In France the predominant pattern is one of nonpartisanship, while in Italy party membership is nearly universal. Among the mayors he interviewed (117 in France, 131 in Italy), 45 percent of the French mayors were currently members of a party as against 89 percent in Italy. Party membership per se is a crude indicator of party involvement, since one may have been a party member in the past or may be an unaffiliated sympathizer. Tarrow, therefore, develops a more comprehensive indicator of partisanship that he calls the index of party experience (IPE).[50] The results for the two countries are summarized in Table 9.4.

Three things need to be observed with reference to Table 9.4. First, the degree of partisanship is much larger in Italy than in France. While in Italy 84.4 percent of the mayors scored in the two highest categories of the trichotomized IPE, the corresponding figure for France is 54.7 percent. Second, in both countries, there is a positive correlation between left-wing radicalism and party experience. Third, the two countries differ most markedly in the party involvement of the conservative mayors. While only 27 percent of Gaullists and giscardiens (French "right") score in the two highest categories of

---

*"Clientelistic state" is a convenient but imprecise expression: in the strict sense, a purely "clientelistic" state is inconceivable since a state always provides collective, that is, nonparticularistic, goods.

the IPE, the corresponding figure for Italian Christian Democrats
(DC, the Italian "center") is 75.6 percent and for the Italian "right"
(Liberals and Neo-Fascists) is 83.3 percent. In other words, the
French conservatives do not seem to feel much need for formal involve-
ment in the party system, while Italian moderates are deeply involved
in partisan life.

What is the reason for the higher partisanship of the latter?
Does it mean that Italian moderates are "encapsulated" into a Catholic subculture of which the DC would be the organized expression?
This is the conclusion that was reached by Almond, Galli, LaPalombara, and a score of other scholars.[51] Tarrow's data, which cannot
be reported here in detail, seem to warrant a different conclusion. In
answering the questionnaire, a number of DC mayors made remarks
such as: "To tell you the truth, even the DC is essentially an electoral party that . . . attracts people politically because it's a party
of government." Another joined the DC because, in his words, it
"helps me in my activities as a mayor." A third added: "It's the
biggest party, I don't see the point of joining any other."[52] These
comments are scarcely congruent with a "subcultural" view of the
party. They rather indicate that the DC is valued less as the Catholic
party than as the party in power.

Once it is demonstrated that party involvement is not necessarily
"subcultural," the next conceptual step is to treat individual partisanship and the relations between parties as two separate variables, not
as part of a single syndrome (political subculture-closed partisanship).
When the partisanship of local elites in France and Italy is measured
in terms of the degree of exposure to nonparty information and affec-
tive orientations that transcend party boundaries, and when these
measures of "openness of partisanship" are cross-tabulated with the
level of partisan involvement, Tarrow's local elites conform to the
following four types:

- Open partisanship and low psychological-organizational involvement
  in a party (the case of the DC)
- Open partisanship and high partisan involvement (the case of the
  PCI—Italian Community Party)
- Closed partisanship and low partisan involvement (the case of the
  Gaullists)
- Closed partisanship and high partisan involvement (the case of the
  PCF or French Communist Party).

What accounts for these divergent national patterns of partisanship: open partisanship in Italy, closed partisanship in France? One
answer lies in the nature of the bureaucracy or, more precisely, in
the nature of the channels linking the state and local administrators.

TABLE 9.4

Level of Party Experience of Italian and French Mayors on Left,
Center, and Right

Ideological Position	Index of Party Experience (IPE) (percent)			Number*
	Low	Moderate	High	
Left				
Italy	6.1	42.9	51.0	49
France	11.1	41.7	47.2	36
Center				
Italy	24.5	42.9	32.7	49
France	51.5	36.4	12.1	33
Right				
Italy	16.7	62.5	20.8	24
France	73.0	21.6	5.4	37
Total				
Italy	15.6	46.7	37.7	122
France	45.3	33.0	21.7	106

*Nine Italian and 11 French mayors could not be included because of insufficient information.

Source: Adapted from Sidney Tarrow, "Partisanship and Political Exchange in French and Italian Local Politics," Sage Professional Papers in Contemporary Political Sociology 1 (1974): 15, 21.

A "substantial part of the indifference of French mayors to the party system," writes Tarrow, "stems from the perfectly reasonable conviction that . . . the job they were elected to do . . . can best be accomplished . . . by developing good relations with the prefect, the subprefect and the field agencies of the ministries."[53]

If a strong and professional bureaucracy like the French one discourages partisan involvement, a politicized and inefficient one such as Italy, exalts the role of the party:

In a political system in which administration is as cumbersome, slow-moving and irrational as the Italian one, local elites have had to utilize their only channel of communication to the centres of resource allocation in the capital—the party system. And because the Italian party system has had to absorb many of the functions of administrative brokerage that ought, by right, to belong to the state, it

had developed primarily . . . as an elaborate structure
of hierarchical clienteles which nestle within, and reach
across, the formal structures of the mass parties like
unofficial systems of power.[54]

This is a good functionalist explanation of bureaucratic clientelism in Italy. I accept it with the following qualifications. First,
it is by no means the only explanation. Clientelism may also be
viewed, as has been shown in the section, "Clientelism as Political
Emancipation Manqué: National Integration and Political Development
in Italy," as a power control device and not merely as an adaptation
to a backward bureaucracy. Second, Tarrow extends his conclusion
to all Italian parties, while his data warrant this conclusion only for
the more moderate ones.[55] It should be added that recourse to the
same technique for resource mobilization means different things depending on whether a party is a true party or a collection of factions.
Also relevant is the link between party and society, about which Tarrow says nothing. There is a world of difference between a politician
who is open to other politicians (both local and national) and cut off
from the mass of the population, and one who does not shun political
exchange and still maintains links with society. As Pizzorno has
demonstrated in his study on Sassari, the former behavior is typical
of the DC, the latter of the PCI.[56] Generally, the DC transmits individual demands in a rather secretive way; the PCI, collective demands to which the party gives great publicity. In other words,
within the universe of types of local partisanship, there are a variety
of subtypes. Some approximate classical mass party militance while
others approach the practices and orientations of political entrepreneurship typical of the political machine.

Furthermore, clientelistic practices in Italy vary from region
to region. It is in southern Italy, as Tarrow has shown in an unpublished analysis, that the political practices and attitudes of the political entrepreneur are most widespread. This can be observed by the
data collected in Table 9.5, which draw upon a sample of southern
Italian mayors. On the whole, southern mayors appear to be only
tenuously integrated into political parties, have relatively few contacts with the public, and seek resources largely through their "special" relations with deputies and in the prefecture. These characteristics are not absent from the mayors in the other three regions sam-
pled by Tarrow. They are simply more noticeable in the Mezzogiorno.
With these qualifications in mind, it is possible to accept Tarrow's
conclusion that "partisanship, in Italy, is a correlate of (local and)
vertical political exchange, and not an inhibition on such exchange."[57]

TABLE 9.5

Italian Mayors' Sample, Selected Elements of Political Involvement and Political Activism, by Region

Percent	North-west	North-east	Center	South	Italy
Who have no organized relations with political parties	20	24	6	42	21
Who have contacts with the public through groups	76	75	74	37	34
Who have contacts with the public through meetings	70	58	85	37	62
With close ties with local deputies	70	64	85	87	76
Who report "special relations" with the bureaucracy	44	43	67	65	54
Who would like to run for higher public office	6	17	18	40	20

Source: Sidney Tarrow, "Mezzogiorno e PCI: Appunti per un aggiornamento," unpublished paper, Ithaca, N.Y., June 1976, cited with permission.

The Social Basis of Clientelism: Role of
the Middle Classes

In the literature on patronage, very little is said specifically about the social strata that are most susceptible to clientelistic incentives. The general assumption is that such incentives appeal especially to those sectors of the population that are no longer "traditional" and not yet "modern."[58] The prototype is the European immigrant in America freed from the primordial ties of peasant Europe but not yet incorporated into the American system. But it can be shown that in Italy there are other groups that play a crucial role in the clientelistic organization of consensus, notably the middle classes.

Broadly speaking, there are three strategies for acquiring consensus: individualistic incentives, collective bargaining, and "overlapping group memberships." The first strategy underlies clientelistic politics; the second, "modern" mass politics; the third, group politics.

The individualistic acquisition of consensus is a "strategy that avails itself of the very inequalities which should be a cause for dissent . . . and uses them as an incentive" in the political distribution of benefits.[59] For instance, where unemployment is widespread and organized action for more jobs would lead to severe conflicts, a degree of consensus may be obtained through a judicious distribution of available jobs. The satisfaction of a common need will then be viewed by the workers as a matter of personal privilege granted to the single client. In a situation of great scarcity, chances are that organized action will be discouraged; "exclusive" access to the leaders, actively sought.

Of all the nontraditional social classes, the middle classes are the most responsive to individualistic incentives. Indeed, Pizzorno defines the middle classes as "that ensemble of individuals who are in a position to prefer a project for individual improvement to projects for collective improvement."[60] Why should it be so? And first of all, what do I mean by such an ambiguous term as "middle classes?" The middle classes (or petite bourgeoisie) are a very heterogeneous group of perons who are neither "bourgeois" nor "workers." The bourgeois typically receive profits or rents or both as in the case of large landowners, entrepreneurs, and the like, while workers receive wages.[61] Between these two groups, there is a mittelklassen made up of employees (public and private) who receive salaries; the "independent middle classes" (small farmers, small entrepreneurs, shopkeepers, artisans, and so on) who receive mixed income (profit and wages); and other special groups (military, religious, and so on) who get salaries.

It can be shown empirically that the middle classes are one of the main supporters of clientelism in Italy by investigating, first, the structure of wages and benefits in the public and in the private sector and, second, the social structure in the south. If remuneration in Italy's public sector lies considerably above that in the private sector, as is in fact the case, this constitutes indirect evidence of the pervasiveness of clientelism in Italian politics. Further, if the middle classes occupy a position in the social structure of the south that is more prominent than in the north, which also turns out to be the case, the importance of clientelistic politics should be more important in the south than in the north.

The Structure of Wages and Benefits in Italy

The best single work on the structure of wages and benefits in Italy is Ermanno Gorrieri's La Giungla retributiva.[62] It is an inquiry into the structure of wages and salaries, that is, the income of the employed population. The assumption is that in a country like Italy, income differentiation is not only due to private ownership of means of production, it is also affected by the bargaining power of various occupational groups and by political interventions favoring some of these groups.

A fairly complete picture of the structure of wages and salaries in Italy is provided by Table 9.6. It shows that state employees and those working in state-run services (railroads, telephones, and so on) are paid from 40 percent to 75 percent more than workers in the private sector. For example, an unskilled worker in the parastato (public hospitals, local administrations, and so on) earns 80 percent more than an unskilled industrial worker. A skilled railroad worker gets 70 percent more than a skilled worker in industry, and so on. In higher positions, the gap is much narrower. It is in fact reversed for top executives, who are better paid in the private sector. (This fact, incidentally, may explain why the Italian bureaucracy is overstaffed in its lower ranks but very deficient in top administrators.) But for the bulk of the workers, the privileged position of the public sector is unquestionable. For example, for no reason on earth, an usher of the state telephone company earns 55 percent more than a skilled automobile worker, 75 percent more than a skilled worker in the ceramic industry, and twice as much as a skilled worker in the garment industry.

Pay is not the only discriminating factor. Job stability is even more important. A public employee never loses his job, which is more than can be said for industrial workers during economic crises. Highly valued everywhere, job stability is seen as the supreme goal in areas of chronic unemployment, such as the south. Lastly, the

TABLE 9.6

Monthly Pay in Italy in the Private Sector and in Public Administration, 1971
(thousands of lire)

Area of Employment	Unskilled Workers	Low-Level Employees	Skilled Workers	Higher Level Employees	Executives	Top Executives
Agriculture	98	185	124	256	—	—
Industry	128	189	153	297	323	897
Construction	125	206	156	331	445	—
Commerce	134	149	150	200	296	468
Private sector (average)	121	182	145	271	354	682
State employees	182	192	218	246	334	470
State-run concerns (railroad, and so on)	211	209	249	288	—	—
Parastato	236	260	285	341	462	581
State telephones	—	352	—	389	399	—
Public sector (average)	209	253	250	316	398	525
Bank employees	—	345	279	390	585	1,271

Source: Ernesto Gorrieri, La giungla retributiva (Bologna: Il Mulino, 1972), p. 195.

rhythm of work in the two sectors (industry and the public bureaucracy) is just too different to be compared, with most functionaries in the public service working a half day, if that much. And, although public administration in Italy pays better salaries, this does not mean that the bureaucracy has worked out a uniform and coherent pay policy. Quite the contrary. Table 9.7 demonstrates that Italian public bureaucracy is characterized rather by "remunerative chaos," to use Gorrieri's words.

Table 9.7 requires a few clarifying comments. In Italy there is not just one bureaucracy, but many. The basic distinction is between stato and parastato (para = beside the state). The stato is the state bureaucracy, and includes the ministries, their field agencies, and concerns directly run by the state (post office, state railroads, state telephones, and the like). In Table 9.7, state telephones are not listed under state concerns in order to stress the particularly privileged position of the telephone workers. The total number of state employees is about 1,700,000. In the table, the state bureaucracy is listed under column 1 (state employees) and 2 (state-run concerns). The parastato is made up of public institutions other than the state. It includes something like 60,000 institutions (enti pubblici) that employ almost 2 million people. Of these, the most important are economic concerns such as IRI, ENI, and other public holdings, employing about 1,000,000 people; enti-operated old-age pension schemes and the National Health Service, about 9,000 in number; and about 13,600 local administrations. In Table 9.7 the administrations who belong to the parastato are listed under column 3. Of this collection of institutions, one author has said, quoting Richelieu, "their disorder is part of the order of the state."[63]

Consider now the data in Table 9.7. On the whole, state employees (1-2) are paid an average 20 to 25 percent less than parastato employees. Within the state bureaucracy, workers in state-run concerns (for example, the post office) receive better salaries than personnel of the ministries. Within the parastato, the better paid employees are found in municipalized concerns (local transportation systems, gas companies, and so on), hospitals, and local administrations. This is not mere coincidence, since these enti are known as key centers of clientelistic power, especially in the Mezzogiorno.

Here is one example from my fieldwork in the Salerno area. The director of the hospital in Eboli (30,000 inhabitants) qualified his hospital as the largest industry in town, together with the city administration. Each employed about 220 people in 1974. He reported that before he became director in 1972, personnel were recruited by chiamata diretta, that is, without public competition. He had stopped such a "clientelistic method for hiring people." At the time of the in-

TABLE 9.7

Pay Inequalities in Public Employment, 1971
(monthly pay, in thousands of lire)

	Ushers	Unskilled Workers	Clerks	Skilled Workers	Higher Level Employees
1. State employees	162	182	192	218	246
Post office	—	229	209	—	—
Railroad	—	201	—	249	288
State tobacco industry	—	204	—	—	—
2. State-run concerns	—	211	209	249	288
Municipalized services	258	255	275	310	386
Hospitals	262	230	269	275	386
Local administrations	206	214	238	246	286
National health service	209	—	268	—	326
Chambers of commerce	205	—	244	—	315
National electricity board	—	245	266	312	352
3. Parastato	228	236	260	285	341
State telephones	285	—	352	—	389

Source: Ernesto Gorrieri, La giungla retributiva (Bologna: Il Mulino, 1972), p. 134.

terview, he had decided to enlarge the personnel of the hospital by adding 60 new jobs (60 new jobs that "could be increased up to 100"). He also commented on the drastic change in the employees' behavior before and after their hiring. Once they were hired, they would not behave submissively any longer.[64] Among other things, this must have meant a tendency to press for higher salaries. Such behavior is understandable since it is the exact counterpart of the "individualistic" (nonbureaucratic) aims that motivated the director's decision to hire new people.

Under which conditions can such a system of individually acquired consensus function and what happens when these conditions change? It "may function only if there is somebody who is excluded from the benefits, or . . . who receives less than others, in the case of a growing economy. . . . Until the beginning of the 1960s, the excluded ones were the unemployed and the wage earners."[65] In a full employment situation, not only does the system cease to work; but instead of generating consensus, it produces dissent on a mass scale. This occurs for two reasons.

First, if inequalities tend to disappear, the beneficiaries of the old system try to reproduce them. This is the root of corporativismo, one of the "evils" most frequently blamed for the present crisis. Corporativismo, the organized form of individualism, is the tendency of "each group . . . to use its own power in order to consolidate and improve its position regardless of the consequences for other [groups]."[66] Corporativismo is certainly not due to clientelism alone—far from it. But clientelism, based as it is on a double blackmail (of the patron vis-a-vis the client and vice versa), exacerbates the evil.

Second, clientelistic consensus implies a waste of resources that becomes intolerable as the system approaches full employment. When the bargaining power of industrial workers as well as the level of their salaries increases, industrialists become more and more concerned with the "rationalization" of the system, starting with the political system. They ask that its parasitic branches be cut off. One of these, as has been shown, is bureaucratic parasitism. For instance, criticism of the national health system has recently become more vocal and authoritative: "The administrative costs of the mutue [agencies that run the health service] is the factor which is responsible for the gap between wages and the cost of labor, and one of the factors which has most affected the sharp decline in profits."[67] These words by Giovanni Agnelli, the head of FIAT, explain why industrialists have become increasingly critical of the DC. They also provide an indication of the strength of a class, the bureaucratic middle class, which so far has been the main support of the parties in power.[68]

TABLE 9.8

Italy: Class Structure, North, Center, South
(in percent)

Class	North	Center	South
1. Bourgeoisie	2.5	2.9	2.4
2. Middle classes	45.8	55.6	51.6
2a. Employees	16.8	23.4	13.3
1. Private employees	10.2	11.7	5.2
2. Public employees	6.6	11.7	8.1
2b. Independent middle classes	26.0	27.8	34.7
1. Farmers, and so on	9.7	10.4	17.0
2. Merchants	8.8	8.3	8.6
3. Artisans	7.5	9.1	9.1
2c. Special categories	3.8	4.4	3.5
3. Working class	51.7	41.5	46.0
1. Agriculture	2.9	3.9	13.0
2. Industry (including construction)	40.9	27.8	23.9
3. Other activities	7.9	9.8	9.1
4. Working population over total local population	38.5	37.2	31.2

Source: Adapted from Paolo Sylos Labini, Saggio sulle classi sociali (Bari: Laterza, 1975), pp. 157–60.

The Social Structure of the South

The place of the middle classes in the social structure of Italy and their especially prominent position in the south are shown in Table 9.8, which concludes this section.

When compared to the country as a whole, the social structure of the south presents some peculiar features:

• The middle classes are more important in the south than in the north (51.6 percent and 45.8 percent of the local working population, respectively), but not uniformly so. Private employees are much more numerous in the north, while the contrary is the case for public employees (8.1 percent in the Mezzogiorno, 6.6 percent in northern Italy). Since there is no reason to believe that the tasks of the administration are any greater in the south than in the rest of Italy (except for Rome, of course), it can be inferred that south-

ern bureaucracy is artificially inflated. Also, the "independent"
middle classes are more important in the south as a result of the
larger number of small farmers and artisans.

- The structure of the working class could not be more different in
  the two parts of the country. It is larger and mainly industrial in
  the north, still predominantly agricultural in the south. If construction workers are excluded from "industry," the contrast is
  even sharper. The northern working class forms 36 percent of the
  local working population as against 12.5 percent in the south.[69]

- The most dramatic contrast of all lies in the size of the employed
  population. When compared to the total local population, the figures are 31.2 percent in the Mezzogiorno, 38.5 percent in northern
  Italy. (The national average is 35 percent, one of the lowest among
  industrialized countries.) In absolute numbers, the employed population in the south is today exactly the same as it was in 1881.[70]
  If poverty, as one author maintains, is "the most fundamental quality shared by the mass clientele of machines,"[71] southern Italy
  qualifies for machine politics just as much today as it did in the
  past.

     It is the existence of such a regional cleavage that makes clien-
telism in Italy an important mechanism of center-periphery linkage.
Its persistence over time calls attention to the structural factors underlying a clientelistic mode of behavior. As has been shown, the process
started in 1860 with the unification of the country and became a distinctive trait in Italian development with Depretis and Giolitti. The
cleavage deepened further since 1945, despite a costly policy of state
intervention in the south. In 1947-48, Italy was reintegrated into the
international economy after three decades of autarchy. Export became the driving force within the Italian economy. The north developed an industrial apparatus geared mainly toward exports. As such,
it was tailored more to the needs of the highly developed economies
of the West than to the needs of the home market. This was well and
good except that the south was cut off from this type of development.
It was cut off because this export-oriented, highly sophisticated industry "could not be . . . grafted onto an agricultural economy which had
not yet experienced its first industrial revolution."[72]
     The result was a new division of labor. The north developed a
massive and very advanced industry. The south specialized in the
provision of industrial manpower and personnel for the bureaucracy.
Apart from the inequality inherent in such a division of roles, there
is a national problem here. A modern country cannot be run by a premodern administration. The point has been argued by an eminent
economist from the south, Augusto Graziani:

The disparity between the technological advancement of industry and the organizational efficiency of public administration is perhaps the greatest bottleneck which the country is facing today. . . . The bureaucracy . . . will have necessarily to concern itself more and more with the management of the . . . economy . . . ; as long as the bureaucracy is compelled to recruit its cadres from the agricultural regions [of the south], I do not believe we shall have an administration capable of managing an industrialized economy. [73]

CONCLUSION

In conclusion, it might be helpful to summarize the main argument and the empirical findings of the study. In Italy the center-periphery problem has manifested itself in the form of territorial dualism. Territorial dualism has meant not only the survival of profound regional cleavages, but also that the most backward sector—the south—has been able to condition the entire course of Italian development.

My argument has been that, when dealing with cases of historic backwardness such as these, current conceptualizations of the political system are inadequate, since they do not address the problem of the historic agents of development (market, state, political parties). The first part of the chapter dealt with this analytical problem. Political development was defined there as a process whereby the state emancipates itself from a backward society by means of autonomous structures (bureaucracy, and so on) and other institutions (mass suffrage, primary education, and so on). By acquiring efficiency and legitimacy, the state may thus act as a decisive factor in the emancipation of the periphery.

The second part was devoted to a historic analysis of the "southern question," which is viewed as a case of political emancipation manqué. In it I discussed some of the conditions that produced and preserved southern inferiority, one of them being the parasitic role of the southern bourgeoisie. The emancipation of the south required a capitalistic revolution, but such a revolution would have undermined the semifeudal power of the ruling class in the Mezzogiorno. Contrary to common belief, the south suffered less from capitalist exploitation than from the lack of it; that is, from the lack of the modernizing processes that the market carries with it.

The weakness of the market is in part responsible for the weakness of bourgeois parties. The data on Italian political personnel after 1860 showed that the structure of this class was not conducive to the development of organized parties. In particular, the predominance

in both Parliament and the government of lawyers and other professional men meant that Italian parties developed mainly as coalitions
of political brokers, with detrimental effects on political development.

Trasformismo is the system of power that made southern inferiority a permanent trait in Italian development. The term stands for
a personalistic method of conflict management which was and still is
very widespread in the south. At a time when the northern elite began to be challenged by peasant and urban unrest, the south, due to
its social backwardness and the late development of organized political
conflict, appeared to be "safe" for bourgeois rule. Hence its increasing role as a factor in political stability. The irony is that the Mezzogiorno became important politically not because the state recognized
the primacy of the "southern question," but precisely because it was
premodern and could thus be manipulated by patronage. Thus trasformismo greatly increased the role of the south without in the least
helping in its modernization.

Some of the implications of this pattern of development for contemporary Italy were explored in the third part of the chapter. Survey data showed that partisanship among local political elites is predominantly clientelistic, especially in southern Italy, and that clientelism may be viewed as a device for dealing with a bureaucracy that
is both inefficient and highly politicized. Although this is more true
of conservative politicians (especially the DC) than of the left-wing
parties, there is little doubt that the structural deficiencies of the
Italian state continue to impose heavy constraints on political behavior
at the local level. [74]

A product, at least in part, of a backward state, patronage also
has important consequences for class relationships. The data on the
structure of wages and benefits in Italy showed the relatively privileged
position of the middle classes, especially in the public sector. The inference here is that the public purse has been used as a means for
acquiring consensus. In terms of our model, this use of public power
may be analyzed as a case of poor boundary maintenance between
state and society, state and party. Following a well-established
practice, the weakness of the ruling parties—in terms of organization,
collective projects, and political legitimacy—has resulted in the partisan use of the state and other public institutions.

Finally, comparative data on the social structure of north and
south demonstrated the persistence of territorial dualism a century
after unification. Two industrial revolutions—the first under Giolitti
around the turn of the century and the "economic miracle" in the
1950s—and a very costly policy of state intervention in the south after 1950 have proven unable to remedy the structural deficiencies
and imbalances that characterize Italian economic and social development. Le mort saisit le vif.

NOTES

1. Alessandro Pizzorno, "Amoral Familism and Historical Marginality," European Politics: A Reader, ed. Mattei Dogan and Richard Rose (Boston: Little, Brown, 1971), p. 96.

2. See "Settentrionali e meridionali," in Bollettino della Doxa, March 10, 1976. Of those born in the south 59 percent regarded themselves as "backward." People born outside the south were less severe in judging southerners than the southerners themselves, except in the northwest of Italy where 65 percent of the interviewed consiered the meridionali "backward." See also Table 8, p. 40. The Doxa poll was based on interviews with 2,054 persons in 150 communes throughout Italy.

3. Rosario Villari, "Liberalismo e squilibrio economico italiano," Conservatori e democratici nell'Italia liberale (Bari: Laterza, 1964), p. 7.

4. Sidney Tarrow, Between Center and Periphery: Grassroots Politicians in Italy and France (New Haven, Conn.: Yale University Press, 1977).

5. See Jane C. Schneider, "Patron and Client in the Italian Political System," unpublished Ph.D. dissertation, 1965. Schneider writes that in the south "even in the presence of state-created . . . modern institutions . . . an 'upward circulation' of patterns of social relations" prevailed over the "rationalizing 'downward circulation' due to the influence of the state," thus conditioning the whole development of Italian politics and society.

6. In a town I studied in the south I found that as late as 1945 the community still bore traces of premercantile structures and a premercantile mentality. See my "Patron-Client Relationships in Southern Italy," European Journal of Political Research 1 (April 1973): 3-34.

7. Emilio Sereni, Il capitalismo nelle campagne (Turin: Einaudi, 1947), and Capitalismo e mercato nazionale in Italia (Rome: Editori riuniti, 1966). Also Villari, "Liberalismo e squilibrio economico italiano."

8. This is the thrust of Villari's seminal article "Liberalismo e squilibrio economico italiano." See also Renato Zangheri, "La Mancata rivoluzione argraria nel Risorgimento e i problemi economici dell'Unità," Studi gramsciani, 2nd ed., ed. R. Cessi (Rome: Editori Riuniti-Istituto Gramsci, 1969), pp. 369-83.

9. See my "Patron-Client Relationships in Southern Italy" for a discussion of the process of formation of landed property in the south.

10. Quoted by Manlio Rossi Doria, "Introduction" to Giustino Fortunato, Il Mezzogiorno e lo stato italiano (Florence: Vallecchi, 1973, originally published in 1911), 2 vols., p. ix.

11. See, for instance, Eric R. Wolf, "Aspects of Group Relations in a Complex Society: Mexico," American Anthropologist 58 (1956): 1065-78; Sidel Silverman, "Patronage and Community-Nation Relationships in Central Italy," Ethnology 4 (April 1965): 172-89.

12. I have elsewhere dealt with the problem of clientelistic methods of resource allocation to the periphery. Luigi Graziano, "Clientelism and the Italian Political System: A Theoretical and Empirical Study," pt. 3 (mimeographed, 1976).

13. For a critical evaluation of the literature on clientelism, see Luigi Graziano, "A Conceptual Framework for the Study of Clientelistic Behavior," European Journal of Political Research 4 (June 1976): 149-74.

14. René Lemarchand, "Political Clientelism and Ethnicity in Tropical Africa: Competing Solidarities in Nation-Building," American Political Science Review 66 (March 1972): 71. Lemarchand is here echoing Myron Weiner, "Political Integration and Political Development," Annals of the American Academy of Political and Social Science 358 (March 1965): 53.

15. Lemarchand, "Political Clientelism and Ethnicity in Tropical Africa," p. 83.

16. Paolo Farneti, Sistema politico e società civile (Turin: Giappichelli, 1971), pp. 18, 54; Juan Linz, "The Breakdown of Democratic Politics," paper prepared for the World Congress of Sociology, Varna, September 1969, pp. 4, 9; David Easton, A Systems Analysis of Political Life (New York: Wiley, 1965), pp. 298-99.

17. Frank Sorauf, "The Silent Revolution in Patronage," Urban Government, ed. E. Banfield (New York: The Free Press, 1961), p. 309, quoted by Alex Weingrod, "Patrons, Patronage and Political Parties," Comparative Studies in Society and History 10 (July 1968): 379. See also Peter B. Clark and James Q. Wilson, "Incentive Systems: A Theory of Organizations," Administrative Science Quarterly 6 (September 1961): 129-66.

18. Linz, "The Breakdown of Democratic Politics," p. 9 (emphasis added).

19. Ibid., p. 3.

20. James N. Anderson, "Buy-and-Sell and Economic Personalism: Foundations for Philippine Entrepreneurship," Asian Survey 9 (September 1969), especially pp. 657-58.

21. Emile Durkheim, The Division of Labor in Society (New York: The Free Press, 1964), pp. 213-14.

22. Stein Rokkan, "Mass Suffrage, Secret Voting and Political Participation," Archives européennes de sociologie 2 (1961): 133. See also A. Pizzorno, "Introduzione allo studio della partecipazione politica," Quaderni di sociologia, 1966, pp. 235-87.

23. Farneti, Sistema politico e società civile, p. 60. See also Linz, "The Breakdown of Democratic Politics," pp. 9-14, and Pizzorno, "Introduzione allo studio della partecipazione politica."

24. Farneti, Sistema politico e società civile, chap. 1.

25. Ibid., p. 6. Same view in Pizzorno, "Introduzione allo studio della partecipazione politica," especially p. 254.

26. Farneti, Sistema politico e società civile, p. 91.

27. Seymour Lipset and Stein Rokkan, "Cleavage Structures, Party Systems, and Voter Alignments: An Introduction," Party Systems and Voter Alignments, ed. Lipset and Rokkan (New York: The Free Press, 1967).

28. Ibid., p. 5.

29. Ibid., p. 6.

30. Ibid., p. 12.

31. Guido Dorso, La Rivoluzione meridionale (Turin: Einaudi, 1972), first published in 1925. Compare also "La Classe dirigente della' Italia meridionale," Dittatura, classe politica e classe dirigente, ed. G. Dorso (Turin: Einaudi, 1949).

32. Dorso, La Rivoluzione meridionale, pp. 45-46.

33. Ibid., p. 47 (emphasis added).

34. Ibid., p. 46.

35. Ibid., p. 294; Dorso, "La Classe dirigente dell'Italia meridionale."

36. Dorso, La Rivoluzione meridionale, p. 115.

37. Ibid., p. 117.

38. Robert C. Fried, The Italian Prefects: A Study in Administrative Politics (New Haven, Conn.: Yale University Press, 1963), chap. 3.

39. The classical indictment of state policies in the south is Francesco S. Nitti's "Il Bilancio dello stato dal 1862 al 1896-97" (1900), in his Scritti sulla questione meridionale, vol. 2 (Bari: Laterza, 1958).

40. Antonio Gramsci, Il Risorgimento (Rome: Editori riuniti, 1971), p. 95.

41. Rodolfo de Mattei, Il Problema della democrazia dopo l'Unita (Rome: Instituto nazionale fascista di cultura, 1934).

42. The 1882 electoral reform increased the electorate more than three times (from 2.2 percent to 7.4 percent of the population). Just before the reform, Depretis agreed to establish a "united party" that would defend Italy against the "dangers threatening its institutions." Quoted by G. Carocci, Agostino Depretis e la politica interna italiana dal 1876 al 1877 (Turin: Einaudi, 1955), p. 270.

43. According to Salvemini, between 1880 and 1900 the south regularly elected to Parliament 200 deputies who were "eternally ministerial." See Gaetano Salvemini, "La Questione meridionale,"

in his Scritti sulla questione meridionale (1896-1955) (Turin: Einaudi, 1955), p. 48; Giampiero Carocci, Giolitti e l'eta' giolittiana (Turin: Einaudi, 1972), especially pp. 22, 51, on the role of the south in Giolitti's system of government.

44. Carocci, Agostino Depretis. R. De Mattei, "Momenti di storia italiana: La 'Pentarchia,'" Studi Politici (1954), pp. 573-85.

45. On the social conservatism of the Sinistra in the south compare Fortunato, Il Mezzogiorno e lo Stato italiano, especially p. 278; Giuliano Procacci, Le Elezioni del 1874 e l'opposizione meridionale (Milan: Feltrinelli, 1956).

46. Carocci, Agostino Depretis, p. 300.

47. Gabriel Almond, "Comparative Political Systems," The Journal of Politics 18 (1956): 391-409. See also Joseph LaPalombara, "Italy: Fragmentation, Isolation, Alienation," Political Culture and Political Development, ed. L. W. Pye and S. Verba (Princeton, N.J.: Princeton University Press, 1965).

48. Sidney Tarrow, "Italy: Political Integration in a Fragmented Political System," paper prepared for delivery at the Annual Meeting of the APSA, San Francisco, September 1975.

49. Tarrow, Between Center and Periphery, chap. 6. Also see his "Partisanship and Political Exchange in French and Italian Local Politics: A Contribution to the Typology of Party Systems," Sage Professional Papers in Contemporary Political Sociology 1 (1974), from which the data in this chapter are drawn.

50. The index of party experience is based on the nature of the mayor's link with a party (unaffiliated, sympathizing, card-carrying member); the number of functions he holds, or has held, in a party; whether or not a party played a role in his recruitment into politics; and the level of his organizational experience within a party organization. Tarrow, "Partisanship," p. 13.

51. See, for example, Almond, "Comparative Political Systems." Also see Giorgio Galli and Alfonso Prandi, Patterns of Political Participation in Italy (New Haven, Conn. and London: Yale University Press, 1970); and Joseph LaPalombara, "Italy: Fragmentation, Isolation, Alienation."

52. Tarrow, "Partisanship," Table 2, p. 23.

53. Ibid., p. 43. See also Jean-Claude Thoenig, "La Rélation entre le centre et la périphérie en France: Une analyse systématique," Bulletin de l'institut international d'administration publique 36 (October-December 1975): 77-123.

54. Tarrow, "Partisanship," p. 46.

55. Ibid., pp. 40, 42, 43.

56. Alessando Pizzorno and Laura Balbo, Studio sulla struttura del potere locale a Sassari-Rapporto sulla situazione politica e sociale, 2 vols. (mimeographed, ca. 1969), pp. 47, 77, 78.

57. Tarrow, "Partisanship," p. 48.

58. See, for instance, E. Wolf, "Kinship, Friendship and Patron-Client Relations in Complex Societies," The Social Anthropology of Complex Societies, ed. M. Banton (New York: Praeger, 1966); Silverman, "Patronage and Community-Nation Relationships in Central Italy"; and James C. Scott, "Patron-Client Politics and Political Change in Southeast Asia," American Political Science Review 66 (March 1972): 91-113.

59. Alessandro Pizzorno, "I ceti medi nei meccanismi del consenso," Il caso italiano, ed. Fabio Luca Cavazza and Stephen R. Graubard (Milan: Garzanti, 1974), p. 322.

60. Ibid.

61. I follow Sylos Labini's classification, which is based on the theory of income distribution in classical economic thought (Smith, Ricardo). Paolo Sylos Labini, Saggio sulle classi sociali, pt. 1 (Bari: Laterza, 1975), chaps. 1-2.

62. Ermanno Gorrieri, La Giungla retributiva (Bologna: Il Mulino, 1972).

63. Sabino Cassese, "Introduction," L'Amministrazione pubblica in Italia (Bologna: Il Mulino, 1974), p. 20.

64. Interview, Eboli, July 3, 1974.

65. Pizzorno, "I ceti medi," p. 332.

66. Gorrieri, La Giungla retributiva, pp. 13-14.

67. L'Espresso, November 19, 1972.

68. M. Dogan, "Political Cleavage and Social Stratification in France and Italy," in Lipset and Rokkan, Party Systems and Voter Alignments.

69. Sylos Labini, Saggio sulle classi sociali, pp. 36-37.

70. Ibid., Table 1.6, p. 160.

71. J. Scott, "Corruption, Machine Politics, and Political Change," American Political Science Review 63 (December 1969): 1150.

72. Augusto Graziani, "Il Mezzogiorno nell'economia italiana degli ultimi anni," Nord e Sud nella società e nell'economia italiana di oggi (Turin: Einaudi, 1968), pp. 32-33.

73. Ibid., p. 37. By contrast, in France the upper cadres of the bureaucracy come mainly from the most developed regions, especially the Paris area. See Ezra N. Suleiman, Politics, Power and Bureaucracy in France (Princeton, N.J.: Princeton University Press, 1974).

74. See Tarrow, Between Center and Periphery, chap. 6, for some of these constraints.

ABOUT THE EDITORS AND CONTRIBUTORS

SIDNEY TARROW is Professor of Government at Cornell University. He is the author of Peasant Communism in Southern Italy and Between Center and Periphery: Grassroots Politicians in Italy and France and is coeditor (with Donald Blackmer) of Communism in Italy and France. Former director of Cornell's Western Societies Program, he is currently working on an interpretation of postwar French and Italian politics.

LUIGI GRAZIANO was trained at the universities of Rome and Paris and has the Ph.D. from Princeton University, Princeton, N.J., where he wrote a thesis on "Clientelism and the Italian Political System," soon to be published in Italian by Feltrinelli. Currently at the University of Turin, he is the editor of Clientelismo e mutamento politico, and has published articles in the European Journal of Political Research and in the Revue Française de Science Politique.

PETER J. KATZENSTEIN is Associate Professor of Government at Cornell University, Ithaca, N.Y. He is the author of Disjoined Partners: Austria and Germany since 1815 and has edited Between Power and Plenty: Foreign Economic Policies of Advanced Industrial States. He is currently engaged in a research project on comparative foreign economic policies.

DOUGLAS E. ASHFORD is Professor of Government at Cornell University and current director of its Western Societies Program. He has written extensively on comparative local politics in both developing and industrial nations. His recent interest is the theory and practice of decentralization, as discussed in his recent Sage paper, "Democracy, Decentralization and Decisions in Subnational Politics." His contribution to this volume is a preliminary analysis for a longer monograph comparing local government reorganization in Britain and France.

PETER GOUREVITCH has been both Assistant and Associate Professor at Harvard University, Cambridge, Mass., where he took his Ph.D. He is currently Associate Professor of Political Science at McGill University, Montreal, Quebec, Canada. He has written articles on European political development, on tariff policies, labor movements, local government and international relations in such journals as <u>Comparative Politics</u>, <u>Political Science Quarterly</u> and the <u>Journal of Interdisciplinary History</u>.

GABRIEL SHEFFER teaches political science at the Hebrew University of Jerusalem and has been associated with the research efforts of the Van Leer Institute. He is the editor of a book, <u>Dynamics of a Conflict; A Reexamination of the Arab-Israeli Conflict</u>, and is the author of many articles in American and European journals, most recently on "Independence in Dependence of Regional Powers" in <u>Orbis</u>.

MARTIN SHEFTER is Associate Professor of Government at Cornell University. He has been both Assistant Professor and Associate Professor at Harvard University, where he did his Ph.D. and wrote a thesis, "City Hall and State House" (1970) from which some of the material in his essay in this volume is drawn. Currently a visiting fellow of the Institute for Advanced Study at Princeton University and the author of a recent article on New York's fiscal crisis in <u>The Public Interest</u>, Shefter is at work on a study of the development of political parties in the United States.

JACEK TARKOWSKI teaches political science at the University of Warsaw. He is the author of "Decision-Making Processes in the Polish Local Political System," published in F. C. Bruhns, F. Cazzola, and J. Wiatr, eds., <u>Local Politics, Development and Participation</u>.

DECISION MAKING IN THE EUROPEAN COMMUNITY
Christoph Sasse, Edouard
Poullet, David Coombs,
and Gerard Deprez

HOUSING IN ITALY: Urban Development and Political Change
Thomas Angotti

INDUSTRIAL POLICIES OF WESTERN EUROPE
edited by Steven J. Warnecke
and Ezra N. Suleiman

THE MULTINATIONAL CORPORATION AND SOCIAL
CHANGE
edited by David E. Apter
and Louis Wolf Goodman